In this series:

1. *The peopling of ancient Egypt and the deciphering of Meroitic script*
2. *The African slave trade from the fifteenth to the nineteenth century*

The African slave trade from the fifteenth to the nineteenth century

Reports and papers of the meeting of experts
organized by Unesco at Port-au-Prince, Haiti,
31 January to 4 February 1978

Unesco

The designations employed and the presentation of material throughout the publication do not imply the expression of any opinion whatsoever on the part of Unesco concerning the legal status of any country, territory, city or area or of its authorities, or concerning the delimitation of its frontiers or boundaries.

First published in 1979 by the United Nations
Educational, Scientific and Cultural Organization
7 Place de Fontenoy, 75700 Paris
Printed by Imprimerie L. Vanmelle, Gent/Mariakerke

Second impression 1985

ISBN 92-3-101672-5
French edition: 92-3-201672-9

Preface

This second volume in the series 'The General History of Africa: Studies and Documents' presents the working documents, a summary report of discussions, and supplementary papers submitted at the Meeting of Experts on the African Slave Trade which was organized by Unesco at Port-au-Prince, Haiti, from 31 January to 4 February 1978.

The purpose of the meeting, which was recommended by the International Scientific Committee for the Drafting of a General History of Africa, was to elicit the authorized views of specialists on the various aspects of the slave trade mentioned in several volumes of the *General History of Africa*. Over and above its immediate results, it also aimed at identifying new lines of research on this subject, since despite the numerous studies and publications that have already been produced, there remain several questions that have not yet been satisfactorily answered.

Discussions centred on the following topics: scale and effects of the slave trade; ideological positions with regard to the problem; abolition of the slave trade, especially in the Indian Ocean; new lines of research.

The authors are responsible for the choice and the presentation of the facts contained in this book, and for the opinions expressed therein, which are not necessarily those of Unesco and do not commit the Organization.

Contents

Introduction   9

Part I: Working papers and summary report

Ideological and political aspects of the African slave trade
Ideological, doctrinal, philosophical, religious and political aspects of
the African slave trade, *S. U. Abramova*   16
Reactions to the problem of the slave trade: an historical and ideological
study, *Michèle Duchet*   31

The Atlantic slave trade
The slave trade and the Atlantic economies 1451–1870,
Joseph E. Inikori   56
The slave trade in the Caribbean and Latin America,
José Luciano Franco   88
Negro resistance to slavery and the Atlantic slave trade from Africa to
Black America, *Oruno D. Lara*   101
Portuguese participation in the slave trade: opposing forces, trends
of opinion within Portuguese society, effects on Portugal's socio-
economic development, *Françoise Latour da Veiga Pinto, assisted
by A. Carreira*   119

The slave trade within Africa and between Africa and the Middle East
The slave trade within the African continent, *Mbaye Gueye*   150
The slave trade and the population drain from Black Africa to North
Africa and the Middle East, *I. B. Kake*   164
Population movements between East Africa, the Horn of Africa and the
neighbouring countries, *Bethwell A. Ogot*   175

The slave trade in the Indian Ocean
The slave trade in the Indian Ocean: problems facing the historian and
research to be undertaken, *Hubert Gerbeau*   184

Summary report of the meeting of experts on the African slave trade   211

Appendixes
    Appendix 1: List of participants   233
    Appendix 2: Opening speech of the Secretary of State for Education,
    Haiti   236
    Appendix 3: Opening speech of the Director-General of Unesco   239

Part II: Supplementary papers

    An account of research on the slave trade in Nigeria, *J. F. Ade Ajayi
and J. E. Inikori*   247
    Portuguese research on the slave trade, *Antonio Carreira*   250
    The Catholic Church and the slave trade, *Luigi Conti*   265
    Supplementary report on slave-trade studies in the United States,
P. D. Curtin   269
    The slave trade and the peopling of Santo Domingo, *Jean Fouchard*   270
    A commentary on the slave trade, *Joseph E. Harris*   289
    The present state of research in Brazil, *Waldeloir Rego*   296
    The state of research in Guyana, *Walter Rodney*   298
    The slave trade from the fifteenth to the nineteenth century,
Y. Talib   299
    Research on African influence in the Dominican Republic,
Hugo Tolentino Dipp and Ruben Silié   306
    Brazilian and African sources for the study of cultural transferences
from Brazil to Africa during the nineteenth and twentieth centuries,
J. Michael Turner   311

Introduction

To facilitate the discussions, Unesco drew up an annotated agenda highlighting the main lines of debate, and invited several experts to prepare working documents on specific topics.

Main lines of debate

Scale of the slave trade

The task here was to use the most recent work in order to establish statistics about the population uprooted from Africa by the traffic in slaves, in particular with a view to providing receiving countries with statistical data about the origin and numerical strength of the people of African extraction.

The figures given and the methods adopted to arrive at these estimates vary from one school of thought to another. The meeting was required to compare the various procedures followed, to make a critical appraisal of them and to suggest a method likely to produce better results. It would undoubtedly be desirable to attempt to take stock of the methods used to evaluate the human losses sustained by Africa as a result of the slave trade (particularly losses suffered at the time of man-hunts on the African continent and deaths in the ports of embarkation and on the slave ships).

Effects of the slave trade

The experts were requested to examine the repercussions of the slave trade both in Africa and in the receiving countries, and also in those countries which organized the slave trade. The aim was to assess not only the numerical importance of the population forcibly removed from Africa, but also the impact of this deportation on the demographic development of the African continent.

The impact of the slave trade on political and social structures, on cultural life and on economic development in Africa, which has not been studied in any depth, was to be discussed thoroughly in order that conclusions could be reached which sum up the question and suggest fresh lines of research.

Furthermore, through discussion of the papers before them, the participants were expected to examine the methods used to assess the new wealth
gained by economies outside Africa as a result of the slave trade. They were
requested to evaluate the growth of that wealth and the role of the slave trade
in the industrial development of the European countries, particularly at the
stage of the initial accumulation of capital. They were also asked to evaluate the
role of the slave trade in the industrial development of the receiving countries.

Lastly, the impact of the slave trade on the attitudes and structures of
the receiving countries was to be examined. In particular, a study was to be
made of the development of relations between the local population and the
new arrivals.

Many studies have been made of African cultural contributions to the
countries where the slaves were settled. The meeting was asked, first, to take
stock of such studies and, second, to examine the consequences of the cultural
mixture on attitudes and on the social and economic structures of the receiving
countries.

Ideological positions with regard to the problem of the slave trade

Although an outline of this aspect of the problem can be found in several
studies, it has never been dealt with in a systematic and exhaustive manner.
The experts were therefore requested to examine the ideological positions
(philosophical, religious or political, *inter alia*) underlying the problem of the
slave trade.

A study was to be made, in particular, of the positions of the Christian
churches and of Islam and of doctrinal developments within them, and of the
standpoints adopted by various political and philosophical schools of thought
on the slave trade and on slavery—especially all the abolitionist movements
of the eighteenth and nineteenth centuries—both in the countries which organized the slave trade and in the countries which stood to gain from it.

Abolition of the slave trade, particularly in the Indian Ocean

A great deal of research has been carried out on what led to the abolition of
the slave trade and the stages through which it passed. The participants were
requested to review the issue.

In particular, they were invited to evaluate the role played by slaves'
uprisings in the abolition process itself, and the participation of slaves in
national liberation movements, especially in North and South America and the
Caribbean.

Special emphasis was to be placed on the Indian Ocean routes, which
have been less thoroughly studied than those across the Atlantic.

The experts were also requested to consider the consequences of the abolition of the slave trade in Africa itself, in Europe and in the receiving countries.

New lines of research

The experts were requested to bring together under this heading all the recommendations concerning the pursuit of research into the slave trade which arose out of the discussions. In particular, they were to: (*a*) list the sources of archives still to be published; (b) suggest forms and directions which further research might take; and (c) put foward suggestions on ways of setting up a system for the exchange of information, researchers and teachers and, when appropriate, students, between universities in the region (Caribbean and the Americas) and Africa.

Working papers

The working papers are grouped in four sections in Part I of this book. The first section contains contributions by S. U. Abramova and Michèle Duchet on ideological and political aspects of the slave trade. In the second section, Joseph E. Inikori deals with the effects of the slave trade on the Atlantic economies; José Luciano Franco examines the slave trade in the Caribbean and Latin America; Oruno D. Lara discusses Negro resistance to slavery and F. Latour da Veiga Pinto, assisted by Antonio Carreira, examines the effects of Portugal's participation in the slave trade on Portuguese society and the country's socio-economic development.

The third and fourth sections deal with the slave trade within Africa itself and in other parts of the world. Mbaye Gueye shows how European participation in the slave trade caused it to swell to huge proportions and discusses the subsequent effects on the internal slave trade. I. B. Kake points out that the peoples of North Africa and the Middle East had been transferring black populations to their territories long before Europeans began trading in slaves and shows how this population drain developed from the fifteenth to the end of the nineteenth century. Population movements between East Africa, the Horn of Africa and the neighbouring countries are examined by Bethwell A. Ogot, and Hubert Gerbeau discusses research to be undertaken on the slave trade in the Indian Ocean.

Part I ends with the summary report of the meeting of experts and recommendations for future action.

Part II of the book contains additional papers which participants were asked to submit, describing research on the slave trade being carried out in various countries. These papers contain mainly bibliographical data, details of work in progress, areas of research to be explored, names of specialists doing research work on the slave trade, statistics, and lists of archives. Some of them also discuss the role and impact of the slaves—economic, cultural, political— in the receiving countries and in the trading countries.

Part I
Working papers and summary report

Ideological
and political aspects
of the slave trade

Ideological, doctrinal, philosophical, religious and political aspects of the African slave trade

S. U. Abramova

'There is no topic in African history on which so much has been written and yet so little known as the Atlantic slave trade.' These words belong to Daaku,[1] the African historian. Indeed, hundreds of studies and popular books have been written on the 400-year-long slave trade. It had a significant impact on man's history: there is hardly a single work on the history of Africa, America or the West Indies and few studies on the history of Europe that do not contain at least one chapter on the export of slaves to the New World.

One hundred years have gone by since Africans ceased to be transported to the New World, but disputes on the slave trade and its place in world history still continue. This paper attempts to give a concise account of the reasons behind the slave trade, its development and appraisal by contemporaries, and what it gave to the peoples involved in it.

Development of the slave trade

In 1441, an expedition headed by Antam Gonsalvez and Nuno Trista brought back ten captives from Africa to Europe. Some of these captives assured their captors that they would be handsomely rewarded if they returned their captives to Africa. Gonsalvez shipped the captives back to Africa where he received in exchange 'ten blacks, male and female, from various countries . . .' and various goods including '. . . a little gold dust'.[2]

Several slaves, with a splendid retinue, were sent as a gift to Pope Eugene IV. The others were sold in Lisbon at an extremely high price.

Following this first profitable sale of Africans the Portuguese sailors began to bring back slaves from every voyage to Africa.

Pacheco Pereira wrote that in his day (late fifteenth century) from the coastal areas embracing Senegal and Sierra Leone alone 3,500 slaves, and at times even more, were carried off yearly,[3] although the capture of slaves was not the main object of the first Portuguese expeditions. At that time, however, the population in some European countries was rather small and slave labour was widely used, for instance, in the countries of the Iberian peninsula. But after the Christian Reconquest the influx of slaves virtually ceased. The marketing of black slaves was probably the first profitable 'outcome' of the costly African expeditions.

One often reads that Portuguese rulers, and among them Prince Henry, known as 'the Navigator', the organizer of Portuguese expeditions to Africa, sanctioned the import of Africans ostensibly to convert them to Christianity. It is true that slaves were baptized, but nevertheless sold.

At that time the Church took quite a different line with regard to Africans. Pope Nicholas V issued a special bull granting the King of Portugal, Alphonso V, the right to seize lands and enslave heathens in regions discovered by that time in Africa, and in those that would be discovered. Moreover, the Catholic clergy, for instance, in the Congo, daily compromised itself and the Church by indulging openly in the slave trade.[4]

In the early sixteenth century, the Spanish established a huge colonial empire in the West Indies and America. In the process of seizing new lands they massacred nearly all of the native Indian population. To obtain cheap manpower they began to bring African slaves, who had proved their worth in Europe as capable and handy workers, to the New World.

By exporting Africans to America the Spanish were not trying to save what was left of the Indians. They were eager to preserve their colonies where there was no manpower to work the mines and plantations. In 1510, the first large group of African slaves, 250 in all, was brought to the Hispaniola gold mines. After that, the Spanish Government regularly concluded *asiento* with other countries for the right to sell African slaves in Spain's American colonies.

In the second half of the sixteenth century, Portugal began to lose its monopoly in Africa, and Spain in the New World. The development of capitalism in Europe prompted an active colonial policy. Holland, Great Britain and then France began conquests in America, Asia and Africa, where they built up their colonial empires.

Having considerably squeezed out Portugal, these countries settled on Africa's western coast where they built forts and established settlements. In the West Indies, Holland seized Curaçao and Aruba; Great Britain, Barbados and Jamaica; France, Guadeloupe, Martinique and, in the late seventeenth century, Santo Domingo, etc. Brazil, Cayenne, Surinam, New Amsterdam (New York) and Virginia were among the colonies that emerged in America at the time.

By the mid-seventeenth century, the main colonies where African labour was soon to be employed were founded. Following the essential organizational period in the colonies the development of plantation economies began. The rapid development of the West Indies and the American colonies would have been impossible in that period without the mass employment of cheap manpower.

Evidence of the European countries' huge interest in African trade as a whole, and particularly in the slave trade, was the founding of numerous trade companies.

This put an end to the first period of development of the slave trade. Two phases are distinguished within this period; different as they are, they form a continuation. The first is the transportation of African slaves from Africa to Europe, mainly to Portugal and partly to Spain. The appearance of Africans in the European slave markets was not merely the continuation of the Mediterranean slave trade. Never before had Europeans indulged in the seizure of slaves on such a huge scale. Never before had the hunt for slaves been so systematic nor had it been carried on solely for the sake of procuring slaves. Never before had Europeans come into contact with such a huge number of slaves belonging to another race and differing from their European masters not only by their outward appearance but also by their inner make-up and their perception of the surrounding world, for the distinctions between European and African reality were drastic.

The second phase is the granting of the first *asiento* and the delivery of slaves to the New World, first from Europe, and later direct from Africa. This was only the beginning of the European–American slave trade.

Formally, the second period of the slave trade began in the late seventeenth century and continued to 1807–08, when Great Britain and the United States of America, the world's two biggest slave-trading powers, abolished the export of slaves from Africa. Actually the borderline was set by the French Revolution of 1789, i.e. during the campaigns of Napoleon that followed, the transport of slaves from Africa was insignificant.

Despite the attempts of monopoly companies to limit the slave trade in one way or another, it was conducted within that period on an unrestricted scale. It was regarded at the time as a branch of trade conducive to the nation's welfare, as 'the first principle and foundation of all the rest, the mainspring of the machine which sets every wheel in motion'.[5] And it is to the eighteenth century that Karl Marx's statement that Africa had been turned into a warren for hunting blacks, refers first of all.[6]

In the late eighteenth century, when a campaign was already in progress to ban the transport of slaves from Africa, defenders of the slave trade produced numerous arguments in favour of its continuation (see below). Here we shall dwell only on the climatic theory advocated by all adherents of the slave trade. The theory alleged that the climate of the West Indies, both Americas and other parts where African slave labour was widespread, was unbearable to Europeans and prevented them from working their plantations. It was claimed that the plantations of European colonists would inevitably fall into decline were it not for the import of Africans, who were used to the tropical climate and, moreover, proved to be splendid agricultural workers. The climatic theory has survived to our day.[7] It has, however, been refuted by the history of the European colonies in America.

After exterminating the American Indians, the British and the French began to employ white slaves to work their plantations. At that time political prisoners and criminals were exiled to the West Indies. The system of indentured servants was also widespread. In Europe, particularly in London and Bristol, people were kidnapped and sold into slavery to the New World.[8]

In the 1640s, when sugar-cane was introduced on a wide scale in the West Indies, and crop areas were extended, the number of white slaves fell short of the demand for manpower. Beginning with the late seventeenth century the import of African slaves into the colonies of the New World rose sharply.

Thus the reason for replacing white slaves by Africans had nothing to do with the hot climate. At that time Europe simply could not supply the colonies with a sufficient amount of cheap manpower. As admitted by all contemporaries, without the enslavement of Africans the colonies of the New World could not have continued to exist. One of the documents of the Royal African Company, founded in 1672, reads: 'The slaves are sent to all His Majesty's American Plantations which cannot subsist without them.'[9]

In the second half of the seventeenth century, the slave trade became notorious as one of the most profitable branches of trade, and each European country, provided it had the opportunity, sought to snatch a profitable share of the slave trade for itself. Great Britain, Holland and France were the leading slave-trading powers of the time. From the late seventeenth century, the British North American colonies, the future United States of America, also sent slave ships to the American coast. Even Denmark and Sweden built several forts on the western coast of Africa with the aim of taking part in the slave trade.

In the seventeenth and eighteenth centuries, the slave trade was considered as respectable as any other branch of trade. Tradesmen from different countries boasted of their successes in trading in 'live merchandise'. Pages upon pages of old books are filled with inventories showing the number of slaves exported from Africa and the number of those who managed to reach the New World alive.[10] These data are only approximate—there were no precise statistics—yet they are sufficient evidence of the importance of the slave trade and its scope in the eighteenth century.

Robert Bisset's *The History of the Negro Slave Trade in its Connection with the Commerce and Prosperity of the West Indies and the Wealth of the British Empire*,[11] one of the most serious works on the subject written by an advocate of the slave trade in the years of struggle for its abolition, when both abolitionists and their opponents spared neither words nor emotions in publicizing their economic, political and religious views on the subject, gives the

precise standpoint on this question: the flourishing and wealth of the metropolitan country depend on the size of the slave trade, the import of slaves to the
plantations.

In *Capital*, Karl Marx quotes a prominent historian, a specialist of the
colonial period: 'It is the agriculture of the West Indies, which has been for
centuries prolific of fabulous wealth, which has engulfed millions of the African
race.'[12] And that was exactly the way things stood. The American colonies,
the slave trade and the 'triangular' trade were a major factor in the primary
accumulation of capital and had a substantial impact on the economic development of the metropolitan countries, but the fabulous wealth of the West
Indies and of the American planters was created by the hands of Africans,
scores of thousands of whom perished in the conditions of plantation slavery.
In distinction to several present-day historians this was well understood by
contemporaries.

To quote a British historian, at the opening of the eigtheenth century:

the African slave trade was the foundation on which colonial industry and the colonial
commerce of European countries rested. It dominated the relations between the
countries of Western Europe and their colonies; it was one of the most important
factors in the warsthe of the century; it played a considerable role in the domestic
affairs of the nations involved in it. [13]

One has only to recall the *asiento*. Being well aware of the profits that would
come pouring in from the delivery of slaves to the Spanish colonies and from
the goods that were smuggled during those voyages, European countries vied
to obtain this contract. According to the Treaty of Utrecht (1713) following the
war for the Spanish inheritance, Great Britain, as the victor, succeeded to the
asiento previously held by France and gained several additional privileges
into the bargain.[14] According to contemporaries, obtaining the *asiento* was a
huge victory for British diplomacy.

In the eighteenth century, the interests of European society were closely
linked with the slave trade, which had a great impact on the growth of European ports and promoted the emergence of manufacturers processing raw
materials cultivated by Africans. In 1796, during debates held in the British
Parliament on the question of abolishing the slave trade, Tarleton and Young,
members of the House of Commons, who represented the interests of ship-
builders and slave-traders, claimed that the abolition of the slave trade would
ruin London, Liverpool, Bristol and Glasgow.[15]

The manufacturers of Nantes maintained in all competence:

The slave trade is the basis of all our navigations. It brings manpower to till the land
of our islands. In exchange the islands give us an abundance of sugar, coffee, cotton
and indigo which are used in domestic and foreign trade.[16]

Certainly, these cities continued to thrive after the slave trade was abolished, but the words of British Parliamentarians and Nantes manufacturers testify once again to their awareness of the economic significance of the slave trade: it provided work for thousands of craftsmen and sailors; many hundreds of people were employed in the textile mills and factories of London, Bristol, Glasgow, Manchester, Nantes, Roanne, etc., working on raw materials from West Indian and American plantations: products of sugar-cane, tobacco, cotton, etc.

Undoubtedly, the greatest profits from the slave trade went to both Americas. No one denies the fact that for several centuries Brazil was actually integrally linked with Africa and that the greatest number of slaves were imported into Brazil. But less is written of the significance of the African slave trade for the United States of America, or of the fact that 'it was the sale of Africans in the New World—the slave trade—that laid the financial foundation of the United States'.[17] Nevertheless, history has preserved the testimony of contemporaries on the importance of the slave trade for the United States economy: when the Declaration of Independence was put up for discussion at the Continental Congress the article denouncing the slave trade was exempted from the text.[18]

In the eighteenth century the export of slaves increased yearly. According to the (exaggerated) data of contemporaries, in the 1780s, when the movement for the abolition of the slave trade began to develop in Europe and America, 100,000 Africans were exported yearly.

The struggle for abolition of the slave trade

Viewing the events of those years from the present time one can single out the following reasons for the abolition of the slave trade in the early nineteenth century: the development of capitalist relations in European countries and America in general; changes in Great Britain's economic policy—the result of the breaking off of its Continental colonies; the impact of the French Revolution with its ideas of liberation; the revolution of African slaves in Santo Domingo; the growing number of slave uprisings in the West Indian colonies as the result of the revolutionary events in France and Santo Domingo; the upsurge of the abolitionist movement in nearly all the European countries.

The struggle to abolish the slave trade continued for several decades. It acquired, to use present-day terminology, an international character and was accompanied by sharp polemics between the abolitionists and their opponents, in the course of which there appeared many books, brochures and pamphlets depicting, often with pro and con exaggerations, the main ideological, political, economic and religious views of that time on the slave trade.

The abolitionists A. Benezet, T. Clarkson and W. Wilberforce proved their demands to abolish the slave trade.[19] They maintained that it rendered Africa lifeless. It had plunged the continent into a chaos of gory internecine wars, and the responsibility for these endless wars and slave hunts lay with Europeans, for it was their constantly increasing demands for slaves that instigated new wars. The Africans had not fought so frequently before the slave trade, and as they had no knowledge of firearms there had been fewer casualties. Tracing the development of the slave trade the abolitionists showed how a new category of successful slave-traders emerged alongside the old chiefs and rulers, and how the Africans' whole life was subordinated to the demands of the slave trade.

The brutal character of the slave trade was sharply denounced. It was emphasized that it embittered both the Africans and Europeans who were involved in it, while the drastic conditions of the transportation of slaves led to high mortality among slaves and sailors.

To impress the reader, the abolitionists took particular pains to show the high mortality rate among European sailors employed on slave ships. Perhaps they exaggerated a little, but today some historians resort to these data to show that, like Africa, Europe experienced a loss of manpower during the time of the slave trade and consequently also suffered from this practice.

The abolitionists consented that African slaves were inferior to European colonists. They asserted, nevertheless, that in the New World slaves were placed in conditions which precluded their further development. In similar conditions Europeans would have remained intellectually at the same level. The abolitionists would exclaim: 'Are there no people in our country who by virtue of the conditions of their life are even less developed than Africans?'

The abolitionists maintained that 'legal' trade—the sale of raw materials to Europe in exchange for industrial goods, would bring more profits. But to achieve this one had to abolish the slave trade which barred Europeans from penetrating the African hinterland.

Planters and manufacturers, who had invested capital in the slave trade, as well as many shipowners and sailors came out in defence of it and of its development, and for preserving slavery in the colonies. Among its protagonists were such figures as B. Edwards, a Member of Parliament and a West Indies planter, Tarleton, a Member of Parliament, a Deputy from Liverpool, and the aforementioned Robert Bisset.[20]

What arguments did they put up against the abolitionists?

First, reasons of a purely economic character: that the slave trade was the source of obtaining slaves; that slave labour formed the backbone of the West Indian plantations, and the number of slaves necessary to work the plantations could be retained only by constantly bringing in new slaves; that if the slave trade were abolished the plantations would fall into decline and the economies of the south of the United States of America, Great Britain and in part France would be undermined; that incomes from mines in Brazil, Cuba and other countries would fall, losses would be suffered by the shipbuilding and textile industries, the makers of firearms and other craftsmen, leaving many people without work.

Its protagonists admitted that the slave trade was a brutal affair but that this brutality was not something peculiar to that trade alone. In conclusion, facts would be adduced showing the brutal treatment of sailors in the British Navy, or the cruellest European laws.

The advocates of the slave trade, like the abolitionists, said much about the Africans' awful life in their homeland, claiming that the slave trade had nothing to do with that side of the question: Africa had always been rent by internecine warfare, slave raids, etc. Idyllic pictures would be given of life in the New World plantations with the following conclusion: in the New World Africans were much better off than at home, as for the state of slavery, they were used to that in Africa. The defenders of the slave trade categorically refuted the abolitionists' arguments on the freedom-loving nature of Africans and explained frequent uprisings on the slave ships only because of brutal treatment.

The advocates categorically claimed that enslavement of Africans and the slave trade were sanctioned by the Bible. They alluded to Noah's damnation of Ham and his progeny as evidence of the fact that Africans were predestined to be slaves. Nevertheless, there was no single opinion on the slave trade among the clergy, and especially so in Great Britain. The Bishop of London, for instance, reminded people that the Bible wrote of slavery in general and not with regard to Africans, and that it did not mention the slave trade or the export of Africans to the New World.[21] At that time these doubts did not become widespread. But in the nineteenth century, when the question of abolishing slavery in the British West Indies was put up for discussion in Great Britain, even the most rabid protagonists of slavery refrained from quoting the Bible. At that time many books were published explaining that the Bible did not sanction the enslavement of Africans.

The Quakers were among those who came out against the slave trade. In the late seventeenth century the American Quakers voiced slogans to abolish it. In Great Britain, the Quakers submitted a petition for the abolition of the slave trade in 1783, and in the nineteenth century they were the first to demand the abolition of slavery in the West Indian colonies.

Beginning of racism

In those years it was widely claimed that Africans in general were intellectually inferior to Europeans, that Negroes, using the expression of those days, stood closer in the line of development to apes than to human beings. This was the beginning of racism in regard to Africans.

We shall not dwell here on racism in general, its origin, or how it was and is manifested in different epochs and among different peoples. This report deals in brief with the times when racialism in regard to Africans began to assume the form of theory.

In the works of Azurara, Cadamosto and Pacheco Pereira, Portuguese sailors who made voyages to Africa before the beginning of the transatlantic slave trade, no racist views are expressed. When Europeans first came into contact with the Negro race, Africans were not looked upon as inferior beings. They could not be regarded as the Europeans' equal partners because priority belonged to those who were stronger. But if the newly discovered lands had been inhabited by non-black people having the same level of development as the Africans encountered there, relations between the Europeans and the local population would have developed in much the same way. At that time the stress was not on racial but religious intolerance. And historians are well aware that religious intolerance was displayed not only with regard to Africans and not only in those times.

After the extermination of the Indians in the French and British West Indies, white slaves were brought there to work alongside Africans (see above). In the writings of those years we do not find any racial pronouncements against African slaves. White and black slaves worked shoulder to shoulder on the plantations and were subject to equally brutal treatment.

In the late seventeenth and early eighteenth centuries many works were published by slave-traders and clerks employed in the numerous African trade companies. Among these authors one finds Barbot, Snelgrave, Bosman, Phillips et al.[22] Serving first as guidebooks (with the exception of Phillips' book in which he openly pities African slaves), informing slave-traders of the most profitable slave markets and means of delivering slaves with the least possible losses to the New World, they were written in a business language. Books written at the time by slave-traders contained no racialist views.

Discourse on the alleged inferiority of Africans as compared with Europeans took place not among slave-traders but in quite different quarters.

In 1781, the work of P. Camper, a Dutch physician and naturalist and a well-known scientist of his time,[23] appeared. Employing in his studies of skeletons of human beings and apes the facial angle, a measure he introduced, Camper concluded that the facial angle of Africans came nearer to that of apes rather than of Europeans. Camper merely stated his conclusions, but his followers, including C. White,[24] used the distinctions between skeletons or people belonging to different races and apes to claim that Europeans were in general superior to Africans not only physically but also intellectually. The protagonists of the slave trade were quick to make use of this conclusion.

Neither before the beginning of the slave trade nor while it was conducted freely and legally did any doubt arise as to the Africans' inferiority to Europeans. But when it became necessary to prove the need for its continuation, economic and religious arguments lacking sufficient conviction were augmented by racialist theory. All the basic racialist provisions against Africans were put forth during the struggle for abolition. From its very beginning racialism had a purely auxiliary character. It was needed to legalize the continuation of the slave trade and sanction slavery in the American colonies, as well as to prove that Africans, owing to the inferiority of their race, were fated to be slaves of the superior Europeans.

The slave trade and racism engendered by it turned the concept of 'slave' from a social distinction into a racial one. Racism is the most odious heritage of the slave-trade epoch.

In the early nineteenth century two of the biggest slave-trading powers abolished the slave trade: Great Britain in 1807 and the United States of America in 1808.

Illegal export of slaves

The year 1808 ushered in the third and last period in the history of the slave trade, that of illegal export of slaves from Africa. The official abolition of the slave trade in Great Britain and the United States did not reduce the number of slaves coming from Africa. In the early nineteenth century, the labour of slaves in New World plantations and mines was just as profitable and enabled planters and manufacturers to receive high profits. The retention of slavery in the New World after the slave trade was abolished predetermined the large-scale development of the illegal slave trade, for not a single slave-trading country was ready to substitute hired labour for the work of slaves.

These factors determined the attitude of different States to the slave trade in the nineteenth century. Of the big slave-trading countries Great Britain was the only one that found it more profitable to struggle against the slave trade than to take part in it. By that time its main colonial interests had switched from the West Indies to the East Indies. Besides, British industry called for increasing amounts of raw materials and new markets, and in this respect its interests became concentrated on Africa. Great Britain headed an international campaign to abolish the export of slaves from Africa. This allowed her to preserve till today the reputation of an allegedly disinterested champion of Africans' freedom. Foreseeing the emergence of its future colonies in Africa, Great Britain found it highly profitable to pose as a liberator in the eyes of Africans.

Undoubtedly the anti-slave blockage played a substantial role in curbing the export of slaves. Moreover, the first African scientists and public leaders

(S. Crowther, J. Horton), whose names are widely known even now, came from among the emancipated Africans who studied later in different missions and in Fourah Bay College.

In the seventeenth and eighteenth centuries the Church had connived in the slave trade; in the nineteenth century the missionaries concentrated their activities on helping emancipated Africans and victims of the trade.

The anti-slavery blockade also enabled a thorough study to be made of the situation on the western and eastern coasts of Africa, and when the time of direct colonial seizures arrived the slogan 'Abolition of the Slave Trade' was used to justify annexations.

In the nineteenth century the abolitionist movement in Europe was aimed at curbing the slave trade and abolishing African slave labour in the West Indian colonies. T. Clarkson, W. Wilberforce and T. F. Buxton in Great Britain and V. Scholcher in France did much to solve these problems. Other slave-trading countries, in utter disregard of their declarations to the contrary, continued to export slaves in keeping with the needs of their colonies' economies. The United States of America, which had abolished the slave trade, regularly imported new groups of slaves. According to the materials of the United States Senate, the works of several nineteenth-century authors and documents of the British Foreign Office, the United States carried on the slave trade until the Civil War. Many southern planters and northern manufacturers regarded the import of slaves as a necessary requisite for the successful development of the plantation economy (the internal slave trade could not cope with the growing need for manpower).

It is common knowledge that the attitude to slavery of Africans split the country into two hostile camps. The history of abolitionism in the United States has its heroes and martyrs. Seeking to justify the right to own people, the adversaries of abolitionism did not confine themselves to economic reasons but resorted to racism. In the nineteenth century the United States became the centre of racism with regard to African slaves. The works of Morton and Nott[25] published there viewed Africans as second-rate people, good only for serving the white man.

In the nineteenth century, following the routing of Napoleon's army, the international prestige of Russia increased substantially. Russia had never exported slaves from Africa. But the Russian Government began to take an active part in international negotiations on measures to put an end to the export of slaves from Africa. In 1841 it signed together with the Great Britain, Prussia and France *The Treaty of the Abolition of the Slave Trade*. In the mid-nineteenth century the movement for the abolition of serfdom was gaining momentum in Russia. In those years the progressive Russian public devoted much attention to questions dealing with the slave trade and the position of African slaves, namely in the United States, drawing a silent parallel with the position of serfs in Russia. The magazine *Sovremennik*, edited at the time by the great Russian democratic poet Nekrasov, published H. Beecher-Stowe's *Uncle Tom's Cabin* and *Life among the Lowly*. The outstanding Russian pedagogue and public leader Vodovozov translated H. Heine's poem 'The Slave Ship', etc. At that time the Russian press subjected racialist provisions to severe criticism. The pronouncements of N. G. Chernyshevsky, the Russian revolutionary democrat, are well known. Neither in the eighteenth nor in the nineteenth century was a single work published in Russia advocating racism against Africans.

After 1850, the general development of capitalism, the growing emigration from Europe and transition to an active colonialist policy reduced considerably the export of slaves from Africa. In the United States the victory of the northern States in the Civil War put an end to the Atlantic slave trade. With the emergence of colonies in Africa, Africans began to be more needed at home than in the New World.

Historiography

A century has gone by since the abolition of the Atlantic European Slave Trade.[26] The international situation has changed as well as the place of African countries among other States: former colonies have become independent. A genuine history of the African peoples is in preparation: *The General History of Africa*, the first volumes of which will soon be published under Unesco auspices. It stands to reason that the slave-trade problem, incorporating numerous complex and often contradictory points, has become in recent years a subject of particular interest to historians in different countries.

The history of the slave trade is now depicted in different ways and sometimes receives a new interpretation (Boahen, Curtin, Duignan, Clendensen et al.).[27] It is clear that the historiography of the slave trade is a separate, highly important and interesting theme.

The history of the slave trade is now studied by African historians, and among them Boahen, Ajayi et al.,[28] and this is particularly interesting. African scholars are able to make a much better evaluation of the scale of the Atlantic slave trade and its consequences in Africa than European historians.

Undoubtedly some questions have to be revised. It is utterly wrong to assert, for instance, that Africans themselves are to blame for the development of the slave trade or to speak of equal co-operation between European and African slave traders, just as it is absolutely incorrect to exaggerate, as has been done in the last few years, the role of the Arab slave trade in East Africa while diminishing the role and consequences of the Atlantic trade.

A point for consideration: for many years historians adopted the figures of Africa's losses from the slave trade given by Dunbar and adduced by

W. B. Dubois in *The Negro*.[29] Historians are well acquainted with Dubois's works, esteem him as a person and scholar, and highly value his work for the welfare of Africa. Unfortunately, Dunbar's materials were probably not critically analysed by the scholar.

Now, however, there is another extreme. New works on the history of the slave trade and among them Curtin's book[30] give 'new' calculations of Africans exported from Africa, and particularly of those imported to the New World. Africanists know that there were, are and will be no exact statistics on the subject. All figures were always approximate. The figures showing the number of slaves exported from Africa and imported into the New World are contradictory and are rarely founded on official documents; in most cases they have been deliberately falsified. That is why all attempts to undertake a complete revision of the numerical aspect of the slave trade without adducing any new sources are highly surprising. Probably the truth lies somewhere in between the figures quoted by Dunbar and the 'new' calculations.

Alongside new works on the history of Africa, new editions are appearing of works on the history of the slave trade by its contemporaries and prominent scholars of the late nineteenth to early twentieth centuries. Books by T. Clarkson, A. Benezet, W. Wilberforce and T. F. Buxton, and Mathieson's trilogy have already come out.

One can say that the history of the Atlantic slave trade has not been studied exhaustively. New studies are being made, new materials are added to the scientific fund. It will also be useful to give a new reading to the works dating from the time of the slave trade. Those who lived in those times saw what the slave trade had done to the African peoples and were quite aware of the true reasons that had engendered and promoted it. A serious unbiased discussion of the basic problems of the slave trade will enable a better investigation to be made of those aspects of its history that until now have been approached by historians of different countries from different standpoints.

Notes

1. T. O. Ranger (ed.), *Emerging Themes of African History. Proceedings of the International Congress of African History held at University College, Dar es Salaam, October 1965*, p. 134, Dar es Salaam, 1968.
2. G. E. Azurara, *The Chronicle of the Discovery and Conquest of Guinea*, Vols. 1–2, p. 57, London, 1896–99 (works issued by the Halkuyt Society No. 95,100).
3. D. Pacheco Pereira, *Esmeraldo de Situ Orbis*, p. 101, 195, 106, London, 1937 (works issued by the Halkuyt Society, 2nd ser., No. 79).
4. A. Brasio, *Monumenta Missionaria*, Vol. VI, Lisbon, Agencia Geral do Ultramar, Ministerio da Ultramar, 1955, d. 132; J. Cuvelier and L. Jadin, *L'Ancien Congo*, Brussels, 1954, d. XIV (Académie Royale des Sciences Coloniales, Section des Sciences Morales et Politiques. Mémoires).

5. E. Williams, *Kapitalism i Rabstvo*, p. 69, Moscow, 1950; *Capitalism and Slavery*, p. 51, Chapell Hill, University of North Carolina Press, 1945.
6. K. Marx, *Capital* (in Russian), Vol. I; 'K. Marx i F. Engels', *Soch.*, Vol. 23, p. 769.
7. J. E. Harris, *The African Presence in Asia. Consequences of the East African Slave Trade*, p. 9, Evanston, Northwestern University Press, 1971.
8. V. Earlow, *A History of Barbadoes, 1625–1655*, p. 295, Oxford, Clarandon Press, 1926; D. J. Owen, *The Origin and Development of the Ports of the United Kingdom*, 2nd ed., p. 129, London, Allman & Son, 1948; J. Latimer, *The Annals of Bristol in the XVIIth Century*, p. 255–6, Bristol, W. George's Sons, 1900.
9. E. Donnan (ed.), *Documents Illustrative of the History of the Slave Trade to America*, Vol. I, p. 193, Washington, Carnegie Institution of Washington, 1930.
10. O. Dapper, *Description de l'Afrique*, Amsterdam, Chez Wolfgang, Waesberge, Boom & van Someren, 1686; J. Barbot, 'A Description of the Coasts of North and South Guinea; and of Ethiopía Inferior, Vulgarly Angola; Being a New and Accurate Account of the Western Maritime Countries of Africa; A. and J. Churchill, (eds.), *A Collection of Voyages and Travels, Some Now First Printed from Original Manuscripts, Other Now First Published in England*, Vol. 5, London, 1746; B. Edwards, *The History, Civil and Commercial, of the British Colonies in the West Indies*, 3rd ed., London, J. Stockdale, 1801.
11. R. Bisset, *The History of the Negro Slave Trade in its Connection with the Commerce and Prosperity of the West Indies and the Wealth of the British Empire*, Vols. 1-2, London, S. Highley, 1805.
12. Marx, op. cit., p. 276; J. E. Cairnes, *The Slave Power, its Character, Career and Probable Designs*, p. 123, New York, Carleton, 1863.
13. Donnan (ed.), op. cit., Vol. 2, p. xiii.
14. 'Assiento, or Contract for Allowing to the Subjects of Great Britain the Liberty of Importing Negroes into the Spanish America', London, 1713.
15. *The Parliamentary History of England*, Vol. XXXII, p. 868.
16. D. Rinchon, *Les Armements Négriers au XVIIIᵉ siècle. D'après la Correspondance et la Comptabilité des Armateurs et des Capitaines Nantais*, p. 6, Brussels, 1956 (Académie Royale des Sciences Coloniales. Classe des Sciences Morales et Politiques. Mémoires).
17. J. A. Rogers, *Africa's Gift to America. The Afro-American in the Making and Saving of the United States*, p. 35, New York, 1961 (distributed by Sportshelf, New Rochelle, N.Y.).
18. *Chronicles of Negro Protest*, p. 47, 49, comp. and ed. with a commentary by B. Chambers, New York, Parents Mag. Press, 1968.
19. A. Benezet, *Some Historical Account of Guinea with an Inquiry into the Rise and Progress of the Slave Trade, its Nature and Lamentable Effects*, London, J. Phillips, 1788; T. Clarkson, *An Essay on the Slavery and Commerce of the Human Species*, from a Latin Dissertation, London, 1788; T. Clarkson, *The History of the Rise, Progress and Accomplishment of the Abolition of the African Slave Ttrade by the British Parliament*, Vols. 1–2, London, Longman, 1808; W. Wilberforce, *A Letter on the Abolition of the Slave Trade*, London, 1807.
20. R. Bisset, op. cit.; Edwards, op. cit.
21. *Substance of the Debates on a Resolution for Abolishing the Slave Trade which was Moved in the House of Commons 10th June 1806 and in the House of Lords 24th June 1806*, London, 1888; *The Parliamentary History of England*, Vol. XXIII, p. 1026.
22. J. Barbot, *A Description of the Coasts of North and South Guinea . . .*; G. Snelgrave, *Nouvelle Relation de Quelques Endroits de Guinée, et du Commerce d'Esclaves qu'on Fait*, Amsterdam, 1735; G. Bosman, *Voyage de Guinée*, Utrecht, 1705; T.

Phillips, Journal of a Voyage Made in 'the Hannibal' of London from England to Cape Monse-Radoe in Africa, and thence along the Coast of Guinea to Whidaw, the Island of St. Thomas, and so Forward to Barbadoes', in A. and J. Churchill (eds.), *A Collection of Voyages and Travels . . .*, Vol. 6, London, 1764.

23. P. Camper, *Dissertation Physique sur les Différences réelles que Présentent les Traits du Visage chez les Hommes de Differents Pays et de Different Ages; sur le Beau qui Caractérise les Statues Antiques*, Utrecht, B. Wild & J. Althear, 1791.

24. C. White, *An account of the Regular Gradation in Man and in Different Animals and Vegetables*, London, 1799.

25. S. Morton, *The Crania Americana*, Philadelphia, J. Dobson, 1839; J. Nott, *Types of Mankind, or Ethnological Researches*, Philadelphia, Lippincott, Grambo, 1845.

26. In the author's opinion the term Negro Slave Trade is seldom used nowadays. Rejecting the expression European Slave Trade, the term 'Atlantic Slave Trade' seems to suit the content of this concept much better.

27. A. Boahen, *The Topics in West African History*, London, Longman, 1966; P. D. Curtin, *The Atlantic Slave Trade : A Census*, Madison, Wis, University of Wisconsin Press, 1969; P. Duignan and C. Clendenen, *The United States and the African Slave Trade, 1819–1862*, Stanford, University Hoover Institution on War, Revolution and Peace, 1963.

28. J. Ajayi and M. Crowder (eds.), *The History of West Africa*, London, Longman, 1971.

29. W. E. B. Du Bois, *The Negro*, p. 155–6, London, Williams & Norgate, 1915.

30. Curtin, op. cit.

Reactions to the problem
of the slave trade:
an historical and ideological study[1]

Michèle Duchet

The problems of trading and dealing in black slaves, and slavery as such, can clearly not be dissociated: the various anti-slavery movements indeed also denounced the inhumanity of the traffic in human beings that drained ever-increasing numbers of blacks from Africa over to America and the West Indies. The petition submitted to the French National Assembly in 1790 by the Amis des Noirs (Friends of the Black People) refers to both 'the slave trade *and* slavery', and this is true of most of the works quoted,[2] if only because the initial step towards stamping out slavery was to put an end to the slave trade. But experience has proved that it was perfectly possible to abolish one without doing away with the other, whence the persistent resurgence of slavery. They can therefore be seen as two distinct forms of human exploitation which are probably closely linked but must not be confused. Indeed, they never were in the minds of those who fought either to preserve or abolish them. I shall try to explain why this was, and review the arguments put forward and the interests at stake.

It would be impossible here to relate the whole history of the slave trade[3] but a few relevant facts must be recalled. The Spaniards were the first to take black slaves across to the New World at the beginning of the fifteenth century. But it was particularly from the seventeenth century onwards, with the development of the great plantations—especially in Brazil—and the sugar economy, that the slave trade really reached its zenith. It is estimated today that some 9 to 12 million Africans were embarked on the slave ships in the period from the fifteenth to the end of the eighteenth century, the yearly average being 60,000. The mortality rate on these vessels was high, but the profit to be made was such (300 per cent) that this traffic was a significant factor in that era of capital accumulation which preceded the Industrial Revolution. The slave trade was profitable for two reasons: not only was this triangular traffic a source of rapid enrichment for those who were involved in it, but it also brought prosperity to the colonies with the steady flow of labour it provided. For the first of these two reasons, countries to which a particular colony did not even belong could be seen to invest in the slave trade there, as did the Dutch in Brazil.[4] For the second reason, companies were founded with the backing of the various mother countries and vied with foreign nations for the monopoly of the trade: the French Compagnie du Sénégal et de Guinée was an example. The combination of these two factors meant that the whole of Europe was involved in this abominable traffic, deriving enormous profit from it. Having thus attained world-wide proportions, the slave trade overstepped the boundaries of the slave economy as such; true, it was the keystone to that economy, but it developed as an independent form of commerce, one of many, and a particularly lucrative one. It had its own trading stations and trade routes in Africa itself, involved in the buying and selling of a new kind of merchandise, the black slave. A whole set of practices grew up around it, both on land and at sea, designed to keep the cargo alive, the value of the shipment being carefully assessed in terms of the price it would fetch at the auction sales.[5] The fact that people had become accustomed to such high rates of profit, and the very existence of the 'system' explain up to a point why the slave trade has subsisted to this day.

For the abolition of slavery did not by any means imply the abolition of the slave trade. Slavery was abolished by Great Britain in 1807, Brazil in 1836, France in 1848, Argentina in 1853 and the United States in 1865, to give only a few examples. But the slave trade continued to exist to satisfy the demand for labour in certain countries, and subsequently the demand for 'forced labour', the modern brand of slavery. Furthermore, in some places, 'a fusion of the two forms of slave trade, the Atlantic and the Arabized trade', had occurred; Moorish traders took their slaves to the Niger delta or the Upper Sangha basin and sold them to European traders.[6] With the slowing down of slave traffic to America, the older routes were revived and the caravans simply changed direction without the trade itself being affected.[7]

Thus it was that shiploads of slaves continued to pour into the Dutch colonies until as late as 1862, and into Brazil until 1887. Thus it was that men like Savorgnan de Brazza and later Monseigneur Augouard had reason to report numerous cases of transactions in human lives in the Oubangui region at the end of the nineteenth century.[8] And thus it is that to this day, the United Nations still receives reports attesting to the continued existence of slavery and the slave trade in the Arab countries. And yet from the fifteenth to the twentieth century, there has been no dearth of protests, decrees and laws on the subject, which ought to have succeeded in eradicating such practices, whilst the countries of Africa, with their accession to independence, were at last freeing themselves from the fear of servitude, forced migration and exile. This calls for a re-examination of history, an investigation of anti-slavery 'opinion': Of what did it consist? Who spoke out against the slave trade and slavery? What did they say? What were their arguments and what reasons did they give? Why this struggle? Was it purely a matter of defending the cause of black slaves, or was there some other underlying cause? What part did the black people themselves play in that struggle? These are all questions that can only be answered by ignoring details of facts and events and going in each case to the heart of the matter: the overall conjuncture, constraints, official attitudes, the issues at stake, ideologies. I shall therefore deal separately with two distinct periods, divided in terms of the prevailing 'conjuncture':

From the fifteenth to the end of the eighteenth century. This was the age of slavery as an institution and the economic system to which it was linked. The 'abolitionist' trend was very slow to develop, and only reached its peak with the independence of the American colonies.

In the nineteenth and twentieth centuries, there was a strong anti-slavery movement and it had won the legal battle, but 'forced labour' and the slave trade gained momentum in defiance of human rights. The fact that they were carried on clandestinely meant that the anti-slavery cause became a humanitarian battle.

The slave trade and anti-slavery from the fifteenth to the end of the eighteenth century

It should not be forgotten that the introduction of African labour to America and the West Indies was a direct consequence of the extermination of the Indians. This is why Las Casas, the Roman Catholic Bishop of Chiapas, was accused of causing the downfall of the Africans by taking up the cause of the Indians. In fact, he should be given credit, as he was by the eighteenth-century philosophers, for having been 'more of a man than a priest', for having been more intent on defending the Indians than on converting them.[9] Because, before his time, the Church had scarcely concerned itself with the enslavement of the Indians, as long as they were converted. The arrival of the African slaves was that much less of a problem in that they had already been reduced to slavery in accordance with the laws of their own countries, and had been bought as such by the slave traders and planters. There was nothing in the Holy Scriptures (Old or New Testament) forbidding Christians to own slaves. In 1836, a theologian, Monseigneur Bouvier, Bishop of Le Mans, declared that the slave trade was permissible, on condition—the only condition—that the blacks were justly deprived of their freedom, that they would be treated humanely and that there would be no unlawful transactions.[10] Once these prescriptions had been complied with, slaves were to be instructed in the true precepts of religion, a task that was easier than it would have been, had the slaves remained in their own countries, free.

In fact, to the theologians,[11] the right to spread the Gospel came first: slavery was deemed legitimate as long as it contributed to the propagation of Christianity. Thus the various missions all had their slaves, playing on the fact that they truly needed them to carry out their task effectively, and that the slaves would, moreover, be their most zealous disciples. There is little evidence of any concern in the matter, and when in 1557 the Jesuit Manuel de Nobrega requested permission to buy more slaves, the Order blamed Miguel Garcia, who had dared to protest against it.[12] The fact that the clergy in the Spanish and Portuguese colonies owned thousands of slaves was regarded as proof of the so-called legitimacy of the slave trade by the Council of the Indies. In addition it was imperative not to let the slave trade fall into the hands of 'heretic' nations. With a clear conscience, Catholics and Protestants vied with each other to secure the market for themselves. Thus it was that the problem of the slave trade came to the fore in a case which took place in 1685, when a German Protestant, Balthazar Coymans, upon request for a concession, met with the reply from the Spanish theologians Molina, Sanchez and Sandoval, who had been consulted on the matter, that there was nothing to be said against trading in slaves if it served the true Faith, but that the souls of the blacks were in grave danger of being contaminated by a voyage on board a heretic vessel![13]

It may be said, however, that Protestants and Catholics shared the same evangelical ideal and that the image of the faithful servant subject to divine law and the authority of a kindly master was enough to reassure a Christian conscience. But there still remained the problem of persecution of the individual—in Africa, on board the slave ships, at the slave markets—in short, within the actual framework of the whole slave system. The deliberately sustained myth of men taken as slaves and then sold to dealers by the Africans themselves, the alleged care taken by slave traders to look after their shipments of slaves, was all cast in doubt when it came to the third stage of proceedings, the slave markets, whose iniquities could not be disguised. The rest transpired through accounts by missionaries and travellers. In 1571, a theologian from Seville, Tomas de Mercado, showed just how far the slave trade was contrary to proper commercial practice and humanitarian principlès. Although he acknowledged the fact that slavery and the sale of African slaves by the Africans themselves did exist, he spoke out against the way traders would foment internecine conflicts as a means of capturing prisoners. He described conditions on board the ships and protested against the alarming mortality rate. His protest was all the more significant in that it was aimed at the slave trade and not simply slavery as such. Other theologians[14] were to express similar views, challenging the 'good faith' of the traders to whom the prisoners were handed over, and who would undiscriminatingly carry off men, women and children. Christian tradition, as we know, holds that any business transaction must be legitimate, and proscribes fraud or excessive profit; the black slave trade was therefore inadmissible, even if one of its functions was to supply the plantations with slaves who would ultimately become Christians. Traders whose consciences were not clear were therefore urged by Mercado to speak to their confessors![15]

It would be pointless to deny the fact that the theologians' standpoint had the advantage of keeping the system fundamentally intact (the plantation and mission economy, and the tacit approval of the local clergy) and only attacking traders and company agents whose lucrative ventures could deservedly cause an outcry. Nevertheless, by drawing attention, through the very arguments they put forward, to the fact that the system depended entirely on a form of commerce which consisted in trading in human lives, and in which slaves of both sexes and of all ages exchanged hands in lots as though they were commodities and not human beings belonging to the same ethnic group or family, a form of commerce in which people were treated on the slave-ships as no animal would ever have been treated, those who raised these questions sowed the seeds of doubt in many a mind: could one take delivery of these slaves without another thought for the inhumanity of the whole process?

The Protestants had inherited the same 'dualistic'[16] tradition as the Catholics, accepting the existence of slavery but not the fact of reducing a man to slavery by unjust and violent means. They believed even more firmly than the Catholics that in a world fraught with sin, slavery was a means of redemption for those whom God had reduced to that state. They, too, proposed to spread the Word to the servile masses, but their far more rigorous doctrine dictated other means of achieving this end. They did their utmost to improve master–slave relations, preaching charity and moderation to the former and submission and respect to the latter. Richard Baxter would say to the slaves:

reverence that providence of God which calleth you to a servant's life, and murmur not at your labour or your low condition, but know your mercies, and be thankful for them.[17]

This ideology of the 'good slave' and the 'good master' was based not only on a theological precept (the proper exercise of 'servitude'), but was also in keeping with the moral standards of everyday life, so typically Protestant; in keeping, too, with the ideal of Christian brotherhood.

At any rate, far from being opposed to the slave trade, the Protestants saw in it a means to serve the cause of evangelization; and it must not be forgotten that in the Protestant world the success of commercial undertakings was evidence of divine approval, and that when it came to deciding who was to blame, to put all the onus on the greedy, ruthless dealer rather than the planter, was positively unthinkable. We shall see, moreover, that the concept of sin plays a decisive role in religious ideology. Let me simply say at this juncture that whereas for the Catholics, the wicked trader was more to blame than the master who owned the slaves, Protestant ethics required that the master be held responsible for the slaves whom God had bestowed on him for their mutual benefit.

Sects

It was here that the anti-slavery movement, based on an ideology of protest
and rupture, first came into being. I agree with D. Brion Davis that the leaven
of the crusade against slavery and the slave trade is not to be sought in religious
tradition, but rather in the birth of a new concept which refused to regard the
established order as a compromise with sin, and gave God and the faithful the
power to transform the world.[18] It was this philosophy that was to give the
different sects the desire and the strength to put an end to what they regarded as
the most dire injustice, and by no means a road to salvation for the pagan
blacks. Moreover, sects like the Moravian Brethren and the Quakers had had
their share of persecution and exile, and their experience made them more alive to
the black slaves' lot. The Quakers' work, so highly praised by the philosophers,
is well known. But it should be recalled, if only to illustrate how powerful the
institution and force of habit were, that at the beginning the Quakers, too,
bought slaves; one can even go as far as to say that the prosperity of their
communities in the New World depended on slave labour, as did the wealth
of a large number of English traders who became Quakers. William Penn
himself owned slaves, and as late as 1730 the slave trade was practised in
Philadelphia.

The Quakers were 'good masters', but they did not try to convert their
slaves or make them join their society, known as the Religious Society of
Friends. Seen in that perspective, their possession of slaves could not be justified
other than by the profit they derived from it: it became a sin. And if the mere
fact of owning slaves was reprehensible, surely trading in slaves was even more
so, as indeed was the traders' maltreatment of them?[19] The arguments put
forward by 'orthodox' theologians struck at the very heart of Quaker doctrine
on this point, their ideal of a simple, just life. Their very existence was challenged. But it was not until 1769 that the anti-slavery lobby won the battle
and had slavery abolished in Pennsylvania. The Quakers' image was greatly
enhanced by their role in this critical battle, and they were held up as an example
by all those who, for quite different motives, had begun to espouse the cause
of the Negroes. Their selfless action was heralded in the *Ephémérides du
Citoyen* by the French Physiocrats [20] and acclaimed by the Abbé Raynal in his
Histoire des Deux Indes as being the acts of 'humane sectarians', of 'Christians
who sought virtues rather than dogma in the Gospel'.[21]

This does not imply that there was a convergence between the 'humanitarianism' of the enlightenment and the philanthropic leanings of certain sects
or even of the churches themselves. It is more the evolution of religious thought
itself, as we have seen for the Quakers, which accounts for the emergence of
an anti-slavery feeling based on the affirmation of a new set of values and a
new moral code. But in Protestant Britain, it was more common for philan-

thropy and the spirit of the Reformation to find their outward expression in charitable organizations. The Society for the Propagation of the Gospel (or SPG) was one, its object being to aid and educate the American Negroes. It was founded in 1701 and it had considerable influence in Georgia. The Count of Zinzendorf sent a group of Moravians to its leader, Thomas Bray, to help him in his work.[22] Several Huguenots joined the movement, which was particularly active in South Carolina, Philadelphia and New York, where it could expect substantial support from the Anglican Church. In 1710, Colonel Christopher Codrington set about founding two model plantations in Barbados. His idea was to show that by treating slaves in a humane manner, by encouraging them to marry and have children, by bringing down the mortality rate through a reduction in the amount of work and the absence of punishment, it was possible to increase the output of the plantations and, particularly, to run on a closed-circuit economy without having recourse to the slave trade. The results were by no means convincing, but a path had been opened towards the suppression of the slave trade, and as an ideal, at least, the experience had a great deal of influence by proposing an alternative to the abominations of the slave trade which it was impossible to control.

Unqualified condemnation of slavery came mainly from the Puritans. Their belief in personal salvation through a life of righteousness and adherence to a strict moral code made them see slavery as the source of all iniquity. In 1664, Richard Baxter, whom I have already mentioned, denounced the slave traders as 'the common enemies of mankind' and condemned as a 'heinous sin' the fact of buying human beings, even if they were slaves, unless it was for the purpose of setting them free. As for the planters, they were 'incarnate Devils'.[23] Morgan Godwyn regarded the Americans as base materialists who no longer cared for their souls, to the point of putting the slave trade before religion;[24] at the beginning of the seventeenth century, a Puritan called Paul Baynes accused them of living in slavery themselves, as sinners; in 1700, Samuel Sewall, a lawyer, declared that there were no grounds for slavery either *de facto* or *de jure*. The effect of all these protests was admission of the fact that the constant importation of blacks was undesirable, and that white labour might be used instead.[25] It is also true that for the first time it was realized that the emancipation of the Negroes and their integration would present formidable problems.

It is clear that the suppression of the slave trade, a necessary but insufficient precondition for the abolition of slavery, was a problem in itself. If all commerce ceased, it was evident that not only would the existing black labour force have to be employed sparingly, but that in the long run the slaves would have to be freed and integrated into a white society. In other words, the slave trade made it possible to perpetuate slavery, while continuing to be a source of manpower. America's openings to the Ocean, to Africa, to the world of slave-

traders and dealers prevented her from feeling the burden of those black peoples
coming to die on her plantations. A land of exile and frustration, she had
nothing to offer her slaves other than slavery. Thus the abolitionists were
constantly confronted with the eternal logic of the system. At the beginning
of the eighteenth century, the Anglican Church's only answer to the expansion
of the slave trade was a great campaign to 'christianize' slaves, thereby
shelving the issue, as it were, and resigning itself to making Christians of those
of whom it could not make free men.

Humanitarianism, the economists and the Enlightenment

A noble-minded primitivist trend had emerged from within Protestant theology
pointing out that blacks were good, and stressing the depravity of the slave-
owners who lived off their work; their corruption and 'materialism' were as
blameworthy as the 'unnatural commerce' carried on by the slave-traders.
These themes were taken up frequently in sermons during the eighteenth century, as well as in literature, for example by Daniel Defoe and in James Thom-
son's *The Seasons*, which was to be Saint-Lambert's source of inspiration.
Novels, poetry and the theatre were invaded by images of the suffering slave-
victim set against those of the cold-blooded, merciless master, all of which
prepared the ground for the abolition of slavery in people's minds.[26] With their
philosophy of sentiment, Shaftesbury[27] and Hutcheson gave a rational basis
to that active compassion with which God has expressly endowed every human
being so that he may concern himself with the sufferings of his fellow-men. This
gave rise to a tendency to portray in the most gruesome detail the misfortunes of
the black people, wrested from an idyllic life to be plummeted into the hell
of the plantations, such as in John Wesley's *Thoughts* on slavery. But Hutcheson
had himself been distressed by his reading of the accounts of the voyages of
Sir Hans Sloane and Atkins.[28]

However, the influence of Scottish moralist philosophy, of which Hutcheson, and then Adam Smith, were the exponents, was not only due to the
virtuous emotion which was its weapon against the insensitivity of the evil
slave-owners, but can also be attributed to the utilitarianist arguments it used
to such effect: thus Hutcheson demonstrated that slavery and slave labour,
which had every appearance of being in the interests of the slave-holder, were
not so in the long run and were in fact the reverse of the very ideal of happiness
and human progress.[29] But his disciple, Adam Smith, went much further:[30]
for him, slavery was only part of a system which worked badly because it
pitted personal interest against the public welfare. The way in which slaves
were treated prevented them from working, and slavery was the most costly
and unproductive form of labour. In fact, Smith's theories revolve around the
whole relationship between free and forced labour in a changing Western

economy, and these theories were hardly an incitement to use black labour. But in a world in which the law of profit prevailed, the economic argument carried most weight, overriding humanitarian considerations and offering in exchange for 'compassion' a distinctly worldly reward, i.e. better yields. We might ask to what extent this form of anti-slavery was compatible with a code of ethics and how far it was instrumental in preparing for the changes that would inevitably come about.

In France, the realism of the Physiocrats was just as ambiguous; it was chiefly an answer to the actual crisis in the slave system, put into words by its administrators.[31] Some of them were reformists, like Pierre Poivre who in 1766 urged the Ile de France settlers to treat their slaves with 'humanity' and not to lose sight of the fact that they were 'men like themselves'. In exchange, the slave would 'serve his master joyfully and faithfully'.[32] Others condemned the evils of the slave 'system' from the economic standpoint; at all stages of the process there were losses, because of the increased difficulty of carrying on the trade and therefore the higher selling price, because of the overworking of badly cultivated land, the excessively high mortality rate, militia expenses, time wasted, and because of the insecurity, indeed the hostility, of the slaves: 'The slave is lazy because it is his only enjoyment in life, and his only way of recapturing a part of himself robbed wholesale by his master.'[33]

There were others who believed in gradual emancipation, so that over a period of twenty years the slave masses would become free workers. *L'Histoire des Deux Indes*, written in 1780, reflected such a project proposed by Bessner, the governor of Guiana. But Raynal's work gave prominence to the ideas of the economists, set out between 1765 and 1775 in the *Ephémérides du Citoyen*: why not let Africa itself produce the commodities that America now supplied? Why not resettle the black slaves in Africa, where they would be free? Admittedly this solution would entail keeping on the slave trade, but it would do away with slavery which was detrimental to the economy of the plantations.[34] Humanitarianism thus upheld the theories of the Physiocrats, and the poet Saint-Lambert, on publishing *Ziméo* in the economists' journal, wrote to Dupont de Nemours: 'It is an act of charity for you to take up the cause of these poor Negroes; I have always pitied them greatly . . .'.[35]

Pity, humanitarianism, philanthropy—these three words aptly sum up the reactions of the eighteenth-century philosophers to the problem of slavery and the slave trade. But with Buffon, Voltaire and Bernardin de Saint-Pierre,[36] the emphasis was on moral condemnation. Helvétius' critique was consistent with the views of the Physiocrats, but was more political: one must be careful not to destroy the principle of self-interest which motivates men, and seen in that light slavery is a mistake as well as a crime.[37] A horror of the 'system' was the subject of most attacks, and in Voltaire's *Candide*, the Negro of Surinam who was mutilated in compliance with the Black Code on runaway slaves, was a sort of symbol of all the sufferings the black man was made to endure, and with impunity, for the law condoned slavery and all the hardships that went with it. In most cases, their accusations were by the same token an extension of their denunciation of the bloodthirsty, barbaric practices of so-called 'civilized' peoples, of the pervading spirit of intolerance which corrupted all their undertakings, of vain conquests and futile voyages.[38] The cause of the black slaves gave rise to a sense of helplessness reflected fairly accurately in this quotation from Helvétius:[39] 'Let us avert our gaze from such a baneful sight, which is so shameful and abhorrent to mankind.'

It is as though the very universality of enlightened philosophical thought deterred it from undertaking a 'charitable action' at a time when a radical change in mankind and society was imminent, from serving a cause which was not sufficiently in the interests of progress, as was, for example, the case of Calas, a victim of religious intolerance.

There is a well-known chapter in Montesquieu's *Esprit des Lois*, in which he questions what 'right we had to make the Negroes slaves' and in which there is this sentence, showing how injustice (in the strongest meaning of that which is unlawful) follows injustice: 'The peoples of Europe, having exterminated those of America, had to reduce the peoples of Africa to slavery, in order to use them to clear all that land for cultivation.'[40]

'Might is right' is the only law here. This was clearly stated, but the 'point of law' was not dealt with, for the fact that there was nothing in religious texts debarred a 'jurist' from giving a straightforward opinion.[41] It was not until 1780, in the *Histoire des Deux Indes*, a 'philosophical and political' history, that the principle of freedom was defended against any 'reasons of state'. Freedom is 'the ownership of one's body and the possession of one's mind'. The government does not have the right to sell slaves, the trader did not have the right to buy them, and no one has the right to sell himself.[42] Thus politics and ethics must join together to bring freedom to enslaved peoples, even before the other nations have shaken off their own chains. The idea of a 'one and indivisible' freedom emerges here from the crucible of the Enlightenment, and turns all causes into one great cause. Because of the universal nature of its principles, 'practice' outweighs theory, the defence of the 'rights of man' is in itself an instrument of progress and justice, whether that man be a 'savage' or a 'civilized' being, whether black, mulatto or white, and whatever his nationality or religion may be.

But the *Histoire des Deux Indes* went much further than that humanitarian protest. It emphasized the Negroes' own revolt and the 'maroon' phenomenon, the significance of which has often been underestimated in the history of slavery.

A thorough study of texts and documents on slavery shows that the fear of slaves becoming maroons was a predominant factor in Europe's 'guilty conscience'. We know that the Negroes' resistance to slavery came out in a number of different ways: suicide on board the slaveships or on the plantations, attempts to murder slave-owners, abortions. The history of the 'system' is a long sequence of escape and rebellion, and in some places the number of maroons reached alarming proportions. It happened in Jamaica in 1720 and in 1734–35; then in Guiana, where the 'colonies' of maroons grew to such a size that the authorities were forced to negotiate with them and grant them their autonomy.[43] There are records in the official *Correspondence* of the concern of administrators and settlers; although for the most part the phenomenon was endemic, the slave population outnumbered the whites to such an extent that the worst could be feared.

'Slavery is a violent and unnatural condition. . . . Those who are subjected to it are constantly possessed with the desire to break free, and are always ready to revolt', observed Jean Dubuq, head of the Colonial Office.[44] This gave rise to a policy of reform and efforts to persuade settlers to make the slaves' lives 'bearable' and make them lose 'the desire to be free, by dint of good treatment'. Humanitarianism was a necessity, before it ever developed into the 'active compassion' advocated by Christians and philosophers.

The slaves' refusal to accept their condition, their assertion of their right to be free, which was manifest in their propensity to run away, in itself the negation of slavery, inspired a whole new set of writings, from Mrs Behn's famous *Oroonoko* to Victor Hugo's *Bug Jargal*, and including Saint-Lambert's *Ziméo*. Others are less well known: the speech by Moses Boom Sam (in Abbé Prévost's *Pour et Contre*),[45] who is shown as the Moses of the black people and, in the *Histoire des Deux Indes*, the appeal for a 'new Spartacus' to lead his brethren on to 'vengeance and slaughter', the advent of a new leader being a certainty now that the fugitive black slaves had succeeded in gaining their independence.[46]

Two distinct trends thus emerged from within the anti-slavery movement: 'humanitarianism' (a term first used by a Physiocrat, Abbé Baudeau)[47] and militant humanism. The first, inspired by Christian compassion, sought to find a cure for an inescapable evil in the charity of the slave-owners and the submission of the slaves. The second condemned the master–slave relationship as an unnatural violence, and saw a possible issue in revolt: 'Your slaves need neither your generosity nor your advice to throw off the sacrilegious yoke that oppresses them. Nature speaks louder than philosophy and self-interest.'[48]

But the world then entered upon the 'revolutionary' era; in 1776, the thirteen American colonies shook off British domination, in 1781 they drew up a constitution for themselves. In 1789 there was the French Revolution and in 1794 the abolition of slavery by the National Convention, shortly after the revolt in Santo Domingo led by Toussaint Louverture. But none of these revolutions, although embarked upon in the name of liberty, really brought freedom to the Negroes. In 1802, Napoleon was to restore the slave trade and slavery in the French colonies. In America, where the whole economy depended on slave labour and slave traffic, the question was raised of how to reconcile the founding of a new nation with an institution which implied non-citizenship. In 1787, the Northwest Ordinance prohibited slavery in a third of the territory, and there were many separate instances of manumission in some of the states. But of the thirteen states, eight were to maintain slavery. After Independence, abolitionist literature abounded, refuting the racist arguments. 'Christian and humanitarian motives combine with the principles of liberal ideology' to prove that the new nation could not act against the very precepts on which it was founded.[49] But most of them trusted in democracy to bring about the gradual decline of the institution.

The principles which are the basis of the Government of the United States will unerringly lead to the extinction of slavery throughout the empire, as soon as it is compatible with public security and the welfare of the slaves themselves.[50]

But there was still no question of slaves being integrated into the American nation, we have the example of Thomas Jefferson accepting the emancipation of the Negroes but proposing to dispatch them to Sierra Leone[51] or even to Santo Domingo. The English philanthropist, Thomas Clarkson, had written a pamphlet which was republished in Philadelphia in 1788. Written for the British public for the sole purpose of condemning the slave trade, it also proposed a means whereby the Americans could 'carry on the Transatlantic trade while ethicizing it'.[52] The blacks would be sent back to Africa, and thenceforth there would no longer be a slave trade, but a trade in the products of their labour. It is of some significance that at this decisive point in its history, the United States had only economic, if humanitarian, solutions to offer, and that no mention was made of slavery in its Constitution. As Elise Marienstras so aptly puts it: 'Recognized in theory as a member of the human species, the American Negro was granted none of the prerogatives universally attributed to mankind by current ideology.'[53]

As we know, it was Great Britain who, with the loss of her American colonies, was the first to launch an abolitionist campaign, in 1787. The London Anti-Slavery Society (Wilberforce, Clarkson, Pitt, Grainville, Fox and Burke) prompted the founding of the French Society in 1788 (Condorcet, Brissot, Lafayette, Mirabeau, a number of *fermiers-généraux* (tax-farmers) and administrators and a few merchants). The main target was the slave trade; but here again, economic and humanitarian motives were inextricably linked: Great Britain wanted to put an end to a form of trade which brought wealth to the Americans, and the French saw the abolition of the slave trade as a means to stamp out slavery. In the documents of the Société des Amis des Noirs—

speeches, addresses, etc.—the slave trade is spoken of as an 'act of barbarism and inhumanity' and slave ships as 'floating coffins' in which atrocity is the prerequisite for profit.[54] They denounced the capture of slaves in Africa itself, the way in which hostilities were deliberately kindled as a source of captives for the slave shipments, looting and corruption; because of the slave trade, 'mankind has become a commodity'.[55]

But beneath the violence, the crisis of the 'system' as such was making itself felt. The issue of slavery, 'which probably should be eradicated only by hardly perceptible degrees so as not to endanger public order or personal property'[56] was approached with circumspection and, it is added, must not be 'confused' with the slave trade. The latter should, it was thought, be replaced by a more profitable form of trade which would channel the commodities produced in Africa towards Europe. What it amounted to was to go from one form of slave trade to another, from the black slave trade to what is known as the 'economy of exploitation', which thrived from the nineteenth century onwards. With the decline of the sugar plantations and the onset of the Industrial Revolution began a long process which in fact culminated in the end of slavery and subsequently of the slave trade. The official dates marking their abolition in the various countries are meaningful only if they are compared with each other and seen in the relevant context. In Great Britain, where the Industrial Revolution was a speedier process and where, furthermore, there was the desire to do harm to the former American colonies, events went faster; in France, Napoleon restored slavery but prohibited the slave trade in 1815. For a long time, slave traffic towards the United States and Brazil persisted, although slavery was abolished in the latter country in 1836. There were Spanish, French, Brazilian and American vessels involved in the traffic, British ships having more or less ceased slaving operations. From the humanitarian viewpoint, virtually everything that was to be said had been said, and the black peoples had been placed under the protection of the law by the Declaration of the Rights of Man. But the colonial system and the exploitation of the working masses were to set all these speeches and decrees at nought.

Slave trade, slavery, forced labour

After being a vast reservoir of slaves, Africa was to become the battleground for European imperialism. Each country carved out its own stronghold, and the old trading stations were often used as a launching ground for prosperous settlements. Colonization was an excuse for every possible form of intervention: military expeditions bought slaves from local traders to use them as 'volunteers'; when villages were taken, their inhabitants were also captured, and shown little mercy. And when the need arose, African labour continued to be exported, especially to the United States and Brazil. The nationality of the ships was immaterial: Spanish, French, Brazilian or American. If one compares the growth of the slave population in the two main countries involved in slavery on the American continent, namely the United States and Brazil, it appears that at the beginning of the nineteenth century there were approximately 1 million slaves in each of them, but by the beginning of the War of Secession the figure had grown to nearly 4 million in the United States as against 1.5 million in Brazil. The United States had thus amassed sufficient human 'capital' to develop its new cotton fields without being unduly hard on the slaves. In Brazil, where there was a steadily increasing demand for labour on the sugar plantations and on the recently developed coffee plantations, the intensive use of slave labour caused a rise in the mortality rate. Hence the need, after a while, to resort to local labour and, from the 1860s onwards, to a policy of immigration.[57]

The slave trade was now no longer an answer to a steady, guaranteed demand for African labour, but was subject to market fluctuations, economic changes and the relative importance of sugar, cotton or coffee. As it was mostly clandestine, there were no longer the enormous profits to be earned that had attracted the slave-traders. And yet it was to persist until it was finally deprived of its clientèle by the defeat of the southern states and the suppression of slavery in Brazil, that is until such time as it could no longer fulfil the basic function it had had in the pre-industrial economy.

But just as in Africa the colonial powers were reducing to 'slavery' whole sections of the local population by forcing them to do all kinds of labour, drudgery and compulsory service, it was inevitable that the slave trade should continue to exist in other forms. The best-known example is São Tomé, a Portuguese island off the coast of Angola.[58] It is probably not the only case of its kind, but it is significant for the way in which the whole 'system' was carried over there without appearing to transgress the 'law'. For the Code of 1878 specified labour conditions in the Portuguese African provinces: free labour and a five-year contract. But from the 1860s onwards, 2,000 to 4,000 Africans were shipped to São Tomé (and also to the island of Principe) each year; hunted down in the Angolan interior, chained together, embarked as contractual labour, they were shipped off to the cocoa plantations, whence they never returned. Public opinion was first roused in 1865 by protests from members of the 'Anglo-Portuguese Commission on Slavery'. An English journalist, Henry W. Nevinson, spoke of a new slave trade (*A Modern Slavery*, 1906) and succeeded in having a commission of inquiry sent out to investigate.[59] Other 'workers' were exported in this way from Mozambique to the Transvaal: there were approximately 80,000 of them a year, and they were rounded up by an association comprising 250 'recruiting agents'. Assimilation laws passed in 1926, 1929 and 1933 failed to put an end to 'forced labour'.

Another example: when in 1894 and 1895 decrees were issued prohibiting the entry of 'slave' captives and caravans into the Sudan, the slave-traders promptly declared that the 'captives' were 'free, wage-earning' porters.[60]

The facts were there: but how to put a stop to the slave trade and slavery when there were 'contracts', 'salaries' and an apparent lack of constraint? More than ever, to preserve the rights of individuals, it was the slave trade which had to be attacked. Even if there were no coercion, deportation with no chance of return constituted in effect a state of slavery, since the 'contractual' labourer was at the mercy of his employers. He was alienated, hence he was no longer 'free'; slavery had wrested him from his home, made him an exile, a captive. In West Africa, the decree of 1905 was aimed at 'any person who has entered into an agreement whose object is to deprive a third person of his liberty'.[61] It is clear enough from the terms of the decree that the legislator's words should, by looking beyond the actual facts of the case, be taken to mean the intention of the guilty party to reduce a man to slavery, even if that man's status was not that of a slave. And yet the traffic continued, especially in the more remote parts of the globe, and only changes in the economic situation finally brought about its extinction.

There was, of course, no lack of humanitarian protests, but the colonial system was not concerned about slavery save in the case of 'household' slaves, and so it was easy to denounce traditional practices in Africa which had been the basis of the Atlantic slave trade. As for the export of labour for the purpose of 'depriving a third person of his liberty', it was far too useful to be prohibited, as was illustrated only too well when, in 1947, the inspector of the Angolan Colonial Service, who was a member of the Portuguese Parliament, submitted a report on 'forced labour' in Angola,[62] only to be given a seven-year prison sentence for his courage.

As for the 'missions', it is extremely difficult to assess their role. Their common ideology was to spread the Gospel, but charity often prompted them to make 'humanitarian' gestures, and the fact that they were settled permanently in the colonies facilitated their action.[63] As far as the Roman Catholic Church was concerned, Pope Gregory XVI had condemned the slave trade as being an 'inhuman . . . commercium' in 1838, and Leo XIII denounced slavery in 1888, instructing Monseigneur Lavigerie to oppose its establishment in the French colonies. But on the whole, churches and missions supported colonization, preferring to focus their attacks on slave trading in the Muslim countries, thereby killing two birds with one stone. The Protestant missionary Fowel Buxton [64] led an expedition into the interior in an attempt to sap the very foundations of the slave trade (around 1840) but the discovery at this time of a route to the Sudan by a Turkish captain opened up new trade outlets, and some 60,000 slaves fell victim to the new trade. As in the earlier period, opposition to the slave trade and slavery came chiefly from religious sects, particularly the Evangelicals. One of the most fervent activists was Sir Thomas Fowel

Buxton, who drew up a proposal to 'civilize' Africa, urging Great Britain to use the influence and power 'which God had thought fit to bestow on her to raise Africa up out of the dust and enable it to draw upon its own resources to wipe out slavery and the slave trade'.[65] As for the official missionary effort, it was restricted to the spread of the faith and the education of the people, leaving the settlement—or the neglect—of these difficult problems to the discretion of the administrative authorities.

Taking the declarations of the Rights of Man, and the Law of Nations as the basis for its ideas, the liberal, philanthropic and humanitarian trend developed, led by such prominent figures as Lamartine, Benjamin Constant and Tocqueville. Victor Schoelcher, who had been one of the chief architects of the Act for the abolition of slavery in 1848, denounced the persistence of the slave trade in Natal in 1877.[66] In many countries, from France and Great Britain to Brazil and the Cameroons, anti-slavery societies were founded to defend the rights of the human being against all forms of slavery, in the widest possible sense that the historical context dictated. But this liberal tradition, inspired by faith in the progress of the human mind and in a certain sense of the white race's 'civilizing' mission, was superseded by socialist thinking which cherished no illusions about 'man's inhumanity to man', and set about demonstrating that the evils of the colonial system were to be found in the logic of its own existence, and that the only way to put an end to slavery 'in all its forms' was to put an end to European hegemony in Africa:

The discovery of gold and silver in America, the extirpation, enslavement and entombment in mines of the aboriginal population . . . the turning of Africa into a warren for the commercial hunting of black-skins, signalized the rosy dawn of the era of capitalist production. These idyllic proceedings are the chief momenta of primitive accumulation . . . slavery . . . is the sole natural basis of colonial wealth.[67]

Within a comprehensive theory of capitalism, Karl Marx defines the slave trade as one form of primitive accumulation, as a traffic in human beings which has specific characteristics and which, at a particular point in history, yields a maximum rate of return.

Liverpool waxed fat on the slave-trade. This was its method of primitive accumulation. And, even to the present day, Liverpool 'respectability' is the Pindar of the slave-trade which . . . has coincided with that spirit of bold advent which has characterized the trade of Liverpool and rapidly carried it to its present state of prosperity; has occasioned vast employment for shipping and sailors, and greatly augmented the demand for the manufactures of the country.[68]

The profit derived from the slave trade itself is compounded by the profit made out of menial labour: merchants, slave-traders and planters share the gains of a system which pushes human exploitation to limits hitherto unknown.

Treated as a mere commodity, bought, sold and exchanged, the slave still provides the labour power needed for the production of colonial wealth. Whereas the wage-earner sells his labour 'freely' (even if that freedom is illusory), it is 'the labour-power itself which is sold' (by a third party) with the body of the slave. Hence:

'The horrors of overwork, that product of civilization, serve to augment the barbarity of slavery and bondage',[69] and the slave trade, prompt to supply needs, makes it unnecessary to ensure that the individual slave survives. Only his productivity counts. Slavery sanctions the slave trade, but the slave trade sanctions slavery: this is the logic of the system which fostered the transition to industrial capitalism. This, in turn, was to throw men-as-commodities on to the market, perpetuating the trade in human flesh and the overwork resulting from it. Although he denounces the atrocities of the slavery system, Marx demonstrates the vanity of humanitarian idealism [70] which depicts the revolt of the slave as a triumph of a certain concept of mankind. 'The rebellious negroes of Haiti and the fugitive negroes of all the colonies' wanted to free themselves, not mankind, and their fight becomes an example for all who are exploited.[71] Nor is it possible to humanize an inhuman system; one must expose its economic causes and the social relationships brought about by the circumstances of the quest for profit and by overwork;[72] the struggle against menial work must be harnessed to the struggle against the exploitation of free workers, and to the struggle against capital.

However, at the international level, liberalism had a useful role in carrying on the combat against the wrongs of the system, until such time as the peoples were able to throw off the colonialist yoke for themselves. But the problem lay in knowing whether it was the abolition of slavery and the slave trade in the strict sense they were fighting for, or whether that included all forms of slavery and the trade in human beings stemming from the exploitation of the African labourers. An International Labour Office report published in Geneva in 1953 rightly recalls that even though the slave trade and slavery had been condemned by conferences and conventions throughout the nineteenth century, there had never been any mention of 'forced labour as an institution distinct from slavery'. Hence the existence of some confusion both in terminology and in people's minds. The 1890 Brussels anti-slavery conference condemned the Arab-centred slave trade, the 1885 Berlin conference prohibited slavery and the traffic in human beings. Article 22 of the League of Nations Covenant (1920) mentions together 'the prohibition of abuses such as the slave trade' and the prevention of compulsory service in certain mandated territories. The Temporary Slavery Commission placed slavery on a par with 'similar forms of servitude'. It provided for compulsory repatriation in the event of work involving the removal of a labourer from his usual place of residence, thereby defining forced labour unequivocally as a form of servitude when the trade in human beings imposes the further insuperable obstacle of the distance between the place of work and the place of residence.[73] In 1926, the Slavery Convention recommended that no amendment should be made to this except when the work is necessary for 'public purposes', such as the construction of the first African railways.[74] A commission of inquiry sent out to Liberia in 1930 reported that 'conveying groups of indigenous captives' to the coast was tantamount to a form of slave trade, and that forced labour was therefore nothing but slavery in disguise, and yet in 1932 the 'Standing Advisory Committee of Experts on Slavery' did not deal with forced labour.[75] What is undoubtedly at the root of all this lack of decision is the difficulty of reconciling humanitarianism and politics, of speaking up in the name of human rights when the interests of the great colonial powers are exacerbated to such a degree that while pretending to reject slavery, they accept forced labour, which they need.

The International Labour Office then decided to deal more specifically with 'forced labour' by trying, if not to stop it, at least to restrict the powers of those who had recourse to it.[76] The danger is inherent in any country where workers are 'recruited or engaged through a system of voluntary migration'. This manpower drain is dangerous because it 'tends to perpetuate conditions of servitude', gives rise to extremely poor conditions of output and remuneration, and finally because it hinders the development of the villages left deserted. However the practice was so widespread that the 'Recruiting of Indigenous Workers Convention' (No. 50) was ratified only by the countries which did not feel directly concerned. In 1949, the statute on 'migrants for employment' (Migration for Employment Convention, No. 97) sought, by the choice of a neutral term to describe them, to protect workers recruited in the so-called underdeveloped countries, in particular the Africans. The United Nations General Assembly had just, on 10 December 1948, adopted the prohibition of slavery and the slave trade 'in all their forms' (Article 4), but without referring to forced labour, even though it asserted that everyone has the right to 'free choice of employment'. This 'Universal Declaration of Human Rights' marked the victory, at the international level, of an ideal, frail though the Second World War had shown it to be. Deportation, slavery and extermination had been the lot of many of those peoples who had formerly been conquerors and colonizers. In the advocacy of human rights, with no discrimination on grounds of race or religion, there was a sort of consensus which reflected both the strength and the weakness of the liberal humanism that had been the legacy of the Age of Enlightenment. Its strength lies in a certain idea of man, of his freedom and dignity, which, after a bitter struggle, has been accepted ever since the eighteenth century. Its weakness lies in the fact that it is a principle, nothing more, a mere 'statement' which is not binding upon those who manipulate men and words, with whom 'forced' labour spells servitude and slavery, and 'migratory labour' means migrant or emigrant workers who do not have the 'free choice' that they, as 'voluntary' recruits, are allegedly given. Words, and history, can be treacherous.

In 1957, an International Labour Office Convention (No. 105) declared the abolition of forced labour, one year after a United Nations Supplementary Convention of 1956 had reaffirmed the abolition of slavery and the slave trade. But the two issues constantly overlap, 'forced labour' being the substitute for slavery in colonial countries, and the slave trade remaining the means of meeting manpower requirements. The inquiry carried out by the United Nations in 1963 on the specific question of slavery and the slave trade provides ample proof of this.

Mohamed Awad's report shows that there were seventy-six replies,[77] and was based on the premise that where there is no slave trade, there is no slavery.[78] He points out that the abolition of slavery has been adopted in principle by most countries at different times, Saudi Arabia being the last to have officially abolished it in 1962. The Mali report gives three distinct periods in the history of slavery in Africa: (a) domestic slavery and prisoners of war in feudal times; (b) the slave trade with the establishment of trading posts; (c) the replacement of the slave trade by a 'system of exploitation'. 'Consequently the abolition of slavery and of institutions or practices similar to slavery only became a fact with national independence.' Finally, anti-slavery societies in Saudi Arabia and India claim that there are still slaves in these two countries,[79] although this is denied by their official representatives. Clearly the word 'slavery' covers a variety of practices, in a variety of different contexts: traditional slavery (which could be taken to include short-distance trading); slavery in the Arab countries which is associated with the caravan trade and which still exists; slavery linked with the Atlantic slave trade; servitude for debt (as in the case of India, for example); and forced labour in the colonial countries, a form of slavery imposed on individuals who are not officially regarded as slaves. To say that the slave trade creates slavery emphasizes the common link in all these practices which successively or together have shattered human freedoms and disrupted ethnic identities throughout the course of history. The slave trade does not only help to preserve slavery as an institution, to the mutual advantage of both dealer and slave-owner; it imposes on the slave the added burden of exile, takes away any hope he may have of ever returning home, and even has the effect of depriving him of the will to regain his freedom. Africa has endured every form of slavery, every form of servitude, her fate seemed to her to be unchanged when the slave trade gave way to 'voluntary' migration.

At the international level, humanitarian efforts are still active. Slavery, the slave trade, forced or compulsory labour have been officially banned: Will they one day be a thing of the past? With decolonization, the conditions of man's exploitation of man have become extinct; sporadically they reappear; there are still 'anti-slavery' societies, and there is still some traffic, though on what scale or through what channels it operates we do not know. We have gauged how long it takes for a positive 'awareness' to develop, and again the distance to be travelled before that awareness is translated into 'humanitarian' action, and we have seen that the evils wrought by man can be undone by man, if only he is prepared to denounce their true causes and realize that there are a thousand ways of exploiting human beings. But who can forecast the day when no men will be slaves, when no men will do trade in their fellow men, when nowhere will men be reduced to the ignominious status of marketable commodities?

Notes

1. Certain original English texts being unobtainable, a free English translation has been given.
2. *La Révolution Française et l'Abolition de l'Esclavage, Textes et Documents*, Vol. VIII, Part 2, Paris, EDHIS, 1968. See Clarkson's *Essai sur l'Esclavage et le Commerce de l'Espèce Humaine*, Falconbridge's *Tableau de la Traite*, etc.
3. Data taken from P. D. Curtin, *The Atlantic Slave Trade*, 1969; See also H. Deschamps, *Histoire de la Traite des Noirs et l'Antiquité à nos Jours*, Paris, Fayard, 1971.
4. See Celso Furtado, *La Formation Économique du Brésil, de l'Époque Coloniale aux Temps Modernes*, The Hague, Mouton, 1972. The Dutch were also to seize the monopoly of the slave trade in the Spanish territories.
5. These practices are described in the ships' logs, and in some accounts by travellers.
6. Pierre Kalck, *Histoire de la République Centrafricaine des Origines Préhistoriques à nos Jours*, Vol. I, p. 140, note 276.
7. According to some historians, it was because of the reconversion of the Atlantic slave trade that the Saharan trade grew to unprecedented proportions. See J. Suret-Canale, *L'Afrique Noire*, Vol. I, p. 162 (Ed. Sociales).
8. P. Kalck, op. cit., p. 139–40.
9. *Histoire Philosophique et Politique des Établissements des Européens dans les Deux Indes*, IV, 20, Abbé Raynal, Éd. de Neuchatel, 1783.
10. Quoted in P. Larroque, *De l'Esclavage chez les Nations Chrétiennes*, p. 31–2, Paris, 1864.
11. Francisco de Vittoria, Francisco Suarez; but these sixteenth-century documents, like those of Paul III or Pius V, relate to the Indians.
12. Serafim Leite, *Historia da Companhia de Jesus*, II, p. 347 et seq.
13. G. Scelle, *La Traite Négrière . . .*, I, p. 708–11.
14. Bartolomé de Albornoz, Tomas Sanchez; see David Brion Davis, *The Problem of Slavery in Western Culture*, p. 189–90, Cornell University Press, 1966.
15. *Summa de Tratos, y Contratos . . .*, Chap. 20, Seville, 1587.
16. David Brion Davis, op. cit., p. 198. My analysis is very close to that of D. B. Davis in his remarkable work.
17. Quoted in Davis, op. cit., p. 204. Baxter was an English Protestant who had been sent out to Barbados. Appalled by the evils he saw in the colonies, he wrote a 'Summ of Practical Theology and Cases of Conscience'.
18. Davis, op. cit., p. 294.

19. ibid., Chap. 10. See Elbert Russell, *The History of Quakerism*, New York, 1942, on all these points.
20. 1769, IX. Letter from Dr Benjamin Rush to Barbeu-Dubourg.
21. Vol. VIII, p. 235.
22. Davis, op. cit., p. 213.
23. Quoted by Davis, op. cit., p. 338.
24. The title of his pamphlet is significant: *Trade Preferred before Religion . . .*, London, 1695.
25. Davis, op. cit., p. 345.
26. Hoxie N. Fairchild, *Religious Trends in English Poetry, I. Protestantism and the Cult of Sentiment*, New York, 1939–49.
27. *Inquiry Concerning Virtue or Merit*, translated into French by Diderot in 1745: '. . . the eternal wisdom governing this universe has linked the personal interest of God's creature to the overall good of his system, so that he cannot pass one by without stepping aside from the other, or fail in his duty to his fellow-men without doing harm to himself.'
28. His *System of Moral Philosophy* dates from 1755. Sloane was the author of a *History of Jamaica*, Atkins had published an account of a *Voyage to Guinea and Brazil. . .*, London, 1735, in which he depicted the atrocities of the slave trade.
29. *System of Moral Philosophy*, II, p. 202 *et seq.*
30. *The Theory of Moral Sentiments*, 1759; *An Inquiry into the Nature and Causes of the Wealth of Nations*, 1776.
31. See Michèle Duchet, 'L'Idéologie Coloniale, la Critique du Système Esclavagiste', *Anthropologie et Histoire au Siècle des Lumières*, Paris, 1971, I. 3.
32. ibid., Discours quoted, p. 148–9.
33. Dupont de Nemours, *Ephémérides du Citoyen*, VI, p. 216 et seq., 1771.
34. *Histoire . . . des Deux Indes*, V, p. 266, Ed. Neuchatel, 1708.
35. *Ephémérides du Citoyen*, VI, p. 180–1, 1771.
36. See Duchet, op. cit., 'L'Anthropologie de Buffon', p. 278–9; 'L'Anthropologie de Voltaire, p. 318–21. Racial prejudice in fact prevented Voltaire from going any further.
37. *De l'Homme*, Section VI, Chap. I.
38. *Essai sur les Mœurs*, Chap. CXLIX, 1756.
39. *De l'Esprit*, I, Chap. 3.
40. Book XV, Chap. 5, 1748.
41. Hence the use of irony which permitted an indirect attack, but had the drawback of being understood only by the initiated. Even in the eighteenth century, several noteworthy misconceptions confirm the 'aristocratic' nature of this form of argument which came to be interpreted as a justification of slavery.
42. Vol. V, p. 275, et seq.
43. See Duchet, op. cit., p. 142–3 and 155–6. These 'colonies' subsisted; they are now the Boni, from the name of their leader, Bonnie.
44. *Instructions* of 30 November 1771.
45. Vol. VI.
46. Vol. V, p. 288.
47. E. D. Seeber, 'Humanism, Humanitism and Humanitarianism', *Modern Language Notes*, XLIX, 1934. By the same author, see *Anti-slavery Opinion in France during the Second Half of the Eighteenth Century*, Baltimore, The Johns Hopkins Press, 1937.
48. *Histoire des Deux Indes*, Vol. V, p. 288.

49. On all these questions, see E. Marienstras, *Les Mythes Fondateurs de la Nation Améri-caine*, p. 209 et seq., Paris, Maspéro, 1976.
50. Z. Swift, 'An Oration on Domestic Slavery', 1791, quoted by Marienstras, op. cit., p. 257.
51. Where the English had founded a settlement of free Negroes who had fought during the War of Independence.
52. Marienstras, op. cit., p. 267.
53. ibid., p. 275.
54. Petion, *Discours sur la Traite des Noirs*, op. cit., Part I, p. 1.
55. ibid., Part II, p. 2. (Frossard, *Observations sur l'Abolition de la Traite des Nègres*, 1793.)
56. ibid., p. 26–27.
57. See Celso Furtado, *La Formation Économique du Brésil, de l'Époque Coloniale aux Temps Modernes*, p. 101 et seq., Paris and The Hague, Mouton, 1972. Furtado points out that between 1827 and 1830, the slave trade increased, since the agree-ment with England was due to come to an end at that date. There was a further increase prior to the ceasing of the trade in 1851–52. Between 1800 and 1860, approximately 300,000 slaves were imported into the United States, most of them clandestinely since the slave trade had been abolished since 1808 (p. 102, note 33).
58. See J. Duffy, *Portugal in Africa*, Harmondsworth, Penguin, 1962.
59. Comprising the leaders of the Aborigines Protective Society and the British and Foreign Anti-slavery Society. The missionary, Charles Swan, published *The Slavery of Today*, in London in 1909.
60. J. Suret-Canale, op. cit., II, p. 87.
61. ibid. The 1831 law applied only to sea traffic. It was the first decree in Africa to prohibit any kind of slave trade. But it was, of course, concerned only with the former territories of French West Africa.
62. James Duffy, op. cit., p. 185. Henrique Galvao estimated that 2 million Africans had been 'expatriated' in this way.
63. There is, of course, a good deal of controversy on the subject. Suggested reading: Rev. Joseph Bouchard, *L'Église en Afrique Noire*, Paris, 1958; G. Goyau, *La France Missionnaire . . .*, 2 vols., Paris, 1948; R. Cornevin, *Histoire de l'Afrique*, 2 vols., Paris, Payot, 1966.
64. Cornevin, op. cit., p. 456.
65. *The African Slave and its Remedy*, 1840. Quoted in M. Merle, *L'Anticolonialisme Européen de Las Casas à Marx*, p. 221, Paris, Colin, 1969.
66. *La Restauration de la Traite des Noirs au Natal*, 1877. See also *Esclavage et Colonisa-tion*, selected texts by V. Schoelcher, by E. Tersen. Preface by Aimé Césaire, Paris, PUF, 1948.
67. Karl Marx, *Capital*, p. 1212, Ed. La Pléiade, I.
68. Karl Marx, *Capital*, Vol. I, p. 759, New York, International Publishers. The end of the sentence is a quotation from Aikin, *A Description of the Country from Thirty to Forty Miles round Manchester*, London, 1795.
62. ibid.
70. See in Marx and Engels, *German Ideology*, London, Lawrence & Wishart, 1942, the harsh criticism of the 'liberal' and individualist thesis of Max Stirmer, author of *Der Einziger und sein Eigetum*.
71. ibid.
72. On the specific forms of profit within the slavery system, there are analyses more precise than those of Marx. For lines of research, see the 'Letter on Slavery',

published in the review *Dialectiques*, 1977, No. 21 in which Claude Meillassoux attemps to demonstrate both the uniqueness and the limits of the 'slavery process'
73. *Documents of the League of Nations*, A. 19, 1925, VII, paras. 100–1, 106–7.
74. ibid., A. 104, 1926–VI. Ratified initially by 36 States, subsequently by 41.
75. See ILO *Report*, op. cit. Annex I: 'Historical Review of International Action on Forced Labour'.
76. ILO, 'Studies and Reports', New Series No. 38.
77. New York, 1967. (The replies were sent in by 23 African countries, 20 Asian and Far Eastern countries, 22 from Europe, 9 from Latin America, and 2 from North America.) The questionnaire had been sent out to all Member States of the United Nations in 1964.
78. Page 8.
79. On 'slave raids', see J. Pollard-Dulian, *Aujourd'hui l'Esclavage*, Paris, Ed. Ouvrières, 1967. Regarding Saudi Arabia, the author speaks of caravans from Sudan, Upper Volta and Niger, and of a network of real slave traders, 'dealers in ebony', p. 196.

Bibliography

Historical works

Bouchaud, J. *L'Église en Afrique Noire*. Geneva, La Palatine, 1958.
Cornevin, R. *Histoire de l'Afrique*. 2 vols. Paris, Payot, 1966.
Curtin, P. D. *The Atlantic Slave Trade*. Madison, Wis., University of Wisconsin Press, 1969.
Deschamps, H. *Histoire de la Traite des Noirs de l'Antiquité à Nos Jours*. Paris, Fayard, 1971.
Duffy, J. *Portugal in Africa*. Harmondsworth, Penguin Books, 1962.
Furtado, C. *La Formation Économique du Brésil, de l'Époque Coloniale aux Temps Modernes*. Paris and The Hague, Mouton, 1972.
Goyau, G. *La France Missionnaire dans les Cinq Parties du Monde*. Paris, Plon, 1948.
Kalck, P. *Histoire de la République Centrafricaine des Origines Préhistoriques à nos Jours*. 2 vols., Paris, Berger-Levrault, 1974.
Leite, S. *Historia da Companhia de Jesus no Brasil*. Rio de Janeiro and Lisbon, 1938–50.
Russell, E. *The History of Quakerism*. New York, Macmillan, 1942.
Scelle, G. *La Traite Négrière aux Indes de Castille*. Paris, L. Larese & L. Tenin, 1906.
Suret-Canale, J. *Afrique Noire*. 2 vols. Paris, Éd. Sociales, 1964.

General works

Curtin, P. D. *The Image of Africa; British Ideas and Action (1780–1850)*. Madison, Wis., University of Wisconsin Press, 1964.
Davis, D. B. *The Problem of Slavery in Western Culture*. New York, Cornell University Press, 1966.
Duchet, M. *Anthropologie et Histoire au Siècle des Lumières*. Paris, Masporo, 1971.
Fairchild, H. N. *Religious Trends in English Poetry*. 3 vols. New York, Columbia University Press, 1939–49.
Marienstras, E. *Les Mythes Fondateurs de la Nation Américaine*. Paris, Masporo, 1976.
Seeber, E. D. *Anti-slavery Opinion in France during the Second Half of the Eighteenth Century*. Baltimore, Md, The Johns Hopkins Press, 1937.

Old texts and documents

Éphémérides du Citoyen, Paris, 69 vols., 1765 et seq.
LARROQUE, P. *L'Esclavage chez les Nations Chrétiennes*. 2nd ed. A. Lacroix-Verboeckhoven, 1864.
RAYNAL, G. T. *Histoire Philosophique et Politique des Établissements et du Commerce des Européens dans les Deux Indes*. Geneva, J.-L. Pellet, 1780 ed.
La Révolution Française et l'Abolition de l'Esclavage, Textes et Documents. 12 vols. and 89 titles. Paris, EDHIS, 1968.
SCHOELCHER, V. *La Restauration de la Traite des Noirs au Natal*. Paris, Imp. de E. Brière, 1877. Selected texts (Preface by Aimé Césaire), under the title *Esclavage et Colonisation*. Paris, Presses Universitaires, 1948.
SHAFTEBURY, A. C. *Inquiry Concerning Virtue or Merit*. Trans. by Diderot, 1745.
SMITH, A. *An Inquiry into the Nature and Causes of the Wealth of Nations*. London, 1776.

Official documents

AWAD, Mohamed. *Report on Slavery*. New York, United Nations, 1967.
ILO Reports: 1953, Report of the Ad Hoc Committee on Forced Labour (Studies and Reports, New Series No. 38); 1929 Report, 'Forced Labour—Preliminary Report and Questionnaire'.

The Atlantic slave trade

The slave trade and the Atlantic economies, 1451-1870 [1]

Joseph E. Inikori

This article deals deals with all the regions of Africa directly affected by the external slave trade from that continent across the Sahara, the Atlantic ocean, the Red Sea and the Indian Ocean. Other territories included are South and North America, the West Indies and all Europe bordering on the Atlantic, including those European countries affected by the activities of the Atlantic countries. In some ways this definition of the scope of this paper is arbitrary. It excludes some of the slave-receiving economies of the period, in particular, those of the Middle East.[2] On the other hand, the economies included were not all affected to the same degree by the slave trade; indeed, some were only indirectly affected. However, the coverage of the territories mentioned makes it possible to analyse in one broad sweep the effects of the slave trade on all the economies most significantly affected.

The slave trade and slavery is a subject on which a great deal has already been said and written, starting from the eighteenth century and continuing to the present day.[3]

But the existing studies have failed to fit the slave trade as a causal factor, positive or negative, into a process analysis of economic development in the major countries or territories that participated in it. This is what this article tries to do. For that purpose the external slave trade from Africa is viewed as a form of international trade whose effects on the countries or regions involved in it, directly or indirectly, are analysed in economic terms. The paper is based essentially on development as opposed to growth analysis. The distinction between these two concepts is not always observed by writers. Modern economic growth is usually defined in terms of a sustained annual increase in income per head of the entire population in a given economy, over a long period of time, while economic development relates to the transformation of an economy from a customary, subsistence, rural and regional stage, to a rational, commercial, urban and national stage, with appropriate institutions for the efficient mobility of factors. Often the transformation includes a major structural shift in the economy, from primarily agricultural to primarily industrial. In the context of Rostovian analysis, development belongs to the 'pre-condition' and 'take-off' stages, while growth belongs to the post-take-off stages. The main question

which this article tries to tackle, therefore, is the extent to which the movements
of the various economies under review were accelerated or retarded by the
slave trade in those crucial stages of development. The analysis draws on the
concept of dynamic gains from international trade as opposed to the static gains
of classical analysis.[4]

Magnitude of the external slave trade

One problem which is central to our question is the magnitude of the external
slave trade from Africa during the period 1451–1870. This means a computation
of the total number of slaves actually carried away from sub-Saharan Africa by
way of the Sahara, the Atlantic, the Red Sea and the Indian Ocean, during
that period. From the point of view of the European sector of the Atlantic,
this is necessary because the development of resources required by the trade
forms an important part of the analysis and this will have to be weighted by
the estimated magnitude of the European portion of the trade. For the African
part of the analysis the computed magnitude will form a useful starting point
for an estimate of the demographic impact of the trade and the consequences of
that for economic development in the regions affected.

Most writers dealing with the slave trade across the Sahara and the
Atlantic have always found it necessary to estimate the total number of slaves
involved. For the Atlantic portion, the most recent of these estimates is that
of Professor Curtin,[5] which was based on published data. However, his global
estimates have now been shown to be generally on the low side of the mark.[6]
At present much work is going on relating to the number of slaves exported
from Africa by way of the Atlantic trade. It may take another decade or more
before the outcome can be stated in terms of global figures. For the purposes of
the analysis in this article, the figure of 11 million slaves provided by Professor
Curtin has been taken as representing the barest minimum for the Atlantic
trade. This, together with the European share of the unknown magnitude of
the Indian Ocean trade, makes up the European portion of the external slave
trade from Africa.

For the trans-Saharan trade, a recent attempt to summarize the implications of some of the existing estimates put the total number of slaves taken
away from sub-Saharan Africa to meet the demands of the desert trade, for the
whole period 850–1910, at 10 million. The distribution of this total over time
shows that for our period, 1451–1870, a little under 6 million people were taken
away.[7] These data are extremely weak, and some think the present estimate may
be on the high side.[8] If the trans-Saharan figure should be proved to be an over-
estimate, this may compensate to some extent the underestimate for the trans-
Atlantic trade.

As for the slave trade from East Africa to the Red Sea, Arabia, the Persian

Gulf, India and the islands on the Indian Ocean, no aggregate estimates of the total numbers involved have been made, From the information available,[9] we may not be exaggerating if we put the total figures for the whole of our period at some 2 million.

Thus, the external slave trade from Africa south of the Sahara between the fifteenth and nineteenth centuries, involved the export of not less than 19 million people.

The slave trade and the expansion of international trade

The buying, shipping and employment of over 11 million slaves in capitalistic production for an international market on the one hand, and the shipping and marketing of the commodities produced by those slaves on the other, constituted a very large part, in volume, of all international economic transactions in the period 1451–1870. In order to relate this international transaction of immense proportions to Western development, we shall try to answer the following questions which in some ways are related:

To what extent did the requirements for buying and transporting over 11 million slaves contribute towards development in Western economies?

Was the process of economic development in Atlantic Europe and the Americas critically influenced by the growth of world trade between 1500 and 1870?

To what extent did the expansion of international trade between 1500 and 1870 depend on the slave trade?

Before answering these questions, something must be said about the division of functions in the Atlantic system within which the slave trade and slavery operated. The main functional categories in that system were: trade and finance; transportation; manufacturing; mining; export staple agriculture in plantations; commercial foodstuff agriculture in medium-sized freehold farms; and the sale of labour. Western Europe overwhelmingly dominated trade, finance, transportation and manufacturing. Portuguese and Spanish America also did some trading and transportation, including some manufacturing for internal consumption. But their main function in the Atlantic system was the mining of precious metals and export staple agriculture in plantations. The middle and north-eastern states of North America, right from the colonial days, concentrated on commercial foodstuff production for export to the slave plantations of the West Indian islands, import and export trade, shipping, finance, shipbuilding, lumber production, fishing and, later, manufacturing. The southern states specialized in plantation agriculture, first, mainly tobacco, but later, mainly cotton. The special function of all the West Indian islands was plantation agriculture—coffee, cotton, indigo, but in particular, sugar cane. Africa did not perform any real production function in the Atlantic system. Its function was limited to the acquisition and sale of slave labour. On the whole, of all the territories under review, only the north-eastern states of North America performed economic functions closely resembling those performed by Western Europe in the Atlantic system.

The character of functions performed by a given territory in the Atlantic system was a crucial factor explaining the type of developmental effect which the system produced in that territory. Trade, finance, shipping, manufacturing, and commercial foodstuff production in medium-sized freehold farms tended to produce much greater positive developmental effects than plantation agriculture. However, the character of the functions does not fully explain the differing developmental effects. It is significant that the territories which were ✓ engaged mostly in plantation agriculture were also those in which 'foreign factors of production' were most largely employed, using this concept in Jonathan Levin's sense.[10] As a consequence, a very large proportion of the total income produced in the Atlantic sectors of these economies was remitted abroad. This was particularly so for the West Indian islands. This, together with the character of the functions performed, left little or no room for a self-sustained internal development to accompany the growth of activities in production for an international market. In the Latin American territories the operation of some internal factors, partly connected with the character of the European colonists and the institutions they brought with them, further reduced the overall positive effects of the Atlantic system for the internal development of those economies. For these various reasons, the positive developmental effects of the Atlantic system were largely concentrated in Western Europe and North America.

The buying and shipping of slaves to the Americas formed one of the most important functions fulfilled by Western Europe in the Atlantic system. This proved to be a very demanding task, requiring considerable mercantile skills, highly sophisticated financial arrangements, refinements in shipbuilding technology, and production of new types of goods demanded by the slave-producing regions of tropical Africa. The creative response of the economies of Atlantic Europe to the requirements of this function formed an important part of the development process in those economies. Unfortunately, a detailed study of the character of this response and an assessment of its place in the process of economic development in Western Europe is only just receiving the attention of scholars employing the analytical tools of development economics. The first of such studies, which has been made on the British economy for the period 1750–1807,[11] shows that during this period of about sixty years when Great Britain dominated the buying and shipping of slaves to the Americas, the peculiar requirements of this function stimulated important developments in key sectors and regions of the British economy. The slave merchants were constantly exposed to considerable risks and so their regular and growing demand for insurance cover was important in the development of marine insurance in Great Britain. The trade required the extension of credit [12] at various stages—credit to slave-dealers on the African coast, and more important, credit to the employers of slave labour in the Americas. In addition, a long space of time, usually over a year, elapsed between the time a merchant in Great Britain invested in goods and shipping and the time the slaves were finally sold in the Americas. In consequence, the financial resources of the slave merchants were more than ordinarily stretched. In fact, the commercial capital required by the slave trade—in shipping, in stock of goods, and in trade credits—was far in excess of the annual volume of the trade. Rather than sink the whole of their fortunes in the trade, the slave-merchants always preferred to obtain credit in various forms. They obtained export credit from the producers of goods for the trade, a requirement which in turn compelled the latter to look for sources of credit for their operation. More important, the slave-merchants obtained credit through the discounting to the voluminous bills of exchange they obtained from the sale of slaves in the Americas.

The favourable demand conditions created in this way were important for the development of banking and the discount market in Great Britain. In fact, some of the provincial banks that sprang up at this time, especially in Lancashire, were motivated primarily by the desire to profit from the discounting of slave bills and other bills resulting from the credit relationship between the slave-merchants and producers of goods for the slave trade.[13]

The special shipping requirements of the trade stimulated considerable activities in British shipyards for the building of a special class of vessel and for the repair and costly outfit of slave vessels. From a calculation based on 137 slave-ships, measuring 24,180 tons, it is found that about 60 per cent of British slave vessels were built in British shipyards, the remaining 40 per cent being made up of prizes taken in wartime, and foreign-built ships purchased abroad, mostly in the colonies. After deducting this proportion, an elaborate calculation based on a large amount of shipping data, shows that between 1791 and 1807 about 15 per cent of all tonnage built in Great Britain was destined for the Guinea trade, about 95 per cent of which went into the shipping of slaves.[14] Between 1750 and 1807, an average of £2,625,959 per decade was invested by British slave-merchants in the building, repairing and outfit of their vessels in British shipyards, ranging from an average of about £1½ million per decade for the period 1750–80, to an average of almost £4 million per decade in the period, 1781–1807. The input requirements of these activities had important linkage effects on other industries, particularly the metal and metal-using trades, and hence the mining of metal ore and coal, and their transportation. They also made an important contribution to the process of urbanization.

The manufacturing sectors significantly influenced were the metal and metal-using industries, copper, brass and iron. The manufacture of guns for the purchase of slaves was an important Birmingham industry. The production of special copper and brass goods for the slave trade, and the employment of copper in sheathing the bottoms of slave vessels were important activities in the London, Bristol and Liverpool regions. But the British industry whose development was most critically influenced by the slave trade was the cotton textile industry.

Between 1750 and 1776, the proportion of total annual British cotton exports, by value, which went to the west coast of Africa varied from 30 to 50 per cent.[15] This proportion fell drastically during the American War of Independence, but recovered after the war, and between 1783 and 1792, varied from 11 to 32 per cent. After 1792, the faster growth of exports to Europe and the Americas meant that exports to the African coast formed a diminishing percentage of total British cotton exports, by value. Thus, in terms of volume, exports to the African coast were important for the development of the export sector of the British cotton textile industry. The cotton goods exported to the African coast were the cheap type for common consumers and this made them adaptable to mass production by mechanical methods. But, by far the most important contribution which exports to the African coast made towards the development of the British cotton textile industry was in terms of exposure to competition.

In the early years of the industry, its home market was protected, the sale of East Indian cotton textiles for domestic consumption having been prohibited in Great Britain early in the eighteenth century. Sales in Europe remained insignificant until after 1776. In those early years, it was mainly on the west coast of Africa that the British cotton textile industry faced very serious competition from similar goods from all parts of the world, in particular, East Indian cotton textiles. The industry's response to this competition was very important for its competitiveness from the last years of the eighteenth century onwards.[16]

Thus, as far as the British economy in the eighteenth century is concerned, the requirements for buying and transporting slaves to the Americas made an important contribution to development. No similar studies have been made for the other European countries that performed this same function in the Atlantic system. But the limited studies of Simone Berbain, Gaston Martin and Pierre Boulle, show that, at least, for Nantes, Rouen and Montpellier, the slave-merchants' demand for cheaply produced goods stimulated the growth of large-scale industry in the eighteenth century.[17] And the export of German linens to the African coast through British and other European slave-merchants was an important outlet for the textile industries of Westphalia, Saxony and Silesia.

The buying and shipping of slaves to the Americas represented just a part of the greatly expanded world trade in which the Atlantic economies

participated in the period 1451–1870. It will be shown later that thus phenomenal expansion of world trade was due largely to the availability of African
slave labour in the Americas. But for the moment we have to establish the
relationship between this growth of world trade and the economic development
of Western Europe and North America.

Between the late Middle Ages and the first half of the seventeenth century
some very important internal developments occurred in West European economies, which were due to changes in some internal factors, such as population,
leading to the growth of intra-European trade, particularly in raw wool, woollen
products, metal products and silver, as well as inter-regional trade within the
individual West European countries. These early developments stimulated in
the different West European countries differing institutional changes, political,
social and economic. Particularly in Great Britain and Holland, the changes
which occurred at this time created

a hospitable environment for the evolution of a body of property rights which promoted institutional arrangements, leading to fee-simple absolute ownership in land,
free labour, the protection of privately owned goods, patent laws and other encourage-
ments to ownership of intellectual property, and a host of institutional arrangements
to reduce market imperfection in product and capital markets.[18]

The main contribution of the Atlantic system to these early developments was
in the supply of bullion which greatly promoted the growth of exchange in
all Western Europe, thereby giving a fillip to the expansion of the market
sector of West European economies. Besides this contribution, much of West
European development at this early stage depended on European resources.
The 'hospitable environment' created by these early developments are very
important in explaining the responsiveness of West European economies to
the external stimuli emanating from the growth of world trade from the second
half of the seventeenth century onwards.

But, it is one thing to say that these early internal developments made
West European economies responsive to external stimuli arising from the
growth of the Atlantic system. It is quite another thing to say that from these
early developments the institutional arrangements that evolved in Western
Europe between the seventeenth and eighteenth centuries, and that great
structural transformation called the Industrial Revolution which occurred in
Great Britain during this period, were inevitable. The explanation for those
developments is to be found in the new problems and possibilities created by
the growth of world trade in the seventeenth and eighteenth centuries: the new
problems of regularly carrying large quantities of goods over very long distances
across turbulent seas; of processing and distributing large quantities of products
imported from distant places; of accommodation in a trade system stretching

to every part of the globe; the opportunities offered for developing new industries based on raw materials previously scarce and expensive, or wholly unavail-
able, such as sugar, tobacco, cotton, etc., and for developing new products in
response to new demands and tastes; the economies of scale associated with
production for a greatly extended world market—these and many other factors
stimulated the institutional developments and the radical structural shifts
which occurred in western Europe at that time. They were all produced by the
growth of world trade in this period. The technical developments and the technological innovations of the period were all called forth and made economic
by the practical problems of production for an extended world market. It is
the verdict of a British economic historian that

Colonial trade introduced to English industry the quite new possibility of exporting
in great quantities manufactures other than woollen goods, to markets where there
was no question of the exchange of manufactures for other manufactures. . . . The
process of industrialization in England from the second quarter of the eighteenth
century was to an important extent a response to colonial demands for nails, axes,
firearms, buckets, coaches, clocks, saddles, handkerchiefs, buttons, cordage and a
thousand other things.[19]

It was this which made possible the concentration of large-scale industrial
production at all levels in the small country that England was in the seventeenth
and eighteenth centuries, being peopled by less than 7 million inhabitants by the
mid-eighteenth century, and by just over 8 million by 1790,[20] and with no ususual
endowment of natural resources. The opportunities offered for large exports
of ironwares and later of cottons 'played a vital part in the building of those
industries to the point where technical change transformed their momentum
of growth'.[21] For Europe generally, and for France in particular, a French
Economic historian wrote:

The eighteenth century can be truly called the Atlantic stage of European economic
development. Foreign trade, and especially trade with the Americas, was the most
dynamic sector of the whole economy (for instance, French colonial trade increased
tenfold between 1716 and 1787), and furthermore the demand from overseas was
stimulating the growth of a wide range of industries as well as increased specialization
and division of labour. Owing to the superiority of sea transport over land transport,
the eighteenth-century European economy was organized around a number of big
seaports, the most prosperous being those with the largest share in the growing colonial trade, such as Bordeaux or Nantes; each of these had, not only its own industries,
but also its industrial hinterland in the river base of which it was the outlet.[22]

He further points out that if

'Americanization' of trade and industry was the most pronounced for countries which owned a colonial empire (such as Great Britain, France, Holland and Spain), its influence extended also farther to the east, to countries which had no colonies but were able to send goods to America as re-exports from the colonial powers, especially through Cadiz; so German linens, cutlery, and hardware reached the West Indian and Spanish American markets.[23]

For North America in the colonial period, it has been shown that the proportion of total economic activity devoted to production for overseas markets was relatively large at the beginning of the eighteenth century, being about one-fifth of total output, and that though that proportion declined over the century, it still remained about one-sixth in 1768–72.[24] This was made up of shipping and other commercial services sold by the north-eastern colonies to the West Indian islands and southern Europe, export of foodstuffs, horses and lumber from the middle and north-eastern colonies to the West Indies and southern Europe, and the export of tobacco, rice and other minor crops from the southern colonies to Great Britain and other European countries. From this analysis of the colonial economy of North America, it is concluded:

While overseas trade and market activity may not have comprised the major portion of all colonial economic activity, the importance of the market was that of improving resource allocation. . . . We argue that while subsistence agriculture provided an important base to colonial incomes and was a substantial part of average per capita income, changes in incomes and improvements in welfare came largely through overseas trade and other market activities. Not only did improvements in productivity occur primarily through market activity, but the pattern of settlement and production was determined by market forces. This pattern changed slowly and unevenly, spreading from the waterways and distribution centres along the Atlantic seaboard into the interior.[25]

For the period, 1790–1860, Professor D. C. North has shown that the export of raw cotton from the southern states was the most crucial factor in the growth and development of the United States economy. As the southern states concentrated all their resources on the production of raw cotton for export, they had to buy their foodstuffs from the producers in the west, and this stimulated the settlement of the west and its specialization in foodstuff production. Also, the south had to depend on the north-east for its transportation, financial and other commercial services. Incomes earned from the production of cotton for export and spent on western food and north-eastern services, provided the base for the growth of import substitution industries in the north-east. And so the north-east graduated from exporting southern cotton and supplying the south and west with imported foreign manufactures, to the domestic production of those goods for consumers in the south and west, as well as in the north-east itself, using southern cotton as part of the inputs for the new industries. It was

this regional specialization based originally on the production of cotton in the south for export that made economic the establishment of large-scale industries in the United States between 1790 and 1860.[26]

It can, therefore, be concluded that economic development in Atlantic Europe and North America was critically influenced by the growth of world trade between 1500 and 1870. The next question is the extent to which the growth of world trade in this period depended on the slave trade. Since this growth depended almost entirely on the exploitation of the resources in the Americas, the question boils down to whether the exploitation of those resources would have been possible at all, or whether the scale of their exploitation would have come anywhere near to what it was, without the availability of slave labour. This is looking at the problem from the point of view of supply. Another way is to look at it from the point of view of demand and ask whether the employment of non-slave labour would not have considerably advanced the cost of production and therefore have raised the prices of the products in Europe to a level that would have considerably reduced their consumption and therefore the quantity imported into Europe. If this had happened, the level of incomes in the Americas would have been reduced, thereby reducing the volume of goods imported from Europe. The overall effect would have been a drastic reduction in the volume of world trade. All this would have depended on the price elasticity of demand in Europe for the products of the Americas.

Recent publications on the subject of slave labour show that in some cases it was either slave labour or nothing. It has been pointed out that Spain and Portugal, the possessors of the majority of the American tropical colonies, were not in a position to provide workers 'who were prepared to emigrate at any price'.[27] For the capitalistic production of sugar in the West Indies generally, it is stated that 'free labour was simply not available in sufficient quantity and what there was would not (*would* not rather than *could* not) put up with the conditions of work on a plantation so long as cheap farmland was to be had in other colonies. It was slavery or nothing.'[28] As a general statement for all the Americas outside Spanish and Portuguese America, it is argued that

Wage or indentured labour would have been forthcoming in some additional numbers at some high wage. Such wage levels would have been high owing to certain factors impeding labour movement into plantation agriculture, [so that] any attempt at sizeable increases in the production of agricultural staples under the inelastic supply patterns characterizing free and indentured labour would have advanced those labour prices substantially.[29]

Apart from the foregoing arguments, it has been shown that in the decade before the civil war southern slave farms produced 28 per cent more output per unit of input than southern free farms, and 40 per cent more than family-

based northern farms.[30] When this superior efficiency of slave labour over free labour is added to the very much higher labour costs that would have prevailed in the absence of slave labour, it can be easily seen why production costs, even in the areas where it was possible to obtain some additional wage or indentured labour at a high price, would have been terribly high in the absence of slave labour. As Ralph Davis has shown, the phenomenal expansion of European consumption of products imported from the Americas depended largely on the very low levels to which their prices dropped in the course of the seventeenth and eighteenth centuries.[31] European demand for products from the Americas was therefore highly price elastic, so that a manifold increase in the prices of those products in the absence of slave labour would have greatly reduced their consumption in Europe and therefore the volume of trade based on them. Hence, taking into account the large areas in the Americas where no production at all would have taken place without slave labour, and the greatly reduced level of production and sale in areas where some wage or indentured labour would have been forthcoming at a high price, the conclusion can be drawn that the growth of world trade between 1500 and 1870 was due very largely to the availability of African slave labour supplied through the slave trade. It is important to stress that even the growth of trade between West European countries at this time depended greatly on the re-export of American products from one European country to another, and the export of European goods from one European country to another for onward trans-shipment to the Americas. Before these developments, autarchic practices by various West European nations in their efforts to encourage home industries militated against the growth of intra-European trade.[32] Even the greatly enlarged trade with the East Indies during this period still depended largely on the Atlantic system, for a large proportion of the oriental goods was re-exported to Africa and the Americas.

Economic consequences of the external slave trade from Africa

This question has just begun to receive the attention of scholars.[33] One recent attempt in this field is based on a static model derived from the classical theory of international trade. The costs and benefits of the slave trade for Africa were computed on the basis of the difference between as estimated total amount of goods that would have been produced (at the subsistence level of production) in Africa by the estimated number of all slaves that were exported and the total value of import goods received in exchange for the slaves. If the former exceeds the latter than the material welfare of Africans deteriorated as a result of the slave trade; but if the latter exceeds the former, then the material welfare of Africans improved as a result of the slave trade.[34] Apart from the conceptual weaknesses of this model, it has no power to determine the dynamic

gains or losses that may be associated with the slave trade. As John H. Williams points out:

the relation of international trade to the development of new resources and productive forces is a more significant part of the explanation of the present status of nations, of incomes, prices, well-being, than is the cross-section value analysis of the classical economists, with its assumption of given quanta of productive factors, already existent and employed [with fixed technology and fixed market and productive organization].[35]

It is sometimes said that the slave trade brought from the Americas to Africa new food crops, such as manioc, sweet potato, maize, groundnuts and some others.[36] If we leave aside the controversy over the American origin of these crops, and accept that as a fact, the argument that those crops came to Africa *because* of the slave trade cannot be sustained on any ground, since these crops are said to have been introduced into West Africa 'by Portuguese traders early in the sixteenth century',[37] a period during which Portuguese slave trade in West Africa was far less important, in volume and value, than Portuguese trade in West African products, such as gold, pepper and so on.[38]

Another way of relating the slave trade positively to African economic development may be through the investment of profits made in the trade by African dealers. It is possible that after the effective abolition of the external slave trade late in the nineteenth century, profits earlier accumulated from it by some African dealers may have flowed into the development of trade in African products, such as palm oil, then in demand. This could be regarded as a positive contribution by the slave trade to African economic development. But during the 400 years or so of the slave trade before its abolition, profits from that trade added nothing in terms of capital formation to the production capacity of African economies.[39] Duke Ephraim, one of the greatest Efik traders of pre-colonial times, 'peopled the vast agricultural area of Akpabuyo to the east of Calabar with slaves purchased from the profits of his trade, not so much to produce oil or even food, but to strengthen the power of his house or ward.'[40] In general, this was how slave-trade profits were employed in the Cross River region of present-day Nigeria. It would seem, therefore, that the economic conditions associated with the slave trade provided no demand incentives for capital formation to take place. Hence economic development in Africa was not stimulated by the slave trade. Indeed, it can be argued that institutions and habits inimical to economic development, which developed and became hardened during over 400 years of slave trade, became, in later years, great obstacles to economic transformation in Africa.

If it is so difficult to isolate any positive contribution by the slave trade to African economic development, two other propositions remain to be examined. First, we propose to show that the slave trade had an ascertainable direct negative impact on the economic development processes in Africa; secondly, that, while it lasted, it prevented the growth and development of 'normal' international trade between Africa and the rest of the world.

The first direct negative impact was its retardative or contractionary effects on African population during a period of over 400 years. This is an issue on which historians hold differing views.[41] With regard to Africa south of the Equator, there seems to be a general consensus of opinion among them that external slave trade led to an outright depopulation in the Congo–Angola region, broadly defined. As for West Africa, there is disagreement as to whether it led to an outright depopulation, but what no one seems to contend is that, at best, the population there was stationary during the period of the external slave trade—that is, the rate of population growth was equal to the rate of population loss due to that trade.

One general weakness of the existing studies of the subject is that population movements in Africa have been related only to the Atlantic slave trade. A proper understanding of African demographic processes in the period 1451–1870 requires an assessment of population losses due to the external slave trade in all its branches. Also, even in the Atlantic trade, only the numbers of slaves actually exported are considered, when it is known that the processes leading to the export of those numbers—the wars, raids and other methods of slave gathering; the long march to the coast; the 'warehousing' of slaves on the coast awaiting shipment; the long keeping of slaves in ship holds before the vessels actually departed the African coast with their full cargoes—involved population losses that probably have been far in excess of the numbers actually exported. The most serious weakness, however, is that no effort has been made to assess, albeit roughly, the additional population the slaves exported would have produced in Africa had they been left there.

It is difficult to make such an estimate. In the first place, no data exist on birth rates and survival rates in Africa at this time. Even if they existed the data would not have reflected the effects of the slave trade on birth and survival rates through its retardative effects on economic growth and the high incidence of war. On the other hand, the Africans exported were all people in their prime of life so that the rate of reproduction among them should have been higher than that of the rest of society left behind.

One way of getting round the problem would have been to employ the reproduction rates among the Africans received in the slave-importing territories of the Americas. But this, again, poses problems. Of all the slave-receiving territories in the Americas it was only in the United States that the imported Africans achieved some rate of net natural increase during much of our period. In the other territories, the effect of a lengthy journey from Africa by sea, strange disease environment, the harsh conditions of plantation slavery, particularly on the sugar-cane plantations, etc., actually led to rates of net natural decrease among the slave populations. Since rates of net natural decrease did not operate in the African territories from which people were exported,[42] the only usable rate is that among the Africans in North America. For this territory, Professor Curtin's calculations show that about 430,000 Africans imported, largely between 1700 and 1810, produced a black population of about 4.5 million by 1863.[43]

Before this rate of reproduction can be refined to provide a rough approximation of the numbers that would have been reproduced in Africa by the people exported, some qualifications are necessary. The North American imports were concentrated in the second half of the eighteenth century so that it actually took the 430,000 imported Africans very much less than a century to produce a population of 4.5 million by 1863. By the time a large number of Africans began to arrive in North America in the second half of the eighteenth century, the first million people to leave Africa as a result of the external slave trade in all its sectors had done so for more than 100 years. On the other hand, the harsh conditions of slavery, its psychological effects on the fecundity of female slaves and the strange disease environment still reduced to some extent the rate of reproduction among the imported Africans in the United States.

On the other side of the coin, it may be argued that the mortality rate in tropical Africa during our period was higher than that of North America during the same period. If this was the case, then the survival rate among the children of Africans in North America, from about the second generation onward, would be higher than that in Africa. In addition the slaves in North America did receive some modern medical attention, however minimal the effect may have been on their health. Another consideration is the fact that the population of Afro-Americans in 1863 was produced with the input of some white fathers. It has been shown that the proportion of mulattos in the total slave population of the United States of America in 1860 was 10.4 per cent.[44]

When these two sets of opposing factors are matched it is not easy to decide the direction of the net result. To be conservative let us assume that, notwithstanding all the points made above, the reproduction rates which prevailed among the Africans imported into North America were higher than the rates that would have prevailed among the 19 million Africans exported had they been left in Africa. Let us even assume that, when all the facts stated earlier have been considered, only 50 per cent of the North American rates would have prevailed in Africa. Applying this rate to the 19 million earlier estimated, the result is that had those Africans not been exported they would have produced an additional population of at least about 99,420,000 in Africa by about 1870. This calculation does not take into account the fact that the large number of Africans who were exported several years before North

American imports started would have produced proportionately far more descendants in Africa than those imported into North America produced in that territory by 1863.

It must be understood that this estimate is a very rough one. It is likely that Professor Curtin underestimated United States slave imports to a greater extent than he did for imports into other territories. If so, reproduction rates based on Curtin's United States figures will be an exaggeration which will make our estimates somewhat too high. On the other hand, in our estimate we have not included the numbers lost in the various stages of producing the 19 million actually exported. Besides, an assessment of the demographic consequences of the external slave trade for Africa has to take into account the indirect effects as well. The unsettled conditions produced by the slave trade and its retardative effects on economic growth had adverse effects on population growth in Africa during a period of over 400 years. It is significant that, from 1500 to 1870, the growth of the African population lagged far behind that of any other continent during the same period. When the external demand for Africans as slaves was cut off in the late nineteenth century, peaceful conditions prevailed, international trade in the products of the African soil developed, the flow of goods within Africa expanded and became more regular, and general economic improvement took place. Under these conditions, population growth rates in Africa came to be among some of the highest in the world between 1900 and 1950. No one should be misled into thinking that this population growth in Africa was due to the availability of modern medicine, whose contribution was minimal, because only a tiny proportion of the total population benefited from the limited modern medical facilities that existed. 'Traditional' African medicine remained the only means of treatment for most people, and 'traditional' African midwives remained the only physicians known to most expectant mothers, as was the case during the slave-trade period. The only new elements that were significant as far as population growth was concerned, were peace and economic improvement.

Thus, however rough it may be there is no doubt that the figure we have produced is a very conservative estimate of the additional population that would have existed in Africa by 1870 in the absence of the external slave trade. It should be pointed out that the operation of the Malthusian checks could not have made it impossible to maintain this additional population since the amount of land in Africa suitable for food production completely eliminates the possibility of their operation. The inescapable conclusion to be drawn from the foregoing, therefore, is that the extremely low ratio of population to cultivable land which prevailed in Africa south of the Sahara up to the present century was the direct repercussion of the external slave trade from Africa.

This underpopulation prevented for several centuries the growth of a virile market sector in the African economies by eliminating population pressure that would have led to internal colonization, taming the forests, and greater population concentration. Internal colonization would have led to interregional differentiation of economic functions arising from climatic differences, differential natural-resource endowments, and differing population densities. The taming of the forests and greater population concentration would have led to a reduction in distribution costs by lowering costs of transportation. All this would have stimulated interregional trade and therefore the growth of production for the market and all the institutional developments associated with that growth. But because the ratio of population to land remained extremely low, population remained largely dispersed, the forests remained untamed, extensive, rather than intensive, cultivation was encouraged, and subsistence production and local self-sufficiency remained the rule. Because land was never a scarce resource no market for land developed and agriculture generally remained uncommercialized. The land-tenure system which became hardened under the conditions produced by the slave trade is one of those institutions inimical to the growth of capitalism which took root in Africa as a result of the external slave trade. In most of Africa, this system if often talked about as if it were something inherently African, without it being realized that the persistence of the system has its history in the slave trade, which prevented the growth of demand for land that would have made it a scarce and, therefore, marketable resource. The present development of a market for urban land in many African countries, following the pressure of population in the urban centres, shows clearly why a land market (urban and agricultural) failed to develop in much of Africa many years ago. In the absence of a large population, the existence of a very great and growing external demand for African products that were land-intensive in production would gradually have reduced land to a scarce and marketable resource and hence led to the commercialization of agriculture and the whole rural economy. This was what the export of raw wool and wollen cloths did for British land tenure and agriculture in the sixteenth century and after; what the export of foodstuffs to the West Indies did for the agriculture of the middle and northern colonies of North America in the seventeenth and eighteenth centuries; and what the export of cocoa is doing for the western State of Nigeria.[45] But, as we shall show later, the opportunity cost of the slave trade made impossible the growth of such an external demand during the period of that trade. Dr Hopkins suggests that, in the absence of population growth, technical innovation would have encouraged the growth of market activities by reducing production costs.[46] This is rather a case of putting the cart before the horse since, historically, the growth of market activities preceded technical innovation. This is to say that, historically, technical innovation was not an autonomous variable, having always been stimulated by demand pressures, although in its turn, it later stimulated the growth of market activities.

The other direct negative effect of the external slave trade on African economic development is associated with the general socio-economic and socio-political conditions created by the trade. Every economic activity has a way of creating such conditions which not only help to sustain its earlier levels but provide it with further momentum. This is the major idea behind Professor Rostow's 'take-off' analysis. That self-reinforcing process was crucial in sustaining the slave trade. The socio-economic and socio-political forces created by the slave trade in Africa which sustained it for several centuries, operated in the form of increased warfare based on the use of firearms and horses supplied by the European and Arab slave-merchants, the emergence of professional slave-raiders or man-hunters, the gearing of political, social and economic institutions to the needs of slave acquisition and marketing and so on. The incentives behind all these innovative activities were the increased variety of European and Oriental products available to those with slaves to sell.

The mechanism of this self-sustaining process is well elaborated by many writers on the slave trade. The account by Leo Africanus shows that the king of Bornu (Borno) at the beginning of the sixteenth century sold slaves to Barbary merchants and received horses for use in his cavalry in return. With these horses the king carried out his annual slave-raiding expeditions.[47] The horses may also have been used to acquire territorial fiefs through which tribute slaves were obtained. In fact, the important slave market of Kuka is said to have been supplied with slaves captured in government raids in the surrounding non-Muslim territories south, west and south-west of Bornu (Borno), and with tribute slaves paid by vassal princes who, in order to discharge this obligation, carried on continuous warfare against their non-Muslim neighbours.[48]

In the Atlantic sector, firearms took the place of horses, and the proliferation of firearms in the coastal and forest states was an important part of the self-reinforcing mechanism. The firearms gave steam to imperial ventures aimed at controlling the sources of slave supply. The conflict between these nascent empires over the control of slave supply on the one hand, and the need for self-defence against their activities by their victims or potential victims on the other hand, created a slave–gun circle. This is why it does not make much sense to talk of these wars as being politically motivated, for beneath what one may describe as a political motive lay what was primarily economic. This is not to say that all the wars of the slave-trade period were caused by the conditions created by the trade, nor that some non-economic motives were not also present in wars that were largely due to the slave trade. But it does mean that the self-reinforcing conditions created by the trade were responsible for much of the wars of the period. As one writer puts it:

The two-way pressures of the ocean trade—European demand for captives and African demand for European goods—worked powerfully toward the institutionalization of the system. Whether making wars in order to capture prisoners for sale or defending themselves against neighbours with similar ambitions, coastal and near-coastal rulers found firearms indispensable to their security. The firearms did much to fasten powerful rulers, as well as weak ones, into a trading system which required the sale of captives.[49]

Of central and eastern Africa it is said:

The opportunity for gaining durable material wealth from the slave trade obviously encouraged rulers to expand their possessions and increase the number of people over whom they ruled. Such expansion often took place by warfare which initially provided prisoners of war, a ready source of slaves, and subsequently provided new subjects on whom taxes could be levied in the form of men. By expanding his fief the ruler also acquired a position of being the final arbiter in judicial matters. This position brought the ruler export slaves through a manipulation of the judicial processes. Thus, for various reasons, the gains to be derived from the slave trade provided one of the sharpest incentives to imperial expansion in Central Africa.[50]

On the other hand, while the European and Arab slave merchants may not have openly encouraged inter-State wars in Africa, apart from Portuguese military activities in Angola, their willingness to loan firearms to warring groups in return for war captives may have played an important role among African States in reaching decisions to make war or peace. For example, a European slave merchant, resident on the Guinea coast, wrote to his co-partner in Great Britain in August 1740:

We have been greatly disappointed in our trade. Ever since the Fanteens went to engage Elmena no thinking man that knew the coast could have expected otherwise; all the trading paths were stopped; nothing going forward but thieving and panyarring; had the said Fanteens become conquerors it's certain we should for our own parts have got eight hundred or one thousand slaves at pretty easy terms; but as they came back repulsed and were even forced to run away, we have suffered to be sure considerably, for I credited the headmen pretty largely to secure their interest on their return that I might have the preference of what slaves they took in the war.[51]

Earlier on this same merchant had written:

General Shampoo is encamped at the head of the River Vutta [Volta] with 20 thousand men ready to engage Dahomee King of Whydah; the said king has an army equal to the other's, encamped within two miles of each other. On the success of the former we have a large interest depending and until that battle is decided in some shape or another there are no trade to be expected. Young in the *Africa* I am loading him with a proper assortment of goods and to dispatch him with all expedition for Little Popo to attend the result of the Battle.[52]

These are not isolated cases, for similar references can be found in the works of other writers on the subject.[53]

Historians have always tried to relate the socio-political and socio-economic conditions created in Africa by the slave trade to political processes, particularly those connected with the rise and decline of States, kingdoms and empires. What has been neglected is an analysis that will explicitly relate those conditions to the process of economic development in Africa. In the matter of State formation, for instance, if the slave trade gave rise to some larger and more powerful States, one would like to know whether such States directed or took part in economic activities likely to bring about economic development; whether they made conscious efforts to provide peaceful conditions under which private enterprise could have helped to bring about economic development; or, finally, whether they consciously made any efforts to evolve or encourage the evolution of institutional arrangements essential for economic development. If the answers to all these questions are negative, one would like to know why.

It is well known that during the period of the slave trade not only did the States whose rise may be associated with that trade fail to do any of the things specified above, but even others, like the kingdom of Benin failed to do so. The explanation is simple. The former remained largely slave-trading States and so had no political or economic incentives to develop other resources, or to encourage private enterprise to do so by providing peaceful conditions, while the other States also became largely involved in the slave trade, or in defending themselves against the activities of slave-trading States. On the other hand, the requirements of the slave trade were such that they could not stimulate any infrastructural developments in the slave-trading States. For instance, the fact that the slaves transported themselves along bush paths eliminated any possible pressure to build good roads and to encourage artisans to build 'the wheel' to facilitate the flow of trade.

From the point of view of the private sector, the chaotic conditions which the slave trade created and which helped to sustain its momentum for several centuries raised transaction costs enormously and so retarded the growth of market activities. Any reading of the European company records bears this out. In a letter to the Royal African Company in Great Britain, an official of the company resident on the African Coast wrote:

at best the Waterside Kings, and Great Cabbasheers (so called) are but poor great rogues, for when they do not disturb the traders, and are not at war with one another for a livelihood combine and lay their heads together to contrive how to abuse and cheat your honours and the Dutch West India Company.[54]

Obviously, the slave trade was not a gentleman's trade, and what the Europeans say about the African dealers, the former also say about each other, for the same writer quoted above had cause to say:

Were I to characterize the Dutch as I by experience have found them to be, I should give the same character of them, as I have herein given of the Natives of this country, for I have often seriously considered with myself whether they or the Natives here were of the most villanous, falsest temper and could never come to a resolution thereon.[55]

No doubt the Dutch and the Africans had much the same thing to say about the British.

What is more, the wars and raids of the slave trade encouraged the location of settlements

in good defensive positions and their location in relation to natural obstacles makes settlements inaccessible at the cost of ease of communications or even good building sites [and good agricultural land].[56]

This encouraged subsistence and discouraged market activities. But what is more serious, by hiding away from slave gatherers these settlements were also hiding away from the flow of modernizing ideas.

Thus, it is hard to exaggerate the consequences of the chaotic conditions created by the slave trade for African economic development. For Central and Eastern Africa, in particular, it has been shown that 'the pre-colonial economic tragedy' consists of the 'dissipation and disruption' of industrial and specialized skills developed in pre-slave-trade days, 'under the impact of violence and the slave trade'.[57]

Not only did the external slave trade retard the development of African economies through its demographic and disruptive effects, but it also prevented the growth of a 'normal' international trade between Africa and the rest of the world at a time when such trade was acting as a powerful engine of economic development in a number of territories. The loss to Africa of the developmental effects of this type of international trade represents one of the most important opportunity costs of the slave trade for African economies.

There is evidence to show that opportunities for the development of international trade in commodities capable of being produced in Africa did exist and that the foreign merchants who came to Africa in the period 1451–1870, were aware of those opportunities, and there is proof that the operation of the slave trade prevented in various ways the development of such a trade.

In the trans-Saharan sector of African international trade, transport costs prevented the development of trade in commodities with low value-to-weight ratio. In fact, it is possible that the problem of finding suitable commodities with which to pay for goods coming across the Sahara may have compelled people in the western Sudan to look for slaves as the preferred commodity. It was in the Atlantic that the first opportunity appeared to develop international trade with Africa in bulky goods.

It is important to note that all the Europeans who came to Africa following the Portuguese discovery of an ocean route to that continent were attracted in the first instance by the desire to develop trade with Africa in the products of her soil—gold, pepper, ivory, etc.—and for a time these remained the most valuable commodities in the Atlantic trade between Africa and Europe. In addition, the European merchants even acted in those early years as distributors of African products from one African region to another. Between 1633 and 1634 the Dutch alone imported about 12,641 pieces of Benin cloth into the Gold Coast, present-day Ghana.[58] Again, in 1645, a Dutch vessel brought to the Gold Coast from Ardra and Benin, 588 pieces of Ardra cloth and 1,755 pieces of Benin cloth, respectively.[59] Between 1486 and 1506 the Portuguese developed an important trade with Benin in Benin pepper.[60] The latter example clearly shows that the rulers of the coastal States took keen interest in this early trading in African products. For instance, when large-scale importation of European and oriental cotton cloths reduced demand for Benin cloth on the Gold Coast, and the Dutch, therefore, failed to buy Benin cloth as they did previously, the king of Benin protested and forced them to take at least 1,700 pieces a year.[61]

Apart from gold, pepper, ivory and some other minor products, the European merchants, quite early in their contact with Africa, were aware of the possibilities of producing in Africa a wide range of products for which there was a demand in Europe. The records of the European companies that traded with Africa are full of correspondence from their officials on the African coast relating to such possibilities. For example, in July 1708, the governor of the Royal African Company resident on the coast, wrote to the Company:

The ground of this country is as fertile as any ground in the West Indies, taking places according as they lye nearer or farther from the sea, but the natives are such scothful sordid wretches, and so given to stealing from one another rather than labour that little or nothing is made of it . . .[62]

The governor recommended that the company should establish a settlement at Fetue on the Gold Coast, which 'will be an inlet to all manner of Plantations'. The success of such company-owned plantations would encourage people to apply to the company 'to come and settle here upon such terms as you may think convenient to permit to settle on'. The company's plantations were to contain corn, sugar cane, indigo, cotton and cattle. The governor refers to the Dutch 'laying out ground on the River Butteroe near their fort there' for the development of a sugar-cane plantation, 'for to make sugar and rum here they have lately sent to Whydah for two hundred slaves, and they expect by their next shipping all sorts of materials for their making sugar and rum . . .'[63]

Later in the eighteenth century, when the Royal African Company's

slave trade became increasingly unprofitable due to long credits and bad
debts in the West Indies, the company made some frantic efforts to develop
trade in African products, not only with the coastal States but also with States
in the far interior. In March 1722 the company wrote to its officials on the
coast:

We have already in divers letters acquainted you with our thoughts concerning the
carrying on of our trade, and as the negroe branch of it grows every day less and less
profitable it is from the article of the home returns we see our chief advantage must
arise.[64]

From then on, the company endeavoured to make its officials on the coast
open up trade with Africa along these lines. It suggested a number of ways
of doing so, from the development of company plantations and encouraging
Africans on the coast to cultivate sugar cane, cotton, indigo, tobacco and
other crops, to the questioning of slaves brought from the interior about the
opportunities for opening up trade with them in the products of the soil. It
was even suggested by the company's officials on the coast that 'from the notion
we have of the Whydah natives industry', the cotton grown on the company's
plantations and by the Africans could be sent to Whydah and

be worked up there into assortments proper for the West Indies and as you have
encouragement or profit by that branch of trade your honours slaving vessels will be
capable of taking on board such quantities as you shall please to direct from hence to
be wrought up at Whydah.[65]

Thus, from the available records, it is clear that not only were the European
merchants aware of the possibilities of developing trade with Africa in the
products of the African soil, but also they made some efforts to develop such
trade. However, they all tended to see the trade in African products as subor-
dinate to the slave trade, which they were unwilling to give up in favour of
devoting full attention to the development of trade in the products of the soil.
Hence, the zeal and enthusiasm with which late-nineteenth- and twentieth-
century European merchants encouraged the development of trade in the
products of the African soil throuth trial and error were completely lacking
in the slave-trade period.

The explanation for the European merchants' attitude is that the development of trade in products of the African soil would have been a slow process
compared with the development of trade in commodities produced in the Americas with African slave labour, and such development would have required a
mass withdrawal of factors from the exploitation of the American resources
and the shipping and marketing of the output. In other words, the exploitation

of the American resources was making a very heavy demand on the same production factors that were needed for the development of African resources. But as long as African slave labour was available, production factors from Europe could be more profitably employed in the exploitation of American resources than in the development of trade in the products of the African soil.

This was so because the employment of African slaves by European planters to produce tropical products in Africa on the scale that prevailed in the Americas would have been very costly in terms of resistance by African governments, the ease with which the slaves employed in Africa could escape from their white masters (possibly with the connivance of African governments), and, most seriously, in terms of mortality among whites in Africa at a time when tropical medicine was unknown to Europeans. The most likely method would have been through co-operation between the European merchants and African rulers to encourage African peoples to cultivate the crops in demand, as was done in the late nineteenth and twentieth centuries. But this method would definitely have been slow in producing a trade on the scale then prevailing in commodities being produced in the Americas with African slave labour.

In this circumstance, so long as African slave labour was available, the Americas remained far more attractive to European production factors. The buying and shipping of the slaves to the Americas, the exploitation of the American resources, and the shipping and marketing of the American commodities internationally, absorbed so many production factors from Europe and Africa that little or nothing was left for the development of trade in the products of the African soil. That development was further hampered by the unsettled conditions which attended the acquisition of captives for sale as slaves.

But the important point is that the advantages of the Americas depended very largely on African slave labour. If there had been no slave trade from Africa to the Americas, the advantage would have been on the side of encouraging Africans to produce a wide range of commodities in Africa for an international market. From the evidence before us, it is clear that this is what would have happened. But the conditions which prevailed under the slave trade made that trade more profitable both to a majority of the European merchants and to the African rulers and entrepreneurs whose talents would have been required for the production and marketing of these commodities in Africa. Consequently, African products imported into Europe during the slave-trade period remained those which required very little entrepreneurship and little or no capital investment to produce—ivory, gum, palm oil, redwood, etc.—being all commodities that were either hunted or gathered from wild trees.

Some European governments fully realized that the development of international trade in the products of the African soil would mean a mass withdrawal of production factors from the exploitation of the American resources. Since they saw this as conflicting directly with what they thought to be their own true interests [66] they did all they could to discourage such development. Thus following the recommendation in 1708 to the Royal African Company by the company's governor in Africa to encourage the cultivation of sugar cane, tobacco, cotton and indigo in Africa, a bill was introduced into the British Parliament to prohibit the cultivation of those crops on the Gold Coast.[67]

Again, in the 1750s, when the officials of the Company of Merchants Trading to Africa tried to encourage the cultivation of some of the American crops in Africa, the British Board of Trade quickly summoned the members of the company's ruling committee and told them,

That the introducing of culture and Industry amongst the Negroes was contrary to the known established policy of this trade. That there was no saying where this might stop and that it might extend to tobacco, sugar & every other commodity which we now take from our colonies, and thereby the Africans who now support themselves by war would become planters & their slaves be employed in the culture of these articles in Africa which they are now employed in in America. That our possessions in America were firmly secured to us, whereas those in Africa were more open to the invasions of an enemy, and besides that in Africa we were only tenants in the soil which we held at the good will of the natives.[68]

The members of the company's committee were therefore ordered to ask their officials on the coast to put an end to this type of activity. Thus, in order to ensure that Africa provided a regular supply of slaves required for the exploitation of American resources, the British Government through the Board of Trade had to discourage the development of African economies. In a letter to the British Treasury in April 1812, about five years after the slave trade had been abolished in Great Britain, the Committee of the Company of Merchants Trading to Africa summed up the whole matter thus:

It is a lamentable but certain fact, that Africa has hitherto been sacrificed to our West India colonies. Her commerce has been confined to a trade which seemed to preclude all advancement in civilization. Her cultivators have been sold to labour on lands not their own, while all endeavours to promote cultivation and improvement in agriculture have been discouraged by the Government of this country, lest her products should interfere with those of our more favoured colonies.[69]

Conclusion

In conclusion, it is clear that the phenomenal expansion of world trade between 1451 and 1870, depended largely on the employment of African slaves in the exploitation of American resources, and that the development and growth of West European and North American economies during this period were greatly influenced by the expanded world trade. This leads to the inference that the slave trade was a critical factor in the development of West European and North American economies in the period of this study. The benefits of the Atlantic system to Latin America and the West Indies generally were minimal, due to the type of economic functions performed, the large amount of 'foreign factors of production' employed and some other reasons. But, the clear losers in the growth of the Atlantic system, and woefully so, were the African economies. The demographic and disruptive effects of a trade which required the forceful capture and sale of human beings retarded the development of market activities and the evolution of institutional arrangements essential for the growth of capitalism. What is more, the operation of the slave trade prevented in various ways the growth of a 'normal' international trade between Africa and the rest of the world. From the evidence presented above, it is clear that, without the supply of African slave labour to the Americas, European merchants and governments would have been compelled by purely economic considerations to encourage the production of a wide range of commodities, including some of the American commodities, in Africa. This would have meant that the growth of world trade in the period under review would have been very much slower, and hence the rate of development in Western Europe and North America. But the History of Africa would have been entirely different. The level of economic and social development would not have been the same in all the regions of Africa, south of the Sahara. But all of them would have been far richer, the regions poorly endowed with resources benefiting from the development of the better endowed ones through trade and other contacts. In the final analysis, it can be said that the Atlantic economies that developed between 1451 and 1870, did so at the expense of the African economies.

Notes

1. I am grateful to Professor Michael Crowder of the Centre for Cultural Studies, University of Lagos, Professor R. J. Gavin of the Department of History, Ahmadu Bello University, Zaria, and Dr E. J. Usoro of the Department of Economics, University of Ibadan, for reading through the first draft of this paper and making helpful criticisms and suggestions. They are, however, not responsible for any errors there may be in the paper.
2. It is not easy to assess the contribution of slavery to the Middle East economies.
3. A great deal of the literature centres round Eric Williams' *Capitalism and Slavery*. A Seminar held at the Centre of African Studies, University of Edinburgh, on 4–5 June 1965, dealt with the issues of abolition raised by Eric Williams. The proceedings of the seminar have appeared under the title *The Trans-Atlantic Slave Trade from West Africa*, University of Edinburgh, Centre of African Studies, 1965. Some of

the papers are of particular interest: Roger Anstey, 'Capitalism and Slavery—A Critique'; John Hargreaves, 'Synopsis of a Critique of Eric Williams' *Capitalism and Slavery'*; C. Duncan Rise, 'Critique of the Eric Williams Thesis: "The Anti-Slavery Interest and the Sugar Duties, 1841–1853"'; Christopher Fyfe, 'A Historiographical Survey of the Transatlantic Slave Trade from West Africa'. The latter is a useful survey of the literature and the type of study available on the slave trade. Also to be noted are, Roger T. Anstey, 'Capitalism and Slavery: A Critique', *Econ. Hist. Rev.*, Vol. XXI, 1968, p. 307–20; Roger T. Anstey, *The Atlantic Slave Trade and British Abolition, 1760–1810*, London, Macmillan, 1975.

Some of the literature on the private profitability of the slave trade antedated Eric Williams' book: James Wallace, *A General and Descriptive History of the Ancient and Present State of the Town of Liverpool*, Liverpool, R. Phillips, 1795; Gomer Williams, *History of the Liverpool Privateers and Letters of Marque with an Account of the Liverpool Slave Trade*, London, W. Heinemann, 1897; S. Dumbell, 'The Profits of the Guinea Trade', *Economic History* (Supplement to *Economic Journal*), Vol. II, January 1931. But since the publication of Eric Williams' book the literature on this aspect of the slave trade has grown enormously. Some of the more important works include: F. E. Hyde, B. B. Parkinson and S. Marriner, 'The Nature and Profitability of the Liverpool Slave Trade', *Econ. Hist. Rev.*, Vol. V, No. 3, 1953; K. G. Davies, 'Essays in Bibliography and Criticism XLIV. Empire and Capital, *Econ. Hist. Rev.*, 2nd Ser., Vol. XII, 1960–61, p. 105–10; R. B. Sheridan, 'The Wealth of Jamaica in the Eighteenth Century', *Econ. Hist. Rev.*, 2nd Ser., Vol. XVIII, August 1965; Robert Paul Thomas, 'The Sugar Colonies of the Old Empire: Profit or loss for Great Britain?', *Econ. Hist. Rev.*, 2nd Ser., Vol. XXI, April 1968; R. B. Sheridan, 'The Wealth of Jamaica in the Eighteenth Century: A Rejoinder', *Econ. Hist. Rev.*, 2nd Ser., Vol. XXI, April 1968; Stanley L. Engerman, 'The Slave Trade and British Capital Formation in the Eighteenth Century: Comment on the Williams Thesis', *The Business History Review*, Vol. XLVI, No. 4, Winter 1972, p. 430–3; Roger T. Anstey, 'The Volume and Profitability of the British Slave Trade, 1761–1807', in Stanley L. Engerman and Eugene D. Genovese (eds.), *Race and Slavery in the Western Hemisphere: Quantitative Studies*, Princeton University Press, 1975; David Richardson, 'Profitability in the Bristol–Liverpool Slave Trade' (paper read at the VIth International Congress of Economic History, Copenhagen, 19–23 August 1974).

See Stanley L. Engerman, 'The Effects of Slavery upon the Southern Economy: A Review of the Recent Debate', *Explorations in Entrepreneurial History*, Vol. 4, 1967; R. W. Fogel and S. L. Engerman, *Time on the Cross: The Economics of American Negro Slavery*, London, Wildwood House, 1974; Stanley L. Engerman, 'Comments on the Study of Race and Slavery', in Engerman and Genovese (eds.), *Race and Slavery*, p. 495–526.

K. Onwuka Dike, *Trade and Politics in the Niger Delta, 1830–1885: An Introduction to the Economic and Political History of Nigeria*, Oxford University Press, 1956; A. Akinjogbin, *Dahomey and its Neighbours, 1708–1818*, Cambridge University Press, 1967; K. Y. Daaku, *Trade and Politics on the Gold Coast 1600–1720*, Oxford University Press, 1970; Walter Rodney, *A History of the Upper Guinea Coast 1545–1800*, Oxford University Press, 1970; A. J. H. Latham, *Old Calabar 1600–1891: The Impact of the International Economy upon a Traditional Society*, Oxford, Clarendon Press, 1973; M. D. Kilson, 'West African Society and the Atlantic Slave Trade, 1441–1865', in N. I. Huggins, M. Kilson and D. M. Fox (eds.), *Key Issues in the Afro-American Experience*, Vol. I, New York, 1971; David Birmingham, *Trade and Conflict in Angola: The Mbundu and their Neighbours under the Influence of the Portuguese, 1483–1790*, Oxford University Press, 1966; Phyllis Martin, *The External Trade of the Loango Coast 1576–1860*, Oxford Clarendon Press 1972; Edward A. Alpers, *Ivory and Slaves in East Central Africa: Changing Patterns of International Trade to the Later Nineteenth Century*, London, Heinemann, 1975.

4. See John H. Williams, 'The Theory of International Trade Reconsidered', in Lord Keynes, Joan Robinson, *et al.* (eds.), *Readings in the Theory of International Trade*, p. 253–71, London, 1950, where this distinction is clearly made.

5. P. D. Curtin, *The Atlantic Slave Trade: A Census*, Madison, Wis., University of Wisconsin Press, 1969.

6. J. E. Inikori, 'Measuring the Atlantic Slave Trade: An Assessment of Curtin and Anstey', *Journal of African History*, Vol. XVII, No. 2 (1976); D. Eltis, 'The Direction and Fluctuation of the Trans-Atlantic Slave Trade 1821–43: A Revision of the 1845 Parliamentary Paper' (paper presented at the Mathematical Social Science Board Seminar on the Economics of the Slave Trade, Colby College, Waterville, Maine, 20–22 August 1975); Roger Anstey, *The Atlantic Slave Trade and British Abolition 1760–1810*, London, Macmillan, 1975.

7. Ralph A. Austen, 'A Census of the Trans-Saharan Slave Trade, or approximating the uncountable' (paper presented at the Mathematical Social Science Board Seminar on the Economics of the Slave Trade, Colby College, Waterville, Maine, 20–22 August 1975).

8. This view was expressed by some of the participants at the Colby College Seminar.

9. C. S. Nicholls, *The Swahili Coast: Politics, Diplomacy and Trade on the East African Littoral 1798–1856*, London, Allen & Unwin 1971.

10. Jonathan Levin emphasized the proportion of total income from export production, which is remitted abroad by 'migrated factors' of production, as one of the important determinants of the magnitude of the contribution of export production to internal development processes in export economies. Consequently, he applied the term, 'foreign factors of production', only to those factors which remit their income abroad. Conversely, he applied the term, 'domestic factors of production', to 'those factors which spend their income within the economy in which it is earned, for consumation, investment, imports, or any other purpose'. See Jonathan V. Levin, 'The Export Economies', in James D. Theberge (ed.), *The Economics of Trade and Development*, p. 17–18. New York, London, Wiley, 1968. In the case of Latin America, remittances (especially bullion remittances) to imperial governments in Europe form parts of factors' remittance abroad.

11. J. E. Inikori, 'English Trade to Guinea: A Study in the Impact of Foreign Trade on the English Economy, 1750–1807'. (Ph.D. thesis, University of Ibadan, 1973.)

12. In some aspects, the credit requirements of the British slave trade are similar to those required today by the trading of capital goods internationally.

13. Inikori, 'English trade to Guinea', op. cit., Chap. VII.

14. Inikori, 'English Trade to Guinea', op. cit., p. 234–41; J. E. Inikori, 'Measuring the Atlantic Slave Trade'.

15. Inikori, 'English Trade to Guinea', op. cit., Chap. IV.

16. See Inikori, 'English Trade to Guinea', op. cit., Chap. IV, for more details.

17. Simone Berbain, 'Études sur la Traite des Noirs au Golfe du Guinée: Le Comptoir Français de Juda (Ouidah) au XVIIIᵉ Siècle', *Memoires de l'Institut Français d'Afrique Noire*, No. 3, 1942, p. 85–6; Gaston Martin, *Nantes au XVIIIᵉ Siècle: l'Ere des Negriers, 1714–1774*, Paris, 1931; Pierre M. Boulle, 'Slave Trade, Commercial Organisation and Industrial Growth in Eighteenth Century Nantes', *Revue Française d'Histoire d'Outre-Mer*, Vol. LIX, No. 214, 1st quarter, 1972.

18. Douglas C. North and Robert Paul Thomas, *The Rise of the Western World: A New Economic History*, p. 18. Cambridge University Press, 1973.
19. Ralph Davis, 'English Foreign Trade, 1700–1774', *Economic History Review*, 2nd ser., Vol. XV, 1962, p. 290.
20. Phyllis Deane and W. A. Cole, *British Economic Growth, 1688–1959*, 2nd ed. Table 2, p. 6, Cambridge University Press, 1967.
21. Ralph Davis, *The Rise of the English Shipping Industry in the Seventeenth and Eighteenth Centuries*, p. 393, London, Macmillan, 1962.
22. François Crouzet, 'Wars, Blockade, and Economic Change in Europe, 1792–1815', *Journal of Economic History*, Vol. XXIV, No. 4, December 1964, p. 568.
23. Crouzet, op. cit., p. 569.
24. James F. Shepherd and Gray M. Walton, *Shipping, Maritime Trade, and the Economic Development of Colonial North America*, p. 44, Cambridge, Cambridge University Press, 1972.
25. Shepherd and Walton, op. cit., p. 25.
26. D. C. North, *The Economic Growth of the United States, 1700–1860*, Englewood Cliffs, N.J., Prentice-Hall, 1961.
27. Henry A. Gemery and Jan S. Hogendorn, 'The Atlantic Slave Trade: A Tentative Economic Model', *Journal of African History*, Vol. XV, No. 2, 1974, p. 229, quoting C. Padro, Jr, *The Colonial Background of Modern Brazil*, p. 19, Berkeley, Calif., University of California Press, 1967.
28. K. G. Davies, 'Empire and Capital', p. 107.
29. Gemery and Hogendorn, op. cit., p. 229–31. For some other aspects of the slave-labour issue, see Robert P. Thomas and Richard N. Bean, 'The Adoption of Slave Labour in British America' (paper presented to the Mathematical Social Science Board Seminar at Colby College, Waterville, Maine, 20–22 August 1975).
30. Robert W. Fogel and Stanley L. Engerman, *Time on the Cross: The Economics of American Negro Slavery*, p. 192, London, Wildwood House, 1974.
31. Ralph Davis, *A Commercial Revolution, English Overseas Trade in the Seventeenth and Eighteenth Centuries*, p. 10, London, Historical Association, 1967. Professor Davis shows that the large reduction in the prices of the products brought them within the reach of more consumers and made them 'near-necessities rather than luxuries'.
32. For the points made here, See W. E. Minchinton (ed.), *The Growth of English Overseas Trade in the 17th and 18th centuries*, London, Methuen, 1969, Chapters 2 and 3 by Ralph Davis on English foreign trade, 1660–1774, and Chapter 5, by H. E. S. Fisher, on Anglo-Portuguese Trade, 1700–70. See also Allan Christelow, 'Great Britain and the Trades from Cadiz and Lisbon to Spanish America and Brazil, 1759–1783', *Hispanic American History Review*, Vol. XXVIII, No. 1, February, 1948, Part 2; and Jean O. McLachlan, *Trade and Peace with Old Spain 1667–1750*, Cambridge, Cambridge University Press, 1940.
33. Walter Rodney, *How Europe Underdeveloped Africa*, p. 103–12, London and Dar es Salaam, Bogle-L'Ouverture Publications, 1972; Henry A. Gemery and Jan S. Hogendorn, 'The Economic Costs of West African Participation in the Atlantic Slave Trade: A Preliminary Sampling for the Eighteenth Century' (paper presented to the Mathematical Social Science Board Seminar at Colby College, Waterville, Maine, 20–22 August 1975); H. A. Gemery and J. S. Hogendorn, 'Technological Change, Slavery, and the Slave Trade', forthcoming in C. J. Dewey and A. G. Hopkins (eds.), *Studies in the Economic History of India and Africa*, London, Athlone Press, in press; A. G. Hopkins, *An Economic History of West Africa*, London, Longman, 1973.

34. Gemery and Hogendorn, 'The Economic Costs of West African Participation in the Atlantic Slave Trade'.
35. Williams, op. cit., p. 255.
36. Gemery and Hogendorn, 'Technological Change, Slavery, and the Slave Trade'.
37. ibid.
38. John W. Blake, *European Beginnings in West Africa, 1454–1578*, p. 23, London, Longman, 1937.
39. It is said that the plantation economy of Zanzibar and Pemba developed in the 1820s following restrictions imposed by the British on the slave trade of the Swahili coast. Thereafter profits from the slave trade contributed to the expansion of those plantations: Nicholls, *The Swahili Coast*, p. 203.
40. A. J. H. Latham, 'Currency, Credit and Capitalism on the Cross River in the Pre-Colonial Era', *Journal of African History*, Vol. XII, No. 4, 1971, p. 604.
41. J. D. Fage, 'Slavery and the Slave Trade in the Context of West African History', *Journal of African History*, Vol. X, No. 3, 1969; Peter Morton-Williams, 'The Oyo Yoruba and the Atlantic Trade, 1670–1830', *Journal of the Historical Society of Nigeria*, Vol. III, No. 1, December 1964; Michael Mason, 'Population Density and "Slave Raiding"—the Case of the Middle Belt of Nigeria', *Journal of African History*, Vol. X, No. 4, 1969; M. B. Gleave and R. M. Prothero, 'Population Density and "Slave Raiding"—A Comment', *Journal of African History*, Vol. XII, No. 2, 1971; Roger T. Anstey, *The Atlantic Slave Trade*, p. 58–88.
42. If that had been the case those territories could not have sustained the slave trade for over 400 years.
43. P. D. Curtin, 'The Slave Trade and the Atlantic Basin: Intercontinental Perspectives', in N. I. Huggins, M. Kilson and D. M. Fox (eds.), *Key Issues in the Afro-American Experience*, p. 39–53, Vol. I, New York, 1971.
44. Fogel and Engerman, *Time on the Cross*, p. 132. The factor of slave breeding is dismissed by the authors as an erroneous idea disseminated by the anti-slavery movement. In fact, they argue that if slave-breeding methods were adopted by the slaveholders the effects on reproduction rates would have been negative due to the psychological effects they would have had on the female slaves. See Fogel and Engerman, op. cit., p. 78–86.
45. Sara S. Berry, *Cocoa, Custom, and Socio-Economic Change in Rural Western Nigeria*, Oxford, Clarendon Press, 1975.
46. Hopkins, op. cit., p. 77.
47. Allan G. B. Fisher and Humphrey J. Fisher, *Slavery and Muslim Society in Africa: The Institution in Saharan and Sudanic Africa and the Trans-Saharan Trade*, p. 59, London, C. Hurst, 1970.
48. Fisher and Fisher, op. cit., p. 160.
49. Basil Davidson, 'Slaves or Captives? Some Notes on Fantasy and Fact', in Huggins, Kilson and Fox (eds.), op. cit., p. 69.
50. J. R. Gray and D. Birmingham, 'Some Economic and Political Consequences of Trade in Central and Eastern Africa in the Pre-Colonial Period', in J. R. Gray and D. Birmingham (eds.), *Pre-Colonial African Trade: Essays on Trade in Central and Eastern Africa before 1900*, p. 18–19, London, 1970.
51. C.103/130: 'Captain George Hamilton to Thomas Hall', Annamaboe, 3 August 1740.
52. ibid., 24 December 1738.
53. K. Y. Daaku cites two cases among British slave-merchants in 1689 and 1706, respectively: K. Y. Daaku, *Trade and Politics*, op. cit., p. 30.
54. C.113/274 Part 4, folios 275–6. The letter is undated, but it should be early eighteenth century.

55. ibid., folios 277–8.
56. Peter Morton-Williams, 'The Oyo Yoruba', p. 27; See Mason, op. cit., and Gleave and Prothero, op. cit., for a discussion of this subject in connection with the Middle Belt of Nigeria.
57. Gray and Birmingham, 'Some Economic and Political Consequences of Trade in Central and Eastern Africa', p. 12.
58. Daaku, *Trade and Politics*, op. cit., p. 24.
59. J. K. Fynn, *Asante and Its Neighbours 1700–1807*, p. 11, London, Longman, 1971.
60. Blake, *European Beginnings*, op. cit., p. 84.
61. Fynn, *Asante and Its Neighbours*, op. cit., p. 12.
62. C.113/273: Part I, Sir Dalby Thomas to the Royal African Company, Cape Coast Castle, 30 July 1708, folios 17–18. What this statement shows clearly is the absence of opportunities for the gainful employment of available resources.
63. ibid., folios, 27–9.
64. C. 113/272 Part 2, folio 235: 'Court of Assistants to James Phipps and Others', African House, London 13 March 1721–22.
65. C.113/274 Part 3, folios 216–17: 'Cape Coast Castle to Royal African Company', 2 July 1722.
66. The thinking of these governments was that the Americas belonged to them as colonies while Africa did not. Therefore, while they could control the exploitation of resources in the Americas they were not in a position to do the same in Africa.
67. T.70/5 folio 64: 'Abstract of Sir Dalby Thomas's letter to the Royal African Company', 29 November 1709.
68. C.O.391/60, p. 66–71: 'Minutes of the Board of Trade Meeting of Friday, 14 February 1752.'
69. T.70/73, p. 139–40: 'The Committee of the Company of Merchants Trading to Africa to the Treasury, 9 April 1812.'

Appendix: Archival sources for a study of the external slave trade from Africa

A large amount of the materials relating to the slave trade which are available in European archives has recently been listed among other materials for African history in foreign archives in two parallel sets of series, one of which deals with only West Africa, as follows:

Patricia Carson, *Materials for West African History in the Archives of Belgium and Holland*, London, 1962.

Patricia Carson, *Materials for West African History in French Archives*, London, 1968.

Noel Matthews, *Materials for West African History in the Archives of the United Kingdom*, London, 1973.

A. F. C. Ryder, *Materials for West African History in Portuguese Archives*, London, 1965.

A very large proportion of the unpublished archival materials relating to the slave trade will be found listed in the above booklets and it is unnecessary to duplicate them here. But these booklets do not list all the materials relating to the slave trade that may be found in European archives. For example, the list for United Kingdom archives does not contain the very important *British Parliamentary Papers*, in particular, the 'Accounts and Papers' in the British Museum which contain a large amount of materials relating to the slave trade; the important Tarleton Papers in the Liverpool Record Office, and the Records of the Heywoods Bank of Liverpool, in Barclays Bank, Heywoods Branch, are also not included. Lloyds Corporation Archives in London also contain some materials relating to the slave trade and are not included in the list by Matthews. The Chancery Masters' Exhibits in the London Public Record Office, mentioned by Matthews, include a very large amount of materials relating to the slave trade, but because of the way those records are described it has not been easy to detect which of them relate to the slave trade. Some of those not mentioned by Matthews are:

C.109/401: 'Accounts of Five Slave Voyages by Samual Sandys & Co. of Liverpool, 1771–1772'.

C.114/1–3 and C.114/154–8: 'Records of Thomas Lumley & Co., of London, Guinea Merchants and Dealers in East India Goods, 1801–1807'.

C.103/130–3: 'Papers of Thomas Hall & Co., of London, Slave Merchants, 1730–1743'.

Recently, some of the records of the Royal African Company of Great Britain have been discovered among the Chancery Masters' Exhibits (C.113/261–95). These have been described by David P. Henige, 'Two Sources For the History of the Guinea

Coast, 1680–1722', *The International Journal of African Historical Studies,* Vol. 2, 1972, p. 271–5.

Apart from the omission of some important sources, all four lists probably contain most of the extant archival sources for a study of the slave trade to be found in Europe.

The second set is more comprehensive. Not only does it deal with the whole of Africa, but it includes sources in a greater number of European archives, and also archival sources in the United States of America. This set, prepared by the International Council on Archives under the auspices of Unesco, contains eleven volumes published under the title *International Council on Achives: Guide to the Sources of the History of Africa.*

One of the frustrations of studying the slave trade, however, is that there are records on the subject in private hands. But because people are very concerned about the moral aspects of the trade, owners of such records are very reluctant to allow scholars to see them. Professor F. E. Hyde of Liverpool University once mentioned this to me about such records in Liverpool. It is possible that as the moral aspects of the trade become less emphasized, scholars may be able to reach more of such materials in private hands.

For central and eastern Africa, the various works by David Birmingham, Phyllis Martin, Edward A. Alpers and others referred to in this paper, contain references to a large number of the unpublished archival sources relating to the slave trade.

The slave trade in the Caribbean and Latin America

José Luciano Franco

The beginnings of the trade in African slaves

Spain, like Portugal, in the settlement of its American possessions, showed a singular inclination for hybrid tropical colonies with a slave component. Large numbers of Negro slaves had been introduced into Spain from the west coasts of Africa during the fourteenth and fifteenth centuries. The discoveries made by the Portuguese and, especially, the encouragement given by the Infante D. Enrique of Portugal to blackbirding expeditions at the beginning of the fifteenth century, gave rise to the slave trade which in later years took the Negroes captured in Africa to the territories recently discovered by Christopher Columbus.

The discovery of the New World gave a tremendous impetus to slavery and the slave trade. The African element was required to exploit the enormous wealth of the newly discovered tropical territories in the Caribbean for the benefit of the Spanish colonizers. Before the end of the fifteenth century Negro slaves began to arrive at Hispaniola—as the island of Quisqueya, now Santo Domingo, was then called—coming from the abundant reserves existing in Portugal and Andalusia. But as early as 1501, African slaves were imported into the New World.

The Spanish conquest and dominion very quickly spread from Santo Domingo to the islands of Puerto Rico, Jamaica and Cuba. As the first slaves brought to the Caribbean islands came from Spain or Portugal, and they were regarded as the chief culprits in the constant uprisings of the indigenous Indians or the slaves imported directly from Africa, the King of Spain decreed that Negroes who had spent more than two years in Spain or Portugal should not be sent to his new colonies in the Caribbean; only those brought directly from his African territories should be sent.

The Spanish colonizers also believed (not without some grounds) that the Wolof slaves—whom they called Gelofes—like the Mande and Mandingo largely converted to Islam, were mainly responsible for the running away of slaves and the slave uprisings in Santo Domingo, Jamaica, Puerto Rico and Cuba. A royal decree prohibited the importing of slaves from these African cultural groups. It was for this reason that the slave trade developed along the coasts of Guinea.

The colonizers of the Caribbean islands repeatedly asked the King of Spain to have more African slaves dispatched to them, and he granted Gouvenot, Governor of Bresa, a licence to import 4,000 Negro slaves from the coasts of Guinea into the West Indies. The latter sold this licence to the Genoese, who in turn sold a part of their rights to Portuguese and other traders.

Between 1512 and 1763, some 60,000 African slaves entered Cuba lawfully. Many more were smuggled into the country. The increase in the slave population was concomitant with the development of the cultivation of sugar, for which hundreds of workers were needed on the agricultural side, and also to a lesser extent with the exploitation of the copper mines in the eastern part of Cuba, administered by an agent of the German firm Welser. Slaves were provided by the Spanish monarch himself for this purpose.

The slave trade from the sixteenth to the eighteenth century

This characteristic period in the history of the African slave trade with the Caribbean colonies began on 12 February 1528, when the King of Spain granted Enrique Ehinger and Jerónimo Sayler, agents of the German bankers, the Welsers, who, with the Fuggers, controlled Spanish finance, the first *asiento* or licence to introduce African slaves into his American possessions.

To deal with matters relating to the *asientos*, a special board, the Junta de Negros, was set up in Spain, in the Casa de la Contratación in Seville; it concerned itself with the trade in African slaves and with ensuring full compliance with the terms of the *asientos*.

In fact, the first 'licence to navigate in the region of our West Indies and to bring Negro slaves thereto' was granted to Pedro Gómez Reynel, for a period of nine years beginning on 1 May 1595. However, under the Royal Decree signed at Valladolid on 11 March 1601, this concession was withdrawn from him and awarded instead to the Portuguese Juan Rodríguez Coutiño, merchant and Governor of Loango. The first stipulation was that Rodríguez Coutiño should transport 38,250 slaves from Africa to the Caribbean, sailing with them from the city of Seville, Lisbon, the Canary Islands, Cape Verde, São Tomé, Angola and São Jorge de Mina.

However, several years before the monopoly of the slave trade was formally granted, by *asiento*, to Gómez Reynel, and more particularly from 3 October 1562 to 15 December 1585, the King of Spain authorized various of his subjects to trade in slaves—for instance, Diego de Ayllon (1562) and Diego Pérez Negron (1563)—while on 20 November 1571 it was agreed that Juan Hernández de Espinosa should take 300 African slaves to Havana. Certain Spanish towns also profited from the slave trade: thus, for instance, the town of Seville was permitted to transport Negro slaves to the New World by the Royal Decree of San Lorenzo dated 5 August 1567, countersigned by Antonio de Eraso.

On the death of Rodríguez Coutiño, the *asiento* granted to the Portuguese was handed on to Gonzalo Vaz Coutiño, and subsequently it was held in turn by Agustín Coello, Rodríguez d'Elvas, Rodríguez Lamego, and finally, up to 1640, by Melchor Gómez Angel and Cristóbal Méndez de Sosa.

The exigencies of the *asiento* led the Portuguese to increase the number of their depots and warehouses on the west coast of Africa. Wherever their barters and deals took place, they needed to have astute middlemen to enable them to improve and extend their business transactions through regular exchange channels. Against attacks by their European competitors—Dutchmen, Frenchmen, Englishmen, Danes and Germans—the Portuguese put up a vigorous and skilful defence. Angola was a Portuguese fief with its trading posts, organized slave trade, governors and agents. From 1526 onwards, beside their huts and Catholic chapels, small forts were built, the earliest of them in Sama and the most strongly fortified in São Jorge de Mina, which became the centre of the slave trade. But the Portuguese could not prevent their rivals from establishing themselves opposite and, later on, from ousting them from almost the whole of Guinea. By 1688, not a single fort remained flying the Portuguese flag.

In the absence of direct trade with Africa, it was inevitable that, to obtain slaves for the mines and plantations of her colonies in the New World, Spain should have to depend either on rebels (the Portuguese), or heretics (the British), or both rebels and heretics (the Dutch), or enemies (the French), since no other country was sufficiently interested in the slave trade. From 1640 to 1662, no measures were taken by the Spanish Government to hinder the clandestine importation of slaves supplied by the British, the Portuguese or the Dutch.

The Dutch, who had shaken off the Spanish yoke during the final decades of the sixteenth century, succeeded in the following century in wresting from the Portuguese their most important enclaves in the slave trade, establishing themselves in Gorea, Joaquín and Tacorari in 1620, and in São Jorge de Mina in 1637. By the end of the century, the Dutch were everywhere installed as slave traders, with São Jorge de Mina as their operational centre. Balthasar Coymans of the West Indies Company of Amsterdam, who was secretly the real concessionnaire of the *asiento* granted to Juán Barroso del Pozo and Nicolás Porcio in 1682, managed to obtain the much coveted monopoly on 23 February 1685.

As the Mexican historian Gonzalo Aguirre Beltrán observes, after Coymans' triumph a tendency arose for *asientos* to cease to be contracts concluded between the Spanish Government and a private individual for the leasing of a public revenue and to become, as was soon to be the case, treaties between countries.

The history of British trade in West Africa prior to the establishment of the Company of Royal Adventurers in 1660 is briefly as follows: up to 1630 or 1640 it remained very restricted in volume and had no connection with trade in the West Indies or the American continent. Between 1562 and 1569, het British slave trade was started by John Hawkins. In 1562, aboard his ship *Jesus,* he carried off a consignment of slaves from the shores of Africa which he exchanged for gold, sugar and hides with the Spanish colonists in Santo Domingo.

Hawkins had shown wisdom and cunning in starting his interloper's trade in the Caribbean, but he had not reckoned with the Casa de Contratación in Seville, which would not allow the slightest infiltration in the Spanish trade monopoly, and promptly seized in Cadiz the two ships that Hawkins was naïve enough to send to that port to sell some of the hides exchanged for Negro slaves in Santo Domingo. The king of Spain, Philip II, refused to accede to the Englishman's repeated requests and was sharply called to account by Queen Elizabeth of England.

After Hawkins' failure, English trade in West Africa dwindled. With the defeat of the Invincible Armada in 1588 and the decline of the House of Austria, Queen Elizabeth was that same year able to grant thirty-five London merchants the privilege of slave-trading on the African coast from Senegal to the River Gambia; these promptly set about turning the island of Tortuga in the Caribbean into the favourite haunt of slave-traders, *rescatadores* ('receivers' of slaves) and pirates.

With the occupation of Jamaica, the British—who during the first half of the seventeenth century had given up the slave trade—decided to renew it with greater intensity. On 18 December 1661, the Company of Royal Adventurers obtained the exclusive right to engage in and organize the slave trade from Cape Blanc to the Cape of Good Hope. Queens, royal princesses, dukes and peers were included among the shareholders in this undertaking. The king himself seized the opportunity of acquiring an interest in so profitable a business. However, the war against the Dutch reduced the profits and caused that band of high-born adventurers to wind up their business, the company being replaced in 1672 by the Royal African Company. In nine years alone, from 1680 to 1689, the latter company sent 259 ships to African shores and transported 46,396 slaves to the American colonies.

At the end of the sixteenth century, the French had not yet realized the full economic importance for them of the trade practised by the Portuguese and the Dutch in Africa, and it was only under Cardinal Richelieu that they began to enter the slave trade on a small scale.

Richelieu gave his approval to the plans of the traders and merchant adventurers of Le Havre who, in 1626, organized with d'Esnambuc the Compagnie de Saint-Christophe to exploit the *pétun* (tobacco) and timber of the island of St Christopher in the Caribbean, and occupied the island of Tortuga and part of that of Santo Domingo. In Africa, Brigueville and Beaulieu of Normandy set about trading in Gambia. By letters patent of 24 June 1633, Messrs Rossée, Robin & Company, merchants of Dieppe and Rouen, obtained permission to trade in Senegal, Cape Verde and other places. Thomas Lambert, a seaman, built a few huts at the mouth of the Senegal River. In 1640, a small fort was established on an island which became known as Saint-Louis. Cape López was conceded to a St Malo company called the Compagnie de Guinée.

What the Spanish and Portuguese had long ago discovered, the French were to learn in their turn: the need for acquiring African slaves to exploit and develop the riches of the Caribbean and America. The trade fluctuated in its initial stages. In 1658, the Compagnie du Sénégal went bankrupt.

The African trade declined, being barely sustained by a few private traders or interlopers. The slave trade came almost to a standstill and virtually ceased in Senegal whose inhabitants, being little sought after by slave-traders, supplied barely more than a few hundred slaves a year. No regular slave trade existed between France, Africa and the Caribbean islands. From Cape Verde to the Congo, the whole of the coastline was in the clutch of agents of governments hostile to France or of commercial rivals—not only Portuguese, English and Dutch, but also Germans established at Cape Three Points. The Swedes built the fort of Christianburg but were ousted by the others.

The French slave trade was officially organized by Colbert in 1664. Convinced, initially, of the value of State control, he wished to imitate the example of the Dutch, regulate the slave trade and group together private capital and initiative in trading companies, putting them in charge of overseas trading posts which he bolstered up by monopolies and concessions.

With the growth of the slave trade, slavery had reached such a pitch by the beginning of the eighteenth century in all strata of colonial society in Latin America that even the Peruvian Indians were able to buy, sell and possess African slaves.

The actual number of men, women and children who were snatched from their homes in Africa and transported in slave ships across the Atlantic, either to the Caribbean islands or to North and South America, will never be known. Writers vary in their estimates, but there is no doubt that their number runs into millions. The following figures are taken from Morel's calculations as reproduced by Professor Melville J. Herskovits and cover the period 1666–1800:

1666–1776: Slaves imported only by the English for the English, French and Spanish colonies: 3 million (250,000 died on the voyage).

1680–1786: Slaves imported for the English colonies in America: 2,130,000 (Jamaica alone absorbed 610,000).

1716–1756: Average annual number of slaves imported for the American colonies: 70,000, with a total of 3.5 million.
1752–1762: Jamaica alone imported 71,115 slaves.
1759–1762: Guadeloupe alone imported 40,000 slaves.
1776–1800: A yearly average of 74,000 slaves were imported for the American colonies, or a total of 1,850,000; this yearly average was divided up as follows: by the English, 38,000; French, 20,000; Portuguese, 10,000; Dutch, 4,000; Danes, 2,000.

The African slaves arriving in the New World were concentrated in various towns along the coast where there were *barracones* or slave markets, in the West Indies, Guianas, North and South America, Venezuela, Brazil, etc., whence they were redistributed.

The places of origin of this great mass of slaves are still a matter of conjecture, but it is believed that, in practice, the supply came from all the African regions, not only West Africa but also East Africa and even Madagascar. We have no reliable documentation on the focal points for the capture of slaves. But there is every indication that the vast majority came from specific areas of West Africa.

In 1701, as the result of negotiations conducted by Du Casse, Governor of Santo Domingo and organizer of the slave trade in the French West Indies, His Most Christian Majesty Louis XIV of France and His Catholic Majesty Philip V of Spain signed the so-called Treaty of Asiento, conferring on the Compagnie de Guinée the monopoly for the importation of Negro slaves into the Spanish colonies in the Caribbean and other places in Latin America.

The Compagnie de Guinée undertook to import during the ten years that the treaty was in force an annual consignment of 4,800 African slaves drawn from any part of West Africa except the trading posts of São Jorge de Mina and Cape Verde, bringing them to Havana, Vera Cruz, Cumana and Cartagena de Indias. It should be noted that, during this French period, the cargoes of slaves were transported from Portobelo across the Isthmus of Panama down to Peru.

This privilege—the slave-trading *asiento*—had for a long time been eagerly competed for by the various seafaring nations. The Portuguese had retained it from 1601 to 1640, up to the time they regained their independence. Subsequently the Spanish Government, in order to prevent it from passing into the hands of one of its major rivals, had in 1622 reached an understanding with a Dutch company. But the Dutch in Curaçao and the English in Jamaica succeeded in having a hand in the business of that company. From then onward the *asiento de negros* was the subject of various negotiations.

Following the War of the Spanish Succession, a radical change took place in the correlation of economic and political forces, and gave Britain, seconded by Portugal and Holland, an absolute control over the slave trade with the Caribbean islands, especially with Cuba. And, under the Peace Treaty signed in Madrid on 27 March 1713 and ratified by one of the articles of the Treaty of Utrecht, the monopoly of the slave trade passed into British hands for the next thirty years.

In 1715, Richard O'Farrill of Irish origin, from the island of Montserrat, arrived in Cuba as the representative of the South Sea Company of London and established slave depots in Havana and Santiago de Cuba, thereby giving great impetus to the African slave trade; the majority of slaves were imported into Mexico, but the traffic was almost at a standstill before the second half of the eighteenth century.

The Spanish ports had protested that they were being excluded from the colonial trade (a monopoly exercised by the Casa de Contractación in Seville) while a foreign country had the right to flood the Caribbean and Latin American colonies with slaves.

The outbreak of war between England and Spain in 1740 provided a convenient excuse for abolishing the privilege hitherto enjoyed by the English slave-dealers. To continue the legitimate business of importing slaves, conducted until then by O'Farrill and the English concessionaires, some Cuban and Spanish capitalists founded the Real Compañía de Comercio de La Habana which, in addition to supplying Cuban sugar-cane planters with new slaves, held the monopoly to operate all the foreign trade of the Greater Antilles.

A series of *asientos* were granted until September 1779 when the last monopoly in the history of the slave trade was abolished. To remedy as far as possible the shortage of labour, the slave-dealers of Cuba, Santo Domingo and Puerto Rico were granted, by Royal Decree of 25 January 1780, the right to obtain slaves from the French colonies in the Caribbean. However, as the demand for slave labour went on increasing, under Royal Decree of 28 February 1789, slave trading was made free in Cuba, Santo Domingo and Puerto Rico, and this was subsequently extended by Royal Decree of 24 November 1791, to the slave-dealers of Santa Fé, Buenos Aires and Caracas. In Cuba, these provisions by which the Spanish Government met the demands of the sugar-cane planters and slave-dealers gave an extraordinary impetus to the slave trade. The phenomenal increase in the Cuban slave population at the end of the eighteenth century is closely linked with the establishment of a sugar-cane plantation economy. Hundreds of slaves were needed for the cultivation of sugar cane and the production of sugar, and as exports increased so the productive labour became intensified, bringing about a higher death rate among the slaves, speeding up wastage, and necessitating a faster replacement of the Africans thus destroyed.

Rise and fall of slave trading and slavery in the nineteenth century

In Cuba, the colonial slave-holding regime set up by the Spanish colonizers at the beginning of the sixteenth century brought into being a social class composed of sugar-cane planters and dealers in human flesh, which from 1778 attained its maximum social and economic power, forming a veritable slave-owning and trading oligarchy up to just beyond the first half of the nineteenth century.

In the last years of the eighteenth century and the early years of the nineteenth, this oligarchy had consolidated its privileged position with the support of the Spanish governors and captains-general who exercised absolute power in the island, and its numbers were to be considerably increased. During this period, not only was so repulsive a business as slave trading considered a normal and current practice among the white Creoles and Spanish residents in the island belonging to the nobility and clergy, but the middle classes engaged in it also with the greatest enthusiasm, and even considered it an honour.

The Cuban slave-dealers were not alone in their infamous business. They could also rely on the services of English, French and United States traders and smugglers. Some slave-dealers in Havana made fortunes by selling slaves to North America. Later on, with the approaching 'coming into force' of the United States constitutional clause prohibiting the slave trade from 1808 onwards, the direction of the slave traffic between Cuba and the United States was reversed. For instance, there sailed into the port of Havana between March 1806 and February 1807, thirty ships flying the United States flag and with United States crews aboard, with consignments mostly for traders of that country resident in Cuba. They reproduced to a certain extent the three-cornered trade which in the seventeenth and eighteenth centuries had brought prosperity to Liverpool, Nantes and Bordeaux, shipping trashy goods to Africa and exchanging them for Negroes, and these in turn for raw materials from the Caribbean or Latin America, which were then shipped to European countries to be manufactured.

In the first thirty years of the nineteenth century, the slave trade reached its peak in Cuba. From 1800 to 1820 alone, according to information supplied by Professor Juan Pérez de la Riva, 175,058 slaves were brought over from the shores of Africa to Cuba; by the following decade this figure had dropped to 72,500.

The progress of the Industrial Revolution, the new types of production and exchange, had a decisive influence on the opening of the campaign—necessarily invested with an aura of romance—for the abolition of slavery and the slave trade. In the Caribbean, the revolt in Haiti, under the leadership of Toussaint Louverture, brought slavery to an end not only there but also in Santo Domingo. In 1807, the fitting out of slave-ships was forbidden in the

British dominions, and in 1808 this prohibition was extended to the importation of slaves.

Internationally, the African slave traffic in the Caribbean islands and in Latin America was partly disrupted by the Treaty of Paris of 30 May 1814, which subsequently led in Vienna, to the famous Declaration of 8 February 1815. In September 1817, a treaty was signed by the representatives of the London and Madrid Governments abolishing the slave traffic; this was limited in scope owing to the exigencies of the time but was later amplified by the treaty of 28 June 1835 under which Spanish subjects were forbidden to engage in that unlawful business. Brazil was also to sign similar agreements.

However, in spite of the above-mentioned international treaties and agreements and of innumerable laws passed by the metropolitan countries concerned, the illegal traffic in slaves reached considerable proportions. Faced with the abolitionist campaign carried out by progressive groups in Great Britain and France and the measures taken to suppress the trade, the slave-trading oligarchy in Cuba and the plantation owners in the Caribbean and slave-owning parts of America retorted by mounting a vicious campaign describing the French 'revolutionaries' in the blackest and most sinister terms and accusing the English of perfidy and selfishness. With the consent and support of the colonial governments and the complicity of the reactionary forces in Europe and America, they organized an illegal slave traffic, thus disregarding the various international treaties and agreements.

Karl Marx, commenting on a session of the House of Lords in London on 17 June 1858 when the Bishop of Oxford raised the question of the slave trade, in an article entitled 'The British Government and the Slave Trade' and published by the *New York Daily Tribune* on 23 July of the same year, made some important observations with regard to Cuba and the illegal traffic in slaves. He said that the Bishop of Oxford and Lord Brougham denounced Spain as being the focal point of that nefarious traffic, and called upon the British Government to compel that country by every means in its power to pursue a political course consonant with existing treaties. Already in 1814 a general treaty had been drawn up between Great Britain and Spain under which trading in slaves was categorically condemned by the latter. In 1817 a special treaty had been concluded whereby Spain undertook to abolish in 1820, in respect of its subjects, the right to engage in the slave trade, and by way of compensation for the losses these might sustain through the application of the treaty, was paid an indemnity of £400,000 sterling. Spain had pocketed the money but the obligations had not been fulfilled. In 1835 another treaty had been concluded under which Spain solemnly undertook to promulgate a penal law of sufficient severity to make it impossible for its subjects to continue engaging in the traffic. But that law had not been adopted until over ten years later; moreover, by a strange fatality, its most important clause—for which

Great Britain had fought hard—had been left out, namely, the one which placed the slave traffic and piracy on the same footing. In short, nothing whatever had been done except that the Captain-General of Cuba, the Minister of the Interior, the royal *camarilla* and, if rumour were to be believed, even the royal family, had imposed a special tax on slave-traders and sold licences to deal in human flesh and blood at so many doubloons a head. . . . Lord Malmesbury himself had stated that it would be possible to cover the seas between the Spanish and Cuban coasts with the number of documents uselessly exchanged between the two governments.

In Cuba, before the second half of the nineteenth century, the development achieved by the colonial economy sounded the death knell for the slave regime. From 1860 onwards, the human commodity could no longer be provided cheaply by the slave traffic. Governmental pressure on the latter was intensified in compliance with British demands. To induce the Spanish colonial authorities to allow the clandestine entry of Africans, recourse had to be had to the expensive procedure of bribery which raised the price of the commodity. On the sea, the relentless vigilance of the British ships gave no respite. One only out of every five consignments organized managed to reach Cuban shores. The traffic no longer provided a solution to the sugar-cane planters' difficulties. The Anglo-North American Treaty of 7 April 1862 for the suppression of the slave trade dealt the final blow to the clandestine slave traffic. And the opening of Cuba's struggle for independence on 12 October 1868, with the massive participation of the Africans and their Creole descendants, heralded the end of slavery within ten years. As far as our research enables us to say, the last African slaves from Angola transported through the Spanish colony of Fernando Po, arrived in Cuba in 1873.

The impact of the slave trade on Cuban society

The slave-owning oligarchy in Cuba which, together with the Spanish and Creole slave-traders, smugglers and merchants, formed the exploiting class in colonial society, was solely concerned, until well into the nineteenth century, with crates of sugar and sacks of coffee, with watching on the quayside for the arrival of slave-ships, and with gratifying its insatiable desire for wealth through the productive labour of hundreds of thousands of slaves in the plantations. But it gradually began to be concerned about the activities of free Negroes and mulattos in various sectors of social life capable of leading an armed protest of the mass of slaves which could put an end to their privileges. The urban craftsmen, consisting of Africans and their descendants, were the only people engaged in occupations contributing towards the country's economic development. Carpenters, blacksmiths, bricklayers, shoemakers, tailors, etc., as well as school-teachers (some very notable ones in the eighteenth century, such as Lorenzo Meléndez, Mariano Moya and Juana Pastor), musicians and poets, were either free or enslaved Negroes and mulattos.

In the nineteenth century, thousands of free Negroes and mulattos were engaged in such occupations in Cuba. Many others were small traders and proprietors. Some devoted themselves to literature, teaching or music, and became distinguished, like the educator Antonio Medina, whose school in Havana was the educational centre for the production of coloured figures which were to contribute towards the cultural development of the Negroes; some became world-famous poets like the slave Juan Francisco Manzano and the free mulatto Gabriel de la Concepción Valdés (Plácido), or eminent concert players like Claudio J. Brindis de Salas and José White.

Socially, these formed a small middle class and were anxious to improve their social and political situation. They had a clear right to believe in the collective advancement of the social class to which they belonged. Thousands of Negro and mulatto slaves, inveterate rebels and non-conformists, aspired, with every atom of human justice on their side, to put an end to the oppression of the slave regime.

Many Afro-Cubans, taking advantage of some royal provisions, had bought honorific posts which gave them a certain prestige. And all conspired diffidently in the seclusion of their homes, in the shadow of their workshops, or in some sunny corner of the countryside against the slave trade and the savage system of exploitation. Some bolder spirits did so more uninhibitedly and joined the small progressive minority of white Creoles at their secret gatherings which foreshadowed the advent of popular union in the fight for freedom. It is somewhat ironical to reflect that, in Cuba, it was due to the inhuman slave traffic that the Negro race came to take part in the formation of a new type of human society.

The slave trade across the Atlantic and the slavery in the Caribbean and Latin America, which helped in the formation of the respective multiracial societies, not only provided an extraordinary contribution through the African's active participation in the development of agricultural production, mining and trade on a world scale, but were also important factors in the shaping of the region's cultures and folklore, of which Cuba and Haiti offer examples among the islands of the restless Caribbean and Brazil on the South American continent.

In concluding this modest account, we should point out that, for a research in depth on the subjects with which we have been dealing, it would be necessary to make copies of the fifteenth- to eighteenth-century documents preserved in the District Archives of Funchal, Madeira, as well as of those appearing in the Calendar of State Papers, Colonial Office, London. Accounts of the African diaspora in the Caribbean, in regard both to the legal and to the clandestine trade in African slaves, the revolt of the latter and their contribution towards the formation of a new society, are to be found in documents preserved in the Cuban National Archives, for the most part unpublished. Such research could be supplemented by recourse to the valuable works produced by the Centre for University Studies of Pointe-à-Pitre (Guadeloupe), directed by Henri Bangou and his assistant Mr Yacou, as well as those of historians of the University of the West Indies in Trinidad and Tobago, Jamaica and Barbados.

Documentary sources

FRANCO, José Luciano. *Esclavitud, Comercio y Tráfico Negreros*. La Habana, Academia de Ciencias de Cuba, 1972. (Catalogue of collections in the Cuban National Archives, Serie Archivo Nacional No. 7.)

Guide to sources of African history.

España. *Guía de Fuentes para la Historia de Africa Subsahariana*. Paris, Unesco and the International Archives Council, 1971.

Bibliography

ABRAMOVA, S. *L'Histoire de la Traite des Esclaves sur le Haut Littoral de la Guinée*. Moscow, 1966. (From the second half of the fifteenth to the beginning of the nineteenth century.)
BELTRÁN, Gonzalo Aguirre. *La Poblacion Negra de México*. Mexico, D.F., 1946.
BONILLA, Raúl Cepero. *Azúcar y Abolición*. Havana, 1960.
CURTIN, P. D. *The Atlantic Slave Trade*. Madison, Wis., University of Wisconsin Press, 1969.
DAVIES, K. G. *The Royal African Company*. London, Longman, Grion & Co., 1957.
DESCHAMPS, Hubert. *Histoire de la Traite des Noirs de l'Antiquité à nos Jours*. Paris, Fayard, 1971.
DÍAZ Y SOLER, Luis M. *Historia de la Esclavitud Negra en Puerto Rico. 1493–1890*. Madrid, n.d.
DUCASSE, André. *Les Négriers ou le Trafic des Esclaves*. Paris, Hachette, 1948.
FRANCO, José Luciano. *Afroamérica*. Havana, 1961.
——. *Comercio Clandestino de Esclavos Negros en el Siglo XIX*. Havana, 1971. (Historical series No. 21. Academy of Sciences.)
——. *Las Minas de Santiago del Prado y la Rebelión de los Cobreros. 1530–1800*. Havana, 1975.
——. *Los Palenques de los Negros Cimarrones*. Havana, 1971.
——. *La Presencia Negra en el Nuevo Mundo*. Havana, 1968.
FRANCO, José Luciano; PACHECO, Francisco; LE RIVERAND, Julio. Facetas del Esclavo Africano en América Latina. *Introducción al Cultura Africana en América Latina*. Paris, Unesco, 1970.
HERSKOVITS, Melville J. *Social History of the Negro*. Clark University, 1935. (Handbook of Social Psychology.)
KING, James Ferguson. Evolution of the Free Slave Trade Principle in Spanish Colonial Administration. *The Hispanic American Historical Review*. Durham, February 1942.
LACROIX, Louis. *Les Derniers Négriers*. Paris, Amiot-Dumoz, 1952.
LE RIVEREND, Julio. *Historia Económica de Cuba*. Havana, 1963.

MANNIX, Daniel P.; COWLEY M. *Historia de la Trata de Negros*. Madrid, 1970.

MARTIN, Gaston. *Histoire de l'Esclavage dans les Colonies Françaises*. Paris, Presses Universitaires de France, 1948.

MARX, K.; ENGELS F. *Acerca del Colonialismo*. Moscow, n.d.

ORTIZ, Fernando. *Los Negros Esclavos*. Havana, 1916.

SACO, José A. *Historia de la Esclavitud desde los Tiempos más Remotos hasta Nuestros Días*. Paris and Barcelona, 1875–77, reprinted Havana, 1937.

——. *Historia de la Esclavitud de la Raza Africana en el Nuevo Mundo y en Especial en los Países Américo-Hispanos*. Barcelona, 1879, reprinted Havana, 1938.

SCELLE, Georges. *La Traite Négrière aux Indes de Castille*. Paris, L. Larose & L. Tenin, 1906.

DE STUDER, Elena F. S. *La Trata de Negros en el Río de la Plata durante el Siglo XVIII*. Buenos Aires, 1958. (Publicaciones del Instituto de Historia Argentina 'Doctor Emilie Racignani,' No. 101.)

VERGER, Pierre. *Flux et Reflux de la Traite de Noirs entre le Golfe de Bénin et Bahia*. Paris and The Hague, Mouton, 1968.

VERLINDEN, Charles. Les Débuts de la Traite Portugaise en Afrique. 1443–1478 *Studia Historica Gundensia*. Ghent, University of Ghent, 1967.

WILLIAMS, Eric. *Capitalismo y Esclavitud*. Havana, 1975.

Negro resistance to slavery and the Atlantic slave trade from Africa to Black America

Oruno D. Lara

Introduction—approaches to the problem

In order to study the Atlantic slave trade and the slave system one must first review a number of problems and order them according to the way they link up. Before such research is undertaken a preliminary remark is called for: central to this vast set of problems is their common denominator—which should be studied in the general *History of Africa*—the Negro. Captured in the course of wars or raids, dragged on foot, stocked and then embarked on slave ships, an African was treated as a piece of merchandise before being sold into slavery on the American plantations. This human merchandise has been written about in two connections: (a) in connection with the slave trade, from the time it seized the African in Africa up to the time it sold him in America; and (b) in connection with the slave system in which the African was forced to work under a colonial regime.

At the beginning of any survey of the slave trade, mention must also be made of the historical links between sugar, monoculture and Negroes. These three elements in combination remain a constant of the slave system and colonial society. The slave trade is approached by historians in two ways, according to their geographic and social environment. In the first case, the heritage of colonial history weighs heavily, the mother country and the colony being regarded as forming a whole. With this approach, interest is centred on Europe, and the various questions are considered separately instead of being seen as a whole in relation to the different government policies. For example, the French West Indies are regarded as appendages of France in French history and there is no link with the other West Indies or with the American mainland. They are studied, casually, in connection with the economic history of a port such as Marseilles, Bordeaux, Nantes or Saint-Malo where an attempt is made to follow the fortunes of natives of these towns after they went out to the Indies. Adopting this approach, the Negro workers may be totally disregarded and only the colonists studied.[1] Or again the study may be centred on the slaves, but without seeing the dynamics of the system and wondering, after summing up a whole series of case histories, whether the fate of the slaves was not improved at the end of the eighteenth century.² Colonial historians do not merely give statistics of slaves living in huts and domestic servants. They attempt to extrapolate and construct mathematical models. With some authors it becomes a matter of quantities and series; with others, 'new economic history', in which an attempt is made to measure with mathematical formulae the profits to be gained from slaves and slavery. This serves two purposes: the social and historical role of the Negroes is minimized and the advantages of colonization are set forth in a strictly scientific fashion with the help of mathematics and political economy. The use of mathematical formulae in economics and economic history has already been strongly criticized by Professor Tinbergen and Professor P. Vilar. Such procedures, even if used only for statistical purposes, lead to disastrous results when applied to the history of the slave trade.³

From the scientific standpoint, three processes are involved: (a) stating the problem in such a way as to place the emphasis on the form of slave exploitation and relating it to a particular geographical area; in this geo-historical totality ⁴ the productive forces and the social relationships of production are studied; (b) listing the sources, subjecting them to critical scrutiny, then using them by considering them from the same angle; (c) adopting a set of methods based on scientific criteria in keeping with the geo-historical totality.

Few authors have so far approached the rational study of the slave trade from this scientific standpoint. Limited by the traditional framework of colonial history, whether they realized it or not, research workers have found it difficult to tackle the subject impartially, that is, to centre the discussion on the dynamics of the form of slave exploitation. Two complementary research procedures can be envisaged.

One procedure consists in studying this form of slave exploitation as seen from inside, that is, by the Negroes. This view of the bases of slave society implies a radical reversal of the colonial outlook. The history of the West Indies, for instance, of the slave system on the West Indian plantations, should be based on a specifically West Indian approach to the problem, on West Indian archives preserved in Denmark, France, the Netherlands, Portugal, Spain, the United Kingdom, the United States of America, etc. This specificity should not be interpreted too narrowly; it is a question of structural specificity. For instance, in studying the slave trade and slavery in the West Indies, research already effected or under way on colonial Brazil must be taken into account; for Brazil and the West Indies have histories which are structurally inseparable owing to the Dutch hegemony in the seventeenth century.

The other procedure consists in recognizing the Negro as a person who never accepted slavery, contrary to what is implied by a number of authors writing history from the colonial standpoint.⁵ The Negroes always refused to submit to the slave system, as is stated by Alejo Carpentier, who is very familiar with the history of the Caribbean. Anyone who is willing to refer to the sources will see that the whole history of the slave trade and slavery is a sequence of revolts. Seen in this light, marginal elements [6] such as the Maroon Negroes assume decisive importance. Studying them makes it possible to clarify the economic and social aspects of the slave system. Centring the problem on the Maroon Negroes and the slave revolts [7] has the advantage of allowing one to deal with the whole question of the method of slave exploitation without getting involved in the intricacies of sectoral analysis.

This is the procedure adopted here. The history of Africa and the black Americas extends from the fifteenth to the nineteenth century along many lines of emphasis—extrema, as the mathematicians would say—which have economic, political, sociological and cultural aspects. At a time when several African and American countries are freeing themselves from colonial tutelage, it is necessary to go back to origins, to the beginning of a process of revolts extending over several centuries. It is impossible to understand the liberation movements in various African countries without going back to the violent revolts which broke out sometimes as soon as the Europeans arrived in Africa.[8]

Approaching the problem from the standpoint of the Negro, in opposition to the slave system, the protagonist in a long process starting in the fifteenth century and continuing up to our own time, is tantamount to founding a new historical anthropology.

The basic records

The first essential step is to go methodically through the tremendous volume of scattered documents recording the main feature of the revolts in English, Spanish, Portuguese, French, Dutch, Italian, Danish, Latin, etc. Some record offices appear to have more material than others: the Public Record Office, London; the Archives Nationales, Paris; and Torre do Tombo, Lisbon. Other centres, less well known to research workers, hold additional material which must be consulted: the Rigsarkivet, Copenhagen; Algemeen Rijksarchief, The Hague; and Det Kongelige Bibliotek, Copenhagen. It is also important, of course, and often advantageous to consult records in provincial towns, overseas territories and the Vatican Archives in order to obtain different viewpoints and see the problem more clearly.

Some archives sources that have not been used and which afford different approaches to the problem are listed in the Appendix (p. 115).

Research to be undertaken

It would be desirable to undertake a research programme centred on different topics.

African resistance to European expansion of the slave system

The Jaga problem comes under this head, or what I have called 'the long transit of the Jaga, from Africa to the New World'. The Jaga broke in upon a foursome already at loggerheads: Portugal, Congo, Ndongo and São Tomé. They were very cruel warriors enjoying political, religious and military superiority. Operating from *kilombos*, or stockades, they invaded the Kongo and laid waste the country when Don Alvaro I (1568–87) came to the throne. He was obliged to abandon his capital, São Salvador, and take refuge on an island in the Zaire. Their invasion disorganized the Portuguese slave trade.

The Jaga invasion should be considered in conjunction with an invasion of Sumbas and that of the Mane of Sierra Leone at the end of the sixteenth century and the beginning of the seventeenth. In Guinea, a very belligerent people, the Bijagos, who inhabited the Rio Grande islands, also inflicted great destruction and took many captives at the same period. Slave revolts have been mentioned as taking place in the Cape Verde region, at Cacheu, in the seventeenth century (1661).

Diogo Gomes relates in *De Prima Inventione Guinéé* that the Portuguese were stopped from pursuing the slave trade in the vicinity of Cape Verde and the Guinea islands by the men of Besagichi, who greeted them with poisoned arrows. Some caravels were burned. This happened towards the beginning when the system was getting started, in the middle of the fifteenth century.

The Jaga invasion, in which the Kwango was crossed in 1568 and the Congo invaded, was also connected with migrations which completely changed the African interior and upset the balance of power on the Atlantic seaboard: (a) migration of the Imbangala, who set out from Luanda to found the Kasanje Kingdom in Angola at the end of the sixteenth century; (b) Luba migration from the old Songai empire; (c) Lunda migration, which followed closely that of the Imbangala; and (d) Pende migration from the coast eastwards into the interior in Angola, under pressure from the Portuguese occupying the Luanda salt-marshes, which were worked by the Pende, and the Imbangala and Jaga invasions.

The following points might be mentioned:

These migrations were spread over the sixteenth century, starting at the end of the fifteenth and continuing into the seventeenth, that is, a period which brought the inhabitants of the African seaboard into contact with the European slave-traders.

They were not mass migrations in which a whole people was displaced, but military expeditions with specific targets to be destroyed. When the Jaga arrived to the west of the Kwango, they lived on a war-footing in their fortified camps or *kilombos* between brief and effective raids. Men and women fought side by side, newborn babies apparently being put to death so as not to hamper the progress of the expedition. According to Battell, the youngest and finest-looking prisoners were made to go through the ordeal of being used as targets.

The object of these invasions, whether or not they brought to a close an earlier phase of migration, was to conquer and destroy the coastal kingdoms which owed allegiance to the Europeans.

When the Dutch took possession of Luanda in August 1641, they became the allies of the Jaga, who cleverly exploited the conflict within the European camp between the Portuguese and the pirates.

Four lines of research are therefore strongly advocated: (a) the Jaga problem ('an African reaction to the slave trade'); (b) internal migrations—origins and movements—causes. Some migrations had their origins in the Sudanese—Moslem conflicts of the ninth and tenth centuries; (c) related invasions—Mane, Sumba, Imbangala; and (d) recording oral traditions and comparing them with any written sources.

A final comment: the Jaga problem is connected with that of the Angolese of São Tomé, who apparently had the same origin, and also that of the *kilombos* of colonial Brazil.[9] The study of the Jaga *kilombo*, as described by Cavazzi, with its seven sections carefully oriented and with several Nganga to run it, helps us to understand the structure of its Brazilian counterpart, whichh as similar features.

Sugar industry and slave uprisings in the African archipelagos

After Cape Verde and Bijagos, the Portuguese tried to occupy São Tomé *c.* 1470–86. The island of Fernando Po, the largest, which was already inhabited at that time by Bubis Negroes, triumphantly resisted the Portuguese invaders. 'Formosa' remained theoretically under Portuguese sovereignty right until 1777, which, as the population of São Tomé increased, enabled the colonists to draw on fresh supplies of slaves. Under a treaty between Spain and Portugal ratified on 11 March 1778, Spain was granted rights over Fernando Po and Ano-Bom and entitled to engage freely in the slave trade along the African coast from Cape Formoso at the mouth of the Niger as far as Cape Lopo Gonçalves, south of the Gabon estuary, in exchange for Catarina Island and the Sacramento colony in South America, which came under Portuguese rule. It was not until 1858, however, that Spanish sovereignty was established firmly by an expedition led by Commander Carlos Chacon.

Through the development of the sugar industry in São Tomé in the sixteenth century, at the instigation of the Jewish element in the population, the island had a considerable export trade with ramifications in the Mediterranean and Europe. As early as 1574, there were sixty *engenhos* producing over 150,000 arrobas of sugar. During the years 1575–80, the production had increased to 200,000 arrobas. By the end of the century it had reached 300,000 arrobas and, in 1624, according to an account given by Garcia Mendes, some twenty big ships loaded 400,000 arrobas of sugar aboard in São Tomé harbour. After this there was a decline, caused chiefly by the destruction wrought by the Dutch and the Angolese.

Tradition has it that a vessel loaded with slaves from Angola was wrecked between 1540 and 1550 near the Sete Pedras Islands not far from the south-east coast of São Tomé. Most of the Negroes were drowned or eaten by sharks. Only a few dozen survivors reached land. The fine bay of the Lulas where they landed was uninhabited at the beginning of the sixteenth century, as were the nearby southern regions of the island. They settled to the north-east of the bay in the mountains which were later to take their name and they lived pro- tected by the forest, raising pigs, cutting wood and engaging in a typically African form of agriculture. Furthermore, Cunha Matos states that up until 1550 the island prospered and the Angolese did not become a threat until the second half of the century.

In 1574, he says, they revolted, drawing other Negroes into the fray, and armed with bows and assegais they invaded the *fazendas agricolas*, or agricul- tural estates, and the city, sacking everything, pillaging and destroying the *engenhos* and killing anyone who tried to stop them. The terror was such that years later, in 1593, Philip I commuted the sentence of banishment to five years for those exiles who had participated as volunteers in supressing the revolt. This had already been done in the case of other convicts who fought against the slaves in 1584. Cunha Matos also mentions the last and most destructive revolt of the Angolese, the one which occured in 1693 and ended with the capture of Negro women in the surrounding *fazendas*. It was Mateus Pires, *capitão do mato* or *da serra* who drove them back into the mountains and rescued the captives. However, São Tomé had already lost a large propor- tion of its *moradores* (inhabitants) almost a century earlier, the richer ones having left for Brazil for fear of the Negro revolts.

Two documents dated 1536 lead us to think that the first act of violence of the Angolese did not occur in 1574, as was believed,[10] but around the years 1530–40,[11] at which time the king of Portugal, John III (1521–57), after again receiving alarming reports from São Tomé, wrote that he was sending Paulo Nunes with arms to restore order. Three days later he wrote again—the matter was urgent—to the island authorities to tell them that Paulo Nunes would not be going. In fact he demanded extraordinary privileges to command the *capi- tania*, which could not be granted in view of the fact that a *corregedor* (mayor) had already been appointed with authority 'to act in the island against the rebel Negroes and with the mission of pacifying them'. The revolt had broken out several months beforehand, since the king had had to appoint a *corregedor* and send him out with instructions to deal with it. The king must then have received further information to the effect that the insurrection had spread and was a serious threat to the inhabitants of the city since, feeling that events were likely to be precipitated, he mentioned in a letter the possibility of the colony as a whole embarking with the forces at its disposal. It is not known what turn the situation took after this first insurrection, which lasted more than a year.

In 1574 the Angolese Negroes, who had then taken refuge in the *matos* (forests) in the south of the island, in the present Pico de Cabumbê, came out of their *kilombos* and fell upon the *engenhos*, pillaging and burning them. They next made for the city of Povoaçoa, where they were repulsed by firearms. However, they occupied the whole island and Negroes employed in the *engenhos* joined them. They had their headquarters on the mountain in the centre of the island, the Pic de Mocambo.

The terrified inhabitants found themselves faced with an enemy enjoying the protection of a hostile natural environment enabling it to launch surprise attacks and then withdraw into the forest whose unexplored paths made retreat easy. The cane fields and the *engenhos*, which were so vulnerable, had to be defended, so a long *guerra de mato* had to be waged, a war of attrition which adversely affected the prosperity of the island.

For years, the Negroes in revolt held the maquis all around the home-steads, 'at a distance of three leagues around the town', and from time to time they attacked a *roça* (village) and lit a few fires which devastated a district, caused a disturbance in the town and frightened the colonists still more. When Father Baltazar Antonio visited the island in 1577, the war was still going on, if it can be called a war with an elusive enemy moving through the woods and on the mountain and attacking when and where it willed. He noted that: '*os mais dos moradores della sao pretos, porque os brancos sao poucos* [most of the residents are black; there are few whites]'. The exodus had already begun. Father Diogo de Costa, who reached São Tomé in June 1584 after a four months' voyage from Lisbon, sailed with 'ten quintals of powder and harque-buses to arm some 70 to 80 soldiers'. Little indeed to defend the population against those Angolese devils![12] So it is not surprising under the circumstances that in 1595–96 the Angolese succeeded in taking the city under the leadership of the legendary chieftain Amador, who assumed the title of King of the Island. The Portuguese, with their backs against the wall, managed to capture him by means of a ruse and mete out retribution. The Angolese then left the city for their *kilombos* in the forests, whence they continued to threaten the terror-stricken colonists.

To explain the economic decline which began at the end of the sixteenth century, it is customary to refer to the sugar-cane disease [13] and the promising start of Brazilian development. However, there are other internal factors pecu-liar to the island of São Tomé which must not be overlooked, such as the disor-ganization and permanent political instability.[14] Governors, bishops, commissioners of audit and judges had been quarreling about land and possessions since the time of the last donee, João de Melo (sentenced in 1522). What is more, from 1567 on, foreign pirates, mainly French, then Dutch, began to harass (*apoquentar*) Portuguese shipping. At the end of the century the first Dutch attacks struck a hard blow at the island's trade. In 1599, a Dutch squadron attacked and plundered the city of São Tomé. In 1641, the Dutch took possession of the island and destroyed more than sixty *engenhos de açucar*.[15] Their squadron then ruled the whole of the west coast of Africa, where the São Tomé merchants traded, and made things very difficult for them.

It was in this situation of internal disorder and disturbances due to foreign competition that the insurrection of the Angolese developed. A number of documents discovered by chance in the course of research at Torre do Tombo in the boxes of uncatalogued archives throw light on the tumultuous events which attented these Negro revolts.

For instance, it would appear that 1616 marked the end of one insurrection and 1617 the beginning of another. Negro maquis existed at a distance of three leagues from the city throughout the century. The year 1693 witnessed a dramatic episode referred to as 'the rape of the Sabine women'. Wives of *moradores* were carried off by the Angolese, who attacked the *engenhos*. A foray (*entrada*) organized by the planters to recover their wives was unsuccessful. Most of the women carried off into the woods and taken into the *quilombos* were coloured, if the traditional story is to be believed.

The eighteenth century began with a violent uprising of the Negro maquis in 1709 and it is mentioned in the documents that the Mina Negroes actively participated. Whenever the privateers attacked the homesteads, the Negroes took advantage of the situation and attacked too. In 1709, the Angolese went into action during the invasion of French privateers and unchained slaves from Mina. Garrison mutinies in 1734 and 1736 also favoured these slave revolts.

The Angolese, who were still a constant worry to the population, obtained letters patent giving them a certain autonomy. Their chieftain and his representatives were respected. When Mateus Sampaio climbed to the top of the Pico de São Tomé in 1880 the island began to be 'rediscovered'. From 1884 on, the Angolese started abandoning their difficult existence in the *kilombos*. Anthropometric studies were carried out in 1950 and 1954 by the Anthropobiological Mission of Angola and the Ethno-sociological Brigade of São Tomé respectively.

In 1895, the Angolese formed a community of 2,000 people spread over the area extending from Vila de Santa Cruz to Vila das Neves on the west coast of the island.

Slaves and slave-ships across the Atlantic—life on board—
resistance in the hold

Many revolts broke out on board the slave-ships which transported all these
unwilling workers from Africa to America. Few voyages were completed
without the Negroes in the hold attempting, sometimes desperately, to get
free. Many of them preferred death to captivity and the sources record many
cases of suicide, achieved by a variety of means, after unsuccessful attempts to
escape. A study of the revolts on board the slave-ships remains to be made,
chiefly on the basis of the considerable volume of British records, in particular,
the log books or slave-trade ships' journals and the tales and letters written
by slavers. The greater part of these sources is at present lying dormant in
London, in the National Maritime Museum, the British Library, the Public
Record Office, and in Bristol, Liverpool, Oxford and Edinburgh. The important
place occupied by Great Britain from the time of the first voyages undertaken
by Francis Drake and John Hawkins in the reign of Elizabeth I,[16] but more
especially from 1713 on, after the Treaty of Utrecht and the Asiento, which
gave that country the possibility of providing Hispanic America with an annual
supply of African workers, explains the great wealth of material to be found
in the British records.

In Dutch, French, Portuguese, Danish and American records, too, documents are to be found concerning voyages of slave-ships across the Atlantic,
which sometimes came to a tragic end as a result of the Negroes in the hold
breaking their chains and fighting furiously for their freedom.[17]

The first known landing of slaves from Africa on Brazilian soil took
place in 1552, although the documents lead one to suspect that there had been
earlier ones. Some thirty years later, in 1580, after the founding of Loanda
in 1575 and just before the rise of the sugar industry, there were at least 10,000
Africans in Brazil. Of course this represents far less than the 4,000 slaves
imported annually to Pernambuco fifty years later. Before the time of the
bandeiras (1590–1625), that of the *entradas* was a period during which fugitive
Negroes, few and far between, were captured in the course of 'reconnaissance
expeditions to the interior or along the coast by the Nordeste colonists'. The
Negroes were already mixing with the Indian tribes pursued by colonists in
search of labour, despite the famous 'law on the freedom of the indigenous
inhabitants of Brazil' (1570), which they had amended and revised.

The Negro revolts were a great nuisance to the Governor of Pernambuco,
Diogo de Meneses, for in a letter to the king dated 23 August 1608 he requested
that *aldeas* be organized in the capital near the sugar-mills. In this way the
Negroes, who were so expensive and revolted against their masters, could be
advantageously replaced by Indians.

The dramatic consequences of the 'Negro shortage' (1625–50), which disturbed the market for a long time, must also be noted.

Taking advantage of the fact that the colonists were in a constant state of war, fighting furiously to combat Dutch competition and occupation, the Negroes broke camp and when the opportunity arose fled to the forest, which always offered protection.

During the first phase of the *entradas*, the Negroes rebelled and lived 'in hiding in the forest, concealed by the winding paths of the *serras* shielded by the darkly-massed palm-trees'. To begin with, they lived by robbing and pillaging nearby plantations and sacking the *fazendeiros*, then they settled down to farming themselves. The runaway slaves cleared, planted and cultivated the land which they occupied for a time. As they became better organized, they abandoned their primitive life of pillage and theft and started trading and bartering their produce with the *fazendeiros* and their neighbours, who needed farm tools and weapons.

For several years they lived peacefully enough with their fields, cattle and crops and attracting very little attention until more and more Negroes joined them as *engenhos* and plantations were abandoned, the Dutch invasion having forced the *senhores* to take up arms to defend the Portuguese colony in an epic resistance.

The rebels seized the opportunity to seek refuge in Palmares where a bountiful nature offered a fertile soil and rivers, swamps and woods favourable to hunting, fishing and fruit-picking. They were not the only ones to find a safe refuge in Palmares; E. Ennes assures us that in these times of war, free Negroes, mulattos, *indios mensos*, or 'civilized' Indians, and even white criminals and deserters availed themselves of it.

This was how the famous Palmares Confederation developed. The confederation, in which some saw a strong organized republic and others just another slave revolt, lasted throughout the eighteenth century.

The runaway slaves left many *quilombos* in their wake, but Palmares was the most important among them. The first *quilombo* was founded in the sixteenth century, probably when the slave trade was just beginning. It was destroyed by Luis Brito de Almeida. A number of these camps were formed near Bahia over the seventeenth and eighteenth centuries and the colonists greatly feared them. One such, in 1601, cut the route from Bahia to Alagoâs at Itapicum. In 1650, Captain Mancel Jourdan da Silva destroyed *quilombos* near Rio de Janeiro with difficulty. There is a reference to another *quilombo* in Alagoâs in 1671.

Several military expeditions were sent to Palmares in the seventeenth century: the figure of thirty-five *entradas* has been established beyond doubt. They include the following: Bartolomeu Bezerra, between 1602 and 1608; Rodolfo Baro, 1644, and Jan Blaer, 1645 (Dutch expeditions); Fernão Carrilho,

1676, 1683, 1686, and Domingos Jorge Velho, 1692, 1694 (Portuguese–Brazilian expeditions).

The capital of the *quilombo* of Palmares, Macaco, fell on 26 February 1694 after a siege of twenty-two days. The fighting went on in the other *mocambos*: Una, Catingas and Engana-Colomim.

The death of Nzumbi, who was killed by the Paulistes on 20 November 1695, put an end to this gallant *quilombo*. After the destruction of Palmares, a number of *quilombos* continued to give vent to the threats of the Negroes up to the time of the nineteenth-century insurrections, which broke out in the colonial towns of Bahia and São Paulo.

Maroons and privateers slip through the Hispanic American net— sixteenth to nineteenth centuries

With the Maroon Negroes holding sway at Nombre de Dios on the Panama route and controlling the traffic from Mexico City to Vera Cruz, a whole system was being overturned and America began in the sixteenth century to slip out of the grasp of the Spaniards. With the support of these rebel Negroes, British, French and Dutch adventurers weakened the defences of the Spanish monopoly. The Negroes armed themselves in the process and were better able to hold their own, for example, in the isthmuses. They built fortifications on land, in Venezuela and Colombia, where they constitued a threat, and at the end of the eighteenth century and during the first half of the nineteenth, they played an important part in the liberation movements in those countries. As an example, one has only to mention Venezuela. The insurrections of Maroon Negroes in the Coro peninsula were a determining factor in the building of the nation.

Caribbean Maroon Negroes

Several slave-struggle sectors can be distinguished in the archipelago of the West Indies:

The Lesser Antilles (Leeward and Windward Islands), seventeenth to nineteenth centuries.

The 'Maroon' wars in Jamaica, 1655 to 1860.

The Cuba stockades and the slave uprising in the sixteenth to nineteenth centuries. The wars which took place in the second half of the nineteenth century, the Ten Year War and the 1898 War, in which Negro troops led by Antonio Maceo won renown, must be studied as part of this process of Maroon Negro revolts.

The slave uprising at Santo Domingo, from the time of La Española and the revolt of Enriquillo, at the beginning of the sixteenth century, which Spain had such difficulty in suppressing, to the destruction of the slave system.

The resistance of the Negroes in Haiti during the French occupation, from the second half of the sixteenth century up to the War of Toussaint Louverture (1790–1803), which enabled Haiti to overthrow the colonial regime.

Negro communities in the Guiana woods

Negroes who ran away from the Surinam plantations had been taking refuge in the virgin forest and organizing themselves with the help of the Indians since the middle of the seventeenth century. Under the governorship of Sommelsdijk, the Dutch made several attempts to wipe out bands of Maroons.

The number of rebel slaves was constantly growing, it rose from 6,000 in 1725–30 to 8,000 by the end of the century. The Dutch were obliged to conclude a peace treaty with the Negro rebel chiefs, as were the British in Jamaica, who were vanquished in the field. In 1760, Governor Crommelin set about renewing the peace offers to the Maroons along Djuka Creek. On 22 May 1761, peace was concluded with the Djuka, then in October Major Meyer confirmed the official peace with the two most important Djuka chieftains: Arabi and Pamo. A year later, on 18 September 1762, the Saramaccaners signed a peace under the same conditions. In 1767, the Becu-Musinga group, who were Matwari Negroes, led by the chieftain Musinga, concluded a separate peace with the Dutch and remained on board the *Saramacca*. They secured free passage along the Vanica Creek for their products.

Afro-American insurrections

The history of the United States of America is marked by slave insurrections from the time of the Thirteen Colonies onwards. Starting in the seventeenth century with the outbreaks of 1663 and 1687, going on in the eighteenth century —in 1709, 1710, 1722, 1723 and 1730 in Virginia alone—slave uprisings steadily increased. In New York itself there were two insurrections, in 1712 and 1741. In South Carolina the situation was still worse, the insurrections following closely one another—1720, 1723, 1738, 1739, 1740. A law on slave control tells us that there were many revolts before 1704.

The conspiracies instigated in Virginia by Gabriel in 1800 and by Nat Turner in 1831 are well known. During this period, there were several uprisings in the area—1802 (Nottaway County), 1808 and 1809, 1812, 1814, 1816, 1829, 1856. In Maryland and North Carolina there was a succession of uprisings too—1802, 1821, 1831, 1843, 1859. In South Carolina, after the 1797 and 1816 outbreaks, there was an insurrection in 1822 led by a Negro from Saint-Thomas in the West Indies, Denmark Fesey, which stands out as a landmark in the history of Afro-American resistance. In Georgia, there were threatening disturbances in 1810, 1819, 1831, 1834–35, 1851, 1856 and 1860. The Negroes revolted in Florida in 1820 (Talbot Island) and in 1856 (Jacksonville). Other revolts occurred in Alabama, in 1837, and Mississippi, in 1835.

Louisiana was also the scene of frequent insurrections. There was one in 1804, in New Orleans, two in 1805 and nearly 500 Negroes marched on New Orleans in 1811. There were revolts on the sugar-cane plantations in 1829, 1835, 1837, 1840, 1841, 1842 and 1856. Tennessee, Kentucky and Texas had their share in 1831, 1856 and 1857.

All this is a far cry from the submissive 'Uncle Tom' so readily imagined by American authors.

Conclusion

In recent years some progress has been made in historical research as a result of the studies of a number of African, West Indian and Afro-American research workers, who have tried to analyse slave society in depth. If such studies are to be continued and if these links between Africa and America and these sources are to be taken fully into account, group pluridisciplinary research will have to be envisaged.

The aim should be to build up an historical anthropology bringing in history, geography, sociology, economics and ethnology. A study of the slave trade and of slavery as it relates to Negro resistance is essential to the understanding of the economic, political and ideological implications of the slave trade for Africa and its effect on societies and powers. Incidentally it enables one to measure the demographic implications for the African continent and to evaluate all that the economies based on slavery gained from the slave trade.

Notes

1. Charles Frostin, in a recent thesis, 'Le Sentiment d'Autonomisme des Colons de Saint-Domingue, XVIIᵉ–XVIIIᵉ Siècles', goes so far as to maintain that the Negro slaves accepted their condition and that only the white colonists revolted against the royal power in Santo Domingo.
2. cf. Gabriel Debien, *Les Esclaves aux Antilles Françaises*, Chap. XX, Fort-de-France, Société d'Histoire de la Guadeloupe, Basse-Terre et la Société d'Histoire de la Martinique, 1974.
3. cf. P. D. Curtin, *The Atlantic Slave Trade*, Madison, Wis., University of Wisconsin Press, 1969.
4. We are indebted to Fernand Braudel for the term 'geohistory'.
5. cf. for example, Gilberto Freyre, *Casa Grande e Senzala*, Rio de Janeiro, 1943. (Coleção Documentos Brasilenos No. 36, 36a), in which it is maintained that the slaves were better fed than the whites and that they enjoyed their work.
6. Marginal because they refused to how to the constraints of the method of slave exploitation.

7. cf. Oruno D. Lara, *De l'Atlantique à l'Aire Caraïbe: Nègres Cimarrons et Révoltes d'Esclaves, XVIe–XVIIe Siècles*, Paris, 1971, 4 vols., typed.
8. This was the case in Guinea-Bissau and Angola, for example.
9. As, for example, the Kilombo das Palmares, in the Capitania of Pernambuco, which held out against the attacks of Dutch and Portuguese expeditionary forces for more than a century, from the end of the sixteenth century to 1698.
10. F. Tenreiro, *A Ilha de São Tomé*; Antonio de Aimeida, *Da Origem dos Angolares. Habitantes da Ilha de São Tomé*, Lisbon, 1895; Frédéric Mauro, *Le Portugal et l'Atlantique au XVIIe Siècle*. See also Almada Negreíros, *Historia Ethnographica da Ilha de São Thomé*, Lisbon, 1895.
11. J. D. M. Ford (ed.), *The Letters of the Council of John III, King of Portugal*, Cambridge Mass., Harvard University Press, 1933; letters dated 22 October 1536 and 25 October 1536 from the king to D. Antonio d'Ataide, Count of Castanheira.
12. Paris, Bibliothèque Nationale, 'Fonds Portugais 8 (15)', No. 93, p. 278; Gaston Sousa Dias, *Relaçoes de Angola*, p. 95; cf. *Bol. Soc. Geo.*, Lisbon, 4th ser., No. 7, p. 349. In 1580, Fructuoso Ribeiro wrote to Father Francisco Martins that the Negroes in revolt occupied the mountain in the centre of the island, the Pic de Mocambo. To defend the island and the town against their attacks, the territory was divided up between three captains.
13. 'For a worm has got into the sugar-cane as in Madeira', F. Mauro, op. cit., p. 190; cf. Luciano Cordeiro, Vol. I, Chapter IV.
14. Between 1586 and 1636, for instance, there were twenty governors and seven serious incidents, two of which resulted in excommunications.
15. There were over 300 of them on the island at the time.
16. These voyages were mainly for the purpose of the slave trade.
17. The Fonds de Nantes (A.D. Loire Atlantique) (B 4.584, B 4.585, B 4.592, B 4.595, B 5.004/5) is mentioned as a reminder. A list of United Kingdom sources relating to the slave-ships is annexed.

Appendix

Archives sources that have not been used

Denmark[1]

Rigsarkivet, Copenhagen. Vestindisk-Guineisk Kompagni, 1671–1755. Kompagniets Københavnske arkivalier (Vestindien vedkommende et Guineakysten vedkommende). Hjemsendte arkivalier fre guvernements-sekretariatet for St. Thomas og St. Jan: Guvernørens rad, 1672–1703. Journaler og rapportbøger m.v. Kopibøger m.m., 1673–1740. Vestindiske inventarier, 1680–1752. Hjemsendte regnskaber fra St. Thomas og St. Jan (see especially Partikulaere regnskaber, 1686–1725). Hjemsendte arkivalier fra guvernementet pa Guineakysten 1698–1754.

France

Archives Nationales, Paris. A. N. Fonds Marine: Série B 2 (2.4, 234, 283); Série B 3 (235, 251, 315, 330); Série 4 JJ, Journaux de bord A/Voyages en Amérique 20, 21, 22, 27, 28, 29, 30, 31, 34, 37, 38, 43, 44; B/Voyages sur les côtes occidentales d'Afrique 61, 62, 63, 64, 65, 66, 67, 69, 70, 71; Série 4 JJ Supplément: 144 A, 144 B, 144 D, 144 F, 144 G.

Records in the Departments. Bouches-du-Rhône: Série B and Série C. Gironde: Série B, Série C (navigation and trade). Ille-et-Vilaine: Sous-série 9 B, Amirauté de Saint-Malo; Série C=Série 4 Fg (Navy and Colonies). Loire Atlantique: Série B, Amirauté de Nantes—Records of the reports of captains of ocean-going ships: B 4570 to 4593 (1692–1766). Inventories and documents deposited

---

1. Here I must thank Miss Elena N. Schmidt, who is at present working, thanks to a fellowship from the Danish Government, on the uncatalogued West Indian holdings of the Rigsarkivet. The latter possesses a large collection of historical sources concerning the Danish Antilles (the Virgin Islands) and the slave trade with West Africa. Miss Schmidt has been enabled to work for six months on the collection of local records contained in hitherto unopened boxes kept on the top floor of the Royal Archives, Copenhagen. It is to be hoped that this task of classifying the records concerning the Danish Antilles can be completed.

with the Admiralty Record Office by ships' captains: 4977 to 4995. Logs: 5004 to 5006 (1706–53). Série C, Chambre de Commerce de Nantes: 722, 738 (slave trade) (1671–1790), 739 to 742, 753 (account of a Negro revolt in Jamaica, 1760).

Municipal records. Le Havre: Série HH, 66 (1716–72)—trade with the colonies; 72 (1741–86)—the slave trade. Nantes: Série EE-267 (1691–1788); Série FF-202 (1725); Série HH-205, 206, 241.

Chambers of commerce and industry. Dunkerque: Deliberations and declarations of slave-ships' captains. Marseilles (A.C.C.M.): Série H. La Rochelle (A.C.C.R.): Boîte XIX, Doc. 6511–6767; Boîte VI (Grand Bureau); Boîte XXI, E.g. 7317 and Dossier 102. Municipal Library of La Rochelle: No. 856 (1787) Logs of the Amitié.

Netherlands

Algemeen Rijksarchief (ARA). West Indian Affairs, 1637–1790 (9217–9224). 'Loket-kas'; 120, 145, 114. Records of the first WIC, 1621–74. Records of the second WIC, 1674–1795. Records of the Surinam Company, 1683–1795 (498 entries). Records of the Dutch possessions, Antilles and Surinam, 1669–1845.

Amsterdam Record Office. Brazil, 1647. Curaçao, 1683–1743.

Dordrecht Record Office (seventeenth century).

Hoorn Record Office. 452, 1548–1807.

Leyden Record Office. Records of Daniel van der Meulen, 1573–1648, 684 items.

Rotterdam Record Office. Records of the burgomasters and town clerks of Rotterdam: 83, papers concerning the WIC, 1616–87. 84, papers concerning trade with the Antilles, 1700–10. 85, papers concerning the Surinam Company, 1685–1708.

Zeeland Record Office, Middelburg. 2036, I vol., 1667–76. Private records of the Verheye-Van Citters family. Collection of manuscripts: 83, 1672–74; 277, 1639–40.

Portugal

Archivo Historico Ultramarino, Lisbon. Caixas: Angola, Guinea, São Tomé, Pernambuco, Cape Verde—royalty and insignia of royalty. Many documents in several boxes at the Biblioteca Nacional, Lisbon. General Collection.

United Kingdom

Bristol Record Office, Council House, Bristol. MSS. 08226: Bills of lading, 1719–21; MSS. 16073—H. Bright, slaver, *The Sally*; transporting slaves to the Antilles. MSS. 12162: Ship's logs, 1777–91. MSS. 15326: J. H. Morgan. MSS. 04058: town dues, 53 vols., 1790–1846.

The British Museum, Manuscripts Department. Cotton Manuscripts: C. Otho E. VIII; C. Vespasian C. XIII. Egerton Manuscripts: 742, 929, 1806, 2395, 2543, 2597. 2648. Harley Manuscripts: 35, 39, 253, 280, 1511, 3361, 5101, 6845, 6922, 7021, Lansdowne Manuscripts: 52, 100, 844, 1197. Sloane Manuscripts: 159, 358,

750, 793, 894, 2292, 2496 (ff. 70–112). Stowe Manuscripts: (Stowe MSS. 166–77) Edmondes Papers (Stowe MSS. 256–61) Phelps Papers. Additional Manuscripts: Add. 12428–40 relating to the Negro insurrections and the slave trade. Add. 19049, idem (1733) Newcastle Papers (add. MSS. 3286–33057). Auckland Papers (Add. MSS. 34412–71). Liverpool Papers (Add. MSS. 38190–489), in particular Add. 38343: plan to reduce the number of Caribs in Saint-Vincent, c. 1778. Mackenzie Papers (Add. MSS. 39187–211).

Broadlands Archives. Slave Trade: SLT 1–37.

Cambridge, The University Library. Doc.: Extracts from the G. R. G. Conway Collection. Foreign papers: Asiento Company, slave trade with Hispanic America. Negro Treaty at Jamaica, 1739 (Section 21).

Historical Manuscripts Commission. Weston Underwood Manuscripts.

House of Lords, London (The Record Office). Sessional Papers: slave trade (slave-trade ships' journals and African and West Indies trade accounts, including slaves, 1759–1800).

Liverpool Record Office. Moore Papers: 920 MOO/315; 1641. Norris Papers: 920 NOR, c. 1695–1709. Tarleton Papers: 920 TAR/194–232, 1749–1810. In particular, Kf 7, 1779–1782, Kf 96, 1779–1811, concerning the voyages of different slavers, Liverpool, West Africa, the West Indies.

National Maritime Museum. Navy Board, Lieutenants' logs: 5,205 vols. 1678–1809. Personal papers: logs of ships sailing to the Antilles. Artificial collections, in particular a report on the slave trade in 1730 in the Wellcome Collection. Individual documents: slave-ships' logs.

Oxford, Bodleian Library. Tanner Manuscripts. Ashmole Manuscripts. Clarendon Manuscripts. Rawlinson Manuscripts: logs of several ships trading with the Antilles and North America (Virginia). Miscellanea: MS. Eng. misc. b. 4, 1799.

Public Record Office, London. The key items are the log books. Captains' logs, 1669 to 1852, 4,563 vols., Admiralty 51. Masters' logs, 1672 to 1840, 4,660 vols., Admiralty 52. Ships' logs, from 1799 on, Admiralty 53. Two additional series: Series I, masters' logs, 1837 to 1871, 339 vols. Adm. 54. Series II, Explorations, 1766 to 1861, 162 vols. Adm. 55. Slave trade: 1816 to 1892. F.O. 84, 2,276 vols. Slave trade: archives of commissions: F.O. 312 to 315, Cape Town, Havana, Jamaica, Sierra Leone.

Atlantic slave trade : documents concerning the slave-ships' voyages from Africa to America

United Kingdom

Archives of Commissions. Slave Trade. Cape Town: (F.O. 312) 1843 to 1870. 43 vols. Havana: (F.O. 313) 1819 to 1869. 67 vols.

Berkshire Record Office. Leicester manuscripts: D/EKm B2 and B3 (1724, 1734).

Bodleian Library, Oxford. MS. Eng. misc. b. 44 ff. 50–1 (1799). MS. Eng. misc. b. 44 ff. 93–4 (1792).

Bristol Record Office. Bills of Lading: 1719–21 (08226). Elbridge family, estate papers:
  AC/WO/10 (1744–1800). Bright, Henri, Insurance policy: 1762 (16073).
  Robinson, John and Tench, John: 1772 (10931). Morgan, James H: 1778
  (15326). Town dues, 53 vols: 1790–1846 (04058).
British Museum, Department of Manuscripts. Harley Manuscripts. Lansdowne Manu-
  scripts. Sloane Manuscripts. Stowne Manuscripts. Additional Manuscripts.
Broadlands Archives, London. Slave trade: SLT 36 (1859).
Hampshire Record Office, Winchester. Blachford papers: 8M 57 (1725), 8M 57/194–
  226,235 (1852, 1853).
House of Lords original papers. Slave trade: slave trade ships' journals (1789–1800).
Individual documents. 1743; 1793–94; 1833–36.
Lancashire Record Office. DDX 22/8 (1774–78); DDd 239/3–14; DDX 428/5 (1833–36).
Liverpool Record Office. Tarleton papers: Kf 7, 1779–82; Kf 96, 1779–1811; 380
  MD 33–6 (1754–69).
The National Maritime Museum. Natural Collections: Section I. Central Records.
  Merchant Navy: shipping records 1787–1856, 44 vols.; ships' log books and
  crew lists, 34 vols.
Public Libraries, Bristol. Jefferies Collection: Vol. XIII letters *c.* 1722–36.
Public Record Office. Legal Records: C.108/280 1606, 1746. High court of Admiralty:
  slave trade—government reports (H.C.A.35) 1821 to 1891, 89 vols.; slave
  trade: additional papers (H.C.A.36) 1837 to 1876, 8 cartons; treasury papers:
  (H.C.A.37) 1821 to 1897, 229 boxes; warrant books: (H.C.A.38) 1541 to 1772,
  77 vols.; miscellanea: (H.C.A.30) 1531 to 1888, 803 boxes and vols. Admiralty:
  log books; station records: Africa, North America and West Indies. Colonial
  Office: colonies, general—colonial papers, general series (C.O.I.) 1574 to 1757;
  America: original correspondence (C.O.5) 1606 to 1807. Antigua and Mont-
  serrat: (C.O.7). Bahamas: (C.O.29). Barbados: (C.O.28). Curaçao: (C.O.66).
  Dominica: (C.O.71). Grenada: (C.O.101). Guadeloupe: (C.O.110). Guiana,
  British: (C.O.111). Jamaica: (C.O.137). Leeward Islands: (C.O.152). Marti-
  nique: (C.O.166). Montserrat: (C.O.175). St Christopher: (C.O.239). San
  Domingo: (C.O.245). St Vincent: (C.O.260). Surinam: (C.O.278). Tobago:
  (C.O.285). Trinidad: (C.O.295). Virgin Islands: (C.O.314). West Indies:
  (C.O.318). Windward Islands: (C.O.321).
Scottish Record Office Edinburgh. Seaforth: GD 46/17/24 (1803–06). GD 46/17/2a
  (1804–05).
C. E. Turner, Esq., Messrs E. W. Turner and Son, Liverpool. Letter books of instruc-
  tions to masters of slaving ships with replies from captains, principally concerned
  with West Indian voyages, eighteenth century.

Portuguese participation in the slave trade: opposing forces, trends of opinion within Portuguese society: effects on Portugal's socio-economic development

Françoise Latour da Veiga Pinto assisted by A. Carreira

The origins of the slave trade and Portugal's monopoly

Slave trading went hand in hand with the great Portuguese discoveries of the fifteenth century. It was probably not initially one of the purposes of trading expeditions; but it was in keeping with the spirit of the time, and people took naturally to it. Its progressive growth was the result of changes in the economic motives underlying Portugal's expansion.

The conquest of Ceuta in 1415 marked the beginning of Portugal's maritime adventure, which subsequently started other nations off on the road to the conquest of new continents and led to the expansion of Europe.

The earliest navigators to round the coast of Africa were prompted mainly by two economic motives: to discover the source of production of Sudanese gold, which had so far reached Europe via North Africa, and to find the sea route to India and her silk and spice markets.

But the ideals of the crusades also played their part, and gave moral and religious backing to the expeditions. When the first sailor-knights rounded the coast of Africa, they were also in search of the kingdom of Prester John, in the hope of making common cause with him against the infidel. Taking Muslim prisoners was in any case regarded as a deed of valour deserving the Church's indulgence. Thus the first Negroes to be captured were taken by men convinced that they were doing a great feat—and also a virtuous deed, since every one of the 'wretches' baptized meant a soul won for God. The technique initially used to acquire the first slaves, *filhamento* or kidnapping, was likewise inherited from the Middle Ages: surprise attacks were made on isolated nomad camps and the captives brought back to Portugal, with—as recorded by Gomes Eanes de Zurara in his *Guinea Chronicle* (1453)—the 'holy purpose of saving lost souls'. It was Nuno Tristão who in 1441 had the dubious honour of bringing back the first Negroes direct from the west coast of Africa, south of Cape Bojador: they were Zenaga nomads.

The island of Arguin was discovered in 1443, and on 8 August 1444 (writes Zurara) the first public sale of slaves was held at Lagos in the presence

why they needed home slaves labor force

of Prince Henry, instigator of the African expeditions. The choicest slaves had previously been offered to the Church.

P. using Africans as for agricultural labor

From this time on, slave trading came to be regarded both as a means of providing a commodity exportable to Spain and Italy and as a source of domestic and agricultural labour for Portugal itself. The latter aspect became increasingly important during the fifteenth and sixteenth centuries, as Portugal's expansion called for more and more manpower. At that time Portugal had a population estimated at only around 1.5 million. Men who went to sea or settled in the colonies needed to be replaced; and Negro slave labour met this need. A third factor very soon came into the calculation when it was realized how useful the blacks were for sugar cultivation. This commodity, still extremely rare, had been introduced into Europe by the Arabs. Attempts had been made to grow it in Portugal itself, in the Algarve, but with only very limited success because it took too much out of the soil. The discovery of the Atlantic islands, however, was to bring about the rise of the sugar-cane industry and pave the way for the introduction and development of its corollary, the Atlantic slave trade.

The Spaniards had earlier introduced sugar cultivation into the Canary Islands, using the Guanches as slaves. Prince Henry, who had been granted by the crown a trading monopoly for the newly discovered territories, followed their example in Madeira and the Azores. The Negroes turned out to be more docile as labourers than the Guanches, and were very soon being re-exported from Portugal to the islands. Demand grew rapidly in consequence, compelling the traders to introduce a less 'primitive' method of acquisition than kidnapping. They had quickly realized that the *filhamento* system was excessively bad for trade: for the coastal peoples had soon learnt to beware of ships, and avoided going on to the beach so as not to be taken prisoner. The traders therefore sought to establish normal trading relations on a barter basis; and for this they very early used the first captives as interpreters. The role of the latter was very important for the development of the trading system. The Venetian Cá da Mosto, employed in the service of the Portuguese crown, records that some slaves, once they had been baptized and could speak their masters' language, were put aboard caravels and sent back among their kinsmen: they then became freed men when they had brought in four new slaves. They also furnished valuable information, both geographical—e.g. about deposits of precious metals—and commercial, such as lists of goods in demand among the natives, and their habits and customs. Once the Portuguese realized that they could acquire slaves by a peaceful exchange of goods which the chiefs and their go-betweens were avid for, a regular trade began to operate. There was, after all, a meeting of supply and demand: for slavery formed part of the social system among the peoples of Senegambia and Guinea, and it was normal to sell one's own kind if they were prisoners of war or were under sentence for adultery, felonies or magical reasons. It was also a more refined way of getting rid of hot-heads and undesirables than by putting them to death. The traders were therefore to find the same ease of exchange all round the coast of Africa.

The Portuguese, moreover, were also reaping the benefit of the much more long-standing internal trade which had been set up by the Arabs. Trans-Saharan trade started from the Sudan, which furnished gold and slaves taken by the Islamized Sahel peoples in forays on the area to the south. One route was via the staging-post of Hoden in the Sahara, where the captives were split up: some were bound for Barco, on the coast of Cyrenaica, whence they were sent on to Tunis and Sicily, while others were taken to Arguin to be sold to the Portuguese in exchange for horses, wheat and textiles.

This trading system led the Portuguese crown in 1455 to build a fortress at Arguin. As Jaime Cortesão has shown, the foundation of Arguin marked a turning-point in the organization of Portuguese trade. Conquest and its corollary, the kidnapping and forcible taking of slaves, were replaced by peaceful trade accompanied by a show of force in the shape of the building of a fortress —which could in case of need serve as a refuge. The establishment of Arguin was also to set the pattern for buildings subsequently erected all along the coast of Africa, not only by the Portuguese but also by their European rivals. Arguin likewise served as a port of call for ships sent to reconnoitre the south; and the trade soon began to thrive. Cá da Mosto in 1455 reckoned the number of slaves brought to Portugal annually at 700–800. A special administration, the Casa dos Escravos, was set up in Lisbon, and the customs house in the capital recorded the entry of 3,589 slaves from 1486 to 1493, not including arrivals from Lagos. C. R. Boxer puts the number of slaves captured by the Portuguese in Africa between 1450 and 1500 at 150,000.

Then, as territories suitable for colonization were discovered, sugar-cane cultivation was introduced into them, entailing a need for manpower which had to be brought from the coast of Africa. This was why, after the discovery of the Cape Verde archipelago, the king of Portugal in 1466 granted the first settlers a monopoly of the slave trade on the African coast opposite the archipelago, both to provide labour for the plantations and also to help populate these uninhabited territories. They were, however, forbidden to sell the slaves outside.

As the trade increased, the crown wished to control it—without, however, being able to take it in hand directly. It therefore sought to derive profit from the trade while keeping its own risk to a minimum; accordingly it set up a farming-out system, the *contratos*. In 1469 Afonso V granted Fernão Gomes the first contract, giving him the exclusive right to the Guinea trade for five years (subsequently extended for a further three) in return for an annual lump-sum payment to the crown and an obligation to discover a hundred leagues of coast a year, working southward from Sierra Leone. The Arguin trade and that of the coastal belt, which had been granted to the inhabitants of Cape Verde, were excluded from the contract. Fernão Gomes was successful in his enterprise, and thanks to his initiative the islands of São Tomé and Principe were dicovered between 1470 and 1472. Thus the contract system, which was to operate throughout the duration of the Atlantic trade, came into being. The Spanish *asiento* was based on a similar system for the delivery of slaves.

Meanwhile the gold traffic was increasing in volume, though the Portuguese failed to reach the mines and had to be content with trading on the coast. In 1482 they built a fortress, São Jorge da Mina, which made possible a great expansion of trade in that area. Ironically, one of the barter items the Portuguese used to obtain gold dust was slaves, brought mainly from Benin.

From 1483 onwards Diogo Cão's voyages of discovery opened the doors of Central Africa to the Portuguese, through the intermediary of the Kingdom of Kongo. Thus another centre of the slave trade came into being contemporaneously with the colonization of São Tomé, where the cultivation of sugar cane quickly developed. The first settlers on the island were deportees and converted Jewish children—'new Christians'—who were married off to slaves brought initially from Guinea and subsequently from Kongo. This *mestico* society soon became slave-traders, after the inhabitants of São Tomé had obtained from the king the privilege of *resgate* or purchase on the African coast opposite the archipelago.

When the Portuguese reached the mouth of the Zaire (Congo) river they found themselves, for the first time in Africa, in contact with a powerful, well-organized kingdom. The first embassy to arrive at the capital, Mbanza, situated upstream in the interior, was well received by the sovereign, who was receptive to European beliefs and skills. Despite some vicissitudes, after the accession in 1505 of the *manikongo* Dom Afonso a very special relationship grew up between the Portuguese crown and this African monarchy. Dom Afonso was genuinely anxious to transform his country with the help of the whites, while preserving its independence. Several members of the royal house went to Lisbon, and Catholicism became the State religion. Nevertheless the real interests of the Portuguese crown in the early sixteenth century were elsewhere; and, although the king of Portugal kept up a correspondence with the *manikongo*, and sent him missionaries and craftsmen, Dom Afonso's hopes were disappointed and his country fell inescapably into a state of decline. There were several reasons for this, all more or less directly connected with the slave trade. Portugal at that time was being pulled in different directions by wide and varied interests. Having made herself mistress of the route to India, her main commercial activity was concentrated on the silk and spice trade. The discovery of Brazil in 1500 led to the introduction of sugar cultivation there in the mid-sixteenth century; and this in turn brought about an increased demand for

African labour, once its superiority to native labour was realized. The Spanish West Indies also began to import slaves for their sugar plantations, while there was still a demand for labour in metropolitan Portugal and its Atlantic islands. Thus the moment when Central Africa, through the kingdom of Kongo, was opening its doors to Western influence coincided with a need for manpower which was to be met by slave trading. It would be hard to find a clearer example of the deep misunderstanding to which the slave trade gave rise between Africa and Europe: here an opportunity was lost and never regained. It is of course true that in Kongo, as elsewhere in Africa, traditional institutions were such as to facilitate the development of the slave trade; but the fact remains that the *manikongo's* hopes of giving his people access to white skills, and so bringing them out of their isolation, were cruelly betrayed. Moreover, the kingdom of Kongo had no other goods to offer except slaves; and, once it engaged in this trade, it was bound sooner or later to be at the mercy of the law of supply and demand, and of various competing interests, both abroad, in the shape of slave-traders, and at home, in the shape of neighbouring peoples also involved in the trade.

The settlers of São Tomé grew more and more active and imported slaves in ever-increasing numbers, not only for their own home market but also for export. At the same time they gradually established themselves in the kingdom and along the river, continually improving their links with the hinterland. During his reign, which lasted until 1543, Dom Afonso managed to curb the trade within his kingdom; and many times he repudiated it in his letters to the king of Portugal. But he could not prevent his vassals from enriching themselves through the trade, while his own enfeebled kingdom became the object of covetousness from across his borders. When he died, his successors were unable to stop either the growth of slave trading or the attacks of neighbouring tribes aimed at making prisoners of war to exchange for the whites' barter goods. The number of slaves being exported from the port of Mpinda around 1530 has been estimated at 4,000 to 5,000 a year. Meanwhile Brazil's manpower needs led the traders to look towards the south. Angola was at that time more thickly populated than Kongo, and was better able to meet this increased demand. Moreover the dealers were interested in having their purchasing areas closer to their embarkation points, so as to reduce as much as possible the loss of slaves in transit, which was always heavy. Early in the sixteenth century, traders developed the habit of going direct to the Angolan coast: they first reached Ambriz, then the Dande and the Cuanza. In so doing they were acting against the interests both of the Portuguese crown, to which they paid no taxes, and of the *manikongo*, by encouraging his vassals to deal with them direct. With the decline of the kingdom of Kongo, Portugal's focus of interest shifted to Angola. In 1571 the king of Portugal granted Paulo Dias de Novais a deed of gift over Angola: in so doing he abandoned his policy of exercising loose sovereignty, and for the first time in Africa adopted the sytem of direct rule. Dias de Novais, who hoped to find silver mines in the interior, was appointed governor for life and donee of the area between the Dande and the Cuanza rivers. The crown, as it had done in Brazil, also granted him a captaincy, while itself retaining the monopoly of the slave trade. But Paulo de Novais' hopes of finding precious metals were disappointed; and Angola, in its turn, lost any means of arousing Portugal's interest except through her manpower. The slave trade was in fact to make rapid strides at Luanda and, from 1617 (the date of its foundation), at São Filipe de Benguela.

Thus by the sixteenth century the triangular trade, which was to continue until the nineteenth century, was already established. Apart from Mina gold, and a few secondary products, Africa was regarded solely as a reservoir of manpower for the sugar plantations of the Atlantic islands, Brazil and Spanish America: Europe supplied the manufactured goods.

But the size of the sugar-cane industry, and with it of the slave trade, aroused the envy of the European powers; and from the end of the sixteenth century onwards they did everything in their power to break Portugal's monopoly. For, after the Treaty of Tordesillas in 1494, the Pope had divided the world between Spain and Portugal: Africa, Asia and Brazil went to Portugal, and the rest of America to Spain. The disparity of these rights led to a change in international law, and the authority of the Pope came under attack from the Protestant schism. With the enunciation of the Grotius doctrine, the freedom of the seas was proclaimed; moreover, in practice, the British and Dutch shattered the maritime hegemony of Spain and Portugal by the end of the century.

Up to then, Portugal had nevertheless held the monopoly of the slave trade, although smuggling had been going on from the beginning. But, up to the end of the century, attacks by foreign powers—Britain and Holland—had been mainly directed against the monopoly of Mina gold rather than against that of slaves. The Dutch–Portuguese war at the beginning of the seventeenth century, and the foreign competition that followed, finally broke Portugal's monopoly.

However, despite domestic difficulties caused by the crisis over the monarchy, and foreign wars, Portugal succeeded in keeping an important role in the slave trade. This was due to the connections she had built up between the centres of supply—Africa—and of demand—Brazil; and also to the systems instituted by the crown for controlling the trade. There were three such systems. The commonest was that of farming out to a *contratador* (the first being Fernão Gomes), who did virtually nothing but collect an indirect tax, for he was authorized to issue licences *(avenças)* to slave traders. The *contratadores* usually lived in Lisbon, while the *avençadores* were the actual slave-traders. Secondly, the crown itself, quite apart from farming out under contract, issued licences direct for the purchase of a specified number of slaves against the payment of a *per capita* duty. Lastly, the crown sometimes had recourse to direct management through an administrator. This system was rarely used, and was only a temporary measure to tide over the interval between two contracts. At certain times these systems co-existed. Farming-out contracts and licences came within the purview of the royal institutions, such as the Casa da Guiné (later known as the Casa da Guiné e Mina, and then as the Casa da India), of which the Casa dos Escravos was one section. Persons authorized to deal in slaves were also allowed to deal in imported barter goods.

Table 1 is a list drawn up by Antonio Carreira of the main farming-out contracts from the end of the fifteenth century to the beginning of the seventeenth:

Table 1. Farming-out contracts, 1486–1642.

Date	Area farmed out	Contractor	Notes
1486–93	Slave River	Bartolomeu Marchione	—
1490–95	Guinea rivers	Bartolomeu Marchione	—
1500–03	Gambia and Cantor rivers	João Rodrigues Mascarenhas	This contract was cancelled after two years, at the contractor's request, in favour of Filipe and Diego Lopes.
1502–03	Slave River	Fernão de Lorenhas	—
1504–06	São Tomé	João de Fonseca and Antonio Carneiro	
1505–07	Guinea rivers	João Rodrigues Mascarenhas	Mascarenhas died before the expiry of the contract, and it pas sed in 1607 to Afonso Lopes dos Couros
1509–12	Guinea rivers	Francisco Martins	—
1510–13	São Tiago and Fogo Islands (Cape Verde) and Guinea	(unidentified)	Payment was to be made in slaves
1510–13	Sierra Leone	João de Castro and João de Lila	—
1511–13	São Tomé	João Fonseca	—
1511–13	Senegal River	(unidentified)	—
1527–30	Cape Verde	Ascenso Martins	—
1536–37	Guinea	Afonso Lopes de Torres	—
1562–68	Guinea	Antonio Gonçalves de Gusmão and Duarte de Leão	—
1574–80	Guinea, São Tiago and Fogo	Francisco Munes de Beja and Antonio Munes do Algarve	—

Table 1—*contd*

Date	Area farmed out	Contractor	Notes
1583–89	Cape Verde and Guinea rivers	Alvaro Mendes do Crato and Diogo Fernandes	Because of the great drought of 1585–87, the contractors were granted an extension of the contract to the end of 1590 by way of compensation.
?–1591	Cape Verde (Windward Islands)	Alvaro Vieira	—
1587–93	Angola, Congo and São Tomé	Pedro de Sevilha and Antonio Mendes de Damego	—
1600–03	Angola	João Rodrigues Coutinho	—
1613–14	Angola and Cape Verde	Antonio Fernandes de Elvas	—
1607–08	Cape Verde	(unidentified)	—
1609–14	Cape Verde	João Soeiro	—
1615–?	Cape Verde	Duarte Pinto de Elvas	—
1616–?	Cape Verde	João de Sousa	—
1617–23	Cape Verde	Antonio Fernandes de Elvas	—
1624–27	Cape Verde	Jácome Fixer	—
1627–32	Cape Verde and Angola	André da Fonseca	—
1632–42	Cape Verde	João Gonçalves da Fonseca	

There are some gaps in the list. It gives the dates of the drawing-up of the contracts but not of their signature. It also shows how vaguely geographical areas were defined, thus demonstrating: (a) the lack of accurate geographical knowledge of the African hinterland (only the points on the coast are stated); and (b) the fact that the crown had no control over the contractors.

Examples of licences granted by the king north of the Equator, quite apart from and contemporaneously with farming-out contracts, include one to Lourenço Alvares for 100 Negroes in 1563; to Dento Vaz for 600 Negroes in 1565; to Manual Caldeira for 2,000 Negroes in 1568 (he also had a farming-out contract for São Tomé and Mina); to Alvaro Mendes de Crasto for 3,000 Negroes in 1583; to João Batista Ravalesca for 1,800 Negroes in 1583; and to Joseph Ardevicus for 600 Negroes in 1680 for Pará and Maranhão. It is interesting to note that these *avenças* were issued in large numbers: thus, from 1604 to 1608 the *contratador* for Angola issued 17,000 licences, while himself remaining in Lisbon.

The royal monopoly did not extend to Brazil, where slaves could enter freely, in contrast to the Spanish West Indies which were subject to the *asiento* system. The original law providing for the collection of export duty on slaves is not extant: the most plausible document on the subject is one by Abreu de Brito (1592), in which he gives a figure of 3,000 reis a head when the destination was Brazil and 6,000 reis for the Spanish West Indies. João Rodrigues Coutinho seems to have arbitrarily increased the duty by 1,000 reis a head during the 1600s. The vagueness of the texts and the lack of other sources led Antonio Carreira to the conclusion that the contractors altered the rate of duty to suit their own interests and convenience.

Portugal and the slave trade in the seventeenth and eighteenth centuries

At the end of the sixteenth century, Portugal underwent a great political change with the union of the crowns of Spain and Portugal in the person of Philip II of Spain. The sixty years (1580–1640) of Spanish rule over Portugal were far more important than this item of domestic politics might at first sight suggest: indeed, the period marks a turning-point in European colonial history, and in the development of the American colonies and its corollary, the slave trade.

During the sixteenth century, Portugal's rivals had tried to break her maritime supremacy in the Atlantic. These attacks were the work of pirates and traders, and were successfully repulsed. There had been attempts at occupation and even raids against the coasts of Mina, Guinea, Cape Verde and Brazil; and though they were pointers to the envy aroused by the trade in gold, slaves and sugar, they were no more than sporadic. The French had tried to establish themselves in Brazil in 1555, and often carried out attacks on shipping. Cape Verde likewise underwent regular assaults by the French and British: in 1578 Drake even went so far as to try to occupy Mina.

But after the union of the two crowns these activities, which had hitherto amounted to nothing more than smuggling and piratical forays, became international conflicts. Attacks directed against the presence of Portugal in Africa were obviously designed to wrest her trade from her. The wars which Spain and Portugal faced with the powers of northern Europe had three main objects as far as Portugal was concerned: to supplant her in her trade with the Orient, to take over the sugar plantations of Brazil, and (as a sequel) to take over the sources of African labour.

The union of the two crowns enabled Spain's enemies to turn also against Portugal; for, though Philip II had decided to leave internal affairs in the hands of the Portuguese, foreign policy was joint. In this struggle, the most relentless foes were the United Provinces. Incursions into Africa started in 1598. Then a twelve-year truce was signed with Holland, in return for the freedom of Portuguese ports to Dutch trade. But when the truce ended, fighting broke out afresh. The Dutch systematically attacked the vital centres of the empire, disrupted the trade with the Orient, and occupied one by one the key points of sugar production in Brazil and their sources of supply of slaves in Africa. From 1630 to 1641 north-eastern Brazil, including Recife, Pernambuco and Maranhão, fell into the hands of the Dutch, while Bahia was twice compelled to surrender. After the signature of the peace treaty with Britain in 1635, Holland continued the war and made themselves masters of the Portuguese possessions in Africa: Mpinda, São Tomé, Luanda and Benguela fell into their hands in rapid succession in 1641.

The Dutch then gained the support of the African chiefs, who were anxious to shake off the Portuguese yoke. The *manikongo* Garcia II and the Governor of Sonho dealt direct with the Dutch East India Company, even sending emissaries to Brazil and Holland to establish closer trading relations. Angola, moreover, was very far from being pacified or colonized, and took advantage of the Dutch–Portuguese conflict; the uprising there was personified by the legendary Queen Nzinga, who succeeded in rallying around her the Mbundu peoples of Ndongo and Matamba. Caught between two fires, the Portuguese in Angola seemed to be in a desperate situation. Events turned in their favour, however, after the restoration of a Portuguese dynasty in 1640. The Dutch refused to make peace, for Portugal in her weakened state seemed doomed to lose her Atlantic empire. But the Portuguese settlers in Brazil rebelled against the Dutch and drove them out of the country. Then, following the liberation of the American colony, the great landowers were soon concerned to re-establish the slave trade on a normal footing so as to provide their plantations with slaves. Thus it was from Brazil that the three expeditions set out that were to drive the Dutch from the coasts of Angola and the mouth of the Congo. In 1648 the Portuguese reoccupied the main centres of the slave trade south of the Equator.

From that time onwards, Brazil became the mainstay of the Portuguese empire. Trade with India having become secondary, Portugal's economic sphere of influence was to be centred on the Atlantic through the triangular trade: the two poles of attraction being Brazil with its plantations (and later its mines) and Africa as the supplier of manpower. Portugal's role was merely to provide manufactured goods and to serve as a staging-post between her two colonies.

Portugal then directed all her efforts towards her American colony, which was rapidly developing. Sugar was now in everyday use in Europe. The plantations needed slaves, and the Brazilian Indians (who had the protection of the Jesuits, and were not such good workers as the Africans) were replaced by Negroes. The industrialization of sugar-cane cultivation was to lead to a great 'slave famine' from the second half of the seventeenth century onwards, not only in Brazil but throughout America.

All the great powers of Europe then organized themselves to engage in the slave trade. By the Treaty of Utrecht in 1713 the British obtained from the Spanish crown the *asiento* contract for the Spanish West Indies, thus securing the cream of the slave trade for themselves. The French came next, encouraged by Colbert who, in setting out to develop the plantations in the French Antilles and the French possessions in the Indian Ocean, gave a fillip to the slave trade.

In the face of this competition the Portuguese had lost their hegemony on the West Coast, and the majority of their settlements there had fallen into foreign hands. But Cape Verde remained a centre of the slave trade, for farming was hard and unprofitable, and the colony, composed of half-castes, lived mainly by slaving. In the course of the seventeenth century the increased demand for slaves led to a resurgence of Portuguese activity north of the Equator: this took the form of the building between 1677 and 1680 of the fortress of St John the Baptist at Ajudá (Ouidah) in Dahomey, while a small factory was set up in 1696 at Bissau. The population of Angola was decimated at about that time by great smallpox epidemics, the most lethal being that which raged from 1685 to 1687. But this resurgence was incidental: Portugal's slave-trading activity was really concentrated on Angola. São Tomé was declining due to the competition of Brazilian sugar cane with its poorer-quality crop; and the half-caste population, in defiance of the central government in Lisbon (which had great difficulty in imposing its authority), took up smuggling and slave-trading. Since the Dutch occupation at Mpinda, Portuguese influence in the now disintegrated Kingdom of Kongo was reduced almost to nil; and foreigners traded freely on the coast of Loango, at Cabinda, at the mouth of the Congo, and on the Angolan coast as far as Ambriz. The Portuguese several times tried to re-establish themselves at Cabinda, even going to the lengths of starting to build a harbour—which was destroyed by Admiral Marigny's fleet in 1783. The authority of the Portuguese crown was really exerted only on the coast south of the Dande as far as Benguela, and it was even so unable to check the smuggling that was rampant out of Luanda and Benguela.

The history of Angola up to the nineteenth century was entirely dominated by the slave trade, for all attempts to encourage agriculture and mining ended in failure. The climate, for one thing, was lethal; of 2,000 soldiers sent out between 1675 and 1694, only 300 survived; and, in contrast to farming, slave-trading offered the appeal of a quick profit. Unlike what had happened in Brazil, the Portuguese came up against organized populations who would not let them through into the interior, where the climate was healthier. Native brokers formed a screen between the coast and the hinterland so as to be able to act as middlemen in the trade; consequently the only way inland was up the rivers.

At the end of the seventeenth century the discovery of the gold mines of Minas Gerais, in Brazil, led to an increased demand for slaves; and it was

Angola that supplied the bulk of them. The mine-owners needed strong men, and the yellow metal allowed them to pay higher prices for them than the planters did. There was thus more incentive to import slaves through Rio de Janeiro —for Minas Gerais—than through Bahia, and this led to conflict between the two towns. To end the dispute, the crown eventually had to introduce an import quota system as between Rio de Janeiro, Bahia, Recife and Paraiba. Thus Angola, forsaken by the mother country, and with a population made up of slave traders, convicts, adventurers and slaves, was nevertheless, as C. R. Boxer has pointed out, 'the corner-stone of the Portuguese Empire'. For Brazil's prosperity depended on Angolan manpower, and Portugal's prosperity depended on Brazilian sugar, tobacco, gold and diamonds.

However, foreign competition and the extent of smuggling led the Portuguese crown to attempt some reforms. Following the example of its competitors, Lisbon was to set up large companies to counter the decline of the Guinea trade and to make good the military forces, which were inadequate to protect the slave trade. None of these companies was ever as successful as their foreign counterparts, but they are still worth mentioning. The oldest, the Guinea Coast or Port Palmida Company, was founded on 1 September 1664; little is known about its activities, which were of no great importance. The same applies to the Companhia de Cacheu, Rios e Costa da Guiné, set up in 1676, which was granted a six-year monopoly of the transport of slaves from this area for Brazil. But the people of São Tiago viewed the setting up of this enterprise with deep mistrust, thinking (no doubt rightly) that it was directed against them and would deprive them of their freedom of action. On 12 February 1682 it was succeeded by the Companhia do Estanco do Maranhao e Pará, with a twenty-year concession: it undertook in that space of time to introduce 10,000 slaves (i.e. an average of 500 a year) into that part of Brazil. It also had a monopoly of trade in that province. Produce for export was exempt from duty for ten years. The purchase of slaves had to be carried out in Angola. This enterprise aroused such hostility among the settlers that it was disbanded after three years of operation and its property was confiscated.

On 14 January 1690 the Companhia de Cacheu e Cabo Verde was set up, with a lifespan until December 1696: a clause was included in the contract forbidding the sale of slaves to 'heretics'. Its powers were limited, and consequently its activities were of no great importance. When the contract expired, the crown negotiated with Spain the transfer of the company's powers and part of its property to the (Spanish) Royal Commission for India, which on 12 July 1699 obtained the *asiento*, for a period of six years and eight months, for the following ports: Cumana, Caracas, Havana, Cartagena, Puertovelo, Honduras and Vera Cruz. Purchasing had to be carried out on the Guinea Coast to a total of 10,000 tons (of slaves), each estimated at three 'India pieces' (i.e. a strong full-grown man) of uniform seven-foot stature, the old and those with physical defects being excluded. The Spanish crown associated itself with the enterprise, contributing 200,000 pesos towards the building up of its fleet This company was as short-lived as the rest, for it was dissolved in 1706.

It was only with the Pombal government that well-structured companies made their appearance. As far as the slave trade was concerned, they were intended to reorganize the triangular trade and to combat the smuggling that had prevailed on a large scale since the demand for slaves had increased in Brazil. Ship-owners in the service of Brazilian planters had got into the habit of obtaining supplies direct, outside the contracts allocated by the crown— even, in times of acute shortage, going as far as Mozambique. Two companies were set up almost simultaneously: the Companhia Geral do Grãu Pará e Maranhão in 1755 and the Companhia Geral de Pernambuco e Paraiba in 1759. They divided the slave-trade area between themselves, the former company operating in the Guinea coast and Cape Verde area, the latter in Angola and on the Mina coast. They both had exclusive rights to the slave and other trade for twenty years. The Companhia do Maranhão was in 1757, by a secret rider, granted additional powers authorizing it to exercise military and political authority for twenty years in the part of Africa for which it had a concession. These powers entitled it to organize the trade in Guinea and Cape Verde, where it likewise fostered the production of subsidiary exports such as cotton goods and archil. It also took the praiseworthy step of giving a great impetus to agriculture (particularly the growing of rice, cotton and cocoa) in the Maranhão area. One of the aims in setting up the company was to ensure a regular supply of slaves; and the policy was therefore adopted of making a profit not so much on the sale of slaves as on the produce of their labour. Hence, though both companies were reasonably prosperous and could distribute regular dividends to their shareholders, the Companhia de Pernambuco e Paraiba showed a loss on the slave trade, and the Companha do Maranhão a slight profit. The goods supplied by Brazil in exchange were mainly tobacco and rum. These two companies were dissolved, the former in 1778 and the latter in 1787, without having been able to eliminate the smuggling, which remained considerable both in slaves and in overseas produce. It was carried on from Brazil, mainly by the British. The setting up of these companies is clear proof that the triangular system and the so-called 'colonial pact' inspired by mercantilism, which together formed the basis of the Portuguese empire's prosperity, were threatened by the free trade which the British were beginning to practise.

Portugal and the abolition of the slave trade

Just as, at the end of the sixteenth century, Portugal had been confronted by one of the greatest crises in her history, as the result of failure to adapt herself to the nex order of the freedom of the seas which had replaced the Papacy's arbitrary division of the world between two nations, so, at the beginning of the nineteenth century, she was unprepared to face the new economic order dictated by Great Britain on the basis of free trade. This system again threatened the existence of her empire, based as it was on the triangular trade and the colonial pact. The slave trade, with its rules and its organized markets, was inimical to free trade; and the atrocities that had followed one another endlessly for centuries in the course of the trade were beginning to revolt public opinion. It would perhaps be more accurate to say that the voices that were raised in opposition were beginning to get a hearing—others raised earlier having fallen on deaf ears—and this was happening in Great Britain. Following a long humanitarian campaign in which such men as Sharp, Wilberforce and Macaulay won renown, Great Britain abolished the slave trade on 25 March 1807. Thenceforth, the British Government did its utmost to persuade the powers that practised it to make an end of it. Under pressure from Great Britain, Portugal, on 19 February 1810, signed a treaty of alliance and friendship, under Article X of which she undertook

to co-operate in the cause of humanity and justice, by adopting the most efficacious means for bringing about a gradual Abolition of the Slave Trade throughout the whole of her territories ... while reserving to her own vassals in the African territories of the Portuguese Crown the right to purchase and deal in slaves.

The Portuguese Government, however, had only given in to Great Britain out of weakness. It had had to take refuge in Brazil, and British support was its only hope of reconquering its metropolitan territory. The abolition of the slave trade in so rapid and radical a way raised problems that were practically insoluble. Portugal at that time had virtually no industry; and the economic transformation of the country was bound to be slow, laborious and beset with great difficulties.

At the congress of Vienna, Portugal managed to make her case heard. Under the treaty of 22 January 1815 she obtained the annulment of the previous agreement. From then on the prohibition applied only to the slave trade north of the Equator, thus exempting Brazil's trade with Angola, the Congo and Mozambique. The powers that Great Britain was urging to abolish the slave trade confined themselves to declaring that they were animated

by the desire to co-operate in the most prompt and effective execution of this measure by all the means at their command, and to use these means with all the zeal and perseverance due to so great and fine a cause; [adding that] ... the fixing of the time when this trade must universally cease shall be a matter for negotiation between the Powers.

This clearly shows that, with the exception of Great Britain, no country at that time genuinely desired to take immediate or decisive steps.

But the slave trade as a method of recruiting manpower was doomed in the medium or long term. The planters and slave-traders realized this—so much so that the trade took on a spectacular new lease of life.

At the same time, Portugal's Atlantic Empire was undergoing profound and irreversible changes. Since 1808 Portugal had been brought by Great Britain to take a series of measures that were to impair her future relations with Brazil. They entailed the opening to trade of all Brazilian ports, and the ending of the rules reserving to Portugal the processing of colonial raw materials. Then, in 1810, Great Britain obtained 'most favoured Nation' treatment; and finally, in 1811, all ports in Portuguese colonies were opened to trade. But these liberalizing measures, which were particularly advantageous for Great Britain, were also highly beneficial to Brazil: for the presence of the government and the court at Rio de Janeiro, and the liberalization of the economy, gave rise to an unprecedented development in the colony: administrative, political, economic and cultural. In 1815, Brazil was elevated to the status of a kingdom, and became aware of her national identity for the first time. Portugal, on the other hand, was passing through a severe crisis, aggravated by the effects of a ruinous war and invasion, and was still under occupation by the British army. The mother country had become virtually a colony of her former colony, while Portuguese Africa became daily more dependent on Brazil. In this situation independence seemed inevitable, and it was consummated when the king returned to Lisbon. Passed into law in 1822, it cut Portugal off from the motive power of her economy. Once trade had been liberalized, Brazil no longer needed the mother country: only Africa was essential to her, to keep her plantations going. But, because of the slave trade, the development of the Portuguese possessions in Africa had been completely neglected, thus reducing Portugal's economic role to one of slave-trader. The prohibition of the trade north of the Equator had benefited smuggling and the trade in the south. Angola and the Congo were the main suppliers. Great Britain, however, tried as far as possible to check infringements.

A supplementary convention to the treaty of 1815, signed in London in 1817, established the distinction between licit and illicit trading, while Portugal and Great Britain agreed to a reciprocal right of search by their warships of vessels flying their flags. Joint commissions were also set up to try prizes.

But, despite these measures—or perhaps because of them—the slave trade flourished more than ever. It became clear that the only possible step was absolute prohibition: this would make it possible to prosecute smugglers who sheltered behind the Portuguese flag. Great Britain, faced with continual changes of government in Portugal, had several times to break off negotiations. Finally, on 10 December 1836, barely two months after coming to power,

Sá da Bandeira announced the complete abolition of the slave trade throughout
the whole of Portuguese territory. His intentions were sincere; and, though
humanitarian motives came into the decision, so also did political and economic
ones. For the slave trade had impeded the development of Portugal's African
colonies while helping Brazil's; and the object of Sá da Bandeira's policy,
given that Portugal had lost her American colony, was to make Angola into
another Brazil.

But before Angola's huge territory could be developed, the trade in
human beings would have to be stopped, the tribes pacified, and the traditional
pattern of emigration from Portugal to Brazil switched to Africa. The Portuguese Government, however, lacked the material resources for carrying out
this enormous task. As far as the slave trade was concerned, there were not
enough ships to maintain effective surveillance, for the fleet was hopelessly
depleted; and the slave-traders had great influence both in Africa and outside
it. In fact, the slave-trading powers stood to gain by the secession of Portugal's
African colonies. In 1838, therefore, Sá da Bandeira formally requested Great
Britain's help. In view of 'the depleted state of the Portuguese navy . . . and the
Exchequer's lack of resources', he sought in return for Great Britain's right
of surveillance 'an explicit formal guarantee of the possessions of the Portuguese crown against any uprising that may take place in these provinces, and
against any attempt whatsoever by foreign powers to foment rebellion or seek
to take over the said possessions'. Spain and Brazil were specifically mentioned.
But Great Britain shrank from such an undertaking, which could have involved
her in defending the Portuguese colonies, and proposed a two-year limit, which
Sá da Bandeira rejected. Great Britain's anxiety was not altogether without
foundation, for already in 1824, in the midst of the crisis in metropolitan
Portugal, Brazil had suggested federation to the African settlers, her associates
in the slave trade. This suggestion had been sympathetically received in Benguela, which led Lisbon to take steps to promote trade between Angola and
Brazil by granting a reduction of customs duty ranging from 50 per cent to
complete remission.

The negotiations dragged on; and meanwhile the slave trade continued
with renewed vigour from the Congo and Angola, because of the Portuguese
authorities' inability to enforce the prohibition, and despite Great Britain's
expenditure of money and effort.

To overcome the shilly-shallying of the Portuguese negotiators, Palmerston passed a bill through the British Parliament authorizing the Royal
Navy to stop and search Portuguese slave-trading ships and indict their crews
for piracy before an Admiralty court. This measure was taken as a grave
affront by Portugal, while, on account of the instability of the government,
the negotiations were not concluded until 1842. London gave Portugal no
guarantee regarding the preservation of her colonies; and joint commissions

with British and Portuguese members were set up to try the crews of vessels apprehended. These tribunals were set up in British as well as Portuguese territories: namely at Luanda, Boa Vista, Cape of Good Hope and Jamaica. The naval patrol responsible for the surveillance of the trade increased in size: in a single year, from April 1846 to April 1847, fifty-eight cruisers—British and Portuguese, but also French—were recorded as entering Luanda harbour.

The machinery for enforcing the prohibition had been adopted as the result of laborious diplomatic negotiations: but many difficulties remained to be overcome in practice before the slave trade as a whole, and in Portuguese Africa in particular, could actually be stopped. For one thing, there was no certainty that these measures would succeed in eradicating the habits of centuries; and furthermore two types of slave trade had grown up, with a home market and an overseas market. The former gave rise to disguised forms of slavery, or at any rate forced labour. The latter, which resulted from the Atlantic trade, was hardly likely to disappear until the slave-owning nations gave up using this form of labour. The profits being higher every time, the slave traders, who had well-organized networks of agents both at home and overseas, naturally found it hard to resist the appeal of gain: especially since smugglers could always shelter under the flags of countries not liable to checking by the naval patrol.

At the time of abolition there was a clash of opposing interests in Portuguese Africa: on the one hand, those of the government, which for various economic and foreign-policy reasons genuinely desired abolition, and, on the other, those of the traders, who continued their smuggling with the connivance of the Brazilian and Cuban planters. It is undeniable, however, that up to 1842 the slave trade had had the benefit of a good deal of complicity at the highest levels, and that the Portuguese administration in Africa was riddled with corruption. Officials at Luanda found it hard to resist the temptation of easy money. Nevertheless, thanks to the energy and integrity of several governors (the most notable example being Pedro Alexandrino da Cunha, Governor from 1845 to 1848), the slave trade in Angola was eventually eradicated. His predecessor, on the other hand, had been relieved of his office, having come under strong suspicion of being implicated with the slave-traders.

One of the main centres of the slave trade was still the Congo area, together with the coast of Loango, Cabinda, Molembo, Ambriz, etc., where slave-traders of all nationalities came to get their supplies. Portugal wished to occupy this area, and one of the subsidiary reasons she adduced, in addition to her claim to 'historic rights', was the abolition of the slave trade. This question dominated Anglo-Portuguese relations for more than a quarter of a century.

Meanwhile, in July 1850, in the face of strong opposition, the Brazilian Parliament passed the abolition law; and, for the first time, the government was strong enough to enfore such a measure. From that time on the Atlantic trade dwindled.

But the slave trade left many after-effects; and it continued in various forms throughout the Portuguese colonial period. There are several reasons for this. One derived from the habits that had been formed, and the existence of a home market organized by the Africans themselves. Another was the need to solve the problem of 'pockets' of slaves still collected together for sale. A third was the colonial administration's intention of improving the land, which led it to 'engage' labourers on terms very similar to those of their forebears who had been transported across the Atlantic. Slavery was abolished in 1858, though with a twenty-year transitional period. But before that, on 23 October 1853, a decree had been promulgated authorizing the transport of slaves from Angola to the island of Principe to develop coffee and cocoa growing there. After being baptized, they were marked on the right arm with a mark signifying that they 'were freed' (*sic*). According to the law, they had to serve for seven years in the plantations; in other words, they were free by right and slaves in fact. In one form or another, the laws of 1875 and 1878 and the decrees of 1899, 1903 and 1909 countenanced disguised forced labour in the Portuguese African colonies and the transfer of labour to São Tomé and Principe.

So shocking was this institutionalized state of affairs that Norton de Matos described and denounced it in 1912. He was Governor of Angola at the time, and tried to change conditions of work in Africa: but the Portuguese colonial administration continued to engage African labour on terms very close to slavery. This led Henrique Galvão, then Inspector-General of the Colonies, to write in 1947: 'The situation is worse than simple slavery. . . . The native is not bought, he is hired by the State. . . . And his employer cares nothing whether he falls ill or dies: he merely asks for a replacement.' This courageous voice was not the only one to be raised against a disgraceful state of affairs, and several colonial careers were cut short because of protests by officials unwilling to fall in with this system. But, as Antonio Carreira testifies, having had direct experience of it, the majority were willing to be cogs in a machine in which corruption arose from collusion between the administration and private interests.

And, as always happened when the slave trade was flourishing, public opinion only heeded the protests raised against abuses when it was ready to do so, and only when conscience was no longer stifled by the interests at stake.

Trends of opinion within Portuguese society

Slavery formed part of the way of life of the Mediterranean peoples from antiquity. In the fifteenth century it was a consequence of the wars against the infidels, and drew its justification from that. The Church differentiated between just and unjust wars. The prisoners of a just war could be reduced to slavery, and if they embraced the Christian faith all the cruelties associated with their condition were justified. Nevertheless, it is clear from accounts that have come down to us that some charitable souls strove to draw attention to the horrible fate of the poor wretches who were uprooted from their homeland and separated from their kin in conditions of unspeakable misery. For instance, Zurara in his *Chronica da Guiné*, while exalting Prince Henry's virtues, records how the slaves were split up quite without pity, the sole criterion for the division being equality between 'lots', in turn subdivided into 'pieces'. It was not until a century later, however, that a voice was boldly and vehemently raised in opposition. It was that of Fr Fernando de Oliveira, who in 1555, in his book *Arte da Guerra do Mar*, severely criticized the slave trade in general and denounced the criterion of the just war. He asserted in substance that it is wrong to make war on people who are not warring and who want peace; that a slave should only serve for a time limited by law; that slave-traders do not seek only the slaves' conversion, for if 'their advantage were removed, they would not go in search of them; and slaves serve their masters much more than they do God, since they are compelled to carry out certain tasks which are contrary to divine law'.

Down the centuries, there is no lack of descriptions of the violence involved in the capture of slaves in Africa and at the depots while awaiting shipment, and then the horrors of the crossing in the *tumbeiros*, or coffins, as the slave-ships were called. The level of losses, initially as high as 20 per cent, fell as time went out, reaching an average of 5 per cent towards the end. The rebellions and the ensuing punishments, the epidemics, the disasters in storms— all this has come down to us in eye-witness accounts, often imbued with horror or compassion. Yet the slave trade was only enabled to last so long because there was a convergence of economic interests, coupled with a religious justification, and because circumstances in Africa were propitious. Few African chiefs were averse from taking part in a trade from which they stood to gain.

Paradoxically, the Jesuits, in protecting the Indians against the Brazilian colonists, encouraged the slave trade. When they first arrived on the American continent the colonists enslaved the native Indians, who were neither as tough nor such good workers as Negroes. The Jesuits took their part successfully, thanks to their influence at Court and the eloquence of the most famous of their number, Antonio Vieira. He also protested, along with other Jesuits, against the despotic attitude of the slave-masters towards their Negro slaves; but they never condemned the principle of the Negro trade. The ban on the enslaving of Indians, proclaimed by the government in Lisbon in 1570, served on the contrary to give it a new lease of life.

The Church's attitude with regard to the question was moreover ambivalent. Whereas under the Papal Pull of 1639 all Catholics who engaged in

slave trading with Indians were excommunicated, it was not until 1839 that
a similar measure was taken in respect of the Negro trade. In addition, as far
as Portugal was concerned, the Church had a material interest in the business
from the start, through the dues she collected for the baptism of slaves. Every
slave shipped had to be baptized; and, though the ceremony of baptism was
carried out in groups, the officiating priest made his charges on a per capita
basis. In the eighteenth century the rate was 300 to 500 reis for adults and
50 to 100 reis for children and infants in arms. The payment of these dues
often led to conflicts between the traders and the clergy (notably in 1697 and
1719), so that the civil power was compelled to intervene. In other words, the
State religion, which in Portugal was ruled by the Inquisition up to the eighteenth century, not only gave its moral sanction to the traffic in human beings
through baptism, but also made a profit out of it. In such circumstances public
opinion could hardly have been expected to condemn a situation which enabled
the maintenance of the economic system responsible for the prosperity of
Brazil and the Kingdom. When, therefore, Pombal abolished slavery in Portugal, in 1773, the aim was primarily to avoid drawing off the manpower that
was desperately short in the mines and plantations of Brazil.

It was not until the nineteenth century that Portuguese public opinion
revolted against the slave trade. Unlike Great Britain, where it was extremely
vehement and was led by great humanitarian figures, in Portugal it was led
by a liberal political élite. Admittedly Portugal was so torn by domestic strife
up to the middle of the century that it would have been difficult for her to
turn away from her immediate conflicts and concern herself with an overseas
problem. On the other hand, politicians such as Sá da Bandeira saw the advantage to Portugal, after the loss of Brazil, of developing Africa, and the imperative need to halt the manpower drain which the slave trade represented.
Humanitarian opinions also found expression, in keeping with the spirit of
the age. Naval officers posted to the coast of Africa were as a rule genuinely
shocked at the continuance of the trade. Later the Lisbon Geographical Society,
which was founded in 1875, conducted an anti-slavery campaign. Accounts by
Portuguese explorers from the interior of Angola, like those of their foreign
predecessors, told of the horrors of the internal trade—sequels of the Atlantic
trade and of that with the Arab countries.

But, above all, opinion was extremely alarmed at the international
campaign directed against Portugal. The various diplomatic vicissitudes that
had marked the negotiations between Palmerston and the Portuguese Government in favour of abolition had aroused British public opinion against Portugal; and its conviction of Portuguese insincerity was strengthened by the
accounts of explorers such as Livingstone, Cameron and Stanley, who on
their travels in Central Africa had witnessed gangs of slaves being escorted
by Portuguese *pumbeiros*. Portuguese public opinion was outraged at the accu-

sations, which were taken up again by Leopold II when he was seeking to counter Lisbon's ambitions at the mouth of the Congo. The Geographical Society, under the leadership of Luciano Cordeiro, was at that time at the hub of the controversy; it published articles rebutting the accusations from Great Britain, which took the form of a press campaign skilfully conducted by the king of the Belgians just when Portugal was seeking to take her place in the European economic order. These attacks were obviously inspired by political motives, and were manifestly insincere: for Portuguese explorers were every bit as indignant as the others at the abuses they witnessed, which resulted from a state of affairs that was past. Moreover various incidents that took place seemed to the Portuguese to show that the powers were themselves continuing a clandestine trade. Thus, Portuguese opinion was particularly incensed in 1858 by a serious diplomatic incident between France and Portugal. Portuguese warships stopped and searched the French ship *Charles et Georges* off the coast of Mozambique, where it had gone to pick up 'free emigrants'. Her captain, accused of slave trading, was arrested and taken to Lisbon, as was the *Charles et Georges*. The incident was turned into a matter of prestige by the governments in Paris and Lisbon, and France sent a squadron up the Tagus which made the Portuguese give way.

Hence, during the nineteenth century, public opinion in Portugal was very often indignant at the attitude adopted towards her by the powers, and developed a real persecution complex where the other European nations were concerned. This came out sharply over the question of the Congo at the Berlin conference of 1885.

Nevertheless, she was, as indicated above, the European country that despite numerous international protests carried on a clandestine slave trade for longer than any other. The explanation is no doubt to be sought in a shortage of the necessary capital and human resources for the development of her African colonies, which was offset by the used of cheap labour.

Lastly, the Portuguese Government's desire to develop these territories resulted from the loss of Brazil, which, as we have seen, was the main recipient of the influx of humanity supplied by Africa. The next question that arises is the socio-economic influence of the slave trade on Portugal itself.

The effects of the slave trade on Portugal's socio-economic development

It is impossible to make a proper appraisement of this question in the present state of our knowledge: more especially as the slave trade was never more than a secondary aspect of primary activities such as the improvement of land for agriculture (especially plantations), mining, the peopling of desert or underpopulated areas, and so on. It is very difficult to assess it in isolation, since it has always been indissolubly linked with these other activities. We can, however,

try to pick out the areas in which its influence made itself directly and specifically felt; and we accordingly propose to take the demographic and the financial
aspects.

Some writers, such as Joël Serrão, consider that the population influx
arising from the slave trade was essential in the fifteenth and sixteenth centuries,
in that it made up for the population losses caused by the discoveries and overseas expansion. C. R. Boxer estimates that in the course of the sixteenth century,
2,400 men, mostly young and fit, left Portugal annually. This is a large number,
considering that—according to the 1527 census—the total population of Portugal at that time varied between 1 million and 1.4 million.

On the opposite side, it is generally reckoned that imported slaves made
up a tenth of the population of the large cities, and this proportion seems to
hold good for the duration of the slave trade. We have no accurate figures
for the rural areas.

At the beginning of the sixteenth century the slaves imported into Portugal were as heterogeneous as the discoveries themselves: Moors, Chinese,
Indians and Negroes were all to be found in Lisbon. The last named were in the
majority: they were employed in the hardest agricultural work, sent when
necessary to unhealthy parts of the country, used for clearing the ground and
also in domestic service. The growth of a society based on slave labour undoubtedly had a variety of consequences. Moralists attributed the laxity of morals
to it, and down the centuries kept up a barrage of criticism of the licentiousness
and frivolity of all classes of society, accompanied by a highly developed taste
for idleness—the heavy work being left to slaves.

Nor must we overlook Brazil's influence on Portugal: for Brazil was
herself profoundly marked by the centuries-old influx of African labour. This
factor, however, is virtually impossible to evaluate, because it is, so to speak,
'two-way'.

It is interesting to note, on the other hand, that, after abolition, white
Portuguese emigration to Brazil to some extent took the place of the slave
trade, being in a way a clandestine form of it similar to those mentioned above.
What happened was that Brazilian planters 'engaged' Portuguese workers on
terms very similar to those of the Negroes shipped to the plantations of São
Tomé. This is borne out by a very marked increase in Portuguese emigration
to Brazil from 1850 onwards. These Portuguese, mostly from the northern
provinces were indebted almost for life to their bosses for the cost of their
passages; they took the place of the Negroes on the plantations, and led exactly
the same sort of life.

Turning now to the financial effect of the slave trade on Portugal's
socio-economic development, the most reliable data available from existing
sources are those concerning the profits made by the crown. These can be
calculated from the duties collected on contracts and the various charges and

taxes levied to meet particular items of expenditure: for instance, the levy introduced in 1664 to cover expenditure on the celebration of the peace between Portugal and the Netherlands, and to help pay for Catherine of Braganza's dowry on the occasion on her marriage to Charles II of England, originally intended to be applied for sixteen years, this levy was subsequently extended for a further twenty. In 1724 a tax was introduced to pay for the construction of the fortress at Ajudá; while in 1757 the rebuilding of Lisbon, which had been destroyed in the earthquake of 1755, was charged to the slave trade. Thus the royal treasury received a substantial return throughout the duration of the trade. It is, however, very difficult to attribute it to this or that particular activity, except in the case of taxes levied for specific purposes, as mentioned above.

In regard to the financing of the slave trade, and hence the question of those who made money out of it, Frédéric Mauro has drawn attention to the part played by the Jews—and the 'new Christians' from the sixteenth century onwards—in the formation of the Portuguese upper middle class. There is room for a thorough study not only of the general question of their importance for Portugal's commercial vitality at the time of the expansion, and their role in the early stages of development of Brazil's sugar economy, but also of the slave trade, which is inextricably bound up with those topics. After all, there were many Jewish and 'new Christian contractors' whose commercial activities were never confined to the slave trade. Moreover, while it is difficult to assess the profits that were made out of legal slave trading, it is impossible to estimate those made by smugglers. The latter played a considerable part over the centuries, but we can only guess at the purpose for which the capital thus acquired was used in Portugal itself.

Once again, the question of the slave trade is inseparable from the overall problem of a given economic system. In very general terms, the main beneficiaries were not so much those who engaged in the trade as those who turned cheap labour to account to improve their land and their mines. In this sense the effects of the slave trade on the socio-economic development of the country were greater, and are much more apparent, in Brazil than in Portugal.

Bibliography

Archives

Arquivos de Angola. Vol. I, Nos. 5–6, March 1936, Vol. II, No. 7, April 1936; No. 8, May 1936; No. 9, June 1936; No. 11, August 1936; No. 13, October 1936; No. 14, November 1936; No. 15, December 1936. Vol. III, Nos. 16–18, January–March 1937; No. 19, April 1937; No. 22, July 1937. Vol. XIX, Nos. 75–8, January–December 1962 (2nd series).
Archivos dos Servicos de Financas (Praia, Cabo Verde). Livro de Entrada de Navios de Longo Curso no Porto de Vila de Praiai (1812–27).

BRASIO, Antonio (Padre). *Monumenta Missionaria Africana (Costa Ocidental Africana)*. Vol. I (1342–1499), Lisbon, 1958; Vol. II (1500–69), Lisbon, 1963; Vol. III (1570–1600), Lisbon, 1964; Vol. IV (1600–20), Lisbon, 1968; Agéncia Geral do Ultramar.

CUVELIER; JADIN, *L'Ancien Congo, d'après les Archives Romaines 1516–1640*. Brussels, Mémoires de l'Académie Royale des Sciences Coloniales, 1954.

Livro Grosso do Maranhao, 1 Partst, Vols. 66 and 67, Biblioteca Nacional do Rio de Janeiro, 1948.

Contemporary studies

ADAMS, Captain John. *Remarks on the Country Extending from Cape Palmas to the River Congo*. London, 1823.

ALVARES, Manuel (Padre). *Etiopia Menor ou Descriçao da Provincia da Serra Leoa (1616)*. (Unedited manuscript in preparation by Teixeira da Mota.)

ANON. *Estabelecimentos e Resgates dos Portugueses na Costa Ocidental da Africa. Colecçao de Viagens, Exploraçoes e Conquistas nos Portugueses*. Lisbon, Imprensa Nacional, 1881.

——. *Bosquejo sobre o Comercio em Escravos, e Reflexoes sobre este Trato Considerado Imoral, Politica e Cristamente*. London, Ellerton & Henderson, 1821.

ASSUMPCÃO, Lino d'. *Exploração d'Africa. Bol. de Sociedade de Geografia de Lisboa*, 5th series, No. 6, 1885.

BERREDO, Antonio Pereira de. *Anais Historicos de Maranhao*. S. Luis do Maranha, 1864–65 (4 vols.).

BETTENCOURT, C. Pacheco de. *Memoria sobre e Abolição da Escravidão nas Colonias Portuguesas e Organização do Trabalho Agricole*. Lisbon, 1867.

BOTELHO, Sebastião Xavier, *Memoria Estatistica sobre os Dominios Portugueses na Africa Oriental*. Lisbon, Tipografia de José Baptista Morando, 1835.

——. *Escravatura. Beneficios que Podem Provir as Nossas Possessoes de Africa da Proibação deste Trafico*. Lisbon, 1840.

BRITO, Domingos de Abreu de. *Inquerito a Vida Administrativa e Economica de Angola, e do Brasil, em Fins do Século XVI (1592)*. (Preface and notes by Alfredo de Albuquerque Felner.) Coimbra, Imprensa da Universidade, 1931.

CADAMOSTO, Luiz de. *Navegaçoes. Colecçao de Noticias para a Historia das Naçoes Ultramarinas que Vivem nos Dominios Portugueses*. Vol. II. Lisbon, Academia Real das Ciencias de Lisboa, Tipografia da Academia. 1867.

CADORNEGA, Antonio de Oliveira. *Historia Geral das Guerras Angolanas* (manuscript of 1680 annotated and corrected by José Matias Delgado). Lisbon, Agencia Geral das Colonias, 1940; New edition by Imprensa Nacional/Casa da Moeda, Lisbon, 1972 (3 vols.).

CARDIAL SARAIVA. A Origen da Escravatura . . . (1829). *Obras* 325/347, Lisbon, 1975.

CAVAZZI, João Antonio. *Descriçao Historica dos Três Reinos: Congo, Angola e Natamba*. Lisbon, J.I.U. Agrupamento de Cartografia Antiga, 1965 (2 vols.).

CORDEIRO, Luciano. *Viagens, Exploraçoes e Conquistas dos Portugueses, 1516–1619. Escravos e Minas de Africa, Segundo Diversos*. Lisbon, Imprensa Nacional, 1881.

CORTE-REAL, J. A. *Respoata a Sociedade Anti-esclavagista de Londres*. Lisbon, 1884.

COUTINHO, D. José Joaquim da Cunha Azevedo (Bishop of Elvas). *Analise sobre a Justiça do Comercio do Resgate de Escravos na Costa da Africa*. Lisbon, Nova Oficina de João Rodrigues Neves, 1807.

Documentos Acerca do Trafico da Escravatura Extraidos dos Papeis Relativos a Portugal Apresentados ao Parlamento Britânico. Lisbon, 1840.

DOENELAS, André. *Descriçao da Costa Ocidental d'Africa*. (Unedited manuscript, dated Santiago, 7 November 1625. Teixeira da Mota Collection.)

FERNANDES, Valentim. *Description de la Côte Occidentale d'Afrique (Sénégal) au Cap de Monte, Archipels, 1506–1510.* Memoria No. 11. Bissau, Centro de Estudos da Guiné Portuguesa, 1951.

FREIRE, J. J. *Projecto para a Abolição do Trafico da Escravatura.* Lisbon, 1840.

LIMA, José Joaquim Lopes de L. *Ensaio sobre Estatistica das Possessoes Portuguesas na Africa Ocidental e Oriental, na Asia Ocidental, na China e na Oceânia.* Lisbon, Imprensa Nacional. (5 vols.: I and II, 1844; III, 1846; IV, 1859; V, 1862—the last two continued by Francisco Maria Bordalo.)

MALHEIROS, Agostinho Marques Perdigão. *A Escravidao no Brasil (Ensaio Historico-Juridico-Social).* Brasilica series Nos. 9 and 10. São Paulo, Ediçoes Cultura, 1944. (Facsimile 1866 of edition.)

MENDES, A. L. *Abolição da Escravatura en Angola e a Organizaçao do Trabalho.* Lisbon, 1867.

MENDES, Luis Antonio de Oliveira. Discurso Académico lino da Sessão da Academia das Ciencias de Lisboa a 12 de Maio de 1973. *Memcrias Economicas da Academia Real das Ciencias de Lisboa.* Vol. IV. Lisbon, 1812.

OLIVEIRA MARTINS, Joaquim P. *O Brazil e as Colonias Portuguesas.* 6th ed. Lisbon, 1953.

PEREIRA, Duarte Pacheco. *Esmeraldo de Situ Orbis (Côte Occidentale d'Afrique du Sud-Marocain au Gabon) 1506–1508, por Raymond Mauny.* Memoria No. 19. Centro de Estudos da Guiné Portuguesa, 1956.

PIGAFETTA, Filippo; LOPES, Duarte. 1591: (Rome): *Relatione del calme di Congo,* Trans. Cahum Léon, Brussels, 1883.

PILOTO ANONIMO. Navegaçao de Lisboa à Ilha de S. Tomé. *Memorias de Academia das Ciencias de Lisboa.* Vol. II, 2nd ed., 1867.

PIRES, A. de Oliveira. *Algumas Reflexoes sobre a Questão do Trabalho nas Possessoes Portuguesas de Africa.* Lisbon, 1874.

——. *Apontamentos para e Historia da Aboliçao da Escravatura nas Colonias Portuguesas.* Lisbon, 1880.

ROCHA, Manuel Ribeiro da. *Etiope Resgatado, Instruido, Libertado.* Lisbon, 1758.

SÁ DA BANDEIRA. *O Trafico da Escravatura e o Bill de Palmerston.* Lisbon, 1840.

——. *O Trabalho Rural Africano e a Administração Colonial.* Lisbon, 1971.

SANDOVAL, Alonso de. *Naturaleza, Politica Sagrada e Profana, Costumbres e Ritos, Disciplina e Catechismo de Todos los Etiopes.* (Published in Seville in 1627 by Francisco de Lira.)

Books

ALMADA, André Alvares d'. *Tratado Breve dos Rios da Guiné.* Lisbon, 1946.

ANDRADE, Elisa. *Les Iles du Cap Vert: de l'Esclavage à l'Immigration 'Spontanée' (les Migrations Capverdiennes à Dakar).* Dakar, United Nations, 1973.

ANTONIL, André João. *Cultura e Opulência do Brasil (1690–1701).* Salvador, 1955.

AZEVEDO, João Lucio de. *Epocas de Portugal Economico.* Lisbon, 1929.

BALANDIER, Georges. *La Vie Quotidienne au Royaume de Kongo du XVIe au XVIIIe Siècle.* Paris, Hachette, 1965.

BARRETO, João Melo. *Historia da Guiné.* Lisbon, 1938.

BIRMINGHAM, David. *Trade and Conflict in Angola: The Mbundu and their Neighbours Under the Influence of the Portuguese, 1483–1790.* Oxford, 1966.

——. *The Portuguese Conquest of Angola,* London, Institute of Race Relations, Oxford University Press, 1965.

BOXER, C. R. *Relaçoes Raciais no Imperio Colonial Portugues—1415/1825.* Rio de Janeiro, 1967.

BOXER, C. R. *The Portuguese Seaborne Empire, 1415–1825.* London, 1965.
——. *A Idade do Ouro do Brasil.* São Paulo, 1969.
——. *Portuguese Society in the Tropics.* Madison, 1965.
BUARQUE DE HOLLANDA, Sergio (ed.). *Historia Geral da Civilização Brasileira.* São Paulo, 1960. (4 vols.)
CAPELA, José. *Escravatura—a Empresa de Saque—o Abolicionismo (1810–1875).* Oporto, 1974.
CARDOSO, Francisco Henrique. *Capitalismo e Escravatura.* São Paulo, 1962.
CARREIRA, Antonio. *Panaria Cabo-Verdino-Guineense.* Lisbon. Junta de Investigaçoes do Ultramar. 1968.
——. *As Companhias Pombalinas de Navegação, Comercio e Trafico de Escravos do Occidente Africano para o Nordeste Brasileiro.* Oporto, 1969.
——. *Cabo-Verde—Formaçao e Extinçao de uma Socieda Escravocrata 1460–1870.* Oporto, 1972.
——. *Angola, da Escravatura ao Trabalho Livre.* Lisbon, Arcadia, 1977.
CARVALHO, Arthur de Moraes. *Companhias de Colonizaçao.* Coimbra, 1903.
CARVALHO, Tito Augusto de. *As Companhias Portuguesas de Colonização.* Lisbon, 1902.
CHAUNU, Huguette and Pierre. *Séville et l'Atlantique (1504–1650).* Paris, 1955–60. (8 vols.)
COELHO, Francisco de Lemos. *Duas Descriçoes Seiscentistas da Guiné.* Lisbon, 1953.
COELHO DE SENNA, Nelson. *Africanos no Brasil.* Belo Horizonte, 1938.
CORREIA, Elisa Alexandre da Silva. *Historia de Angola.* (Manuscript dated Rio de Janeiro, 1782.). Lisbon, Atica, 1937. (2 vols.) (Series E. Imperio Africano, notes by Manuel Muria.)
CORREIRA LOPES, Edmundo. *A Escravatura.* Lisbon, 1944.
COUTO, Carlos. *Os Capitaes-mores en Angola no Século XVIII (Subsdios para o Estudo da sua Actuaçao).* Luanda, 1972.
CURTIN, P. D. *The Atlantic Slave Trade: A Census.* Madison, Wis., University of Wisconsin Press, 1970.
DAVIDSON, Basil. *Black Mother: The Years of the African Slave Trade,* London, Gollanecz, 1961.
DEERR, Noel. *The History of Sugar.* London, Chapman & Hall, 1949–50. (2 vols.)
DESCHAMPS, Hubert. *Histoire de la Traite des Noirs de l'Antiquité à nos Jours.* Paris, Fayard, 1971.
DUFFY, James. *A Question of Slavery: Labour Policies in Portuguese Africa and British Protest 1850–1920.* Oxford, Oxford University Press, 1967.
DUNCAN, T. Bentley. *Atlantic Islands—Madeira, the Azores, and the Cape Verde in Seventeenth-century Commerce and Navigation.* Chicago and London, University of Chicago Press, 1972.
FELNER, Alfredo de Albuquerque. *Angola—Apontamentos sobre a Ocupação e Inicio do Estabelecimento dos Portugueses no Congo, Angola e Benguela.* Coimbra, Imprensa da Universidade, 1938.
FRIEDERICI, Georges. *Caracter da Descoberta e Conquista da America pelos Europeus.* Rio de Janeiro, 1967.
GODINHO, Vitorino Magalhaes. *Os Descobrimentos e a Economia Mundial.* Lisbon, Arcadia, 1963.
GOULART, Mauricio. *Escravidão Africana—das Origens à Extinção do Trafico.* São Paulo, 1949.
HELENO, Manuel. *Escravos em Portugal.* Vol. I. Lisbon, 1933.
HERSKOVITS, Melville J. *The Myth of the Negro Past.* Boston, Beacon Press, 1958.

IANI, Octavio. *As Metamorfoses do Escravo (Apogeu e Crise da Escravatura no Brasil Meridional)*. São Paulo, 1962.

KUCZYNSKI, Robert R. *Demographic Survey of the British Colonial Empire*. London, published under the auspices of the Royal Institute of International Affairs. 1948–53. (3 vols.)

——. *Population movements*. Oxford, 1936.

LOPES, Admundo Correia. *A Escravatura—Subsidios para a sua Historia*. Lisbon, 1944.

MACEDO, Sergio D. T. *Apontamentos para a Historia do Trafico Negreiro no Brasil*. Rio de Janeiro, 1942.

MANNIX, Daniel P.; COWLEY Malcolm. *Black Cargoes: A History of the Atlantic Slave Trade, 1518–1865*. New York, Viking, 1962.

MAURO, Frédéric. *L'expansion Européenne (1600–1870)*, Paris, Presses Universitaires de France, 1964.

——. *Études Économiques sur l'Expansion Portugaise (1500–1900)*. Paris, Calouste Gulbenkian Foundation, 1970.

——. *Le Portugal et l'Atlantique au XVIIe siècle (1570–1670)*. Paris, Étude Économique, 1960.

MURDOCK, George Peter. *Africa: Its Peoples and Their Culture History*. New York, McGraw, 1959.

OLIVEIRA, Mario Antonio Fernandes de. *Alguns Aspectos da Administração de Angola na Epoca das Reformas 1834–1851*. Lisbon, 1971. (Mimeo.)

——. *Aspectos Sociais de Luanda Inferidos nos Anuncios Publicados na sua Imprensa (1851)*. Instituto de Investigação Cientifica de Angola, 1964.

ORLOF, A. S. *Institution de l'Esclavage dans l'État du Congo au Moyen-Age (XVI–XVIIe Siècles)*. *International Congress of Anthropology and Ethnology*. Moscow, Naouka, 1964.

OTT, Carlos. *O Negro Baiano (Les Afro-Américains)*. Dakar, IFAN, 1953. (Paper No. 27.)

PARREIRA, Henrique Gomes de Amorim. *Historia do Açucar en Portugal, Estudos de Historia da Geografia da Expansão Portuguesa*. Anais da J.I.U. Lisbon, 1952.

PINTO F. Latour da Veiga. *Le Portugal et le Congo au XIXe Siècle*. Paris, Presses Universitaires de France, 1972.

RAMOS, Arthur. *O Negro Brasileiro*. Rio de Janeiro, 1934.

——. *As Culturas Negras no Novo Mundo*. Rio de Janeiro, Civilizaçao Brasileira, 1937.

REBELO, Manuel dos Anjos da Silva. *Relaçoes entre Angola e Brasil 1808–1800*. Lisbon, 1970.

RODNEY, Walter. *A History of the Upper Gulnea Coast, 1545 to 1800*. Oxford, The Clarendon Press, 1970.

RODRIGUES, José, Honorio. *Brasil e Africa : Outro Horizonte (Relaçoes e Politica Brasileiro-Africana)*. Rio de Janeiro, 1961.

RODRIGUES, Nina. *Os Africanos no Brasil*. São Paulo, 1932.

SÁ, José de Almeida Correa de. *A Abolição da Escravatura e a Ocupação de Ambriz*. Lisbon, 1934.

SALLES, Vicente. *O Negro do Para sob o Regime da Escravidao*. Rio de Janeiro, 1971.

SARAIVA, José Mendes da Cunha. *As Companhias Gerais do Comercio e Navegação para o Brasil. I—Congresso da Historia da Expansão Portuguesa no Mundo, 3e Secçao*, Lisbon, 1938.

——. *Companhia Geral de Pernambuco e Paraiba. Arquivo Historico do Ministerio das Finanças, I*. Lisbon, 1944. *Congresso do Mundo Portugues*, Vol. X, Lisbon, 1910.

——. *A Fortaleza de Bissau e a Companhia do Grao Para e Maranhao*. Lisbon, Arquivo Historico do Ministerio das Finanças. 1947.

SCELLE, Georges. *La Traite Négrière aux Indes de Castille.* Paris, L. Larose & L. Tenin, 1906. (2 vols.)

SIMONSEN, Roberto. *Historia Economica do Brasil 1500–1820.* São Paulo, 1937.

STAMM, Anne. *L'Angola à un Tournant de son Histoire 1838–1848.* Paris. (Thesis.) (Mimeo.)

TAUNAY, Affonso Escragnolle de. *Subsidios para a Historia do Trafico Africano no Brasil.* São Paulo, 1941.

TEIXEIRA, Candido da Silva. Companhia de Cacheu, Rios e Costa da Guiné. *Bol. do Arquivo Historico Colonial,* Vol. I, Lisbon, 1950.

VANSINA, Jan. *Kingdoms of the Savanna.* Madison, University of Wisconsin Press, 1966.

VIANNA FILHO, Luis. *O Negro na Baia.* Rio de Janeiro, José Olympio, 1946. (Documentos Historicos, No. 55.)

——. *O Trabalho do Engenho e a Reacçao do Indio. Establecimento da Escravatura Africana. Congresso do Mundo Portugues,* Vol. X. Lisbon, 1940.

WYNDHAM, Hugh A. *The Atlantic and Slavery.* London, Oxford University Press, 1935.

Articles

AZEVEDO, Pedro A. de. Os Escravos. *Arquivo Historico Portugues* (Lisbon), Vol. I, 1903, p. 290–307.

CARDOSO, Manuel da Silveira Soares. Os Quintos do Ouro de Minas Geral 1712–1732. *Memorias e Communicaçoes Apresentadas ao Congresso Luso-Brasileiro de Historia,* Vol. X (O Ciclo do Oiro e dos Diamentes). Lisbon, 1940.

CARNEIRO, Edison. O Negro como Objecto de Ciencia. *Africa-Asia, Revista do Centro de Estudos Afro-orientais da Bahia,* Nos. 6–7, 1968, p. 91–100.

CURTIN, P. D.; VANSINA, Jan. Sources of the Nineteenth Century Atlantic Slave Trade. *Journal of African History,* Vol. 5, 1964, p. 185–208.

DELAFOSSE; DEBIEN. Les Origines des Esclaves aux Antilles. *Bull. de l'IFAN,* Vol. XXVII, Series B, Nos. 1–2, 1965.

DIAS, Manuel Munes. Fomento e Mercantilismo: Politica Portuguesa na Baixada Marachense 1755–1778. *Studia,* No. 16, November 1965.

FARO, Jorge. O Movimento Comercial do Porto de Bissau de 1788 a 1794. *Boletin Cultural da Guiné Portuguesa,* Vol. 14, 1959, p. 231–58.

LIMA JUNIOR, Augusto de. *O Ouro das Minas Gerais.*

——. A Grande Invasão das Minas Gerais. *Memorias e Communicaçoes Apresentadas ao Congresso Luso-Brasileiro de Historia,* Vol. X. Lisbon, 1940.

KLEIN, Herbert S. O Trafico de Escravos Africanos para o Porto Rio de Janeiro. *Anais de Historia.* (Facultade de Filosofia, Ciencias e Letras de Assis (Brasil)). Year V, No. 5, 1973, p. 85–101.

MARCILIO, Maria Luisa; MARQUES, Rubens Murillo; BARREIRO, José Carlos. Consideraçoes sobre o Preço do Escravo no Periodo Imperial. *Anais de Historia* (Facultade de Filosofia, Ciencias e Letras de Assis (Brasil)), Year V, No. 5, 1973, p. 1–194.

MATOSO, Katia M. Queiros. A Proposito de Cartas de Alforria, Bahia 1779–1850. *Anais de Historia,* (Facultade de Filosofia, Ciencias e Letras de Assis (Brasil)), Year IV, No. 4, 1972, p. 23–32.

MAURO, Frédéric. L'Atlantique Portugais et les Esclaves (1570–1670). *Revista da Facultadade de Letras* (University of Lisbon) Vol. 22, No. 2, 1956, p. 5–52.

MENDES, M. Maia. Escravatura no Brasil (1500–1700). *Congresso de Mundo Portugues,* Vol. X, p. 31–56. Lisbon, 1940.

MORAIS, Evaristo de. A Escravidao Africana no Brasil (das Origens à Extinção). *Brasiliana,* Series V, Vol. XXIII, 1933.

MOTA, Avelino Teixeira de. *A Malograda Viagen de Diogo Carreiro a Tombuctu em 1565.* Lisbon, J.I.U., Agrupamento de Cartografia Antiga, Separata LXII, 1970.

——. *Alguns Aspectos da Colonização e do Comercio Maritimo dos Portugueses na Africa Ocidental nos Séculos XV e XVI,* Lisboa, J.I.U., Agrupamento de Cartografia Antiga, Separata XCVIII, 1976.

OLIVEIRA, Waldir Freita. Consideraçoes sobre o Preconceito Racial no Brasil. *Revista Afro-Asia do Centro de Estudos Afro-Orientais da Bahia,* Nos. 8–9, 1969, p. 1–19.

OTTE, Enrique; RUIZ-BURRUECOS, Conchita. Los Portugueses en la Trata de Esclavos Negros de las Postrimerias del Siglo XVI. *Moneda y Crédito* (Madrid), Vol. 85, 1963, p. 3–40.

POLLAK-ELTZ, Donde Provêm os Negros da América do Sul. *Afro-Asia, Revista do Centro de Estudos Afro-Orientais da Bahia,* Nos. 10–11, 1970, p. 99–107.

RODNEY, Walter. Portuguese Attempts at Monopoly on the Upper Guinea Coast, 1580–1650. *Journal of African History,* Vol. 6, 1965, p. 307–22.

RODRIGUES, José Honorio. A Rebeldia Negra e Abolição. *Afro-Asia. Revista do Centro de Estudos Afro-Orientas da Bahia,* Nos. 6–7, 1968, p. 101–17.

SERRAO, Joel. *Dicionario de Historia de Portugal.* Lisbon, 1963. (4 vols.)

TURNER, J. Michael. Escravos Brasileiros no Daomé. *Afro-Asia. Revista do Centro da Estudos Afro-Orientas da Bahia,* Nos. 10–11, 1970, p. 5–24.

The slave trade within Africa and between Africa and the Middle East

The slave trade
within the African continent

Mbaye Gueye

The slave trade was a very ancient practice in Africa. The Europeans did not invent it. They only exploited it by impelling the Africans to 'derive the greater part of their resources from it'.[1] With the coming of the Europeans, the volume of the trade swelled to huge proportions, causing widespread social upheaval in Africa.

Unfortunately we do not have all the necessary material on the internal slave trade. We cannot attempt to make even a rough assessment of its magnitude from currently available sources. The little information we do possess is either fragmentary or written long after the event, comes mostly from the colonial authorities and deals more with the struggle to suppress the domestic slave trade than with the trade itself.

Prior to foreign intervention, the slave trade was undoubtedly practised in Africa but on an extremely small scale. It was devised chiefly as a means of reintegrating into society individuals who had been cut off from their families following a war or other catastrophe. For the organization of African society does not allow for isolation and individualism. The African ideal is that of a community existence based on powerful family ties with a view to a 'well-ordered, secure life'.[2] People only count in so far as they are part of a harmonious, homogeneous entity. In these conditions, a man on his own formerly had no chance of survival. Enslaving peoples whom natural or other disasters had cast adrift was a useful means of providing them with a social framework relevant to their expectations in life. Those who purchased them gave them a new identity. The slaves would give up their own patronyms for that of their new master. This type of integration did not jeopardize the group and could not fundamentally disturb the original balance of the community for it concerned only a tiny minority of individuals.

It was the steadily increasing demand for slaves a a result of foreign intervention in the affairs of the continent which brought about a fairly substantial increase in the volume of the trade, hitherto restricted to transactions on a narrow local scale. The material advantages to be gained by trading in slaves were an incentive to some of the clans, especially in medieval times, to intensify their raids on neighbouring tribes, to have something to barter for

Mediterranean or Asian goods. 'The people of Lemlem', writes Edrisi, 'are perpetually being invaded by their neighbours, who take them as slaves . . . and carry them off to their own lands to sell them by the dozen to the merchants. Every year great numbers of them are sent off to the Western Maghreb'.[3] Arab traders also took many captives from East Africa and sold them in Arabia, Iraq and as far afield as China. In both cases, however, the number of slaves was actually comparatively small. The traders did not have the transport to carry their human cargoes in bulk. The trans-Saharan crossing precluded the purchase of great numbers of slaves. Arab authors state almost unanimously that it was chiefly women who were purchased to fill the Maghrebian emirs' harems. The Arabs were in fact drawn to the area mainly by gold, regarded at the time as the 'blacks' main commodity'.[4] Slaves were only used as currency in very large transactions. Otherwise cowrie shells and animals were quite adequate for barter purposes.

Between 1441 and the middle of the nineteenth century, the expanding slave trade ultimately became Black Africa's only link with Europe and America. The establishment in the New World of European sugar, cotton and tobacco plantations, as well as mining for precious metals, gave rise to a demand for an abundant, cheap manpower force which could not be met by either the Amerindians or the European workers. The answer was the Black Africans, who were regarded as good farmers. What is more, they would have no difficulty in adapting to the tropical climate. Once they had been enslaved and transported to America, they would find it easy to work the settlers' estates.

The constant rise in demand led the African dealers to set up well-organized trade structures to keep the Europeans supplied in slaves.

The true beginnings of the Atlantic slave trade coincided with the collapse of the last great African Empire, the Songhai. The breaking up of the land into a number of kingdoms and small political divisions at the tribal or small village community level, many of which were hostile to one another, favoured the expansion of the slave trade. Ambition and vanity caused the chiefs to turn on one another. Acute jealousies and sudden retaliation by the defeated led to incessant warfare and raiding. War thus became the simplest means of procuring slaves. After the battle, the victorious side, not content to capture those who had been unable to flee, would penetrate into the defeated tribe's territory and seize captives from amongst the people living in the border areas. Free men who were taken as slaves and were able to pay a ransom were generally freed in exchange for two good-quality slaves.[5]

With the growth of the slave trade, some chiefs finally lost all sense of responsibility. Claiming that some members of a village had said something against them, they would not hesitate to order the guilty parties' village to be razed to the ground and the inhabitants reduced to slavery.[6] In the dead of night the village would be encircled by the chief's warriors. At dawn the attack would be launched. They would set fire to the huts. Any man trying to resist would be put to death. The women and children were taken and put up for auction. The spoils would be shared out evenly between the chief and his warriors.[7]

The recurrent wars and the devastation they brought with them made the hideous spectre of famine a familiar sight. To obtain food, the heads of some families would sell some of their household slaves. If they had none, they would sell their children or pawn them to wealthy people in the hope of redeeming them when times were better.[8]

During periods of famine, chiefs would intensify their raiding forays to procure slaves who would then be sold in exchange for food supplies. The poorer inhabitants of the famine-stricken areas would try to flee to avoid being captured. But usually the chiefs of the territories in which they sought asylum would promptly seize them and sell them without any further ado. This is what happened to some of the inhabitants of Kajor and Jolof who went to Waalo to escape the terrible famine which had swept through their land. The king of Waalo seized them and sold them to the Compagnie des Indes.[9]

The chiefs' desire to acquire European goods at a low price induced them to sharpen the penalties for offences and crimes; the apparently most trivial offences were now severely punished.

Insolvency now became liable to the penalty of slavery. The creditor would take the offender and put him up for auction.[10] Theft, murder and cannibalism were likewise punishable by enslavement. Thieves whose guilt was proved became their victims' slaves. Those guilty of certain offences liable to a fine which they were unable to pay also forfeited their freedom. But although thieves, criminals, insolvent debtors and cannibals were all mercilessly reduced to servitude and sold as slaves, war and slave raids nevertheless remained the main source of slaves.

Caught up in the mesh of the slave trade, which was much more lucrative than trading in kola, ivory or cattle, the African traders progressively went over to trading in slaves, organizing it in such a way as to minimize the risks inherent in such a large-scale business. A category of local traders emerged known as merchants (French: *courtiers*) by the Europeans and as Juula by the Africans. They were mostly to be found among the Sarakole, the Mandingo and the Hausa.

These slave-merchants would go to the various markets where the slaves were bought and sold. Each territory had its market-day, on which all the different dealers would meet. The largest slave markets were Segu, Bambarena, Khasso and Bambuhu.[11]

Every year the African merchants would set off for the regions of Upper Senegal/Niger and Hausaland in search of slaves whom they would then take off to the places where they would be most likely to secure the highest prices for them. As the slave trade developed, particularly in the eighteenth century, the Africans themselves came to organize their commerce on a more rational basis. Because of the risks of all kinds involved in trading independently, they decided to join forces and 'form a caravan led by one or more overseers'.[12] Each slave train was composed of 'two or three slaves chained together, in groups of four to twelve, depending on whether they [belonged] to a single merchant or to several in the same partnership'.[13]

To forestall mutiny or evasion, the African merchants would make their captives carry a stone or some sand, weighing between forty and fifty pounds, for the whole length of the journey; or alternatively trade goods such as sorghum, elephants' teeth, hides or wax, so that sheer exhaustion would rob them of any desire to escape.[14]

Shortly before the date for departure to the coastal markets, where they would meet up with the European slave-traders, the African merchants would begin to round up the slaves who were to be sold along the coast at specific rallying-points. The European goods they had acquired at the previous sale had been used to purchase more slaves. They always had a way of having their fellow countrymen repay them in slaves for loans in kind.[15] In Bambarena, writes Pruneau de Pommegorge, the long-established institution of slavery led the local rulers to set up villages where they kept the captives they had seized during raids.[16] Whenever they wanted European goods they would select a few of them and sell them to the Mandingo and Hausa merchants. According to Mungo Park, the people captured and put in these special villages outnumbered those who were free. They made up three-quarters of the entire population.[17]

The African merchants preferred these people born in captivity to free men who had been made slaves. For they were accustomed to hunger and fatigue and stood up better to the hardships of the long voyages. They were resigned to their unhappy fate. Never having been exposed to the joys of freedom, they probably regarded their lot as the normal course of events. They presented no danger to the African traders for they never attempted to run away.[18]

Once this first batch had been gathered in, the African merchants would fill up their caravans by going around to the various slave markets to buy more slaves. When all was in order, the merchants would set off for the coast or for the markets where they would periodically meet company agents. Those who supplied the French would make for Galam but only when the rainy season was imminent. Those who supplied the British would head for Gambia, but only when the rivers could be crossed and the bush was destroyed by fire.[19] In this way the merchants were less in danger of being attacked by the wild beasts which roamed the lands between Faleme and Gambia.

During the march to the coastal termini or trading posts, the captives were treated harshly. Regarded as nothing but merchandise transporting another sort of merchandise, they were chained together by poles cleft at both ends slung behind their necks.[20] They were given just enough food to keep them going from one stage to the next. At each halt they were put in irons before being allowed to go to sleep.[21] The slave-drivers would take it in turns to keep watch over them until it was time to depart. All along the way the caravan would leave a trail of human beings who were no longer able to endure the fatigue and hunger in its wake, to be devoured by the hyenas and jackals.[22] Those who could not keep up with the rest of the caravan would be driven on with whips, and those who could not go on form sheer exhaustion would be slain in cold blood in front of their terrified companions, and their bodies left to the wild beasts.[23] This implied that the same punishment would be inflicted on any slave showing any signs of ill-will. Human bones laid strewn all along the routes that led from the interior to the trading posts.

These gruesome slave-trains were made up of long lines of

haggard, emaciated men, worn out by the lack of food, dazed by the blows they were dealt, doubled over with the weight of their loads; crippled, spindle-legged women covered in hideous wounds and forced to help themselves along with long sticks; old people completely spent, bent double with fatigue and age.[24]

When after several days' march in the silence of those African desert trails they would reach the trading posts, it was only the first stage in their grim odyssey.

At the trading stations, the African merchants would bide their time over the sale of their slaves in anticipation of substantial profit margins. If the price they were offered was too low they would refuse to sell. While they were waiting for the highest bid, they would deposit their captives in the neighbouring villages, and there the slaves would be chained together, unable to move, until such time as they would be purchased by the agents of the European companies. From there they would be dispatched to the coastal termini where they would be kept until there were enough of them to warrant shipment to America.

As the slaves were bought up by the traders, they were shackled together two by two with collars and chains until their turn came to be sent down to the coast. The device used was 'an iron chain five or six feet long with a flat iron collar at one end which would be fitted around their necks and clasped in such a way that it could not be unlocked without tools' [25] Once the whole operation was settled, the merchants would return home.[26]

The slave trade organized in this way was not the only means of supplying the European traders with slaves. For States like Benin, Ashanti and Dahomey were not prepared to bow to a system in which they were merely middlemen. At the end of the seventeenth and the beginning of the eighteenth century, first Ashanti and then Dahomey resolved to put an end to their inland position and open up a window to the coast in order to trade directly with the Europeans.

They did away with all the merchants who had previously passed through their territories to take their slaves to the coast to sell them to the European slave-traders. From that time on, they became involved in slave-dealing on a large scale.

Periodically they would send troops into the neighbouring countries to capture slaves whom they would then sell in order to secure arms and other European goods. In Ashanti and Dahomey the slave trade became a State monopoly. Most of the slaves were now sold by the State and no longer by private individuals.

In Central and East Africa the internal slave trade was controlled by foreigners. The Portuguese led expeditions inland. From ancient times the Arabs had specialized in hunting down Africans and reducing them to slavery Slave raids and the search for ivory were the two main activities of the Arabs in East Africa.[27]

Alongside this slave trade which served to export captives to America or Asia there was another trade network within the continent itself which helped to meet local labour demands.

For the expansion of the Atlantic trade did not bring about the collapse of the old trading traditions. Although the economic nerve-centres had shifted from the hinterland to the coast, the former trade relations between Black Africa and North Africa were as lively as ever. Only luxury goods were traded. Lacourbe reports that at the end of the seventeenth century an Arab horse was worth twenty-five slaves.[28] Pruneau de Pommegorge claims to have seen an African chief buy a horse for 'a hundred slaves and a hundred oxen'.[29] The emphasis on horses was due to the fact that war had become a truly lucrative industry and cavalry necessarily played an important part in military strategy.

Slaves were also used in marriage negotiations as part of the 'bride price'. In princely marriages, the bride price was mainly composed of slaves, whereas for commoners it consisted simply of a handful of tobacco leaves and a few animals. Since local custom did not allow mastes to part with their own household slaves, they would buy trade slaves or ordinary slaves to give away to their future parents-in-law.

At the time of the overseas trade, slaves captured in raids or purchased, or prisoners of war, were not all sold to the European slave-traders. Some of them were bought by Africans and remained in Africa. They then became part of their master's domestic slave household. But since they had not been born under their master's roof, they were called ordinary slaves. Admittedly they did the same work as the household slaves, but their status was inferior, for their master could sell them without incurring any recrimination, whereas household slaves could not be parted with unless it was absolutely necessary.[30]

Ordinary and trade slaves were regarded as foreigners. They had virtually no legal protection in common law against arbitrary treatment by their masters, who could maltreat or sell them as and when they thought fit. They could be included as part of their master's property in payment of some object purchased by him, or be pawned to a distrustful creditor.[31]

The internal trade by itself was not sufficient to meet domestic labour requirements. With the extension of the Atlantic slave trade, the local rulers became increasingly caught up in the relentless workings of the slave machine. War became their normal occupation. What was needed was a category of people who would cultivate the land to provide food for the local population. Agricultural villages were set up everywhere, peopled with slaves who had been purchased or captured during raids. Thus the Bakuba in the Congo neither maltreated 'nor sold their prisoners of war. They settled them in areas far from their native lands, and called them Mitsungi.'[32] Their masters could pick out any number of them and sell them or hand them over as hostages, 'as pledge for a debt or in payment of the bride price'.[33]

In West Africa, ordinary slaves were used for a variety of purposes. During the rains, they were employed to work in the fields. From dawn to about two o'clock in the afternoon they would work for their masters. From then on they could work for themselves. On Fridays and feast days they were free all day.[34] What they produced on those days was their own, and could be used to buy back their freedom or that of their children. But the price of freedom was extremely high, and cases of self-redemption were extremely rare. And since when they died, 'their sole heir was their master, it was he who reaped the benefit of the extra work'.[35]

In Senegambia ordinary slaves were divided into two categories: slaves who had been captured during the countless raiding expeditions, and slaves bought at the slave markets. The former were kept in special villages both in time of peace and war. After several years in such villages the bravest of them were selected to become warriors, and were henceforth royal slaves. They would fight under the command of the chief, and he alone had the right to punish them. Slaves who had been purchased could be sold at any time. They were part of their master's concession and he had the right to maltreat them. Their existence was often an unhappy and degrading one. Their main preoccupation was to satisfy their 'animal needs: eat when they could, sleep as much as possible and breed when the opportunity arose'.[36] The master's only obligation was to feed and clothe them.[37]

A trade slave who had been in his master's service for some time could request permission to marry. The master would then choose a wife for him without any regard for the candidate's wishes. He could also take her away again as and when he wished. However, a trade slave who was fortunate enough to be given a wife who had been born in her master's house automatically belonged to his wife's category. He was only sold if he tried to escape, was particularly insolent or committed a crime. Marriages between two trade slaves were on the whole only a fleeting source of joy to them, for the imperatives of their existence or the whims of their masters could separate them from each other or from their children. And yet there is no evidence of revolt. It may be that it seemed futile to attempt anything of the kind, although it would appear that individual escapes were not infrequent. At any event runaway slaves made no attempt to form armed gangs to take their revenge or free their brothers who were still in captivity.

Ordinary female slaves were not allowed to do private work. They were permanently at the beck and call of their masters' wives. A child born of ordinary slave parents automatically acquired the privileged status of household slave. He could neither be sold nor maltreated, and was usually given the same upbringing as the master's own children. Nor could his mother be sold until she had weaned him.

As we have already said, we cannot give an accurate appraisal of the extent of the domestic slave trade. Apart from a few references in accounts by travellers, there are no texts giving detailed information on the subject. From a certain time on, the internal trade was probably practised on a very large scale since it served both as a reservoir for the export trade and as a form of currency in commercial transactions at home. It even contributed to the development of household or domestic slavery. We do not know exactly how it operated or how it compared in volume to the export trade.

It would perhaps not be presumptuous to suggest that the height of the internal slave trade was between the end of the eighteenth century and the middle of the nineteenth. By the middle of the eighteenth century, the slave-trading nations of Europe had already organized themselves in readiness for the large-scale export of slaves overseas. The slave trade then went deep into the forest and mountain areas which were as yet untapped. As a result, even remote communities became involved in the trade.

The slave trade engendered a permanent state of internecine conflict. Drawn into its web, the local rulers spent most of their time at war. Plunder, theft, rape, capture of human beings and animals became the order of the day. The air was rent with the wails of the victims.

This atmosphere of violence, hatred and terror affected the spiritual and moral values of society. The ancestral moral virtues were flouted daily. The rulers were no doubt conscious of the danger, but the cogs of the infernal machine made short work of their better thoughts and drove society on to its downfall.

It was for this reason that the Muslims resorted to armed combat to defeat the despotic regimes, in the hope of restoring a more equitable society. They took the offensive as from the end of the eighteenth century. In 1776 came the establishment of theocratic rule in Fuuta Tooro. A few years later, Usman Dan Fodio was victorious in Nigeria, and Ahmadou Cheikou in Massina. In the middle of the nineteenth century, El Hadj Omar took up the combat and islamized the Nigerian Sudan.[38] All these wars, which furthered the expansion of the internal slave trade, coincided with the decision by the Western European nations progressively to put an end to the slave trade.[39] In 1807 Great Britain, and in 1815 France decided to abolish it. Finding no outside market for their slaves, the Africans were compelled to use them at home. Slavery was the natural ransom that conquering armies would demand of those they had defeated.

The sudden slackening of European demand presented the serious problem of how to dispose of the slaves. Around 1843, after a war between the Bambara and the Sarakole in which the latter were defeated, the Bambara king arrived in Bakel with 800 prisoners for sale. But he found no market for them. Not knowing what to do with his prisoners, he

ordered the unfortunate wretches to be systematically slaughtered. As was customary, they were lined up, tied down firmly and gagged so that they could not spit on the executioner, in which case he would have been unable to kill them. The executioner slew nine of them and spared the tenth' who was the executioner's tithe.[40]

In the Podor region, 'laptots' witnessed a similar massacre. Dervish Moors, unable to sell their prisoners for lack of prospective customers killed off the children and cripples.[41]

In spite of the anti-slavery laws, however, the British and the French continued to trade in slaves in order to meet some of their manpower problems. Thus in order to provide Senegal with new sources of income, the French had recourse to agricultural resettlement projects, 'the success of which would add a huge continent to France's possessions'.[42] Since the American colonies had been developed by African labour, there would surely be no dearth of willing workers to do the same in plantations on African soil.[43] France followed the example set by Great Britain and in 1822 established a system of indenture by virtue of which slaves could be used in the European areas by those who had redeemed them. The planters could thereby procure cheap labour for their concessions.

All they needed to do was to buy slaves inland, where they were assured that the slaves' lives were in danger from the harsh treatment they had been subjected to ever since the abolition of the Atlantic slave trade had made it impossible for the African merchants to dispose of their merchandise.[44]

The colonial service also bought indentured slaves for military purposes. In spite of the measures taken by Faidherbe to reorganize the battalion of Tirailleurs Sénégalais (an infantry battalion), most of the conscripts were in fact young slaves who had been purchased and were enlisted for fourteen years in the French army. They were given an intensive military training and were subsequently used during the conquest of French West Africa and Madagascar.

With the adoption of this system by the Europeans soon after the official abolition of the Atlantic slave trade, the purveyors of slaves were given a new incentive to resort to 'every immoral and criminal method of procuring slaves'.[45] The indenture system thus led to a revival of 'surprise raids, kidnappings, plundering and war'[46] in the French and British possessions, just as there had been in the heyday of the Atlantic trade. What was even more serious, the number of slaves taken in by the French and British authorities was minute in comparison with the vast numbers that were offered for sale. In 1845, Breghost de Polignac estimated that 60,000 slaves were put up for sale in the various markets in Upper Senegal/Niger. France's average annual purchases barely exceeded 500. Thus even if this institution potentially saved a few hundred lives, it nevertheless had an extremely prejudicial effect on the hinterland peoples who carried on waging war as a veritable industry. The prevailing insecurity was obviously incompatible with the development of a modern economy.

By 1830 the agricultural resettlement schemes had come to grief. It was suggested that the system be suppressed to put an end to abusive practices. It was thought that when the order abolishing it became known inland, the caravans which would periodically make their way to the trading posts would no longer have any slaves to sell, and the hinterland peoples would cease trading in slaves and turn to other occupations.[47] In 1844 France abolished the indenture system but allowed the colonial administration to carry on buying slaves to swell the ranks of the African battalion.[48] In spite of the precautions taken by the administration to restrict conscription to the numbers strictly required to organize the black troops for the defence and security of the colony, the internal traffic continued to be plied as briskly as before as long as there was some market for at least part of its merchandise. What could not be sold to the Europeans automatically reverted to the category to be put up for sale on the various market-places, to supply the African domestic market. The result was a net increase in the number of ordinary slaves.

The difficulty of finding markets for their trade slaves led some of the African merchants to seek new occupations. Some sought to compensate for the loss of the enormous profits they had earned with the slave trade by going into agriculture. The Sarakole forsook the slave trade for the cattle trade, while the Hausa and Yoruba increasingly devoted themselves to trade in palm oil.

These new ventures meant that the hinterland peoples were at last able to take part in the economic revolution that Europe sought to stimulate in Africa for the benefit of its own captains of industry.

The overall result was a metamorphosis in the outlook of the chiefs in the years following the abolition of the indenture system. Realizing that there would no longer be a market for their slaves, they encouraged their subjects to devote their energy to the production of export crops which would be the only way of procuring European goods. In 1858, one of the hinterland chiefs declared that he had had no slaves to sell since the demand for them had ceased. He now employed them in ground-nut plantations, which was far more lucrative.[49]

With the increased production of lawful export goods, the domestic slave trade progressively declined. The new farmers, who had an ample, assured supply of servile labour in the shape of their household slaves, were quite capable of doing without ordinary slaves, who were always tempted to escape. As the colonial conquest progressed, the internal slave trade lost its vitality.

To give weight to their campaign against slavery, the colonial authorities sought the support of the hinterland chiefs. Each time a trade treaty was concluded with the native leaders, the Africans had to commit themselves to ceasing all slave traffic. Faidherbe adopted this policy in all his dealings with the Senegambian chiefs. The treaties provided that never again would they sell free subjects, nor allow raiding parties to destroy villages, nor capture and enslave foreigners travelling through their lands.[50] But the mere fact of signing the treaties did not mean that the slave trade simply vanished. Only those who had found a suitable substitute really gave it up. The development of export crops alone provided 'a means of alleviating and then gradually eliminating this noxious trade'.[51]

The European authorities were quick to grasp the situation. To begin with they were careful to be extremely tactful with the chiefs over the thorny issue of slavery. Their courts only tried cases of slavery committed by European citizens in the European possessions. In the occupied territories, colonial authorities and African chiefs co-operated to combat the slave trade until its final extinction. In 1892, the governor of the French possessions took a wise decision on slavery: he made all the African chiefs in these territories sign an agreement whereby they agreed to prevent slave traffic in the territories ruled over by them. Ordinary slaves who in principle could be sold out of hand were now given the same privileges as household slaves, who as time went on came to be regarded more as servants than as slaves.[52]

Their subjects did, however, retain the right to buy slaves from foreigners. It was deemed preferable to 'admit slaves from distant, barbaric lands into the homes of people who [53] agreed to treat them as servants, rather than leave them in the hands of people who would truly treat them as slaves'.[54]

As can be seen, the main object was to weaken the internal slave trade. The African chiefs still practised it, to be sure, but less ostentatiously. Some of them, claiming to apply the provisions of the agreement, would confiscate the caravans passing through their territory and keep them for themselves. Caravan drivers would refuse to go through areas where their slaves might be arbitrarily seized at the whim of a chief.[55] They would only move when it was dark.

Because of all the inherent risks, after 1893 it was more often children who fell prey to the slave-traders. Slaves freed by the colonial authorities were kept in 'free' villages where the authorities could requisition them at any time for head porterage.

As from 1898, with their supremacy firmly established, the colonial authorities increased their coercive measures against the African slave-dealers. The definitive abolition of the internal slave trade compelled the Africans to turn to agriculture. Around 1900, numerous directives were issued with a view to ending the slave trade once and for all. For example, a circular promulgated that year provided that 'all caravans of slaves intended for sale, from any part of the colony, should, on being reported, be immediately put under arrest'.[56] The slaves should be freed an placed in free villages, the slave-owner given a penalty of fifteen days' imprisonment and a one hundred franc fine per slave, and his merchandise confiscated.[57]

At the beginning of the twentieth century the slave trade was still practised. But by and large it had declined substantially, owing to the strict application of the administrative directives. In 1905, the Governor-General of French West Africa prohibited all purchase of slaves. In spite of severe sanctions, some Africans continued to derive the greater part of their income from this traffic. Slaves were as a rule exchanged for cattle.[58] But transactions were becoming difficult or even impossible because of the precautions the African traders had to take, and especially because of the scarcity of prospective buyers who were disinclined to run the risk of being involved in illicit dealings, or took advantage of the situation by forcing the sellers to do business at absurdly low prices under threat of denunciation.[59] Although it was an undeniable fact that the slave trade still existed, all the reports by colonial authorities at the beginning of the twentieth century stated that it was no longer the powerful institution it had been. There was a period of calm in internecine conflicts following the colonial conquest. The modernization of the economy meant that recourse to slave labour was increasingly hazardous. It could legitimately he hoped that the domestic slave trade would eventually die a natural death. But the slave trade is an institution that dies hard. It persisted on the African continent for more than a century after the abolition of the Atlantic slave trade.

Notes

1. G. Hardy, *Histoire Sociale de la Colonization Française*, p. 69, Paris, Larose, 1953.
2. James Pope Hennessy, *La Traite des Noirs à Travers l'Atlantique 1441–1807*, p. 37, Paris, Fayard, 1969.
3. Edrisi, *Description de l'Afrique et de l'Espagne*, p. 90, trans. by Dozy and Goeje, Leyden, 1866.
4. Edrisi, op. cit., p. 9.
5. Mungo Park, *Travel in the Interior Districts of Africa in the Years 1795–1777*, p. 433, London, 1800.

6. J. B. Gaby, *Relation de la Nigritie Contenant une Exacte Description de ses Royaumes*, p. 49, Paris, 1689.
7. Binger, *Esclavage, Islamisme et Christianisme*, p. 17, Paris, 1889.
8. Champagne and Olivier, *Le Voyage de la Jeunesse dans les Quatre Parties du Monde*, p. 396, Paris, 1882.
9. Archives Nationales, C.6 14—*Delacombe à Messieurs de la Compagnie*, 3 June 1754.
10. Champagne et Olivier, op. cit., p. 396.
11. Park, op. cit., p. 37, 38.
12. Pruneau de Pommegorge, *Description de la Nigritie*, p. 76, Amsterdam, 1789.
13. ibid., p. 76.
14. ibid., p. 76.
15. Park, op. cit., p. 383.
16. Pruneau de Pommegorge, op. cit., p. 76.
17. Park, op. cit., p. 433.
18. ibid., p. 433.
19. ibid., p. 377.
20. ibid., p. 287.
21. ibid., p. 37.
22. Stanley, *Through the Dark Continent*, 1878.
23. Park, op. cit., p. 493.
24. Frey, *Campagne dans le Haut-Sénégal et le Haut-Niger*, p. 134, 135, Paris, 1889.
25. Pruneau de Pommegorge, op. cit., p. 103.
26. Park, op. cit., p. 37.
27. R. Coupland, *The Slave Trade and the Scramble*, p. 136, London, 1968.
28. Lacourbe, *Premier Voyage du Sieur Lacourbe Fait à la Côte d'Afrique en 1686*, p. 126, Paris, 1913.
29. Pruneau de Pommegorge, op. cit., p. 17.
30. Pelletan, *Mémoire sur la Colonie du Sénégal*, p. 99, Paris, An X (1801).
31. Archives Nationales du Sénégal, K 17, Poulet's report on domestic slavery in French West Africa, 1905.
32. Jonghe (ed.), *Les Formes d'Asservissement dans les Sociétés Indigènes du Congo-Belge*, p. 79, Brussels, 1959.
33. ibid., p. 80.
34. J. H. Saint-Père, 'Les Saracollés du Guidimakha', *BCEHS*, p. 24, A.O.F.
35. ibid., p. 24.
36. Archives Nationales du Sénégal, K 18, Commandant Poder's report, p. 6.
37. Archives Nationales du Sénégal, 13 g. 195, Commandant Bakel's report on slavery.
38. Archives Nationales du Sénégal, K 27, Report on slavery by the President of Tut, 1902.
39. Archives Nationales du Sénégal, 1 g. 283, Chauchon, Report on the area of Nioro du Rip, 1901.
40. Arch. Rég. Sénégal, K 8, Breghost de Polignac's report on slavery, 22 January 1844.
41. ibid.
42. Raffenel, *Nouveau Voyage au Pays des Nègres*, Vol. II, p. 67, Paris, 1856.
43. Schefer, *Instructions Données aux Gouverneurs de 1763 à 1870*, Vol. I, p. 228, 229.
44. ibid., Vol. I, p. 363.
45. Arch. Françaises d'Outre-Mer-Sénégal, XIV-18, Report by Under-Secretary of State for Colonies on temporary recruits.
46. ibid.
47. Archives Nationales du Sénégal, 3 E 17, Governor Bouet's report on the indenture system, 16 January 1844, in privy council meeting.

48. Archives Nationales du Sénégal, op. cit.
49. Faidherbe, Le Sénégal, *La France en Afrique Occidentale*, p. 383.
50. Annales Sénégalaises de 1854 à 1885, p. 407, Paris, 1885.
51. Archives Nationales du Sénégal, 2846 Folio 122, Brière de l'Isle to the Minister of the Navy and Colonies, Anon, 1878.
52. Archives Nationales du Sénégal, K 18, Agreement of 2 December 1892 between chiefs and the governor.
53. ibid.
54. ibid.
55. Archives Nationales du Sénégal, K 13, Letter from Mody Ndiaye to the Governor, 9 January 1893.
56. Archives Nationales du Sénégal, K 16, W. Ponty, Circular to area commandants of Senegambia-Niger, 18 October 1900.
57. ibid.
58. Archives Nationales du Sénégal, K 18, Report by Commandant of Kaolack on slavery.
59. Archives Nationales du Sénégal, K 18, Report by Commandant of Tivaouane area on slavery.

Bibliography

ANENE, J. C. *Slavery and Slave Trade in Africa in the XIX and XX Centuries*. Ibadan University Press, 1962.

CHAMPAGNE AND OLIVIER. *Le Voyage de la Jeunesse dans les Quatre Parties du Monde*. Paris, 1882.

DUIGNAN AND CLENDENEN, C. *The U.S.A. and the African Slave Trade 1619–1862*. Stanford, Calif, Hoover Institution Studies, 1963. 72 p.

DURAND, J. B. L. *Voyage au Sénégal ou Mélanges sur les Découvertes, les Établissements et le Commerce Européen*. Paris, Agasse, 1802–1807. 3 vols. 360, 384 and 67 p.

EDWARDS, B. *History of the West Indies*. Stockdale, 1794. (2 vols.)

GABY, J. B. *Relation de la Nigritie Contenant une Exacte Description de ses Royaumes et de leurs Gouvernements*. Paris, Couterot, 1689. 91 p.

GOLBERRY, S. *Fragments d'un Voyage en Afrique Fait Pendant les Années 1785, 1786, 787*. Paris, Treutel, An X (1801). 2 vols. 512 and 523 p.

KAY, G. *La Traite des Noirs*. Paris, Laffont, 1968. 287 p.

LAMIRAL. *L'Afrique et le Peuple Africain*. Paris, 1789.

PARK, Mungo. *Travels in the Interior Districts of Africa in the Years 1795–1797*. London, Bulmer, 1800. 551 p.

POMMEGORGE, P. de. *Description de la Nigritie*. Amsterdam, 1789.

SAUGNIER. *Relations de Plusieurs Voyages à la Côte d'Afrique, au Maroc, au Sénégal, à Gorée, à Galam*. Paris, Gueffier Jeune, 1791. 341 p.

LA VALLEE, C. *Journal de la Traite des Noirs*. Comments by J. Mousnier. Paris, Éditions de Paris, 1957.

WILLIAMS, E. *Capitalisme et Esclavage*, Paris, Présence Africaine, 1964. 355 p.

The slave trade and the population drain from Black Africa to North Africa and the Middle East

I. B. Kake

It has been customary for historians to study the phenomenon of the slave trade in the perspective of America and the West Indies only. Yet long before Europeans began trading in slaves, the peoples of North Africa and the Middle East had been transferring black populations to their countries.

The slave trade in that part of the world goes back to antiquity, but it was from the fifteenth to the end of the nineteenth century that it was developed on a particularly large scale.

What routes were used to bring the black slaves back? Who organized the expeditions? Where did the slaves come from? Where did they go to? How did they travel? What fate awaited them at their destination?

Attitude of Islam to slavery

Islam, like Christianity, did not do away with slavery but tempered it. Mohammad accepted the Arabs of his time as they were. The Koran, while acknowledging bondservice as an established fact, sought to alleviate its conditions and possibly to prepare the way for its disappearance. To free a slave, says the Book in many of its verses, is one of the most laudable acts a Believer can perform, worthy enough to merit redemption of one's sins. To enslave a Muslim against his will is an offence against God. According to the *shari'ah*, prostitution of captives or even trading in them for purely lucrative ends is no less reprehensible: 'the worst of men is he who sells men,' said the prophet Mohammad, who appointed one freed slave, the Ethiopian, Bilal, to the much-coveted position of Muezzin, and another to the commander of an army.

During his lifetime Othman, the third Caliph, bought 2,400 captives for the sole purpose of setting them free, and was highly praised by the devout for doing so.[1]

Only non-Muslims could be taken as slaves. In practice, it was not easy to make the distinction. After the celebrated Battle of Tondibi, the Moroccans, having defeated the Songhai, took back with them forty camel-loads of gold-dust and 1,200 prisoners. One of them, Ahmed Baba, a famous jurisconsult from Timbuktu rose up in the name of Islamic law and even had the audacity to demand an explanation from the Sultan, who eventually freed him.

In 1611, Ahmed Baba was approached by his admirers from the region of Tuat. They were appalled by the enormous consignments of 'ebony' passing through their oases, and spoke to him of their misgivings.[2]

Could one be involved in this kind of traffic without putting one's soul in peril? In the Sudan, they knew, there were many Muslims; was it not to be feared that there might be some 'brothers' among those poor wretches torn from their families?

In reply to these questions, Ahmed Baba drew up a treatise entitled *Frame-work for an Appreciation of the Legal Position of Sudanese Taken as Slaves*. It contains a wealth of quotations, good intentions, and reservations, and in it the Sudanese jurisconsult declares that although it is difficult to distinguish Muslims from non-Muslims, it is nonetheless a crime for a Muslim to buy a Muslim. Slavery, he goes on to say, is admissible in the context of the Holy War if the slaves are non-Muslim, but the forms must be respected. First, pagans must be called upon to embrace the Muslim religion. If they refuse, they have the option of paying capitation, in exchange for which they are allowed to keep their religion. Only if they refuse to comply with either of these alternatives can they be taken as slaves.

It can be seen that the attitude of Islam to slavery and the slave trade was, like that of Christianity, not very clear. Without going as far as Berlioux, who maintained that to abolish slavery and the slave trade the Koran would have to be torn up,[3] one is forced to face the fact that the Eastern slave trade was carried on solely by the Muslims of the Maghreb and the Middle East.

Routes used to bring the black slaves back

Let us now look at the great routes along which The consignments of 'ebony' were, for centuries, brought back to the Muslim countries via the same trade routes as the other commodities (gold, ivory, etc.) that took the Muslims to Nigritia. Four main routes were followed: the West–East route, from the Maghreb to Western Sudan; from Tripolitania to Central Sudan; from Egypt to the Upper Nile; and from the Middle East—Egypt to Waday-Darfur. Each of these routes had its 'golden age' in the history of the slave trade.

Marcel Emerit has attempted to describe some of these overland routes.[4]

Every two or three years, he writes, a great caravan would leave the Wad Noun for Timbuktu, bearing a cargo of woollen or silk bands, spices and incense. From the Wad Noun it took seven days to reach Seguiet el Haura, a large river that flows into the ocean. Then for three days it would follow its tributary, the River Butana. After another seven days it reached Ouadane. From Ouadane some caravans went on to Senegal by a relatively easy route.

Those caravans going to Timbuktu, took twelve days to reach Tichitt, and another twenty days marching eastwards, to get to Araouan, whence they made their way to Timbuktu. In 1591, it took Pjouder's troops fifty days to go from Wad Noun to Timbuktu.

In the sixteenth century and throughout the period of the Gaoan Empire, the flow of caravan traffic from the West was considerable. It helped to increase the circulation of gold in North Africa and thereby indirectly aided the development of the Barber towns. But by the eighteenth century it had declined considerably.

The central route started from an area extending roughly from Lake Chad to Hausa territory. The slaves were taken northwards via Zinder and Agades. It was a twenty-five-day journey on foot to Ghat.

The caravans, including those bringing slaves from Darfur, would converge on the Fezzan. They were then taken over by the Tuaregs and were either taken off to Tripolitania via Marzuq, or to Ghudamis via Ghat.

At Ghudamis, another staging point, the caravans split up, some bound for Morocco and others for Tunisia. From Kano to Tunis, changing masters at each main halt, the black slaves would cover a distance of 3,000 kilometres on foot, and in what a climate! That hundreds survived the journey at all is to be wondered. For some the adventure was not yet over. From Tunis, or from Tripoli, they were dispatched to the Levant and sold for the fourth or fifth time.

In the East the main centres were Zanzibar and Kilwa, which in the nineteenth century were the principal suppliers of slaves to the Middle East. In March 1826, Ali Khûrshîd Aghâ was appointed Governor of the province of Sennar by the Egyptian authorities; in his 'reign', slave trading became a seasonal and well-organized government activity. Using the thin pretext of military manœuvres, his troops raided the Dinka, Ingassawa and Shilluk tribes and marched them off down river.

Subsequently, in 1870, Zobeir, a notorious slave trader, was appointed Governor of the province of Bahr-el-Ghazâl and devastated both Darfur and Kordofan.

The volume and magnitude of the slave trade greatly increased after 1840 when Sa'id (Ibn Sultan), ruler of Muscat, moved permanently to Zanzibar. He introduced the clove to Zanzibar, and large plantations were developed which demanded a substantial labour force. A third reason for the increase in the slave trade was the instability of the hinterland, which made it easy for the Arabs to side with one or other faction against another and to use the prisoners taken during these internecine conflicts to augment their trade.

The decisive factor in the Arab slave raids was their ample supply of fire-arms, which enabled men like Tippoo Tib to muster well-trained raiding parties against which the bows and arrows of the hinterland tribes were powerless.

The major centres of the slave trade on the coast were Malindi, Mombasa, Tanga, Pemba, Zanzibar, Kilwa and Bagamoyo. Although the latter had become an important terminus by the middle of the nineteenth century, Zanzibar still remained the nerve centre of the trade. Hence the truth of the saying 'When you pipe in Zanzibar, they dance at the lakes.'

Norman R. Bennet mentions three main routes of trade penetration in the nineteenth century:[5] the first, based on Kilwa, extended to the area around and beyond Lake Nyasa. All along this route, the Yao tribe procured slaves for the Arab traders; the second route began at Bagamoyo, opposite Zanzibar, passed through Tabora and the land of the Nyamwezi, and then went on to Ujiji, across Lake Tanganyika and into the interior of the Congo; and the third itinerary began at such ports as Pangani, Tanga and Mombasa, passing by Mount Kilimanjaro across Masai territory to the eastern shores of Lake Victoria.

With the expansion of the slave trade, centres like Ujiji and Tabora became the outposts of the trade, and tribes like the Yao, the Nyamwezi and the Ganda became the sorry intermediaries in that ignoble commerce.

The Arab traders penetrated deep into the Congo and even Angola, according to accounts in 1852 by Portuguese officials who had come in contact with them. Some authors report that up to 10,000 slaves were being sold annually at Kilwa and Zanzibar around 1810, whereas by the 1860s the figure had risen to 70,000 for Zanzibar alone.

The best example of the popular image of the ruthless slave-trader was Tippoo Tib, who ruled supreme in the Congo basin during the last quarter of the nineteenth century. This skilful trader raised a private army, establishing his base first at Ujiji, then moving to Kasongo, Kibonge and Ribariba. His empire stretched from Lake Tanganyika to the Ituri forest and into the Congo basin as far as Basoko. He met and assisted a number of explorers such as Livingstone, Stanley, Wissman and Junker. For a time his position was legalized by the Belgian authorities, who appointed him Governor of the Falls region in the Congo Free State. But he represented such a threat that they took up arms against him, defeating his son Sefu and nephew Rashid in 1893 during the Arab War of 1892–94. Tippoo Tib withdrew to Zanzibar, where he wrote his autobiography in Swahili.

Another *condottiere* of the same ilk was Râbih Ibn Abdullah, who dominated the Chad region between 1892 and 1900. He controlled Bagirmi, Bornu, Kanem, Tibesti and the regions of Borku and Waday. Most of the slaves sold by Râbih were brought from Dâr Fartît, on the northern frontier of the present-day People's Republic of the Congo. Like Tippoo Tib, he clashed with European interests. He was killed in 1900, fighting the French troops at Kousseri in the Baguirmi region west of Lake Chad.

The slave trade in Central and East Africa was thus mainly in the hands of the Arabs, who between 1840 and the turn of the century transformed it into a ruthless, flourishing and well-organized business.

Travel conditions and slave markets

During these voyages, the slaves were treated with great cruelty by the Muslim traders. The *ghellabis* (slave-traders) were utterly inhuman, with more regard for their camels than for their black slaves.

Since the camels in the caravans were heavily loaded with their cargoes of water, gum arabic, elephant tusks, etc., all the black slaves, with the exception of children under the age of 10 or 12 had to follow on foot. Any who lagged behind from sheer exhaustion were goaded on by the *ghellabis* with a whip or *kurbash*.

The caravan would usually set off at dawn and not halt until evening. Water was parsimoniously rationed out, and the wretched slaves would often drink only once a day. They died more from thirst than exhaustion. Berlioux recounts the horror of those desert crossings:

Only by seeing the caravans in the immense solitude of the desert can one imagine how much the heat and the privations must have added to the suffering of those slaves newly deprived of their freedom. . . . Along that interminable route there are a few oases, but sometimes there is nothing but stark desert for several days on end. This is where the slave caravans suffer their greatest losses, not only from exhaustion, but because the slave-traders prefer to economize their provisions rather than save the lives of a few of these poor wretches.[6]

Those who were shipped off to be sold in Arabia or the Persian Gulf Emirates were scarcely better off. They were transported in boats known as dhows. Dhows were usually fairly small, and since they had to cater for a relatively heavy traffic, the slaves were packed into them and made the journey in extremely arduous conditions.

When merchants spoke of the arrival of a caravan, they would assess its size by the number of heads, amking no distinction between camels and slaves. The leader of the caravan used the same expressions to goad on the slaves as the camels.

When a Turk bought a black slave, Frédéric Cailliaud wrote, he would have him circumcised and then choose some bizarre name for him, for fear of giving him a name that a man might bear.[7]

Slaves, when not captured during raids, were acquired at markets specializing in the trade. Some of these were to be found in Black Africa, like the one at Kuka (a town in the Chad region), whose slave market was described by many European travellers in the nineteenth century.

Throughout the year it would be teeming with unfortunate creatures of

all ages and origins—old men, white-haired old women, babies, sturdy ado-
lescents—from Bornu, Bagirmi or Waday, in other words from all the neighbouring regions. It was a wholesale market, and the buyers were chiefly dealers
working for the export market. In the Maghreb, as we shall see, were the retail
markets where the slaves would be sold to private customers.

The difference between the two kinds of sales point was the same as the
difference between a factory warehouse and a department store. The former
was for the knowledgeable and contained nothing but great piles of merchandise,
whereas the latter was dressed up and embellished with all sorts of decorations
in order to attract the public.

In the wholesale markets, the merchandise was displayed in all its sorry
ugliness. The slaves were dirty and clothed in rags. The dealers examined them,
measured them, opened their mouths to look at their teeth, and inquired after
their appetite, for this was regarded as a sign of health.

At the end of the nineteenth century, a young boy was worth 15 to 30 thalers,[8] a girl between 30 and 60 thalers and an old man or a mother between
3 and 10 thalers.

Once they reached the Maghreb or the East, the slaves were first cleaned,
then put up for sale on the market-place. The sales procedure here was rather
more elaborate than at Kuka. In the Fez and Marrakesh markets, public sales
were held three times a week. The prospective customers would be sitting around
the small square on their haunches, waiting for the human merchandise to
arrive. When it did, the *dellal* (town crier) would lead each slave from group
to group, crying out his price. Potential buyers would ask questions, inquiring
about the poor creature's age, antecedents and the various prices he had fetched;
they would touch him and prod him as though he were a horse or a mule. And
when at last, after much discussion and inspection, the deal was concluded,
the purchaser, the *dellal* and the slave would go to the *adoul*, or notary, who
ratified the sale and made out the official deed.

The slave always had with him a sort of identity document giving his
origins, his service record and the successive prices paid for him. Only one or
two lines had to be added to record his entry into a new household. The sale
of a beast of burden or a draught animal would have been no different, apart
from the fact that the man had papers, the animal did not.

The number of Africans transferred from Nigritia
to the Muslim countries

It is not easy to set a precise figure on the drain represented by this traffic,
but an average of 20,000 a year seems a probable figure for the centuries
during which the Muslim slave trade was at its height.[9]

By way of hypothesis, Raymond Mauvy estimates that 100,000 black slaves were taken to the Muslim world in the seventh century, 200,000 in the eighth, 400,000 in the ninth, 500,000 in each of the tenth to the thirteenth centuries, 1 million in the fourteenth, 2 million in each century from the fifteenth to the nineteenth inclusive, and 300,000 in the twentieth century, making a total of 14 million altogether. These are provisional figures pending more detailed studies, which in fact will only be possible for the nineteenth and twentieth centuries.

The Arabs kept no official record of the numbers, nor did they write about their own slave trade as some European authors wrote about the Atlantic slave trade. In any general history of the black slave trade, the role of the Muslims cannot be ignored. Their trade, however, appears to have been on a smaller scale than that of the Europeans, although it lasted longer; indeed some of its consequences are still apparent in the Middle East to this day.

Although the conditions in which the slaves were captured and carried off to the Muslim countries were particularly atrocious, the treatment which the survivors of the desert crossing received on arrival was on the whole reasonably tolerable.

Treatment of black slaves in the Muslim world

The living conditions of black slaves in the Muslim world varied according to their sex and the country in which they were to live.

By and large, women were better treated than men. Those who were not admitted to the dignity of favourites became servants in the harems and resignedly submitted to the whims of the wives.

The brothers Jérôme and Jean Tharaud have left us some picturesque descriptions of the different functions of black women in Morocco.

In Morocco, there is the bedchamber negress, who is more inclined to admire her master; what the Fassi (inhabitant of Fez) likes about his negresses is that their skin is supposed to be warmer than that of white women. And for a Moroccan, every ailment comes from the cold, whereas all healing is the result of heat.

Next to the bedchamber negresses is a category of slave known as the *dada*, or wet-nurse, a person of great importance, a despot even. Finally, there is the dowry slave-girl; when a girl marries, her husband has to give her a slave, who is her mistress's go-between for messages or gifts.[10]

Negresses were sought after by the Moroccans not only as concubines, but also as wives, on a par with white women. This explains the large number of mulattos of every shade in Morocco today. Edmondo de Amicis remarks:

Curious twists of fate! A poor ten-year-old black boy, sold at the confines of the Sahara for a bag of sugar or a piece of cloth, can, if fate is kind to him, find himself

30 years later a Minister of Morocco discussing a trade treaty with the British Ambassador, or, even more likely, the little black girl, born in a filthy hovel and exchanged in the shade of an oasis for a skin of eau de vie, can find herself while still almost a child, bedecked with jewels and richly perfumed, in the arms of the Sultan.[11]

In any case, in Muslim countries the Negress was regarded as an object of pleasure. She was also a musician and a highly esteemed cook.

The fate of the men, with a few individual exceptions, was less enviable. Madame Valensi, in her study of the black slaves living in Tunisia in the nineteenth century, observes that their condition was lowly.[12] There are no known cases of social ascension among them. Some did become saints, and their miracles are reported in the hagiography; but here there was no escape from slavery, no hope of ever being redeemed or repatriated.

At best, they were freed, mainly on the death of their owner. In this way blacks could put down new roots in Tunisia and, before slavery was abolished, merge with the Tunisian population and even own property. But their status was always one of inferiority.

At times even black slaves had to endure hardships reminiscent of those suffered by their brothers in misfortune on the plantations of tropical America.

According to G. Mouette, the black slaves in Morocco during the reign of the Sultan Mouley Archy (eighteenth century) were very badly off.[13] They were put to death for the slightest mistake. The workshops were full of them, in irons and covered in wounds.

But the fate of the eunuch slaves was even worse. At the end of the nineteenth century, there was still a vast establishment at Messfoua (Morocco) preparing eunuchs for the Sultan. Eight out of ten of those who were operated on died. Léon Frank records that between 100 and 200 men were turned into eunuchs annually at Abu Tig, a small town in Upper Egypt.[14]

One of the last bastions of black slavery in the Muslim world was the army. From the earliest days of the Hegira, Islam employed what Mangin calls the 'black force'.[15]

'Amr', the second Caliph's lieutenant, conquered Egypt and Nubia and there raised black troops. It was these troops that were the backbone of the army which invaded North Africa. It was this force that provided the sovereigns of Spain and the Maghreb with the disciplined, loyal and brave element which their armies lacked. In the eighth century, the Omayyad Caliph Adb-ar-Rhaman I (755–87), founder of the Caliphate of Spain, rescued the Spanish peninsula from anarchy with the help of a 40,000-strong black army. The last of the sovereigns of this dynasty also had many blacks brought from the interior of Africa and shaped them into a formidable cavalry corps.

The ostentatious Harun Al-Rashid himself bought a great number of black slaves, whom he armed. In Egypt, the Tulunids and later the Fatimites had black troops.

The role of the black force during the Crusades is a subject that remains to be studied; it must have been an important one and no doubt accounts for the tenacity of Islam.[16]

The black slaves imported into the Maghreb as a result of this flourishing trade were used as guards and soldiers.

The Moroccan Sultan Moulay Ismail (1647–1727) called upon blacks not only for a bodyguard of unswerving loyalty but also to form a large standing army; he also gave them a political role of the highest importance throughout his realm by establishing military colonies.[17] The Turks had done the same before him, when they created at different points groups of auxiliaries who were known as *abids* (slaves) when they belonged to the black race.

Mulay Ismail gathered together, through purchase, tribute or war contribution, all the black slaves in the country, a huge operation that was not conducted without difficulty, particularly in Fez. His nephew Abhed, Governor of Draa, led an expedition as far as the Sudan, bringing back a large number of slaves. He provided them all with wives, then settled them in vast agri cultural colonies established at selected points, such as road junctions or in the middle of turbulent tribes. The Sultan raised a black army under the patronage of an Islamic saint, Sidi el Boukhari.

Ez Ziani, who held an important post at the Sharifian court at the beginning of the nineteenth century, tells us that at the end of Moulay Ismail's reign, 150,000 *abids* were on the army lists. It was these troops who defended Morocco's independence against the Spaniards and the Turks. And after the death of the founder of their corps they were to become king-makers.

Conclusion

All in all, the Muslims, as well as the Christians, contributed through the slave trade to the spreading of the black race beyond its original frontiers.

The Saharan oases and the southern confines of the Maghreb are largely populated by blacks, who constitute a quarter of the population of southern Tunisia, three-quarters of the inhabitants of the Draa valley, and almost the entire population of the Fezzan.

In the Maghreb and in Egypt, negroid types are not unusual. In Arabia there is still a faily strong element of black blood among the coastal population. As noted earlier, the black question is not often spoken of in the Muslim world. This is due primarily to the fact that the black slaves were not confined to ghettos as they were in America; more often than not they mingled with the white families, the black servants living under the same roof as their masters. However, in spite of their integration into social life, the black is still a second-class citizen in the Muslim countries.

No one has summed up the problem of Arab–Black relations better than the Egyptian historian Samir Zoghby:

An abscess can lead to blood poisoning. It may also develop into gangrene which may require amputation of a limb. Yet, if treated surgically it will probably leave an ugly scar and the memory of a throbbing pain. Such have been Arab relations with Black Africa. The past brings forth the ugly image of the Arab slave-trader which mars the present and strains the dialogue, creating awkward moments of embarrassment.[18]

This article should be seen as an attempt to lance the abscess, to open a dialogue and to plan for the future in full awareness of the past.

Notes

1. André Falk, *Visa pour l'Arabie*, p. 169, Paris, Gallimard, 1958.
2. E. Zeys, 'Esclavage et Guerre Sainte', consultation d'Ahmed Baba aux Gens du Touat, XVème Siècle, *Bulletin de la Réunion d'Études Algériennes*, 1900.
3. E. Berlioux, *La Traite Orientale, Histoire des Chasses à l'Homme Organisées en Afrique*, Paris, Guillaumin, 1870.
4. M. Emerit, *Les Liaisons Terrestres entre le Soudan et l'Afrique du Nord au XVIIIème et au Début du XIXème Siècle*, Algiers, 1954.
5. Norman R. Bennet, 'Christian and Negro Slavery in Eighteenth Century North Africa', *Journal of African History*, 1960.
6. Berlioux, op. cit.
7. Frédéric Cailliaud, *Voyage à Méroé, au Fleuve Blanc*, Paris, 1826.
8. 1 thaler = 3.75 francs.
9. Raymond Mauvy, *Les Siècles Obscurs de l'Afrique Noire*, Paris, Fayard, 1970.
10. Jérôme and Jean Tharaud, *Fès ou les Bourgeois de l'Islam*.
11. Edmondo de Amicis, *Le Maroc*, p. 323, trans. from the Italian by Henri Belle, Paris, Hachette, 1882.
12. L. Valensi, Esclaves Chrétiens et Esclaves Noirs à Tunis', *Annales-Economies-Sociétés*, November/December 1967.
13. G. Mouette, *Histoire des Conquestes de Mouley Archy, Connu sous le Nom de Roy de Talifet*, p. 407.
14. Dr Louis Frank, *Collection d'Opuscules de Médecine Pratique avec un Mémoire sur le Commerce des Nègres au Kaire*, p. 202, Paris, 1812.
15. Charles Mangia, *La Force Noire*, Paris, Hachette, 1910, 355 p.
16. See Crusade Historians, *Historiens Orientaux*, Vol. IV, p. 147–8.
17. See Magali Morsy, Moulay Ismail et l'Armée de Métier, *Revue d'Histoire Moderne Contemporaine*, April–June 1967.
18. Samir M. Zoghby, 'Blacks and Arabs: Past and Present', *Current Bibliography on African Affairs*, Vol. 3, No. 5, May 1970.

Bibliography

North Africa and Egypt

BRAITHWAITE, John. *History of the Revolutions in the Empire of Morocco Upon the Death of the Late Emperor Muley Ishmael*. London, J. Darby Brown, 1729. 381 p.

BUSNOT, Père Dominique. *Histoire du Règne de Mouley Ismaël, Roy de Maroc, Fez, Tafilet, Souz, etc.* Rouen, G. Behourt, 1714. 254 p.

FRANK, Louis. *Mémoire sur le Commerce des Nègres au Kaire et sur les Maladies auxquelles Ils Sont en y Arrivant.* Paris, A. Koenig, 1802. 52 p.

HEYD, Wilhelm. *Histoire du Commerce du Levant au Moyen-Age.* Vol. II. French ed., recast and considerably expanded by the author. Leipzig, Furey Raynaud, 1885–86.

JACKSON, James Grey. *An Account of the Empire of Morocco and the District of Suse. To which is Added an Account of Timbuctoo.* London, G. W. Niiob, 1809. 288 p.

KHALDOUN, Ibn. *Histoire de l'Afrique sous la Dynastie des Aghlabites et de la Sicile sous la Dynastie Musulmane.* Paris, Imp. de Firmin-Didot Frères, 1841. 80 p.

DE LAFOSSE, M. Les Débuts des Troupes Noires au Maroc. *Hesperis.* 1st quarter, 1923, p. 1–12.

LEVTZION, Nehemia. *Ancient Ghana and Mali.* London, Methuen & Co., 1973. 283 p.

MORSY-MAGALY, Mouslay Ismaël et l'Armée de Métier. *Revue d'Histoire Moderne et Contemporaine,* Vol. XIV, June 1967.

MOUETTE, Germain. *Histoire des Conquestes de Mouley Archy, Connu sous le Nom de Roy de Talifet; et de Mouley Ismaël ou Sméin son Frère et son Successeur à Présent Régnant, tous Deux Rois de Fez.* Paris, E. Couterot, 1683. 469 p.

PELLOW, Thomas. *The Adventures of Thomas Pellow. Three and Twenty Years in Captivity among the Moors Written by Himself,* London, 1890. 279 p.

PINGNON. L'Esclavage en Tunisie, 1930–1932. *Revue Tunisienne,* p. 18–37, 345–77.

RENAUT, François. *Lavigerie, l'Esclavage Africain et l'Europe.* Paris, Éditions E. De Boccard, 1971. 2 vols.

SAMIR M. ZOGHBY. Blacks and Arabs: Past and present. *A Current Bibliography on African Affairs,* Vol. 3, No. 5, May 1970.

WESTERMARCK, E. *Ritual and Belief in Morocco.* London, Macmillan, 1926. 2 vols.

ZEYS, L. Esclavage et Guerre Sainte, Consultation Adressée aux Gens de Touat par un Érudit Nègre de Tombouctou au XVIIᵉ Siècle.

Middle East

BERLIOUX, Étienne Félix. *La Traite Orientale, Histoire des Chasses à l'Homme Organisées en Afrique depuis Quinze Ans pour les Marchés de l'Orient.* Paris, Guillaumin, 1870. 350 p.

ELBAZ, Elie. *Le Judaïsme Noir. Essai sur les Falachas.* Paris, Sorbonne, 1974. (Mémoires de l'Histoire.)

FALK, André. *Visa pour l'Arabie.* Paris, Gallimard, 1958.

FISHER, Allan G. B.; FISHER, H. J. *Slavery in Muslim Society in Africa.* London, C. Hurst, 1971.

HARRIS, Joseph, E. *The African Presence in Asia.* Evanston, Northwestern University Press, 1971.

MANGIN, Charles. *La Force Noire.* Paris, Hachette, 1910. 355 p.

PERRON, Dr. Précis de Jurisprudence Musulmane ou Principes de Législation Musulmane Civile et Religieuse selon le Rite Halekite par Khalil Ibn Ish'Ak. Traduction, Paris 1848–1849. Réponses des Falachas dits Juifs d'Abyssinie aux Questions. Faits par M. Luzzato. (Extraits des archives israélites no. 5 du 1 avril au 15 mai 1851.)

Population movements between East Africa, the Horn of Africa and the neighbouring countries

Bethwell A. Ogot

Although the African diaspora is of global significance, very little research has been done on the African presence in the Middle East and Asia. How many Africans migrated to Saudi Arabia, Yemen, Aden, Iraq, Iran, Pakistan, India and China? What happened to them? What contributions did they make to the history and cultures of their adopted lands? These are all important questions which deserve the same serious treatment as that given to the Atlantic slave trade.

As on the west coast, the slave trade was the major cause of population movements in the Indian Ocean region. Historians still differ about the volume of the trade before the nineteenth century. Coupland in his *East Africa and Its Invaders* (1938) and *The Exploitation of East Africa 1856–1890* (1939), argued that the trade had gone on between East Africa and Asia for at least 2,000 years. During that period the theme ran 'like a scarlet thread through all the sub-sequent history of East Africa until our own day'. Millions of East Africans were shipped from the region, resulting in a general depopulation of the area. This thesis is repeated in standard school textbooks.[1]

Recently, many scholars have rejected the Coupland thesis. G. S. P. Freeman-Grenville, for example, has contended that it was only after Omani Arabs began to intervene in East African affairs in the seventeenth century that slaves were exported from the Somali region.[2] Edward Alpers goes even further and categorically states:

It is very clear that the east African slave trade as a factor of continuing historical signifance traces its roots no further than the first half of the eighteenth century. Coupland's argument that it was of continuing importance from the earliest contacts with Asia simply cannot be substantiated.[3]

While Coupland might have exaggerated the volume of the traffic in human beings and its duration, it is difficult to accept the modern revisionist theory championed by Freeman-Grenville and Alpers that it was negligible before the eighteenth century. Writing in the same book as Freeman-Grenville, Gervase Mathew shows that slaves were exported from Opone (the southern

Somali coast) to Egypt in ancient times and also that black slave soldiers from
East Africa were exported to Mesopotamia. He concludes that the slave trade
was a constant factor on the East African coast between A.D. 100 and 1498.[4]
A Chinese scholar, Tuan Ch'eng'shih, writing in the middle of the ninth century, refers to slave exports from Po-pa-li which, according to Oriental scholars
such as Fredrich Hirth, J. J. L. Duyvendak and Paul Wheatey, is in Somalia.
According to a document dated 1119, most of the wealthy families of Canton
possessed African slaves.[5] Another Chinese writer, Chan Ju-kua, makes several
references to African slaves in his work published in A.D. 1226. He asserts, for
instance, that African 'are enticed by offers of food and then caught and carried
off from Pemba for slaves to the Ta-shi [Arab] Countries, where they fetch
a high price'.[6] The Arab book *Adjaib al-Hind*, written during the latter part of
the tenth century, stated that 200 slaves were exported from East Africa to
Oman annually and that 1,000 ships from Oman were involved in the trade
with East Africa.[7] R. B. Serjeant, using the Hadrami Chronicles, also confirms
that slaves were being exported from East Africa to Arabia before the Portuguese period.[8] East African slaves were also being imported into the Persian
Gulf, especially into Bahrain, between the tenth and twelth centuries.[9] The case
of India is much clearer. Substantial numbers of African slaves were reported
by travellers in the Middle Ages to be in Gujarat and the Deccan Areas. From
1459 to 1474, King Barbuk of Bengal possessed 8,000 African slaves.[10] Mathew
has argued that most of these slaves came from the present United Republic
of Tanzania.

Slaves continued to be exported from East Africa during the Portuguese
period to Arabia and the Persian Gulf. In 1631, for example, 400 Africans from
Mombasa were shipped as slaves to the market at Mecca.[11]

It is thus clear that from at least the seventh century slaves were being
exported in small numbers from eastern Africa, stretching from Ethiopia and
Somali in the north to Mozambique in the south. They worked on the date
plantations in Basra, Bandar Abbas, Minab and along the Batinah coast;
in the pearl-diving industry in Bahrain and Lingeh on the Persian Gulf; as
slave soldiers in various parts of Arabia, Persia and India; as dock workers and
dhow crews in much of the Arab-controlled Indian Ocean; and as concubines
and domestic servants in Muslim communities throughout Asia.[12]

The African exodus to Asia and the Middle East and the presence of
Africans in the eastern world is a crucial subject which can only be understood
by paying greater attention to the pre-1800 period. What were the specifics of
the Asian economic situation which created the need for slaves? Was there any
difference in status between African and non-African slaves? How did the
Islamic ideas on the institution of slavery affect the slave trade? Why is it
that today there are few socially or culturally separate Afro-Asian communities
in Asia? What was the impact of the African presence upon the indigenous

cultures of Asia and the Middle East? These and other similar questions need to be explored.

Moving on to the nineteenth century, we find that the historians' main concern has been the volume of the slave trade. Scholars such as R. P. Baur, R. W. Beachey and Richard Rensch maintain that several millions of East Africans were sold into slavery in the nineteenth century. Baur, for instance, asserts that 30,000 slaves were exported from the East African coast annually in the 1880s.[13] Professor Beachey affirms that over 5 million east Africans were sold into slavery during the nineteenth century.[14] Three doctoral theses have recently shown that the above estimates were nothing but wild guesses.[15]

Before we can engage meaningfully in a quantitative discussion of the Indian Ocean slave trade, we should emphasize that before the nineteenth century, the majority of slaves were household servants, artisans, soldiers, sailors, common labourers and concubines. They rarely engaged in large-scale production of commodities. (The only known exceptions are the salt works of Persia in the ninth century and salt mines in the Sahara). The expansion of commerce in the late eighteenth and early nineteenth centuries gradually transformed agriculture in eastern Africa. More and more land was brought under cultivation between 1820 and 1870. Traders became farmers, and slave-traders became slave-owners. A slave system fradually emerged in East Africa, in which the ownership of the means of production—land and slaves—defined the principal social groups in society.

The development of European sugar plantations in the islands of Bourbon and Ile de France relied on slave labour. The slave population of Bourbon grew from 387 in 1808 to 30,000 in 1779 and 50,000 in 1809–10, while that of Ile de France rose from 19,000 in 1766 to 55,000 in 1809–10.[16] Most of these slaves came from Mozambique, although about a quarter of them came from Kilwa. Numerically, this slave trade to the Mascerene islands was not large, amounting to about 6,000 per year at the most. Furthermore, it was hampered by the Anglo-French rivalry, which led to the British taking the Ile de France (now renamed Mauritius), a ban on slave importation in 1821, and a treaty with the Sultan of Muscat in 1822 banning the export of slaves by Omanis to Christian nations. But Bourbon (renamed Réunion) remained in French hands and continued to receive slaves from various East African ports—Zanzibar, Mombasa, Takaungu and Lamu. Moreover, in the 1840s and 1850s the French obtained slaves from Zanzibar under the so-called 'free labour' system, according to which slaves had to sign a labour contract affirming that they were going voluntarily before their Arab masters could be paid by French agents. Soon 'free labourers' were coming from Zanzibar, Kilwa and Mozambique in large quantities.

In 1847, Seyyid Said, under strong pressure from the British, signed a treaty banning the exports of slaves beyond his dominions in East Africa. But by the 1850s and 1860s, more slaves than ever were still being exported to Arabia and the Persian Gulf. Moreover, slaves in large quantities were now needed by the expanding agricultural economy of East Africa.

Most of the successful Arab traders had decided to invest their profit in a new cash crop—cloves—which had been imported into Zanzibar from Réunion by about 1820. Between 1835 and 1845, most of the successful Omani traders became large estate owners, possessing 200–300 slaves per plantation. The large profits from the clove industry stimulated migration from Oman. According to estimates, the population of the Omanis in Zanzibar rose from 300 in 1776 to about 5,000 in 1872. In 1877 alone about 1,000 Arabs emigrated from Oman to Zanzibar. In the 1840s, clove cultivation spread to Pemba, where both Arabs and the Wapemba themselves took to it.

The clove trade was not limited to the Indian Ocean market. American and European traders took their share of cloves. For example, in 1841, American traders bought 110,200 pounds of cloves and, in 1859, 840,000 pounds. The French bought cloves worth $47,983 in 1856 and $60,000 in 1859. The British and the Germans also joined in the trade. Nevertheless, India and Arabia remained the most important consumers of Zanzibar and Pemba cloves.

The clove planters invested heavily in slaves. By 1849, Zanzibar alone was estimated to have 100,000 slaves. True, it is difficult to have any accurate population censuses at this time. Nevertheless, all estimates by contemporary observers agree that the slave population in Zanzibar had increased to over 200,000 by 1860 out of a total population of about 300,000. Most of these slaves were owned by the Omani Arabs and numbered less than 5,000.

Seyyid Said who had acquired forty-five plantations had 6,000 to 7,000 slaves on one plantation alone. Indeed, the period of large and steady clove harvests coincided with the time when the export of slaves from the interior of East Africa was greater than ever. According to Cooper, between 15,000 and 20,000 passed through Zanzibar each year. Including slaves that were sent direct to the Persian Gulf and Arabia, the slave trade of the northern section of the East African coast was in the neighbourhood of 20,000 to 25,000 slaves a year. According to Curtin, the Atlantic slave trade did not exceed this magnitude until the eighteenth century.[17]

Throughout the nineteenth century, Kilwa was the major supplier of Zanzibar slaves, drawing them from a wide area, especially from the Lake Nyasa region and northern Mozambique. The neighbouring peoples such as the Wahadimu of Zanzibar or the Mijikenda of Kenya, did not provide slaves. Perhaps the slave traders did not wish to antagonize them because of their proximity.

What kind of a plantation society emerged in East Africa? By 1860, many observers were referring to the Arabs as a landed aristocracy. But not all Arabs were planters, nor were all planters wealthy aristocracy. At the top of the hierarchy was the Sultan. Seyyid Bargash, for instance, earned $25,000 per year from his estates, which were worked by about 4,000 slaves. By 1890, he possessed 6,000 slaves. His sister, Bibi Zem Zem, owned about 600 slaves; and Seyyid Suleiman, another member of the Al-Busaidi tribe, owned over 2,000 slaves. On the whole, the largest landlords owned between 1,000 and 2,000 slaves, while the average landlord owned thirty slaves. At the bottom of the scale was the smallholder who owned one or two slaves. The important point to bear in mind therefore was that free labour was marginal to the Zanzibari economy, and on the plantations virtually all labour consisted of slaves.

By 1870, Zanzibar society had undergone a profound change. The plantation had become important as an investment and as a way of life. But it did not dominate society. Commerce was still important to a large segment of the Omani élite. Moreover, political power was a matter of dynastic and communal politics, not a derivative of plantation ownership.

But the plantation system was not restricted to Zanzibar and Pemba. It extended to the mainland, with old crops such as grain and coconuts as the main bases. What changed was the farming methods—from subsistence farming depending on a family supplemented by a few slaves, to plantations, a large-scale operation based on slave labour. Arabia and the Horn of Africa imported foodstuffs from East Africa. In East Africa, places like Zanzibar with expanding populations and reliance on cash crops had to import food from the mainland.

Grain cultivation therefore expanded all along, the East African coast, from Mrima Coast to Lamu, supplying markets in Somalia and Arabia, as well as Zanzibar.

The significance of this development is demonstrated in the history of Malindi, an old town which had been abandoned. But from about 1860, Malindi soon became an important grain-exporting centre. It also contained thousands of slaves.

By 1874, Malindi was well established. Grain exports were worth about $150,000 a year. Each year, thirty dhows left Malindi with millet, destined for the Hodramant, while fifteen to twenty exported sesame. In the words of John Kirk, Madindi had become 'the granary of East Africa'. The height of Malindi's prosperity was reached in the 1880s.

Thus in fifteen years, Malindi had graduated from being an abandoned town to the granary of East Africa. The main reason was the abundance of land slave labour. By 1873 Kirk estimated that Malindi had 6,000 slaves. By the 1880s, there were about 10,000 slaves, owned by about 2,000 Arabs and Swahili. The richest of them all was Salim bin Khalfan Al-Busaidi, who migrated to Malindi from Muscat in the 1860s, as a man of modest means. He became Governor of Malindi in 1870, and from 1885–87 and again from 1891 until his death in 1920, he was Governor of Mombasa. He became the largest

Arab landowner in Mombasa and Malindi. At the time of his death, his property was worth £175,000.

The important conclusion is that Malindi was built up in a generation by
immigrants with no local roots, but with connections in their places of origin—
Lamu, Muscat, the Hodramant and Zanzibar.

Between 1873 and 1907, several restrictions were placed on the slave
trade in East Africa, resulting in its final abolition in 1907.

Notes

1. See, for example, Z. Marsh and G. W. Kingsnorth, *An Introduction to the History of
East Africa*, Cambridge University Press, 1957.
2. Freeman-Grenville, 'The Coast, 1498–1840', in R. Oliver and Gervase Mathew (eds.),
History of East Africa, Vol. I, p. 152, 1963.
3. *The East African Slave Trade*, p. 4, Historical Association of Tanzania, 1967 (Paper
No. 3).
4. *The East African Coast until the Coming of the Portuguese*, p. 101, 121.
5. G. S. Graham, *Great Britain in the Indian Ocean 1810–50*, p. 148, 1967.
6. 'Loarer's Report, 1849', in C. S. Nicholls, *The Swahili Coast: Politics, Diplomacy and
Trade on the East African Littoral 1788–1856*, 1971, p. 199.
7. L. Krapf, 'On the Slave-Trade within the Iman of Muscat's dominion and the Independent States of East Africa between 2 degrees North and 10 degrees South of the
Equator', C.M.S. Archives, London, (CA5/016, 18 February 1849).
8. Graham, op. cit., p. 148, footnote 2.
9. Nicholls, op. cit., p. 204.
10. *Alpers, Ivory and Slaves in East Central Africa*, p. 252, 1975.
11. M. W. Jackson Haight, *European Powers and South-East Africa*, p. 264, 1967.
12. Joseph E. Harris, *The African Presence in Asia*, p. 3–25, 1971.
13. R. P. Baur, *Voyage dans l'Ondoé et l'Onzigona*, p. 91, 1882.
14. 'The African Diaspora and East Africa'—an inaugural lecture delivered at Makerere
University, Kampala, Uganda on 31 July 1967, p. 14.
15. Abdul Sheriff, *The Rise of a Commercial Empire: An Aspect of the Economic History
of Zanzibar, 1770–1873*, University of London, 1971 (Ph.D. thesis); Fred James
Berg, *Mombasa Under Busaidi Sultanate : The City and Its Hinterland in the 19th
Century*, University of Wisconsin, 1971 (Ph.D. thesis); Fred Cooper, *Plantation
Slavery on the East Coast of Africa in the 19th Century*, Yale University, 1974
(Ph.D. thesis).
16. Auguste Toussaint, *Histoire des Iles Mascareignes*, p. 335–6, 1972.
17. *The Atlantic Slave Trade: A Census*, p. 266, 1969.

Bibliography

ABDURRAHIM MOHAMED JIDDAWI. Extracts from an Arab Account Book, 1840–1854.
Tanganyika Notes and Records, Vol. 33, 1953, p. 25–31.
African Historical Studies, Vol. IV, No. 3, 1971. (Special issue on connection of Zanzibar
with interior of East Africa.)
AKINOLA, G. A. The French on the Lindi Coast, 1785–1789. *Tanganyika Notes and Records*,
Vol. 70, 1969, p. 13–20.

——. Slavery and Slave Revolts in the Sultanate of Zanzibar in the Nineteenth Century. *Journal of the Historical Society of Nigeria*, Vol. VI, 1972, p. 215–28.

ALPERS, E. A. *The East African Slave Trade*. Nairobi, East African Publishing House, 1967.

——. The French Slave Trade in East Africa, 1721–1820. *Cahiers d'Études Africaines*, Vol. 10, 1970, p. 80–124.

——. Re-Thinking African Economic History. *Kenya Historical Review*, Vol. I, 1973, p. 163–88.

——. Trade, State and Society among the Yao in the 19th Century. *Journal of African History*, Vol. X, 1969, p. 405–20.

BEECH, Mervyn W. Slavery on the East Coast of Africa. *Journal of the African Society*, Vol. 15, 1916, p. 145–9.

BERG, F. J. The Swahili Community of Mombasa, 1500–1900. *Journal of African History*, Vol. IX, 1968, p. 35–56.

——. *Mombasa Under Busaidi Sultanate : The City and Its Hinterland in the 19th Century* University of Wisconsin, 1971 (Ph.D. thesis).

BRODE, Heinrick. *Tippoo Tib: The Story of His Career in Central Africa*. London, Edward Arnold, 1907.

BURTON, Richard. *The Lake Regions of Central Africa*. London, Longman & Co., 1860. 2 vols.

——. *Zanzibar : City, Island, and Coast*. London, Tinsley Bros, 1872. 2 vols.

CHRISTIE, James. *Cholera Epidemics in East Africa, ... from 1821 till 1872*, London, Macmillan, 1876.

——. Slavery in Zanzibar As It Is. In: E. Steere (ed.), *The East African Slave Trade*. London, 1871.

COOPER, Frederick. *Plantation Slavery on the East Coast of Africa in the Nineteenth Century*. Yale University, 1974. (Ph.D. thesis.)

——. The Treatment of Slaves on the Kenya Coast in the 19th Century. *Kenya Historical Review*, Vol. I, 1973, p. 87–108.

COUPLAND, Sir Reginald. *East Africa and Its Invaders*. Oxford, 1938.

——. *The Exploitation of East Africa, 1856–1890: The Slave Trade and the Scramble*. London, Faber & Faber, 1939.

ELTON, James Frederick, *Travels and Researches among the Lakes and Mountains of Eastern and Central Africa*. Ed. by H. B. Cotterill, 1879.

FITZGERALD, W. W. A. *Travels in the Coastlands of British East Africa and the Islands of Zanzibar and Pemba*. London, Chapman & Hall, 1898.

GAVIN, R. J. The Bartle Frere Mission to Zanzibar. *Historical Journal*. Vol. 5, 1962. p. 122–48.

GRAY, Sir John. *The British in Mombasa, 1824–1826*. London, Macmillan, 1957.

——. *A History of Zanzibar from the Middle Ages to 1865*, London, 1962.

HARRIS, Joseph E. *The African Presence in Asia*. Evanston, Northwestern University Press, 1971.

HUTCHINSON, E. *The Slave Trade of East Africa*. London, 1874.

INGRAMS, William H. *Zanzibar : Its History and Peoples*. London, H. F. & G. Witherby, 1931.

JONES-BATEMAN, P. L. (ed. and trans.). *The Autobiography of an African Slave-Boy*. London, 1891.

JONES, M. K. *The Slave Trade at Mauritius, 1811–1829*. Oxford University, 1936.

KELLY, J. B. *Britain and the Persian Gulf, 1795–1880*. London, Oxford University Press, 1968.

——. *Sultanate and Imamate in Oman*. London, Oxford University Press, 1959.

KRAPF, Johann Ludwig. *Travels, Researches, and Missionary Labours During an Eighteen Years' Residence in Eastern Africa.* 1860.

LIVINGSTONE, David. *The Last Journals of David Livingstone in Central Africa from 1865 to His Death,* London, 1874.

LLOYD, Christopher. *The Navy and the Slave Trade.* London, Longmans, Green & Co., 1949.

LOARER, Captain. L'Ile de Zanzibar. *Revue de l'Orient,* Vol. IX, 1851, 240–99.

MACKENZIE, Donald. A Report on Slavery and the Slave Trade in Zanzibar, Pemba and the Mainland of the British Protectorates of East Africa. *Anti-Slavery Reporter,* Series IV, Vol. 15, 1895, p. 69–96.

MARTIN, Esmond B; RYAN, T. C. I. A Quantitative Assessment of the Arab Slave Trade of East Africa, 1770–1896. *Kenya Historical Review,* Vol. 5, No. 1, 1977, p. 71–91.

MBOTELA, James Juma. *The Freeing of the Slaves in East Africa.* London, Evans Bros, 1956.

MBARAK, Ali Hinawy. *Al-Akida and Fort Jesus Mombasa.* London, 1950.

NEW, Charles. *Life, Wanderings and Labours in Eastern Africa.* London, 1873.

NEWMAN, Henry Stanley. *Banani: The Transition from Slavery to Freedom in Zanzibar and Pemba.* London, Headley Bros., 1898.

NICHOLLS, C. S. *The Swahili Coast: Politics, Diplomacy and Trade on the East African Littoral, 1798–1856.* London, Allen & Unwin, 1971.

PEARCE, F. B. *Zanzibar: The Island Metropolis of Eastern Africa.* London, T. Fisher Unwin, 1920.

PHILLIPS, Wendell. *Oman: A History.* London, Longman, 1967.

RASHID BIN HASSANI. The Story of Rashid bin Hassani of the Bisa Tribe, Northern Rhodesia. (Recorded by W. F. Baldock). In: Margery Perham (ed.), *Ten Africans.* London, Faber, 1963.

RUSSELL, C. E. B. (ed.). *General Rigby, Zanzibar, and the Slave Trade: With Documents.* London, Allen & Unwin, 1935.

SHERIFF, Abdul Mohamed Hussein. *The Rise of a Commercial Empire: An Aspect of the Economic History of Zanzibar, 1770–1873,* University of London, 1971. (Ph.D. thesis.)

SULIVAN, G. L. *Dhow Chasing in Zanzibar Waters.* London, 1873.

TIPPOO TIB. *Maisha ya Hamed bin Muhammed el Murjebi yaani Tippu Tip.* Trans. by W. H. Whiteley. *Supplement to the East Africa Swahili Committee Journal,* Vol. 28–9, 1958–59.

TRIMINGHAM, J. Spencer. *Islam in East Africa.* Oxford, Oxford University Press, 1964.

The slave trade
in the Indian Ocean

The slave trade in the Indian Ocean: problems facing the historian and research to be undertaken

Hubert Gerbeau

Problems facing the historian

Disruption, violence, silence—keywords conveying the suffering which the laws of the slave trade seemed to inflict on their victims. Keywords, too, which the traditional historian of the Atlantic slave trade was able to use without compunction when he wrote a paragraph of commercial history, in so far as he was not troubled by the silence of the two-footed commodity transported across an ocean which was more of a barrier than a connecting link between two continents.

These simple observations introduce us to problems with three basic aspects which should be stressed. The first is a truism: the Indian Ocean is not the Atlantic. The second is a question: is it possible to write the history of silence? The third is a postulate: interest in the history of the slave trade grows if we do not insist on reducing it to a paragraph in commercial history but place it at the level of a history of civilizations.

The preponderance of the Atlantic slave trade still weighs heavily on historians because it was on such a large scale, and especially because it has been more thoroughly studied than that of the Indian Ocean. The very dates that have been suggested to me are an additional sign of this. If I were to confine myself to the period from the fifteenth to the nineteenth century, it would mean adhering too closely to an Atlantic pattern. An 'Indian Ocean' perspective implies that the phenomenon should be relocated in a continuous process starting well before the fifteenth century and overlapping into the twentieth. Seeing the subject in this same perspective, we are reminded that while the uprooting from 'Mother Africa' was perpetrated in an identical fashion by way of the oceans to the east and to the west, the receiving countries were quite different. On the one side was a New World, on the other the lands bordering on an ancient ocean. In the latter, there were three stata of unity: 'a kind of racial unity resulting from Malay and other emigrations . . . a cultural unity spreading out from the Indian sub-continent . . . and a religious unity created by Islam' (Allen, 1969).

The historian of the slave trade in the Indian Ocean is concerned with a domain whose global nature cannot escape him. That it should be exceedingly hard for him to grasp its components does not surprise him. The first difficulty he meets with is that of the ill-defined limits of the oceanic area. As an initial hypothesis, he may consider that any phenomenon involving the transport of slaves from Africa or arriving there via the Indian Ocean falls within his purview. More difficult to solve are the problems relating to the immensity of the geographic sectors, the human diversity in the coastal countries and islands, and the length of the periods concerned. Each of these aspects has been dealt with in the works of many specialists who usually have no connection with one another. The historian of Zanzibar or of Mauritius in the nineteenth century had little occasion to do any work on India or China in the fifteenth century, and vice versa. This is a drawback, but not a serious worry; that, as we shall see, stems from the very nature of the subject-matter involved.

The specialist in the slave trade is a historian of men and not of merchandise, and he cannot accept the silence of those transported. Traders, sailors, administrators and planters cannot give him enough information. Would one write the history of Auschwitz drawing only on Nazi sources? This comparison makes us aware of a twofold danger: those who, using only one type of document, see but a part of the picture and are therefore biased, and those who, reacting against deception, put their own interpretation on the thoughts of silent actors and are therefore overbold. The study of the transported slaves is not as simple as that of deported persons during the last war. The zeal of the abolitionists sometimes lights the way, but often obscures it too. Does the historian himself remain uninfluenced by the irrationalism of a history where opposing schools of thought seem to be divided on the basis of colour, where some side with the victims and others with the executioners? Whether this difficulty is felt or not, it is reflected in the tone and arrangement of published works. Those who are more technically minded will be criticized for their dispassionate indifference, others, more givan to polemics, will be taken to task for their unscientific bombast. Those who are concerned about the dearth of records become over-meticulous, counting, standing up and knocking down their Negroes like skittles; others, obsessed by the existence of this forest of fossilized men, of whom only patchy traces remain, launch into bold hypotheses and parade their millions of captives in flamboyant, funereal processions. At best, must the historian not borrow from both schools of thought, introducing a human dimension into the infinitely detailed analyses and building up his general assumptions with scientific accuracy? But even so, will he be able to force the slaves out of their silence? The ways of approach are narrow, and often very indirect, as we shall see in the last part, but the postulate that I have advanced on the content of a history of the slave trade now inclines me in this direction.

If the requested study on the slave trade is taken to mean a history of civilizations, in other words an approach to the 'total history' of which Michelet dreamed, the task becomes more significant. There is then the twofold obligation of broadening the field of investigation and of using working tools with which the historian is not always familiar. It will no longer suffice to date the cargoes and count the men and the piastres; he must think in terms of cooking, religion, magic, dancing, music, population, social organization, agricultural practices and cultural themes. The historian will have to be an archaeologist, an ethnologist, a specialist in oral traditions, a biologist, a linguist and perhaps a psychiatrist. These research techniques should not be excluded on the assumption that the history of the slave trade is but the study of a certain type of transportation, that the human being traded does not concern us before his departure or after his arrival. To limit the subject thus would be like trying to reduce the history of nutrition to the analysis of food: foodstuffs are first of all living substances and they are ingested by human beings who will assimilate this or that nourishment from them. The history of nutrition would be futile if it were not rooted in economics and did not include its social aspects. In my opinion, it is not irrelevant to the subject of the slave trade to inquire into the life of the man who is leaving and of the one who has arrived. This history should be anchored in the history of Africa and the countries concerned, and should go so far as to include the slave society. Its subject, however, remains specific, and is not to be confused either with general history or with the history of slavery.

If the historian of the slave trade were to be refused this scope for his study, he would still be forced to broaden his field and the range of the tools at his disposal. This second requirement springs from his ignorance of many facts concerning the slave trade. When there are no records concerning a large-scale transport of slaves, must he resign himself to a blank page, or can he formulate hypotheses with supporting arguments? I shall return to this point which concerns the research to be undertaken.

Having suggested a certain conception of the history of the slave trade and of the man-object to which it applies, and having drawn a distinction between the Atlantic and the Indian Ocean approaches, I can now turn to two corollaries which will give rise to a number of associated problems. The first concerns the slave trade and the 'Indian Ocean' unity, and the second is an attempt to delimit periods or make a classification outline.

Disruption and violence wrenched the traded slave out of the traditional world in which he lived, often as a free man, and placed him in a new world which was to him a psychological and physical shock. This transition sometimes took him as far as the New World when the ships carrying captives from West Africa to the Indian Ocean and those sailing from the 'Indian Ocean' area towards the Atlantic passed one another while rounding the Cape. But this extreme uprooting was unusual. As a general rule, the slave taken to the heart of India or the Arab countries, or even more so if employed in the coastal regions and islands, continued to form an integral part of an oceanic whole whose unity has been emphasized by Allen.

Here a crucial question arises: was the 'Indian Ocean' slave trade a factor for destruction or construction? Did it alter, strengthen or undermine the three 'strata of unity'? The land and sea networks covered by the slave-trader on the ocean and its precincts must be evaluated with the yardstick of the history of civilizations within the scope of which I have sought to place this study of the slave trade. There are additional questions to be borne in mind: Are those elements which were not originally contained in the crucible going to melt and enrich the alloy, or are they going to introduce the straw that will cause future cracks? Those elements are not only the slaves transported from the heart of Africa but also the Europeans who came late to the Indian Ocean and settled in other lands.

It is not easy to distinguish between those who are actors or objects in the traffic and those who are not. The term 'slave trade' may seem quite clear, yet in fact it is anything but so. At the Unesco meeting of experts in Mauritius,- in July 1974,[1] we expressed the wish that to the Cartesian notions of 'free' and 'slave' should be added the notions of 'half-free', 'subjected', 'dependent', 'quasi-', 'pre-' and 'post-' slave. The exact term has not yet been found, but it does correspond to a real situation which can be outlined empirically. Models exist in Roman antiquity (the client, the freedman) and in the European Middle Ages (the serf). The characteristic of the intermediate models between free man and slave seems understandable in the Indian Ocean in terms of a discrepancy between the legal status and the real position. In Madagascar there were slaves who owned slaves, and in India other slaves legally ran the State as high officials and counsellors, before becoming sovereigns. But in the sugar-producing islands, 'free employees' were marched, with pitchforks at their throats, to the beaches of Mozambique before being crammed into ships as wretchedly as their 'freely employed' companions in India and ended up, like them, in work camps where the commander's stick and the master's arbitrary attitude survived the abolition of slavery. In this intermediate category we must also include the 'patronized' slave of the last years of French colonial slavery and the *affranchi à livret* (freedman with papers) of the first years of emancipation, the 'apprentice' of the English colonies, certain domestic slaves in Madagascar and certain 'family captives' in Africa. These last four or five examples, it will be objected, are admissible in a history of slavery but ill-chosen in a history of the slave trade. In self-defence, I might refer to the sale of punished domestic servants to slave-traders, but the problem on which we must concentrate is more general. In order to define it with greater precision, I shall request a twofold favour: that I be allowed to quote an example chosen some distance away from the Indian Ocean, and that if the slave trade be taken to mean the purchase or capture of a man, followed by his displacement and sale, then certain compulsory voyages, which were the result of slavery and of the greed of masters, were indeed akin to the slave trade. In 1957–58, while conducting research in the Niger Valley, I had occasion to see that the manifold survivals of the phenomenon of 'family captives' sometimes involved compulsory displacements. The most extraordinary one seemed to me to be the annual trip made by a *bellah* doctor, i.e. a captive of the Tuareg, who owed his promotion to the fact that he had been a hostage at school, where he had, against his will, replaced a chief's son. He lived in an African capital, but travelled regularly 2,000 kilometres to visit his former masters in their tents and turn over to them one-twelfth of his average annual income.

When thousands of the emancipated slaves in the sugar-producing islands fled the plantations, were they moving of their own free will to the uplands or the towns where they would die of poverty? Was it not the colonial society which, having always connected working on the land with the stigma of servility, drove them to such a desperate flight towards reintegration in the human species from which, despite baptism and the law, an attempt had been made to exclude them? This was a death-blow dealt them by the social system, because legal emancipation was not backed up by any welfare measure in a free economy and society. A century later, it was discovered that some islands had operated as a population trap and a new migration was organized.

I have alluded to these extreme cases only in order to show that by its extent and its connotations, the slave trade may lead the historian further afield than he had expected. On the immediate fringes of slavery, there are many slave-trade phenomena which he will in any case be unable to overlook and which concern the 'half-free'. It was not by chance, I imagine, that Unesco proposed to me the subject of the *traite esclavagiste* and not that of the *traite des esclaves*.[2] This former term lends itself not only to a value judgement on the trade, but also amounts to an invitation to approach the phenomenon in a broader context. A man with a pro-slavery mentality has no need of slaves in the legal sense in order to carry on his trade. For that reason the slate's substitutes, the 'free employees' and the forced labourers, were to become provender for the slave trade. Their inclusion in my subject is therefore more in order than it appeared at first sight.[3]

There is still the problem of agreeing on what may be regarded as the slave trade. I have already suggested that the traffic in Indian and African 'free employees' who worked on sugar plantations would fall within this category. But there are, too, the Malagasy 'free employees' and the Chinese 'coolies', the political prisoners of Indo-China and Madagascar, the forced labourers on Indonesian plantations, and perhaps even the Indian labourers laying the railways in East Africa or the Mozambique Negroes migrating to work in the Transvaal mines.

While these migrations are still rooted in disruption and violence, the silence of those concerned is less heavy. Research on them would probably be rewarding. To attempt to make an inventory of them would lead me too far from my subject, and I shall therefore confine myself to drawing attention to a problem which is one both of vocabulary and of classification. It would be convenient to exclude from my study all those who were not slaves in the legal sense of the term. But caution is advisable—an unduly meticulous legal approach may distort reality to the point of making a travesty of history.

In the list of research projects to be undertaken—which I shall therefore restrict here to slaves properly so called—I shall have to deal with extensive geographical and chronological sectors in which the state of knowledge varies considerably. Sometimes such knowledge is like a building, strong and firm yesterday, but today rocked by the effects of new research. Often the accumulation of problems to be solved seems overwhelming but the specialists who are going to tackle them will surely manage to clarify them. Yet will light be fully shed on the Arab slave trade, on the slave trade in the Far East and on the clandestine slave trade of the nineteenth (and twentieth) century?

The Bureau of the Scientific Committee for the Drafting of a *General History of Africa*, at its meeting in Fez in February 1975, expressed the wish that we should not 'attempt to sum up the wealth of material already published', but it seems to me that the best way of presenting the 'forms to be assumed by the research on this vast subject and the avenues such research might explore' is to cutline, in a periodic framework relating to the Ocean, what is already known and what might be learned, before concluding with a brief synopsis.

Forms and avenues of research to be undertaken

To the end of the fifteenth century

When H. N. Chittick expresses the opinion that the Indian Ocean constituted the 'largest cultural continuum in the world during the first millenium and a half A.D.' he keeps us to the straight and narrow path of our problem: what place does the slave trade have in this continuum, and is it a factor making for dispersion or for cohesion?

There is no doubt about the age-old nature of the slave trade. Its movements were governed by the regular alternation of the monsoons observed as early as the first century by the Greek, Hippalos. Four months a year, in winter, the north-east winds blew ships coming from Arabia and north-west India towards the east coast of Africa. For about six months in the summer, winds blowing from the south-west favoured the return journey.

The Periplus of the Erythraean Sea, an anonymous work by an Egyptian Greek written between the first and the beginning of the third century A.D., tells us that slaves were taken from the Horn of Africa, in other words present-day Somalia. The Berbera region furnished a small number and the Ras Hafun region even more. Beyond that zone, the *Periplus*, which describes the southern Arabs as being firmly settled along the East African coast, makes no mention of slaves among items traded. From the end of the seventh century onwards, these Arabs were joined by Muslim refugees. The towns of Mogadishu, Brava and Kilwa were founded by the latter in the tenth century. From there they flocked to the island of Mafia, to various points along the coast, and to the Comoro Islands. The earliest contacts of Arab traders with the Malagasy coast seem to date also from the tenth century (Vérin, 1967).

Between the time with which we are familiar through the *Periplus* and Ptolemy, and the turning-point marked by the tenth century, the source materials contain practically no information about the East African coasts and islands which the Greeks called Azania and the Arabs, Sawâhil. But there must have been a considerable slave trade there, if we are to judge by the 'Zendj' or 'Zanj' revolt, in other words the Bantu who were taken to Mesopotamia to work in the sugar-cane plantations and, in the ninth century, played a decisive part for twenty years in the waging of war and the formulation of a new State. The Zendj were finally exterminated, but their revolt contributed to the fall of the Abbassid Caliphate and put an end to the construction of dams in southern Iraq, which H. Deschamps sees as the 'first model of a great tropical construction project involving the labour of hundreds of Negro slaves'.

From the tenth century onwards, the accounts of Arab geographers enlighten us to some extent on the slave trade. Masoudi, about 1050, speaks of trade between Mogadishu and Pemba in slaves, ivory and iron which were exchanged for pottery from China and Persia. Edrisi, in the middle of the twelfth century, tells how children from Zanguebar were lured with dates and captured, and refers to the expeditions that enabled the prince of the Island of Qishus, in the Sea of Oman, to supply himself with captives in the 'Zendj' country.

The prosperity of Mogadishu and Kilwa which Ibn Battuta visited in the fourteenth century is not unrelated to the slave trade practised by the sultans of the east coast. Along this coast, an Islamized mercantile society of mixed blood raised to its zenith a culture which Chittick proposes to call 'primitive Swahili'.

Arab sailing boats from the Red Sea took on slaves in the Comoro Islands from Muslim traders. In the fifteenth century, those traders, with reinforcements from Shiraz, increased their activities and brought wealth to these islands which 'had become slave-trade centres and stores of human flesh between Africa and Arabia' (Faurec, 1941).

However, the mass conversion of the Negro peoples along the east coasts of Africa certainly obstructed the slave trade; indeed, it was much more rife in western Sudan during the same period. For although the practice of slavery had spread despite the recommendation of the Koran, it was still agreed that only non-Muslims could be forced into slavery. The result was not the disappearance of the slave trade, but an extension of the distances travelled by the traders and captives as the non-Muslim territories became more and more remote. All in all, the slave trade was one of the major activities of the Muslim merchants in the Indian Ocean. Their best outlets were in the Near East, which they reached by way of Yemen and the Persian Gulf. (C. Cahen, 1970). It may be that the decline in the exportation of slaves from Malaysia and the Indonesian Islands at the end of the Middle Ages caused an increase in the slave trade along the coasts of East Africa for the markets of Islam. The strong position held by Muslim traders in all the 'South Seas' towards the middle of the fifteenth century, after China gave up her maritime policy in the Indian Ocean, is another factor weighing in favour of this hypothesis (Labib, 1972).

What was the extent of the slave traffic up to that time in the trade between Africa and China? This is a difficult question to answer. Exchanges seem to have been controlled by Indonesian intermediaries and appear to have been considerable, judging by the number of Chinese porcelain pieces discovered by East African archaeologists. The slave traffic, however, is scarcely mentioned in the records. In the eighth century, two Negro slaves were shown to the Emperor of China, and in the twelfth century inhabitants of Canton were using African slave labour. The seven naval expeditions carried out by the eunuch admiral Cheng Ho—the first began in 1405 and the last ended in 1433— attracted considerable attention. They stopped briefly at points along the East Indies, the Persian Gulf and a number of ports on the east coast of Africa, including Brava and Malindi. The exploit became a favourite topic in Chinese popular literature, but the ruling classes found these prestige operations launched by the emperor unnecessary and ruinous (Wang Gungwu). Were African slaves brought back by the Chinese ships on that occasion? It seems reasonable to put the question.

The African slave trade to India was on a larger scale and is better known. When the Muslims conquered the valley of the Ganges in the eleventh and twelfth centuries, a 'slave dynasty' held power for some time. In the thirteenth century, from Ceylon to Gujarat, Ethiopian slaves known as *habshis* or *siddis* were much sought after. They served as soldiers and sailors. There is a record of the arrival in India of a large number of slaves from East Africa in the fifteenth century. A number of them rose to responsible positions, and some even to high office. For instance, in Bengal where the sovereign owned 8,000 African slaves, King Fath Shah tried to get rid of the most influential ones. In return, they killed him. From 1486 to 1493, two slave soldiers of African origin ruled over Bengal. Under the succeeding sovereign, who was an Asian, the Africans had to take refuge in Deccan (Keswani, 1974).

To take stock of the fifteenth century which, in the Indian Ocean, sometimes seems like the rather insipid continuation of exploits of civilization and slave-trade phenomena that had been going on for centuries, would be a very premature undertaking. There are still a great many obscure areas. Specialists in Indian, Chinese and Islamic studies may one day bring new manuscripts to light or propose a 're-reading' of extant documents, concentrating on the problem of the slave trade. Archaeology should also shed further light on places and movements. I shall return to this point later.

When Vasco da Gama's fleet penetrated into the Indian Ocean from Cape Guardafui to Sofala in 1498, the coast was lined with prosperous sultanates. Its Arabization and Islamization made it appear to the caliphs as a dependency of the Muslim world, 'a notion whose full implications were to be discovered by the Portuguese when they came face to face with the Egyptians and Turks' (Otinno, 1975).

From the sixteenth to the eighteenth century

Progress in the Mediterranean area and the first phase of the voyages of discovery across the Atlantic were stimulated by the planting of sugar cane and the concomitant search for slave markets. Profits from the Negro slave trade were a consideration in the financing of later voyages of exploration (J. Heers, 1966). When the Portuguese entered the Indian Ocean, however, they were 'in quest of spices and nothing else' (Godinho, 1969). When they visited the towns along the East African coast at the beginning of the sixteenth century, they noted that slaves there wore simple loincloths, that buildings were beautiful and that the social élite wore silk and jewels. But their goal was farther off. They were interested in East Africa 'to the extent that it lay on the "route to the Indies", and controlled access to it and traffic along it'. This was the Portuguese attitude down to the nineteenth century (Mollat, 1974). Slaves and gold came later. In Sofala, merchants from Gujarat exchanged cotton goods from Cambay and glassware from Melinda, for gold from Monomotapa, ivory and captives which they took home with them. Following their example, the Portuguese entered into relations with the Kaffirs (Godinho, 1969). In the course of punitive expeditions against the Kingdom of Monomotapa, a handful of Portuguese Africans remained behind between the Zambezi and Limpopo rivers and, after 1574, lived largely on the slave trade (Mauny, 1971).

The Portuguese, sailing towards India, recognized a number of islands in the south-west of the Indian Ocean and gave them names. One of Don Sebastian's captains, who took it upon himself to send his sovereign 'a host of slaves for his galleys', had a short-lived plan to conquer the Comoro Islands. More tangible were the slave-traders' activities in Madagascar. In the seventeenth and eighteenth centuries, the Portuguese, through the intermediary of Malagasy chieftains, loaded their ships with slaves from the northern part of the islands. Their preference was to frequent the north-west coasts, which were lay-over points between Mozambique and Goa, and there take on slave cargoes bound for India (Vérin, 1972). Miss Keswani had pointed out that the importation of African slaves was carried on actively in Madagascar during the Portuguese period (Unesco, 1974).

Other slaves were taken away by the various Europeans who penetrated into the Indian Ocean. The Dutch, on their way to Indonesia, began as early as 1596 putting into the Bay of Antongil which was to become the favourite place for their Negro slave trade in Madagascar. Their settlement in Mauritius in 1638 and in the Cape in 1652 stimulated this traffic. But it was for a more distant destination that the *Jacht Sillida* carried off 236 Malagasies on 5 December 1681: they were to join other slaves, mostly from Malabar, to work in a gold-mine in western Sumatra (Lombard, 1971). Here there was a sharing of wretchedness, and a meeting of cultures, but how many acculturations failed to take place because of the 'mandor's' whip?

The English ports of call, the Danes stopping along the coast of Coromandel on their way to their outpost at Tranquebar, and the French settled in Fort-Dauphin, all provided new opportunities for slave trading, but the best ones were seized by the pirates, beginning in 1685, when the European powers temporarily withdrew from Madagascar. Driven out of the West Indies by the advance of colonization, hundreds of freebooters took refuge in the 'Great Isle'. They became the brokers of the slave trade until about 1726, buying Malagasies and reselling them to the English of Bristol, the Dutch of Batavia and the French of Martinique, as well as to the Arabs of Boina and Majunga. The corsairs delivered their own merchandise and slaves to the neighbouring island of Bourbon (Réunion) where a French governor had signed a contract with them to purchase slaves whom he then resold to those under his administration. According to the account of the Provençal pirate, Misson, the founder of Libertalia, 'A slave in Barbados costs from £750 to £1,250, whereas in Madagascar with some £12 of merchandise one can buy all one wants. We can get a fine chap there for an old suit' (Filliot, 1975).

This cynical calculation had been made before Misson, since Barbados Island had received 335 Malagasy slaves as early as 1664. The need for manpower in the West Indies and on the American continent was to keep up this long-distance traffic until the eighteenth century, with a peak period between the years 1675 and 1725. All told, approximately 12,000 inhabitants of Madagascar went to the New World in servitude (Hardyman, 1964). They were soon joined there by slaves from East Africa, for example, in Santo Domingo where the Governor estimated that in 1785, some 3,000 to 4,000 slaves came in from the Mozambique region, as compared with 34,000 slaves from the Atlantic coast (Debien, 1974; Toussaint, 1967).

It is perhaps in the microcosm of the Mascarene Islands that the multiplier effect on the slave trade of the intrusion of Europeans in the Indian Ocean can best be analysed. The colonization of Bourbon and Ile de France (Mauritius) gave rise to a need, as in the West Indies, for manpower from afar, and for some fifty years slaves were brought from India, Senegal and the Gulf of Guinea. At the same time cargoes of slaves were brought from Madagascar. These were increased in the eighteenth century and reinforced by those from East Africa. At first, the only suppliers were the Portuguese trading stations South of Cape Delgado. In the second half of the century, slaves were also purchased from the Muslims on the Zanguebar coast, i.e. from Cape Delgado to the Gulf of Aden. From 1670 to 1810, the Mascarene Islands thus appear to have imported approximately 160,000 slaves, 115,000 of them between 1769 and 1810. Of these 160,000, 45 per cent were Malagasies, 40 per cent Africans from the east coast, 13 per cent Indians and 2 per cent Africans from the west (Filliot, 1974). In Bourbon, which accounted for approximately half the total traffic, the slave population in 1808 is estimated to have been 53,726 persons, 23,013 of whom were Creoles, 17,476 'Mozambiques', 11,547 Malagasies and 1,690 Indians or Malays (Wanquet, in press).

The volume of the traffic stimulated the activity of local slave dealers, but it is difficult to say how many slaves were intended for Europeans and how many went to supply the old traditional markets. Some of the latter operated in an autonomous fashion, as for example the Egyptian markets along the Red Sea which gave rise to a traffic in eunuchs and Abyssinian and Galla girls. Other enterprises had a twofold object, as illustrated by Malagasies and Muslims. From 1785 to 1823 the Malagasies organized their own raids on the Comoro Islands and along the east coast of Africa, between Mafia and the Kerimba archipelago. Froberville describes expeditions of 400 to 500 pirogues carrying over 15,000 men. The extent of the phenomenon can be judged by contemporary accounts and also by the living witness of oral traditions that can still be heard on Great Comoro, Mayotte and along the Mozambique coast, and by the size of the fortresses which were built there to withstand attacks by Malagasy slave traders (Vérin, 1972).

Less spectacular, but part of the long history, was the Muslim slave trade. On the east coast of Africa, Portuguese domination, though discontinuous and unstable, included the capture of a transoceanic commercial system that stretched from Mozambique to Canton. In the sixteenth and seventeenth centuries this resulted in 'an uninterrputed economic and cultural decline' for the Muslim towns (Oliver, 1970). Nevertheless, in the lulls between pillaging expeditions and revolts, Muslim ships pursued their traffic. The slave trade was re-established on a large scale between 1622 and 1650 from the Zendj coast to Bombay by Muslims from Muscat. Muslim ships are reported to have been active at the end of the seventeenth century at Mogadishu, Kilwa and Zanzibar.

The bell tolled for the Portuguese in northern Mozambique when the Jesus Fort in Mombasa fell in 1698. The conquering Arabs from Oman settled along the coast and, in the eighteenth century, there was a rebirth of Swahili civilization. Save in a few exceptional cases, this return in force of Islam was final. The Islamic trading stations in the north-west and north-east of Madagascar had been prosperous since the fifteenth century. In the eighteenth century, operations were divided up—Arab traders on the west coast, particularly at Majunga, imported African slaves, and European traders, mostly French, on the east coast exported them to the Mascarene Islands (Valette, 1970; Vérin, 1972).

The period running from the sixteenth century to the end of the eighteenth is better known in many respects than the previous one. Nevertheless, the slave trade in the eastern part of the African continent from the Cape to the Red Sea still faces us with many enigmas. Research should be focused mainly on the Arab and Portuguese sources, with archaeology still being the most essential auxiliary. The traffic towards the Far East should be studied in detail. An investigation into slavery on the eastern side of the Ocean would be rewarding. For example, slavery seems to have been stimulated in the Indonesian archipelago by the spread of Islam from the sixteenth century onwards and the formation of large sultanates (Lombard, personal communication).

The long nineteenth century

Recent studies on Madagascar and the archipelagos in the south-western part of the Indian Ocean in the eighteenth century give a fairly accurate picture of this area. For the nineteenth century, however, these islands seem to call for more sustained attention. The eastern part of the African continent, which was the centre of a ferocious and massive slave trade at a time when world slavery was dying out, has been the subject of a number of works over a period of more than a century. This does not mean, however, that everything has been clarified.

The measures taken by the French Revolutionaries against the slave trade and slavery had a paradoxical effect in the Mascarene Islands, in that the hindrance to the two systems was offset, to say the least, by the feverish reactions of the advocates of colonial organization. At the end of the eighteenth and beginning of the nineteenth century, slave labour continued to be imported into the islands from Madagascar and especially from the African mainland. The British occupation in 1810 led to a half-hearted application of the prohibition of the slave trade as decided by the British Government in 1807. The return of Bourbon to France in 1815 and the continued possession of Mauritius by Great Britain had little effect on slave-trade activity. Farquhar, the Governor of Mauritius, even tried to persuade the English authorities to grant legal recognition to 'clandestine' traffic. France, which in her turn abolished the slave trade in 1817, was equally tolerant of the slave-traders in Bourbon. Repressive laws became more severe in 1820s but there was a world of difference between theory and practice. Hypocrisy often vied with inefficiency. For every zealous governor, such as Hall in Mauritius or Milius in Bourbon, there were ten accommodating judges, officials who dealt in the slave trade themselves, corrupt police, and inhabitants fanatically supporting slavery. In Bourbon, the gendarmes, who spent more in the taverns than they earned, turned a blind eye when captives were disembarked, and the judges who had interests on the island, demanded a superabundance of proof before they condemned a guilty party, even when all the evidence was against him. In Mauritius, the chief registrar responsible for the slave register, which was the principal means of checking on the illicit trade, was himself an opulent importer of slaves brought in secretly from East Africa. Investigations carried out in Mauritius by a Royal Commission from 1826 to 1828 show that the slave trade was practised there at least up to 1824. This needs to be studied further. Research could be based on the London archives and the voluminous files of the Mauritius Record Office (for example, series IA, IC and series IB which contains the 'Minutes of Evidence and Other Records of the Eastern Enquiry Commission, 1826–1828'.

The Seychelles archipelago played a specific part in this traffic. By virtue of its geographical position, it served as a relay point, and by registering the slaves it facilitated their re-exportation towards Mauritius. Local archives shed light on the slave trade in the archipelago, particularly for the 1823–28 period (Seychelles Government Archives, at Port Victoria, Mahé).

In Réunion, a thorough study of the local archives has led me to conjecture that at least 45,000 slaves arrived secretly, most of them between 1817 and a final date around 1831, although some arrivals apparently continued into the 1840s (Gerbeau, 1972).

After the abolition of slavery, enforced in 1835 in Mauritius and in 1848 in Réunion, latent or derivative forms of slavery persisted. I referred above to the methodological problem thus facing the historian of the slave trade. While the traffic in Indian 'free employees' had its roots mainly in poverty, that of the African coast, Madagascar and the Comoros was linked with the continuance of slavery in those areas. A great deal remains to be discovered about the manoeuvres governing the 'employment' of these slaves. Reports by English consuls might well be supplemented by French archives, e.g. those concerning Nossi-Bé, Sainte-Marie de Madagascar and Mayotte (Dépôt des Archives d'Outre-Mer at Aix-en-Provence).

Mayotte was the only island in the Comoros which was annexed by France in 1843 and was consequently subject to restrictions on the slave trade. Throughout the rest of the archipelago the trade from East Africa continued. On Great Comoro, the Sultan of Itzandra built a walled enclosure in the mountains to hold slaves. Some distance away, Humblot, the director of a company and soon to become the 'Resident', bought slaves at sixty rupees a head, then 'hired' them, allowing them to buy back their freedom in five years by their labour, valued at one rupee per month (Vérin, 1972). On Johanna Island, Sunley, the British Consul, traded in slaves himself and this enabled him to supply manpower for the first of the large plantations which were to prosper on the island. This trade, and the forced labour resulting from it, aroused Livingstone's indignation and after leaving Johanna he persuaded the British Government to remove Sunley (Robineau, 1967). Throughout the archipelago, slavery, which was an integral part of traditional Comorian society, was still being practised in 1912, when union with Madagascar officially put an end to it.

At that time, Madagascar itself had only recently given up slavery. Abolition was contemporary with the transformation of the country into a French colony. The origin and fate of the 500,000 slaves freed in 1896 varied considerably, as the many Malagasy terms used to designate them show (Nolet, 1974). Throughout the entire nineteenth century a clandestine trade, about which little is yet known, continued. The principal effect of the prohibition measures taken by the Europeans and the Malagasies themselves seems to have been to move the centres and make the traffic more covert. In 1817, Radama I forbade the slave trade, and in 1877 Ranavalona II freed the 'Mozambiques'. The slave trade disappeared theoretically in the territories controlled by the Merina, as well as at Majunga, from 1823 onwards. But shipments continued elsewhere, especially from Mozambique, with partial redistribution in the neighbouring archipelagos. As late as 1891, Merina merchants were coming to Maintirano for supplies of recently landed slaves. As for the effects of the emancipation in 1896, they were less radical than expected, not only on the traditional forms of servitude, but even on the slave traffic. In the north-west, and particularly in the Bay of Baly, the clandestine trade seems to have been carried on up to 1900 (Vérin, 1972).

The problem of Arab ships registered under French names and carrying on a slave traffic under the protection of the French flag deserves to be studied further. We have many unpublished details on a number of cases at the end of the nineteenth century concerning Arab ships out of Muscat and Zanzibar that were stopped with slaves aboard, taken on in Madagascar and on the African coast, whom their owners were preparing to deliver to Mayotte or to take back to Muscat (Gerbeau, in press).

Behind the effervescence of the slave traffic discernible in all the islands was the immense human reservoir of the African continent whose east coast offered a feast on which the slave-traders of four continents threw themselves during the nineteenth century. The 'Indian Ocean' area, even more than the Atlantic side, fell increasingly into the hands of the dealers in black flesh as the century wore on.

The Bombay Record Office enables us to follow the last stages of the importation of African slaves into India in the nineteenth century, while the New Delhi archives reveal the struggle of the British against the slave trade during the same period. In 1814, ships from Muscat brought slaves from Africa whom they exchanged for Hindus to be sold in Zanzibar. By the 1840s it would seem that only a few hundred African slaves a year were being brought to India (Keswani, 1974). The huge demand for slave labour came from the islands of the Indian Ocean, to which I have already referred, the Muslim countries where slavery had existed for thousands of years, and the American continent with its adjacent islands.

For the slave trade in the Portuguese possessions, a great deal remains to be unearthed in the Lisbon archives and in those of Lourenço Marques, and these data should be compared with those to be found in the receiving countries and with diplomatic records, especially British ones. Estimates based on Foreign Office documents already reveal the extent of the traffic in Mozambique in the 1817–43 period, both as regards departures from Africa and arrivals in slave countries such as Brazil and Cuba (Curtin, 1969). The existence of slaves in the Portuguese colonies until 1869 undeniably stimulated the clandestine traffic, despite the Anglo-Portuguese Agreement of 1842 prohibiting the slave trade. The incident of the *Charles-et-Georges*, intercepted in 1857 while sailing from Mozambique to Réunion with 110 Negroes aboard, who were theoretically 'free-employees' but claimed to be slaves stolen from their masters, has a certain piquancy when discovered in both the Portuguese and the French archives. A commerce in slaves seems to have been carried on as late as the 1870s along the coasts of Mozambique (Filliot, 1974).

At the latitude of the Islamized towns along the coast, the slave routes penetrated into the interior. In the centre, across from Zanzibar, was the road of the Nyamwezi; to the north that of the Kamba; and to the south that of the Yao. A great deal has been written about this slave trade, its volume, its atrocities and the reactions to which they gave rise. For the record, I would mention the accounts of such European travellers as Burton (1857–59), Livingstone (1858–64 and 1866–73) and Cameron (1873–76). The interior routes were dotted with supply centres and the traffic was in the hands of local chiefs and a few hundred Arabs. The money-lenders were Banyans, i.e. Indian merchants settled in Zanzibar. The slave trade was stimulated on that island when Seyid Said, the Sultan of Muscat, established his capital there in 1832. The cultivation of clove trees, sugar cane and copra in Zanzibar and Pemba created the need for a fresh batch of slaves every three or four years. But this manpower drain does not suffice to explain the annual importation of 15,000 slaves from 1830 to 1873, as recorded in the customs registers of Zanzibar (Marissal, 1970). Some of these slaves, to whom must be added those who arrived fraudulently and those who were disembarked in other ports, were exported. In certain years, as many as 20,000 left Zanzibar, Kilwa Paté and Pemba. Most of them were sent to Arabia and the Persian Gulf, particularly Muscat. There, some of them were taken away by the 'Arabs of the North', whilst othere were re-shipped to Bahrain, Karachi and Bushire, in Persia, and some went as far as Baghdad and Isfahan. The length of the overland journeys and sea voyages, the extent of the traffic despite the anti-slavery struggle, and the serious consequences for Africa are dealt with in studies by Newitt and Alpers, in their articles published in the *Journal of African History*, in Alpers (1967), to which I shall return, and in the thesis by Renault (1971). Touching in places on the borders of the Indian Ocean, the large-scale slave trade on the Red Sea and along the Nile should also be mentioned. R. Pank-hurst estimates that over 25,000 slaves a year were exported on an average from Ethiopia up to 1865. The traffic had by no means ceased at the beginning of the twentieth century. The slave trade declined slowly in the second half of the nineteenth century in Egypt, Arabia and the Sudan, but controversy over the figures continues, and in more than one region disquieting practices were still occurring in the twentieth century.

The danger of persistence of the slave trade and slavery in the present century so concerned the United Nations that it arranged to have the problem studied. I refer the reader to the Engen Report in 1955 and the Mohamed Awad Report. The latter recommended that absolute priority be given to the establish-ment of a committee of experts on slavery.

Forms and avenues of research to be undertaken: a tentative synopsis

As regards the 'slow abolition of the slave trade in the Indian Ocean', there are many avenues beckoning the historian. The period of this study should extend from the second third of the nineteenth century into the twentieth. Before the years 1830–60, with chronological variations depending upon the sectors, it would seem a trifle rash to speak of a 'slow abolition'. The fifteenth century saw the end of a phase of traditional slave trading that had lasted for over a thousand years. It did not disappear, however, but was taken over and stimulated by the colonial slave trade which was at its height in the second half of the eighteenth century and the first third of the nineteenth. Then came the period of secondary and clandestine forms of the Western slave trade accom-panied and then outdone by the Muslim slave trade.

The study of these questions would be greatly facilitated by the publica-tion of new inventories of archive sources. Valuable guides already exist and might be used as models. For example, there are those of M. D. Wainwright and N. Matthews.[4]

The *Guide to Sources of African History*, prepared with the help and under the auspices of Unesco, is invaluable, but unfortunately the volumes are appearing rather slowly and there are still many gaps in the geographical field covered. The authors of this guide themselves are hoping that an inventory will be made of the wealth of documentation preserved in Africa itself. But we should go further and try to secure the participation of all the countries bordering on the Indian Ocean or involved in its history. Portuguese archives are still little known. Godinho's thesis [5] gives an idea of their volume and mentions the enormous amount of inventory work that remains to be done in certain record offices such as that of Torre do Tombe. There is still much material to be discovered and catalogued in the National Archives of India (Keswani, in press). This would seem to be equally applicable to most of the archives in the Far East. A very helpful list concerning the Indian archipelago was drawn up by Denys Lombard at the request of Unesco. Y. A. Talib and H. N. Chittick have stressed the need for new editions of Arab sources. It has emerged from discussions on this subject that it would be useful not only to make inventories and publish new texts, but also to devote specific attention to the texts already available. This applies to the many accounts of travellers as well as to printed documents of parliamentary of legal origin.[6]

However much the inventories of archives in some European countries may have progressed, research on the slave trade encounters a number of difficulties. Since the store of documents has grown with the centuries, those subsequent to the eighteenth century are often abstracted rather briefly and sometimes catalogued in an approximate fashion. The ideal would be to have a common index for all the record offices, and the computer may perhaps make this possible. Then research workers would simply have to press the keys marked 'slave trade' and 'Indian Ocean' in order to receive a plan of the itinerary to be followed round the world, with trails blazed so that they would not get lost in the voluminous but scattered archives obtaining in large cities, such as London, Lisbon and Paris. Sometimes the working tools already exist but funds for their publication are wanting. This is true of the remarkable inventories that have just been made at the French National Archives, Overseas Section, and which relate in Paris to the 'Réunion' series, and in Aix-en-Provence to the 'Madagascar and Dependencies' collection. One example should be cited, namely the *Bibliography of Mauritius (1502–1954)* by A Toussaint and H. Adolphe, published in Port-Louis in 1956. The work includes a list of archives concerning Mauritius to be found in collections throughout the world. This volume, which it is hoped will be updated, is a prototype of what might be attempted for the whole of the Indian Ocean.

An evaluation of the wealth produced by the slave trade in external economic systems could be made only in conjunction with a study of the receiving countries. This question was of concern to those who lived in the years immediately following emancipation of the slaves. They carried out studies on the comparative profitability of free and slave labour. Such studies were conducted in the West Indies as well as in the Mascarene Islands and often show slave labour to be the less economical. However, many assiduous inquiries are still needed before it can be proved that the slave's output was 'uneconomical'. Having read the work by R. W. Fogel and S. L. Engerman,[7] one would be tempted today, on the contrary, to look into the profitable aspects of slavery, even in the mid-nineteenth century. Another point that needs clarification has to do with the financing of the slave trade, and the profits made by the exporter and the carrier. Summary evaluations do exist. I quoted Misson's sally about the price of slaves in Madagascar and the value that was put upon them in Barbados. In the mid-nineteenth century, a slave exchanged for two goats near Lake Tanganyika was sold for $20 in Zanzibar and over $60 in Muscat. These two towns, which were relay points along the slave routes and centres for financing and redistribution, owed their wealth to the slave traffic. The constitution of commercial networks, the profit-and-loss balance, and the share of the slave trade in commerce as a whole are studies which still need to be undertaken in most of the regions in the Indian Ocean. A remaining task would be to study the slaves' descendants—freed slaves or fully fledged citizens. This is not only a demographic problem but also one of integration in society or rejection by it. In what generation is restitution made for the robbery of Africa? At what point is a balance struck between what the slaves' descendants have received from the host country and what they have given it?

The major difficulty is still that of counting the slaves. This is the key both to an accurate answer regarding the enrichment of external economic systems and to an evaluation of the demographic consequences for Africa. E. A. Alpers has criticized Coupland's views on the connections between the slave trade and the low population density in East Africa (1967). The matter does not seem to have been fully settled. While plenty of estimates have been made for the eastern part of the continent from the middle of the eighteenth century onwards, there are virtually none for the previous periods. The contributions made by the slave trade in the islands, many of which were 'population traps', are beginning to be assessed more accurately. But losses in the transportation over land and sea are often still unknown and many generalizations seem to be rash. Internal displacements—a sort of slave trade in a vacuum—are still certainly being minimized, as are the volume and duration of the clandestine traffic in the European colonies and Muslim countries. It is on these last points that the overall evaluations made by Curtin and Deschamps will probably have to be modified most.

A great deal is expected from G. I. Inokori's work on population and the impact of the slave trade on societies and powers in Africa. In the eastern part of the continent, I would suggest only a few avenues of research: up to about 1750, the political and social balance seems to have been very little affected by the slave trade; after that date devastation and anarchy were rampant along the slave routes. But all the regions were not involved to the same extent. Sometimes a strengthening of power was not unconnected with profits from the slave trade, as in the case of Seyid Said in Zanzibar; in other cases, a new power was set up thanks to the trade, as for example that of Tippoo Tib who, about 1872, founded a State on the Lomani River, a tributary of the Congo.

Sometimes the slave trade brought about a certain interpenetration of the African and European social systems, as for instance in Portuguese territories. More often, it accentuated cultural antagonisms and helped to establish a firmer claim to political, social and religious originality, especially in the Islamized portion of East Africa. In casting about for types of research to be undertaken. the need for a methodical correlation between lands of departure and lands of destination becomes evident. The slave trade is sometimes overworked as an explanation of events. Thus 'it is impossible to go on maintaining that the "Africans" of Madagascar who came there before the eighteenth and nineteenth centuries (Makoa, Mozambika) were brought in as slaves' (Ottino, 1974). More often, however, we are afraid of going too far the other way, because the silence about the slave and the silence of the slave are profound. We are afraid of minimizing the economic and cultural influence of the slave in a receiving society by failing to pay attention to the quality of the transplanted African values or by being ignorant of the quantitative extent of the slave trade. Although the slave trade sometimes brought about a reduction in the population when an epidemic was carried by a contaminated ship, it was generally found to add to the population, as the clandestine arrivals alone show. While still aboard ship, the slave in transit gave vent to his feelings by his songs, his rebellion or his suicide. It may not always be possible to locate him in the archives, but he did leave traces of his departure and his arrival. I should like to recall that there are two ways of approaching the phenomenon of the slave trade when written documents are scarce. One way is via archaeology, which may confirm, 'sometimes in a spectacular fashion, realities of ancient times that are reflected in the texts'; and the second is via oral tradition which, although 'a very tenuous Ariadne's clew',[8] may save us from losing our way once and for all. P. Vérin observed in the Boeny area, in Madagascar, the presence of eighteenth-century monuments whose construction was directly linked to slave-trade profits. The excavations currently under way in East Africa and Madagascar, those recently begun in the Comoros, and perhaps even those being planned in the Laccadive and Maldive Islands may yield a wealth of information. No site in the Indian Ocean should be excluded out of hand. The difficulty facing the historian of the slave trade is how to single out the detail which is significant for his subject from the mass of data available, without making arbitrary additions.

At Bangui, in Africa, J. L. Miège collected oral evidence from living witnesses about the slave trade which had been carried on across the continent, from the Kano region as far as Zanzibar, Jedda and Muscat. Inquiries made of old people in Réunion seem to warrant situating the arrival of their forebears at the time of a clandestine traffic, which is later than one would have suspected from the texts.

These remarks lead me, by way of conclusion, to venture a hypothesis: even when there are no texts concerning a slave-trade phenomenon, the historian can sill proceed with his work. He will have to go to the spot himself, i.e. to the land whence the slaves departed and to the one where they arrived. It is essential for him to glean information from the local inhabitants, to search their memories and their land. His archaeology should extend to the sites inhabited by the Maroons. Perhaps then we shall understand better how far the slaves, and more particularly the rebel slaves, have kept Africa alive in the 'Indian Ocean' area. The absence of studies does not necessarily mean the absence of a subject requiring study. The Atlantic side of the continent alone has produced the Boni Negroes of Guyana, the Vodun Creoles of Haiti, and American jazz, whereas the Indian Ocean slave has not so far made history. The *séga* (dance of the Mascarene Islands), short stories, proverbs, Creole languages, cooking recipes and religious beliefs can teach us a great deal about the qualitative and quantitative impact of Africa. Even anthropological blood-group research may shed light on the dominant features of a particular population. And so at the level of forms of research we find this converging of human sciences which I suggested was necessary when I was endeavouring to identify the problems inherent in defining the coverage of a study of the slave trade. In the Indian Ocean, as in the Atlantic, Africa has probably survived the convoys, the plantations and cultural alienation. 'Mediterranean seas—and the Indian Ocean is one such—have always been centres of civilization', writes M. Mollat. The slave made his own contribution to this centre. As part of the 'cultural continuum', he transported Africa eastwards for centuries. As his odyssey drew to an end, hordes of Indian and Chinese 'coolies' began to flow in the opposite direction. The trade in 'free employees' and slaves was an insult to civilization but it was also a feature of civilization; more effectively than ivory, gold, pottery of spices, it forged between the shores of the Indian Ocean a living link—man. Above and beyond disruption, violence, bloodshed and tears, there was acculturation. The islands are beginning to bear witness to this. As for the continental coast lines, scarcely any stones have yet been scabbled in this quarry of history.

Notes

1. Meeting of Experts on the Historical Contacts between East Africa and Madagascar on the One Hand, and South-East Asia on the Other, Across the Indian Ocean, Port Louis, Mauritius, 15–19 July 1974.

2. Translator's note—The English translation of both terms is 'slave trade'. An *esclavagiste* is a partisan of slavery.
3. By way of illustration, I would mention among current studies and recent works written on the same lines, the title of a book by Hugh Tinker, *A New System of Slavery. The Export of Indian Labour Overseas 1830–1920,* Oxford University Press, 1974.
4. *A Guide to Western Manuscripts and Documents in the British Isles relating to South and South-East Asia,* London, 1965; *A Guide to Manuscripts and Documents in the British Isles relating to Africa,* London, 1971.
5. op. cit., p. 49 et seq.
6. For example, the *British Parliamentary Papers,* published by the Irish University Press, or the Recueil Général des Lois et des Arrêts, by J. B. Sirey.
7. *Time on the Cross,* Boston, 1974.
8. J. Ki-Zerbo, Preface to *La Tradition Orale,* Niamey, 1972.

Bibliography [1]

Bibliographies, inventories of source materials, methods

Specal importance should be attached to meetings of experts, symposia and congresses whose proceedings are unfortunately sometimes published much later, and sometimes, too, with the discussions omitted. For a methodological study of the slave trade in the Indian Ocean, a great deal of information will be found in the following:

Beirut Symposium. Sociétés et Compagnies de Commerce en Orient et dans l'Océan Indien, 1966. Paris, SEVPEN, 1970.
Dar es Salaam Congress on the History of Africa, 1965. Nairobi, East African Publishing House, 1968.
Lourenço-Marquès Symposium. Océan Indien et Méditerranée, 1962. Lisbon, Studia, 1963; Paris, SEVPEN, 1964.
Meeting of Experts on 'Les Contacts Historiques entre l'Afrique et Madagascar d'Une Part, et l'Asie du Sud-Est d'Autre Part, par les Voies de l'Océan Indien', Port-Louis, 1974. Paris, Unesco. (Distribution limited.) The papers submitted by Messrs Devisse, Glélé, Mollat, Mutibwa, Ogot, Rabemananjara, Talib and Vérin as well as the Final Report by Jean Devisse are most useful for this subject.
Meeting of Experts on Malay Culture, Bangkok, 1973. Paris, Unesco. (Distribution limited.)
Meeting of Experts on Malay Culture, Kuala Lumpur, 1972. Paris, Unesco. (Distribution limited.)
Saint-Denis de la Réunion, Symposium on 'Les Mouvements de Population dans l'Océan Indien', 1972. In press.
San Francisco Seminar, 'Course et Piraterie' held in August 1975 by the International Commission for Maritime History during the Fourteenth International Congress of Historical Sciences. Foreword by Michel Mollat. Paris, Unesco, 1975. (Mimeo, 3 parts.)
Symposium on the Slave Trade, Colby College, Waterville (USA), 18–22 August 1975. (See particularly 'A Census on the Transsaharan Slave Trade' by R. A. Austen.

1. I have mentioned only those reference works and publications of a general nature which contain important information about the slave trade in the Indian Ocean and I have confined the list of articles and specialized publications, as far as possible, to the most recent ones. Those often contain summaries or critical analyses of previous studies and lists of source materials and bibliographies.—H.G.

Books and articles:

GERBEAU, H. *Les Esclaves Noirs. Pour une Histoire du Silence*. Paris, A. Balland, 1970.

Guide to Sources of African History. Prepared with the aid under the auspices of Unesco, Zug, Inter-Documentation Company AG, 1970.

HOGG, P. C. *The African Slave Trade and its Suppression. A Classified and Annotated Bibliography of Books, Pamphlets and Periodical Articles*. London, Cass, 1973.

LAYA, D. (ed.). *La Tradition Orale. Problématique et Méthodologie des Sources de l'Histoire Africaine*. Niamey, CRDTO, 1972. Preface by J. Ki-Zerbo.

LE BLEVEC, D. L'Océan Indien Occidental avant l'Arrivée des Portugais. Orientation Bibliographique pour une Étude des Côtes Africaines, des Iles et des Routes Maritimes du Sud-Ouest de l'Océan Indien, Antérieurement au XVIᵉ Siècle. *Cahiers du Centre Universitaire de la Réunion*. Saint-Denis, 1976.

LOMBARD, D. Les Études sur le Monde Insulindien. Situation et Perspectives. *ASEMI*, Vol. VI, No. 1, 1975. (Document prepared at the request of Unesco, Kuala Lumpur meeting, 1972.)

MATTHEWS, N.; WAINWRIGHT, M. D. *A Guide to Manuscripts and Documents in the British Isles and Relating to Africa*. London, Oxford University Press, 1971.

MOLLAT, M. Les Relations de l'Afrique de l'Est avec l'Asie: Essai de Position de Quelques Problèmes Historiques. *Journal of World History*, Vol. XIII, No. 2, 1971, p. 291–316.

TOUSSAINT, A.; ADOLPHE, H. *Bibliography of Mauritius (1502–1954)*. Port-Louis, Mauritius, Esclapon, 1956.

WAINWRIGHT, M. D.; MATTHEWS, N. *A Guide to Western Manuscripts and Documents in the British Isles Relating to South and South-East Aasia*, London, Oxford University Press, 1965.

Studies on the Indian Ocean and the slave trade

ALLEN J. de V., Proposition en Vue d'Etudes sur l'Océan Indien. Kampala, 1969, and Port-Louis, 1974.

ALPERS, E. A. *The East African Slave Trade*. Nairobi, East African Publishing House, 1967.

AWAD, M. *Rapport sur l'Esclavage*. New York and Paris, United Nations, 1967.

BEACHEY, R. W. *The Slave Trade of Eastern Africa: A Collection of Documents*. Rex Collins, 1976.

BENNETT, N. R.; BROOKS, G. E., Jr (ed.). *New England Merchants in Africa. A History through Documents 1802 to 1865*. Boston, University Press, 1965.

BONTINCK, *Tippou Tib*, Brussels, ARSOM, 1976.

CAHEN, C. Le Commerce Musulman dans l'Océan Indien au Moyen Age. p. 179–93. *Colloque de Beyrouth, 1966*. Paris, SEVPEN, 1970.

CHITTICK, H. N. L'Archéologie de la Côte Orientale Africaine. *Arabes et Islamisés à Madagascar et dans l'Océan Indien*. p. 21–38. Tananarive, 1967.

——. *East Africa and the Orient: Parts and Trade Before the Arrival of the Portuguese*. Port-Louis, 1974.

COOPER, F. *Plantation Slavery on the East Coast of Africa in the Nineteenth Century*. Yale University, 1974 (Ph.D. thesis.)

COUPLAND, R. *East Africa and its Invaders. From the Earliest Times to the Death of Seyid Saïd in 1856*. Oxford, Clarendon Press, 1938.

——. *The Exploitation of East Africa 1856–1800. The Slave Trade and the Scramble*. London, Faber & Faber, 1939.

CURTIN, P. D. *The Atlantic Slave Trade. A Census*. Madison, Wis., University of Wisconsin Press, 1969.

DEBIEN, G. *Les Esclaves aux Antilles Françaises (XVIIe–XVIIIe Siècles)*, Basse-Terre, Fort-de-France, Sociétés d'Histoire de la Guadeloupe et de la Martinique, 1974.

DESCHAMPS, H. *Histoire de la Traite des Noirs de l'Antiquité à nos Jours*. Paris, Fayard, 1972.

DESCHAMPS, H. et al. *Histoire Générale de l'Afrique Noire*. Paris, Presses Universitaires de France, 1970 and 1971. (2 vols.)

FAUREC, U. *L'Archipel aux Sultans Batailleurs*. 1st ed. 1941; 2nd ed., Moroni, Promo Al Camar, n.d.

FILLIOT, J.-M. *La Traite des Esclaves vers les Mascareignes au XVIIIe Siècle*. Paris, ORSTOM, 1974.

——. Pirates et Corsaires dans l'Océan Indien. *Colloque de San Francisco sur Course et Piraterie*. Part II, p. 766–84. Paris, 1975.

FREEMAN-GRENVILLE, G. S. P. *The East African Coast: Select documents from the First to the Earlier Nineteenth Century*. Oxford, Clarendon Press, 1962.

GERBEAU, H. Quelques Aspects de la Traite Interlope à Bourbon au XIXe Siècle. *Colloque de Saint-Denis sur les Mouvements de Population dans l'Ocean Indien*. In press.

GODINHO, V. M. *L'Économie de l'Empire Portugais aux XVe et XVIe Siècles*, Paris, SEVPEN, 1969.

GRAHAM, G. S. *Great Britain in the Indian Ocean*, Oxford, Clarendon Press, 1967.

HARDYMAN, J. T. The Madagascar Slave-Trade to the Americas (1632–1830). *Colloque de Lourenço-Marquès sur Océan Indien et Méditerranée*. p. 501–21. Paris, SEVPEN, 1964.

HEERS, J. Le Rôle des Capitaux Internationaux dans les Voyages de Découvertes aux XVe et XVIe Siècles. *Colloque de Lisbonne sur les Aspects Internationaux de la Découverte Océanique aux XVe et XVIe Siècles*. p. 273–93. Paris, SEVPEN, 1966.

KELLY, J. B. The Arab Slave Trade, 1800–1842. *Britain and The Persian Gulf, 1795–1880*. p. 411–51. Oxford, Oxford University Press, 1968.

KESWANI, D. G. Archival Documentation on the Indian Emigration to Indian Ocean Countries. *Colloque de Saint-Denis sur Les Mouvements de Population dans l'Océan Indien*. In press.

——. *Indian Cultural and Commercial Influences in the Indian Ocean, from Africa and Madagascar to South-East Asia*, Port-Louis, 1974.

KI-ZERBO, J. *Histoire de l'Afrique Noire*. Paris, Hatier, 1972.

LABIB, S. Islamic Expansion and Slave Trade in Mediaeval Africa. *Colloque de Saint-Denis sur les Mouvements de Population dans l'Océan Indien*. In press.

LOMBARD, D. Un 'Expert' Saxon dans les Mines d'Or de Sumatra au XVIIe Siècle. *Archipel*, Vol. 2, 1971, p. 225–42.

MARISSAL, J., *La Traite Orientale à Zanzibar*. Paris, Centre de Recherches Africaines, 1970.

MAUNY, R. *Les Siècles Obscurs de l'Afrique Noire*. Paris, Fayard, 1971.

MIÈGE, J. L. La Libye et le Commerce Transsaharien au XIXe Siècle. *Revue de l'Occident Musulman et de la Méditerranée* (Aix-en-Provence), No. 19, 1975, p. 135–68.

MOLET, L. Le Vocabulaire Concernant l'Esclavage dans l'Ancien Madagascar. *Perspectives Nouvelles sur le Passé de l'Afrique Noire et de Madagascar*. Paris, Publications de la Sorbonne, 1974, p. 45–65.

MOLLAT, M. *Historical Contacts of Africa and Madagascar with South and South-East Asia: the Rôle of the Indian Ocean*, Port-Louis, 1974.

OLIVER, R. L'Afrique Orientale. *Histoire Générale de l'Afrique Noire*, Vol. 1, p. 423–49.

OLIVER, R.; MATHEW, G. (eds.), *History of East Africa*. Vol. I. Oxford, Clarendon Press, 1963.

OTTINO, P. *Madagascar, les Comores et le Sud-Ouest de l'Océan Indien (Projet d'Enseignement et de Recherches)*. Université de Madagascar, 1974.

OTTINO, P. Le Moyen Age de l'Océan Indien et le Peuplement de Madagascar. *Annuaire des Pays de l'Océan Indien*. p. 197–221. Aix-en-Provence, CERSOI, 1974.

PANKHURST, R. The Ethiopian Slave Trade in the Nineteenth and Early Twentieth Centuries: A Statistical Inquiry. *Journal of Semitic Studies* (Manchester), Vol. 9, 1964, p. 220–8.

RENAULT, F. *Lavigerie, l'Esclavage Africain et l'Europe (1868–1892)*. 2 vols. Paris, E. de Boccard, 1971.

——. La Traite Transsaharienne et Orientale en Afrique. *Godo Godo, Bulletin de l'IHAAA* (University of Abidjan), No. 2, July 1976, p. 25–46.

——. *Libération d'Esclaves et Nouvelles Servitudes* (Abidjan), 1977. (Nouvelles Editions Africaines (B.P. 20615).)

TINKER, H., *A New System of Slavery, the Export of Indian Labour Overseas (1830–1920)*. London, Oxford University Press, 1974.

TOUSSAINT, A. *La Route des Iles*. Paris, SEVPEN, 1967.

VALETTE, J. Considérations sur les Exportations d'Esclaves Malgaches vers les Mascareignes au XVIIIe Siècle. *Colloque de Beyrouth, 1966*. p. 531–40. Paris, SEVPEN, 1970.

VÉRIN, P. Les Arabes dans l'Océan Indien et à Madagascar, *Arabes et Islamisés à Madagascar et dans l'Océan Indien*, p. a–c. Tananarive, 1967.

——. *Histoire Ancienne du Nord-Ouest de Madagascar*. Tananarive, Taloha 5, Université de Madagascar, 1972.

WANG GUNGWU, The Chinese and the Countries across the Indian Ocean. Port-Louis, 1974.

WANQUET, C. *La Réunion pendant l'Époque Révolutionnaire*. In press.

——. La Réunion et la Guerre de Course pendant l'Époque Révolutionnaire. *Cahiers du Centre Universitaire de la Réunion*, No. 8, 1976, p. 23–60.

Summary report of the meeting of experts on the African slave trade

Port-au-Prince, Haiti, 31 January to 4 February 1978

The meeting, which was attented by thirty-three experts and nine observers, was inaugurated by H.E. Dr Raoul Pierre-Louis, Secretary of State for National Education (Haiti) who gave the opening address (see page 236), after the observance of one minute's silence in memory of all the victims of the slave trade. Amadou-Mahtar M'Bow, Director-General of Unesco, then outlined the main features of the experts' task, and stressed the positive spirit of international co-operation manifested by the holding of such a discussion on this difficult subject in Haiti, the scene of great suffering from the slave trade and of the struggle for the liberation of the black man (see page 239).

The meeting selected its officers as follows: Dr Raoul Pierre-Louis (Haiti), Chairman; Professor B. A. Ogot (Kenya) and Professor H. Tolentino (Dominican Republic), Vice-Chairmen; Professor J. Devisse (France), Rapporteur.

This summary report sets out the most constructive suggestions which emerged from the discussion, and includes the most recent information. It is not a point-by-point record of the discussion.

Summary report

Scale of the slave trade

Record and criticism of results so far achieved

Despite serious efforts in recent years to reach a comprehensive conclusion, differences in the assessment of the global extent of the slave trade remain acute, and they emerged during the discussion. According to some participants who wished to take into considerations factors such as losses during capture and land journeys across Africa, and deaths during the sea crossing, Africa's losses during the four centuries of the Atlantic slave trade must be put at some 210 million human beings.

According to others the overall total of slaves transported between the tenth and the nineteenth centuries from Black Africa to the various receiving territories should be put at between 15 and 30 million persons.

In the case of particular receiving territories there is similar uncertainty. For Brazil, for example, the highest estimated figures are four times as large as the lowest.

The majority of the experts considered that, in any event, even now, these figures are not sufficiently exact, since different data series which do not permit of superposition or comparison have been assembled hitherto with no coherent overall plan. Research should therefore be pursued in accordance with the following guidelines.

Account should be taken, for example, of hitherto neglected data such as deaths on capture, during land of sea journeys, and following insurrections. Interesting statistical information was provided concerning deaths on board the slave-ships. Depending on the length of the crossing, percentages varied greatly in the Indian Ocean at the end of the eighteenth and beginning of the nineteenth century. These were approximately 25 per cent in the case of transportation from the west African coast to the Mascarene Islands, 21 per cent when it was from the east coast of Africa, and 12 per cent on ships out of Madagascar.

There should be more extensive research into the transportation of slaves over at least ten centuries towards the Islamic countries, for which very little precise information has been collected up to now.

An evaluation should be made of the slave trade in the Indian Ocean, which lasted from ancient times to the twentieth century, much longer than that in the Atlantic. Here again present estimates vary greatly: they range from 1 to 5 million for the period from 1451 to 1870.

A very thorough study should be made of the post-abolition clandestine slave trade in all its forms, particularly in the south Atlantic and Indian Oceans. Although much good work has already been done, the meeting considered that in too many instances the establishment of the figures used was based on a partial, or even partisan, critique of the sources and that the investigation should therefore be broadened. However there should be preparation for the further research to be carried out by basing it on the adoption of stricter working methods.

While recognizing that regional or global quantification was necessary in order to satisfy the legitimate concern for a proper assessment of the damage caused to Africa, and also to make the requisite economic analysis, the meeting hoped that the research entailed, which would certainly be of long duration, would not block all the discussion and research that needs to be pursued in so many other fields.

The meeting noted that hardly anyone disputed the fact that several tens of millions of black Africans were uprooted from Africa and transported to more or less distant receiving countries and that this drain, quantitatively huge and qualitatively catastrophic, could not be compared, so far as its effects were concerned, to the voluntary or at least free migration of Europeans to North America in the nineteenth century.

Possibilities of improving our present state of knowledge

Two main theoretical approaches emerged during the discussion, with some experts on one side and some on the other. However, these approaches are not methodologically irreconcilable, even though they are linked to different philosophies or historical methods.

The inductive method is to present the slave trade, a logical and not at all accidental phenomenon, in the context of world-wide social and economic evolution.

The slave trade arose from the needs of the capitalist economy to develop outside Africa, and variations in the scale of the drain from the African continent and in the distribution of slaves among the receiving countries reflected the variations in those needs. Very different situations were mentioned as between the Atlantic islands (Fernando Po, São Tomé, Cape Verde, Canaries–Azores–Madeira), the Caribbean area, North and South America, the countries bordering on the Indian ocean and the islands of that ocean. The examples given show that each degree of increased intensity in the production of the colonies was reflected in different degrees of intensification of the slave trade.

Similarly, the introduction of the steam engine and of the cotton-gin were important factors in speeding up the demand for black labour.

In most cases it was necessary for such labour to be renewed very frequently. The life-span of slaves was short and the birth rate very low, thus the maintenance or increase of the labour force required was possible only by increased slave imports to keep pace with the development of economic competition among European countries.[1]

More empirically, the other deductive method would be the further preparation of serious monographs before attempting to generalize and draw together numerical results or make classified assessments.

Those in favour of this method, less concerned with overall explanations, stressed the urgency of certain improvements in the technical methods of research, such improvements were felt to be needed also in the case of the other approach.

The meeting stressed that archives should receive special attention. In certain cases, they had been removed or concealed where they related to the slave trade;[2] in other cases they had not been classified;[3] or insufficient use had been made of them where they were abundant.

In general, the meeting advocated the preparation as proposed by the Director-General in his opening address, of a *Guide to Sources relating to the History of the Slave Trade in the Archives of the Caribbean Area*.

The meeting also considered that a careful re-reading of known sources could provide much new quantitative material (for example concerning deaths at sea) and also linguistic information. While the records were mostly drawn up by and for slave-owners, they could yield much hitherto scarcely used information. A thorough scrutiny of the various kinds of sources would make it possible to classify in the order of its real importance the information published by each of those sources.

Finally, it was considered desirable to carry out a systematic search in certain countries (e.g. Turkey, Egypt, the Maghreb countries, Iran, Arabia, India and Europe) among sources hitherto inaccessible or not sufficiently available to the public and which could provide information on the various aspects of the slave trade. It was thought that private archives and those of European trading companies could also yield important details if their owners agreed to co-operate in the collective search.

Oral tradition was thought to be no less deserving of attention. In Africa itself it could, in particular cases, still provide valuable material. In Brazil, the Caribbean area, the United States, the islands of the Indian Ocean, and among the African communities which had returned from India to Kenya, in Gujarat

and in the region of the Persian Gulf, however, it was important that intense
and speedy action should be taken before the disappearance of elderly witnesses
able to provide both information on the slave trade and important linguistic
material.

To increase our information on the transplantation of African cultures,
a careful survey should be undertaken, rapidly and in depth, of all the traces
of African languages in the three Americas. This study might initially be undertaken through co-operation between African linguistic specialists and American
scholars, pending the creation of institutes of African linguistics, particularly
in the Caribbean area.

In Africa, a systematic mapping should be undertaken of destroyed or
deserted villages wherever they can validly be linked to the slave trade.

In the Caribbean, Brazil and North America, immediate action should
be taken systematically to assemble objects related to the slave trade, or objects
which have African prototypes.

In a more general vein, the present vagueness of definitions relating
to the ethnic origin of the transported slaves led the meeting to recommend
that scholars should not be satisfied with vague epithets referring to the embarkation area in Africa (e.g. 'Congo', 'Angolan') or to a general linguistic group
(e.g. 'Bantu').

Interesting examples were given of the results obtainable when greater
detail is sought. In the Cape Verde Islands between 1834 and 1856, a register
gives 5,890 names of slaves of whom 141, who had not been baptized, were
entered under their African names with an indication of their origin (Mandingo,
Joloff, Mandyak, Flup, etc.). On the other hand, the example of the Malays in
the Indian Ocean should be carefully distinguished from that of the 'Malé'
of Brazil. In connection with these latter the meeting received divergent information. However, the word 'Malé' is synonymous with Muslim, as is 'Fulani'
in Guyana.

More generally still, reference was made on several occasions to the
advantage of having a descriptive graph of the quantitative evolution of the
slave trade. The information provided by recent studies on this point could be
gradually corrected and made more accurate as research methods become more
sensitive. Such an overall picture of the phenomenon, in conjunction with
regional and country graphs, would make it easier to perceive the variations
and contradictions of the slave trade. It would also contribute to emphasizing
the importance of never overlooking chronological factors in any quantitative
assessment of the phenomenon.

Effects of the slave trade

The results so far achieved by research vary considerably. Information becomes ever more scanty the further back one goes in history. The state of knowledge is relatively good concerning the routes used in transporting the slaves and the ports of embarkation, but study of the economic and political impact of the slave trade is much less advanced. It is difficult to break down such work into component parts and dissociate the quantitative elements from the qualitative, the economic from the political.

Demographic repercussions in Africa

It was clear that no one now supports the idea that the slave trade played a positive role by averting a population explosion in Africa, but there are considerable differences of opinion concerning the responsibility of the slave trade for the underdevelopment of the African continent. Investigation of this subject is difficult, because the usual tools for analysis are non-existent.

The meeting recommended that for such studies resort should be had to the techniques of demographers, which would provide indications as to the minimum population density of a particular area capable of ensuring the survival of its inhabitants and as to the optimum population density range within which the best conditions for development were to be found.

Likewise, the study of works on environmental effects in Africa (for example on the tsetse fly or onchocerciasis) could provide interesting evidence as to the secondary causes of depopulation or population movements.

The use of global economic analysis techniques should make it possible to obtain a quantitative and qualitative assessment of the negative influence of the slave trade on African productivity. The preparation of monographs for area of Africa would be useful in obtaining a complete picture of the effects of the slave trade.

Impact of the slave trade on political, economic and social structures in Africa

None of the experts present disputed the idea that the slave trade was responsible for the economic backwardness of Black Africa. Some experts discussed the positive role that might have been played as producers and consumers by the Africans removed from the continent if they had not been transported as slaves away from Africa.

It was found that the external demand for labour became increasingly pressing with time and that in the overall study of the slave trade chronological sequences must be preserved. The demand by the Muslim labour markets was followed, after the fifteenth and sixteenth centuries, by that arising from the first European experiments with plantations. Then, as the major phenomena of the plantation economy and mining developed in the seventeenth and eighteenth centuries in the Americas and later in the Indian Ocean, the slave trade grew to massive proportions. Despite its legal abolition, it was maintained, to a varying extent according to region in the nineteenth and in places even into the twentieth century, and took different clandestine forms.

While the analysis of the pressures exerted on Black Africa by the demand for labour appeared to be relatively well developed today, the analysis of economic and social consequences was found to be far less advanced. In many cases, hypotheses still have to suffice.

It would seem that, before the fifteenth century, there was an economic development that was characteristically African. The accelerated demand for labour abroad impaired and then put an end to this development. This is the most logical explanation for the absence of economic vitality in African societies at the time of the European capitalist expansion.

The slave trade appeared to have provided some already organized African trading societies with the ready-made solution of exchanging human beings for imported goods. Where no specialized trading function existed, those who held political power had to make a choice between accepting the proposed slave trade or refusing, with all the consequences. European pressures in this field continued to increase from the sixteenth century— when they already existed for example in the Congo and in Zimbabwe— to the eighteenth century. In the case of some African societies the choice was often decisive, for instance the Ovimbundu in Angola, in order to survive as an organized group, entered into the system of the Portuguese slave trade.

The import of manufactured articles probably reduced the Africans' incentive to produce: this was no doubt the case of iron production in Senegambia. There was a similarly increasing demand for raw materials—ivory, furs and skins, gum, etc.—which were useful for industrial development in Europe. It is also probable that the diversion of a considerable part of the labour force to slavery and the slave trade prevented the establishment of a pool of manpower available for agriculture and the production of manufactured goods.

Little by little the slave trade acquired the support of a new class of rich merchants, whose origins varied according to the region and who were often able to oppose the African political authorities successfully when the latter showed unwillingness to co-operate in the slave trade. This merchant class should be carefully studied.

It was considered that the development of a deep-seated sense of insecurity and the increase of inter-ethnic or social tensions created an 'anti-economic mentality' in Africa: all that the Africans were concerned about was to survive through modest and routine work in proportion to needs. It was felt that this point should also be the subject of very careful studies.

From another point of view, the experts considered that it would be desirable
   to analyse qualitatively the losses suffered. While it is already known
   that those uprooted from Africa were generally the young people, too
   little is known of their social level and the circumstances of their capture.
It is relatively easy today to map the main places where the slave trade was
carried on. Such a map shows areas whose relative importance varied with the
time and 'collecting areas' related to 'demand markets'. It was considered
that in this field it would be easy to produce fairly quickly a collective publication summarizing the results achieved to date for the whole of Africa between
the tenth and twentieth centuries.

   The experts examined the question of the changes undergone by the
African political authorities owing to the slave trade. Divergent opinions
emerged on certain points.

The idea that the authorities may have shown organized opposition to the
   slave trade has often been put forward in recent years. Recently, oral
   traditions have been found which advance such a reason as one of the
   basic causes of the emergence of the Empire of Mali. It was considered
   that no study had yet been made of the forms taken by such authorities,
   which varied greatly institutionally according to the region and the
   society concerned.

The traditionally organized authorities, for example in Jolof, Cayor, Balol,
   Songhai, Congo and Zimbabwe, were, in various ways and at various
   times, confronted with the pressure of European or Muslim demands for
   slaves. They were all upset by this pressure. They all suffered immediate
   defeat, or such a transformation of their relations with the societies that
   they represented that they became either the forced instruments of the
   traders or the victims of less scrupulous political rivals. The slave trade
   had an indisputably destructive effect on the oldest African authorities.

On the other hand, new forms of authority arose more or less directly out of
   the slave trade. There were some kings who sought, through the formation
   of docile groups of slaves, a means of domination without opposition,
   contrary to traditional customs. Others created a privileged military
   caste as a defence for their group, thus establishing a warrior class
   supported by domestic slaves in greater numbers than formerly. In the
   nineteenth century such authorities emerged all over Africa, even inland.
   Subjected to the aggression of the European slave trade, the black
   Muslims of West Africa reacted by encouraging the organization of
   religious authorities whose primary concern was to defend the Islamic
   communities by refusal to co-operate with the slave-traders, and also
   by the use of force.

The political map of Africa was profoundly modified as a result of such movements. In general neither the authorities nor the societies of the nineteenth

century bore any resemblance to those which had existed at the beginning of the slave trade.

The question arises who best protected those dependent on them and to the detriment of whom, in this redistribution of political factors.

In any event, it seems indisputable that such upsets were accompanied by an increase of social tensions, a worsening of servitude, especially quantitatively and by a transformation of the former processes of social integration that the various forms of personal dependence provided in African society prior to the fifteenth century.

As an extreme case, it must be recalled that, at least in East Africa, and no doubt elsewhere, rulers founded their power and wealth in the nineteenth century on the systematic exploitation of the sale of slaves destined for the Indian Ocean ports or for plantations which were by that time established on the soil of Africa itself.

Economic consequences in the countries benefiting from the slave trade

It was considered that, from the outset, a distinction must be made between the receiving countries and the colonial powers which certainly derived the greatest advantage from the slave trade. The latter controlled the competitive process carried on under cover of the monopoly system and dominated capitalist growth from the sixteenth to the nineteenth century. They benefited twice from the export of African slaves, first through the transportation of slaves and secondly by the production of marketable commodities made possible by the local use of slave labour. The receiving countries benefited much less uniformly from the arrival of their labour force; to a large extent this lack of uniformity is due to the degree of power of the colonists, which varied over the years, and to the varying degree of their participation in competitive trade.[4]

A careful distinction should probably be made between State profits, made mainly out of the slave trade in certain cases and out of the power provided by the marketing of colonial produce in other cases, and private profits, of a more modern kind, made for example in Great Britain and in the United Provinces.

This is a very complex question. First, because it is linked with the development of Western capitalist economy over three or four centuries and because it is difficult to identify quantitatively the proportion of the means of capital accumulation derived from the slave trade. Secondly, because the very question of the role played by the slave trade in this development of pre-industrial and industrial capitalist Europe is in itself a novelty, at any rate for some European scholars. Similarly, methodological changes and perhaps even changes of attitude are required to link the analyses of the economic development in Africa with that of the development of Europe in a single overall perspective. The meeting expressed a strong hope that European historians would co-operate in the research that would have to be undertaken along these new main lines of historical reasoning.

In the area of generalities a place apart has to be given to the Muslin countries of Africa, Arabia, the Persian Gulf and the Indian Ocean. It is difficult to assess the role played in enriching this part of the world by the Africans present from the seventh century in Iraq, who specialized in the difficult processes of cultivating dates and sugar cane, and of pearl fishing. How can an accurate assessment be made of the contribution of black soldiers and African sailors to the power of the Muslim world?

It is only in the nineteenth century that the Muslim slave trade, linked to the labour needs of the Indian Ocean colonies, may be regarded as being integrated in the capitalist system. Thus, for the earlier periods, other approaches and other scales of assessment are needed than for European capitalism.

How can an equitable assessment be made of the contribution of black Africans imported into Europe, first through the Muslim countries up to the fifteenth century, and then directly?

The meeting voiced concern that these phenomena, which are so complex and so full of contradictions, should always be studied in a historical perspective, that is to say as an evolving phenomenon, with chronological references.

The colonizing countries benefited in disparate ways from the consequences of the slave trade.

The countries of the western Mediterranean, which were the richest in capital before the fifteenth century, slowly lost their predominant position from then on to the Atlantic European countries.

Portugal was late in taking the path of modern capitalist economic development, because of the lack of a well-to-do middle class. Brazil benefited more from the slave trade than the mother country. In Brazil, the massive influx of labour from Africa, regarded by the Portuguese simply as a manpower reservoir, made possible the development of the mines and also the plantations, both of which, in the eighteenth century, produced commodities for which there was a large-scale international market. Portugal invested in Brazil alone, and hardly invested at all in Africa before 1930.

Spain was not able to take any better advantage, through development of an entrepreneurial middle class, of the profits made possible by the slave trade. It was unable to keep the monopoly of the slave trade and did not develop any major trade in the produce of the plantations. Its colonies, therefore, did not share in the rapid development of the colonies of its European rivals in the eighteenth century. The importation of manpower was not as necessary in those colonies as elsewhere, and labour was hardly involved in any large-scale production of exportable wealth. From this standpoint, there is a great contrast between the Spanish part of Hispaniola and the part which became French in the eighteenth century and is now called Haiti.

The United Provinces benefited only from the transportation of slaves and from the import of African raw materials. Their colonies in the Caribbean demonstrated no great need for imported manpower nor any particular productive vitality.

France, particularly in the eighteenth century, obviously made considerable real profits from the slave trade, but perhaps even more profits from the intensive exploitation of the Caribbean islands which it owned and which enabled it to take part in the production of sugar and fresh food products for the British North American colonies as well as the French colonies. The basis for an economic and military alliance of converging interests emerged between France and the British colonies.

The extent to which this manpower was exploited and driven, in Haiti for example, created violent tensions in the relations between masters and slaves, relations which constantly worsened with the arrival of more slaves. The rapid reaction to the very success of the French farming economy was what led to the revolt of Santo Domingo and Haitian independence.

Great Britain, which benefited during the eighteenth century from increasing mastery of the seas, would seem to have made greater profits from the slave trade itself than from the plantation colonies.

It is not clear whether it was the northern or the southern colonies in North America which really benefited economically from the contributions of black labour.

In any event, the slave-trade economy brought wealth to the population of the ports and those who worked for them in France, Great Britain and Holland, in which countries it made some contribution to capital accumulation. It certainly increased the wealth and political influence of the West European middle class, but it must be remembered that the riches of Asia and the Indian Ocean also played a part in that prosperity.

In the American islands, in Brazil, and in the sugar-producing islands of the Indian Ocean, the rapid growth of the plantations created conditions for basic development. This development was brought about mainly by black labour, with the co-operation of the few Amerindian groups that survived the massacres of the first colonial period. The receiving countries, looked at from this standpoint, received the Africans not just as objects of trade but as creators of wealth—even though in the eighteenth century that wealth accrued solely to their European masters.

The plantation societies were violently split and racial prejudice created an even stronger barrier there than elsewhere between white masters and black slaves. The tension was made even more dangerous as the quest for larger-scale production made the treatment they received more and more unbearable for the slaves.

In Brazil and in Réunion there gradually emerged a society in which apart from agriculture, most of the 'small trades' were carried on by the slaves. There thus developed a whole series of producing trades which were not under the control of the planters. These are at present being studied by Cuban scholars.[5]

Socio-cultural consequences in the receiving countries, particularly the Americas

While Haiti considers itself born of the slave trade, the societies to which it gave rise became creole by force of circumstances in the course of time. In these culturally and ethnically more or less composite societies, it is still difficult to identify the role of Africa and African cultures. The degree of survival of African influences is quite clearly linked directly with social and political developments in each case under consideration.

Wherever the Black Africans' reaction to protect themselves was not rapid and radical, integration of the slaves into the culture of the European master class took place, more or less quickly. This gave rise to a linguistic and religious fragmentation. The greater the religious, linguistic and day-by-day integration of the slaves into a European type of life, the more one-sided the process of 'creolization', the more difficult it is to find traces of African culture. The meeting considered that these very processes of integration should in themselves constitute a subject of research.[6]

The Muslim societies were in a different category. The religion and the language of the Arabs would appear to be irreversible factors making for integration, at least in the case of Africans removed from the black areas of the continent to the Middle Eastern Islamic countries.

The areas where research should eventually be carried out are enormous. They should include Fernando Po, São Tomé, the Cape Verde Islands, the Azores, the Canaries and Madeira, which were known and populated in certain cases before their discovery by Europeans. It should also include the islands in the Indian Ocean, the Caribbean, Brazil, the United States and Mexico.

Brazil offered many examples of African survivals. In addition to existing inventories, there should no doubt be more thorough and scientific studies.

Bahia has a million black inhabitants; African Muslims set up a resistance movement in the nineteenth century north of Bahia and organized themselves into a theocratic republic linked to the African continent. Afro-Brazilians returned in the nineteenth century to the countries round the Gulf of Benin. An old man of 96, Baba Ijesa,[7] spoke in Yoruba with two of the experts attending the meeting. Special attention should be given to Brazil, which probably constitutes a useful example.[8]

Evidence noted in the Caribbean islands is no less interesting. In the Dominican Republic, in Haiti, in Guadeloupe, in the Guianas and in Brazil, relations between Amerindians and blacks were neither as infrequent nor as bad as the colonists would have it believed. The role of the Amerindians in the early stages of the presence of blacks would seem to have been greater than had long been thought. In Cuba, even today, the vestiges of this prejudice are so strong that it is still stated that the population is entirely Afro-Cuban, and that the Amerindians have quite disappeared. The same was said to be the case in Guyana, whereas there are still Amerindians surviving today, in both cases. It would be of interest to make a study of the real relations of the blacks with the Amerindians.

An avenue of research could be opened up by using the apparently tenuous vestiges of African languages in the social, military or religious life of the diaspora. However, this should not lead to neglecting study of the various creole languages of Central America and the Indian Ocean.[9]

Stories having great similarities with African stories have been found in the Caribbean, Réunion and Mayotte. It would be interesting to undertake a systematic and careful analysis of them, particularly to note the differences between non-African and African versions.

It is undoubtedly thanks to the maroons, of whom there are particularly large numbers in the Spanish colonies, but who also exist in other Caribbean regions, and in the islands of the Indian Ocean, that a large proportion of African cultural tradition has been preserved. The existence of *marronage* as a social, political and military phenomenon should thus be studied along with its cultural implications.[10]

The official cultural doctrine of the Dominican Republic, based on 'Indian-ness' and excluding reference to Africa would seem to put this country in the opposite category from Haiti. History obviously explains this paradox.

Haiti, born of a slave insurrection on the part of those who arrived in great numbers at the end of the eighteenth century, derives the force of its political cohesion from a basic choice made on 14 August 1791 at Bois Caiman. To the careful observer, Voodoo would still appear today to be the focal point of Haitian cultural life.

This people sprang from ethnic groups that were faced with the same problem of freeing themselves from slavery but who had been at loggerheads among themselves until then. Voodoo, as reinterpreted and integrated into the Caribbean situation, is the best preserved heritage of African religious and cultural traditions.[11] On this ground, it deserves careful study. In Haiti, it has taken on a value different from that which it has in Africa where it originated, or in other regions of Central America.

Ideological positions with regard to the problem of the slave trade

This topic was discussed from three different points of view:

First, the discussion of cultural heritages prior to the eighteenth century, the role of the Enlightenment, racialism and Marxism were not pushed very far.

Research needs to be done on the responsibility of classical philosophy and also on certain monotheistic trends which made it philosophically possible to justify the unequal position of the blacks. Perhaps it can at least be said that it was a far cry in fact from the principles proclaimed and those of Christianity, the Enlightenment to the social reality of slavery. A number of experts strongly stressed the historical contradiction between the statements of principle on the part of the authorized representatives of Christianity and the reality of actual support for the slave trade over a long period on the part of churchmen and missionaries, even if they were disavowed by their superiors.

The real centre of interest lies therefore in the conception of slavery held by the societies which practised it to the detriment of the Africans. Clarifying studies must still be carried out in order to arrive at closer definitions of the meaning attaching to the term 'slave' in the different societies involved. Similarly, the meeting decided to refer to the International Scientific Committee for a *General History of Africa* the controversial problem of the terminology that should be used in connection with the topics under discussion.

The circumstances in which anti-black racism arose were not defined with sufficient vigour. How, by what means and at what time did the transition take place from the notion of 'natural inequality' of individuals and the notion of racialism?

The contribution of theoretical Marxism to the discussion of slavery was mentioned; it consists mainly in the denunciation of the labour force and of the surplus profits made possible by the slave trade.

At this initial level, the meeting contributed neither decisive information nor the beginnings of any new thought. It simply noted that the debate remains open.

The question of the theoretical attitude of Indian communities confronted with the presence of African slaves was raised but no answer was forthcoming. Second, whatever the noble intentions and proclamations of churchmen and philosophers, the ideology applied in the seventeenth and eighteenth centuries supported the interests of the European middle class. This explains the contradictions mentioned by many experts.

For example, ideology justified the capture of slaves—who were 'pagan' and thus destined to eternal damnation—by the 'possibility of salvation' conferred on them through baptism or conversion to Islam. This attempt at justi-

fication conceals another inegalitarian, Mediterranean-oriented value judgement regarding 'civilization' as distinct from the pagan way of life devoid of
rules, culture and religion.

There was thus a confrontation of values between one world, that of the
Mediterranean, certain of the coherence of its values and traditions, incapable
of understanding that there were other cultural paths and values than its own,
and the unsung, rejected African cultures, looked down upon because their
values were unwritten, non-imperialistic.

When these two worlds came in contact, two conflicting conceptions
prevailed of man seen as a producer. In the Western view, man was perceived
as pursuing his individual path within the developing capitalist society and
exploiting the work of others to the extent that he was stronger than they were:
in the African conception, the individual producer was a member of a cohesive
production group. These two opposing values of individual work, both of
which had profound underlying religious significance, made any real understanding between the European and the African cultures impossible.

The 'superiority' of the white man, which was 'demonstrated' by his
economic success, proved the 'inferiority' of the black man, which was 'demonstrated' by the fact of his capture and enslavement. The blacks were made to
feel radically inferior in their dependent situation, thus breaking the individual
and collective capacity to put up any resistance. They were only able to regain
that capacity when they had faith in the values of their own society, values
which the enslavement process sought to make them forget as rapidly and completely as possible.

The violence done to the Africans in enslaving them is perceived as
justified by the foregoing arguments. Likewise the contamination of African
society by the violence of the power relationship is perceived as 'justified'
by the success of this inegalitarian violence.

It would be interesting to investigate the ideological reaction of Africans,
so far as it can still be discovered, to the slave trade seen in this light. It would be
also interesting to find out how the slave trade is now interpreted in the African
villages, ethnic groups and regions that were affected in various ways by that
trade.

A third type of ideological analysis should be systematized. It relates to
the change of outlook of the slaves in the receiving countries. How did they
preserve some notion of freedom? In a Spanish document of 1503 the com-
plaint is made from this standpoint that the blacks were contaminating the
Amerindians. How did they preserve the memory of their values and cultures?
How were the maroon societies organized? On what political or military bases?
What was the background of the leaders who led the revolts? What was the
genesis of the successful revolution in Haiti? There can be no doubt that one
of the reasons why the meeting was unable to arrive at clear and concise con-

clusions on this matter was that many of the local studies have not been circulated widely enough—for example, the studies on *marronnage* carried out in Haiti, Cuba and the Caribbean region in general.

Abolition of the slave trade

The dates of abolition of the slave trade and later of slavery vary widely and reflect different factual situations. When their financial interests were at stake, owners frequently found it more economical to free their slaves! Such reasons explain why emancipation began in Cuba and Brazil a long time before slavery was officially abolished. Some of the freed slaves travelled back to what is now Nigeria and to Dahomey (now Benin) at their own expense. The abundance of such examples, particularly in the Caribbean, indicates that a general study of the subject would be worth while[12].

Slave revolts undoubtedly played a part in accelerating abolition and in the development of a wage-earning structure. The Haitian Revolution spread terror in the slave-trading colonies and metropolitan countries and the slaves regarded it as symbolic. During the period between the abolition of the slave trade and that of slavery itself, frequent revolts occurred in the English- and Spanish-speaking Caribbean, with the support of Christian sects or churches. In this respect, and perhaps involuntarily, Christianity encouraged the appearance of emancipation movements and Messianic cults.

Here, too, Islam was in a unique position. Rejecting the idea that a Muslim could ever be a slave, and believing that a 'pagan' one *ipso facto* was, Islam had nothing to say about the two abolitions which were the cause of so much ideological and political discussion in the Christian world.

Whether early or late, abolition of the slave trade hardly ever put an end to the manpower drain of Africa. In the Indian Ocean clandestine slavery continued to exist until late in the nineteenth century. Other means of procuring labour, such as the indenture system, took the place of the slave trade.

Abolition made very little difference. The relations of the masters and the newly emancipated did not improve. The condition of the emancipated was often worse, financially, than before.

Under cover of the new legality, all sorts of schemes were introduced to enable the masters to perpetuate their control of the labour force (the *gourmettes* of Senegambia and the 'freedom villages' of West Africa are examples). The existence of a free labour market meant that the masters could avoid part of the costs they had previously borne in connection with their slaves.[13] Slavery was an obsolete system, but in addition it was now a less economical proposition than wage-earning labour. Moreover, when the labour market was saturated, wages fell.

As a rule, 'official' liberalism considered that freedom was a sufficiently generous gift to absolve the liberators from any further responsibility for the fate of the former slaves. Irrespective of the status of those who organized their return—States institutions, churches, benevolent societies—the Africans who were repatriated to Sierra Leone and Liberia constituted a relatively small minority. The same was true of the blacks repatriated from Bombay to Kenya, whose case merits further study.

The experts were generally inclined to conclude that abolition brought no radical changes, but simply led to the transition from one state of production and exploitation to another. Abolition made it possible to exploit an expanding African labour market. At that point, trade with Europe could have served as an incentive to the development of the domestic economy of Africa. But habits acquired during the period of slavery appear to have limited the stimulus that might have been expected.

Before such a stimulus could make itself felt, it was stifled by the colonial conquest which blocked the development of African industry by introducing foreign business enterprises—and these, once again, exploited the continent so as to meet the needs of other countries.

There is ample room for further economic study, based on these initial reflections, concerning the nineteenth and twentieth centuries.

The abolition of slavery by Portugal in 1888 led Brazil to break off its relations with that country a year later. The Portuguese economy suffered the ill-effects of this secession for many decades.

Lastly, the experts turned their attention to the effects of abolition on inegalitarian attitudes towards blacks. They concluded that abolition had led to an increase in racialist attitudes of all kinds with regard to the Negro world which was regarded as 'uncivilized', a world that had no right to its own culture or its own religion. 'Scholars' were quick to justify this harsh and unjust attitude and to draw a distinction between the 'primitive' Negroes, with whom nothing could be done, and the 'superior' Negroes, who could be assimilated.

New lines of research

The experts recommended the following activities and subjects for research:
Exchanges, with assistance from Unesco, of teachers and students from universities in Africa, the Caribbean and the Indian Ocean region, who are interested in the study of the various forms and consequences of the slave trade.
The establishment of bilateral research teams of Latin American, Caribbean and African scholars to make an inventory of African cultural survivals (linguistic expressions, for example) of African life in the Americas.
The African States should be asked to include the teaching of Caribbean

cultures in their educational syllabuses at all levels and the Caribbean States should do the same with African cultures.

Assistance should be given for the microfilming of documents published all over the world on the slave trade; one collection should be deposited in a university centre in the Caribbean, another in a centre in Africa and a third in a centre in the Indian Ocean region.

Economic studies of the slave trade in the sixteenth, seventeenth and eighteenth centuries should be developed with particular reference to its effects on the history of Africa and the history of the Americas.

The various forms of African resistance to the slave trade should be studied: (a) in Africa itself; (b) on the slave ships; (c) in the Maroon communities; (d) in the form of individual or collective cultural resistance to integration in the receiving country, particularly in Brazil, the Caribbean and North America.

A study should be made of the participation of Africans as soldiers and sailors in the life of the Islamic world in North Africa, the Middle East and India.

The meeting was informed of the decisions taken by the Director-General of Unesco concerning the development of studies of the cultures of the Caribbean region: (a) assistance in the exchange of information between African research workers and those in other countries; (b) organization in July 1978 of a multi-disciplinary conference of experts in the Caribbean region, with the aim of studying the different aspects of the cultures of the region and preparing a research and publication programme; and (c) organization in 1979 of a meeting of experts on 'The African Negro Presence in the Americas and the Caribbean', in connection with Unesco's programme for the study of African cultures.

Closing session

At the end of the meeting, the Director-General stated:

In the last few weeks, I have been approached directly by black communities in various Latin American countries, who are now taking an interest in problems related both to their historical origins and to the situation of their contemporary cultures. I believe this to be evidence of the existence of new aspirations, which Unesco should take into consideration and which academic circles in general can no longer afford to ignore. As far as the future is concerned, I am in a position to assure you that the Organization will do everything in its power, in co-operation with the International Scientific Committee, to find ways and means of ensuring that publications dealing with your discussions are issued without delay, and of increasing our support for the research under way in different universities and institutions. Indeed, we way decide to take further measures to meet your wishes.

Your meeting has shown that specialists from different countries of the world —from Africa, Asia, Europe, the Caribbean, Latin America and America in general—

are capable of examining, with complete lucidity and objectivity, issues that are
extremely controversial because they have a connotation that is in some cases ideological as well as affective, and of arriving at recommendations that are satisfactory from
the scientific point of view . . .

Recommendations

The meeting drew the attention of the Director-General of Unesco to the
following points, and asked him to make their importance known to all the
governments concerned in Africa, the Caribbean, Europe and Asia.

Archives concerning the slave trade

All the archives concerning the slave trade must be made accessible to scholars,
without any restrictions. Unless matters were improved, much archival material
might be lost, and hence international opinion should be alerted.

It is matter of urgency that a scientific classification be undertaken of
public and private archives in Africa, the Americas and Europe relating to the
slave trade.

It would be desirable that Unesco provide rapid assistance in the preparation of a guide to sources relating to the slave trade to be found in collections
of archives in the Caribbean area.

Oral traditions relating to the slave trade

There exist, particularly in Brazil, in the Caribbean area, but also in various
parts of the Indian Ocean region and in North America, persons who possess
traditions concerning the slave trade, as well as surprising vestiges of transplanted African languages. Rapid and vigorous efforts should be made to
record this living evidence of survivals of African influences outside Africa.

Traces of African languages on a large scale (Haiti, Bahia, etc.) or in
more fragmented form must be preserved and recorded, and then studied by
competent experts, pending the establishment, which was also recommended,
of linguistic institutes for the study of the African languages in the countries
of the black diaspora, particularly in North and South America, the Caribbean
and the Indian Ocean region.

Missions by African experts to the Caribbean

Participants in the meeting strongly recommended that African specialists
should be sent to inventory and study the vestiges of African cultures in the
Caribbean.

Education of children and students in African and Caribbean history

The experts strongly hoped that the governments concerned would agree to include the history of Africa in syllabuses in the Caribbean area and the history of the Caribbean in syllabuses in African countries.

Notes

1. It was suggested that the experts pay the greatest attention to the pitfalls of inadequately digested mathematical techniques used on behalf of a dangerous ideology. The following works were recommended by one of the participants: *Calcul et Anthropologie* Paris. (Collection '10/18'); André Regnier, *La Crise du Langage Scientifique*, Paris; *Pourquoi la Mathématique*, Paris (Collection '10/18').
2. Examples were given for Portugal and Guadeloupe.
3. The Copenhagen Archives relating to the Virgin Islands are a case in point. However, Dr Neville Hall, Dean of the History Faculty at the University of the West Indies, Mona (Jamaica), was given access to them recently.
4. It should be emphasized that the benefits of the slave trade accumulated by the receiving countries were a powerful stimulus to international trade, both in volume and in value, and that this commercial development was itself an incentive to modern economic development in Western Europe and North America.
5. See Pedro Deschamps Chapeaux, *Contribución a la Historia de la Gente sin Historia*, Havana, Editorial de Ciencas Sociales, 1974.
6. Scholars in Puerto Rico have begun to undertake research of this kind.
7. Ebun Ogunsanya, *The Yoruba Dialect in Bahian Portuguese*, Romance Languages Department, Radcliffe College, Harvard University, 1971 (Senior Theses, B.A.); Interviews with Eduardo Magobeira (Baba Ijesa), Bahia, June–August 1970.
8. See Jane McDivitt, *From Anguish to Affirmation—A Study of the Poetry of the Afro-Brazilian*, Harvard University, 1976, (unpublished doctoral thesis); Anani Dzidzienya, *The Minority Position of Blacks in Brazil*, London, Institute of Race Relations, 1972.
9. See the final report of the Meeting of Experts on the Historical Contacts between East Africa and Madagascar on the One Hand, and South-East Asia on the Other across the Indian Ocean, held in Mauritius in 1974 (Unesco doc. SHC.74/CONF/ 611/10.
10. See Richard Price, *Maroon Societies*, Ann Arbor, Michigan.
11. See R. Berrou and P. Pompilus, *Histoire de la Littérature Haïtienne Illustrée par les Textes*, Paris, Éditions de l'École, 3 vols.
12. See *Revista la Torre*, special issue published in November 1973 on the abolition of slavery in the Caribbean.
13. See Antonio Carreira, *Angola, da Escravatura ao Traballo Livre*, Lisbon, Arcadia, 1977

Appendixes

Appendixes

Appendix 1 : List of participants

J. F. ADE AJAYI
Vice-Chancellor, University of Lagos
(Nigeria)

Fitzroy A. BAPTISTE
Department of History,
University of the West Indies,
St Augustine, Trinidad (West Indies)

Max BENOIT
No. 19 Turgeau, Port-au-Prince
(Haiti)

Edward K. BRATHWAITE
Department of History, University
of the West Indies, Mona (Jamaica)

Antonio CARREIRA
Rua Maestro Jaime Silva, No. 9-80,
Dto Lisboa-4 (Portugal)

John H. CLARKE
Hunter College, 695 Park Avenue,
New York, NY 10021
(United States)

Philip D. CURTIN
Department of History,
Johns Hopkins University,
Baltimore, MD 21218 (United States)

J. DEVISSE
14 Avenue de la Porte de Vincennes,
75012 Paris (France)

Alioune DIOP
Société Africaine de Culture,
Paris (France)

Michèle DUCHET
ENS Fontenay,
Université de Paris VII,
29 Rue Boussingault,
75013 Paris (France)

L. EDMONDSON
Department of Government
(and Vice-Dean, Faculty of Social
Sciences), University of the West
Mona (Jamaica) Indies,

Jean FOUCHARD
Société d'Histoire de Haïti,
B.P. 64, Port-au-Prince,
(Haiti)

Hubert GERBEAU
Centre Universitaire de la Réunion,
97489 Saint-Denis, (Réunion)

Mbaye GUEYE
Faculté des Lettres et Sciences
Humaines,
Dakar (Sénégal)

Joseph E. HARRIS
History Department, Howard
University,
Washington, D.C. 20059
(United States)

J. E. INIKORI
Department of History,
Ahmadu Bello University,
Zaria (Nigeria)

Ibrahima Baba KAKE
79 Rue Marcadet,
75018 Paris (France)

D. LARA
Institut Caraïbe de Recherches
Historiques
14 Rue Henri-Wallon,
93800 Epinay s/Seine (France)

M. LIMA
  Rua Alves Redol, 17/CV/Esq,
  Lisboa-I (Portugal)
Pierre MONOSIET
  Musée d'Art Haïtien
  P.O. Box 1309, Port-au-Prince
  (Haiti)
D.T. NIANE
  Fondation L. S. Senghor,
  B.P. 2259 Dakar (Senegal)
René PIQUION
  Directeur de l'École Normale
  Supérieur d'Haïti
  2 bis Rue de Bois Patate
  Port-au-Prince (Haiti)
Bethwell A. OGOT
  Director,
  International Louis Leakey Memo-
  rial Institute for African Prehistory,
  P.O. Box 46727, Nairobi (Kenya)
A. F. PAULA
  Head of the Central Historical
  Archives,
  Roodweg 7 bis, Willenstho,
  Curaçao (Netherlands Antilles)
Raoul PIERRE-LOUIS
  Secretary of State
  for National Education (Haiti)
F. L. Veiga PINTO
  37 Avenue Dumas,
  Geneva (Switzerland)

Frank Moya PONS
  Atarazana No. 3 (Altos),
  Santo Domingo
  (Dominican Republic)
Waldeloir REGO
  Ladeira do Desterro, 19,
  Caixa Postal 1023,
  Salvador/Bahía (Brazil)
Walter RODNEY
  186 South Ruinveldt Gardens,
  Georgetown (Guyana)
Rubén SILIE
  Calle Diagonal 'C' No. 54,
  Santo Domingo
  (Dominican Republic)
Y. A. TALIB
  Department of Malay Studies,
  University of Singapore
  (Singapore)
H. F. S. TJOE NY
  Dean of the Faculty of Social and
  Economic Sciences,
  P.O. Box 2611,
  Paramaribo (Suriname)
Hugo TOLENTINO
  Avenida Bolívar 110,
  Santo Domingo
  (Dominican Republic)
J. Michael TURNER
  Departemento Geographia e Historia,
  Fundaçao Universidade de Brasília
  (Brazil)

Observers invited by Unesco

Holy See
Mgr L. Conti,
  B.P. 326,
  Port-au-Prince
  (Haiti)
Frère Raphael Berron,
  B.P. 1,
  Port-au-Prince
  (Haiti)

Menil Foundation
Mrs J. de Menil,
  1506 Branard Street,
  Houston, TX 77006
  (United States)
Mrs Karen Coffey,
  1506 Branard Street,
  Houston, TX 77006
  (United States)

Calouste Gulbenkian Foundation
Mario Antonio Fernandes de
  Oliveira,
  Avenue de Berna, Lisboa
  (Portugal)

*International Council for Philosophy and
Humanistic Studies*
Sir Ronald Syme,
  Unesco House,
  Paris (France)

Other observers

*Association des Historiens et Géographes
  de Haïti*
c/o Ministry of Education,
Port-au-Prince (Haiti)

P. T. Ndiaye, representing the

Leopold Sedar Senghor Foundation
P.O. Box 2035, Dakar (Senegal)
Max G. Beauvoir
  Groupe du Péristyle de Mariani,
  P.O. Box 2187. Port-au-Prince
  (Haiti)

Unesco

Adadou-Mahtar M'Bow,
  Director-General
Nadjm-Oud-Dine Bammate, Deputy
  Assistant Director-General for
  Culture and Communication (atten-
  ded the inaugural and final sessions)

Maurice Glélé, Cultural Studies Divi-
  sion, Culture and Communication
  Sector
Monique Melcer, Cultural Studies
  Division

Appendix 2: Opening speech of the Secretary of State for Education, Haiti

Mr Director-General of Unesco,
Excellencies,
Ladies and Gentlemen,

In opening this meeting, and with the Director-General's permission, I invite the meeting to observe a minute of silence in memory of all the unknown maroons, of all our ancestors, and particularly of a greatly lamented 'Griot' François Duvalier.

We are grateful to His Excellency, the Life President of the Republic for having extended his patronage to this meeting, and we sincerely thank him for all his interest and support in connection with this meeting of experts jointly organized by Unesco and the Haitian Government.

We are very happy and proud, Mr Director-General, to have you among us on this occasion, and it is a great pleasure to be able to express to you directly the respect, admiration and fraternal affection which, for many reasons, we bear you. Your participation in this inaugural sitting is for us a major contribution which we greatly appreciate.

Allow us, Mr Director-General, to present our respectful greetings to one of our own people, your own wife, so modest and yet so distinguished. Both of you are here among your own.

I now welcome the honourable participants and observers to the sunny and friendly land of Haiti, the home of Toussaint Louverture, Boukman, Halaou, Biassou, Jean-Jacques Dessalines, Alexandre Pétion, Henri Christophe and François Duvalier.

A visitor who sees Haiti for the first time from the air is bound to be struck by the craggy nature of the country. If he comes closer, he will, if he looks carefully, perceive the teeming of intense life, he will hear virile songs accompanied by drums, which provide encouragement and support for those working on the land, according to the fantasy of the combite musicians. Here and there, smoke rises from modest cottages, from hamlets scattered on the tops of the mountains, on the hillsides, and in the lush valleys.

The visitor then exclaims: 'This is Haiti', Haiti the country of plateaux and mountains, Haiti the land of places of great suffering, glory and hope, and of unsuspected potentialities. The names of these places are Bréda, Cormiers, Haut du Cap, Arcahaie, Vertières, La Crête à Pierrot, Gonaives, Marchaterre and Bonnet à l'Evêque where rises King Christopher's Citadelle in all its majesty.

There are other secret spots which do not have well-known names; these are the dark caves in our mountains, our steep cliffs and hidden dells in our plains; all of them friendly and impregnable hiding places for the maroons of former times. We can include in this context every inch of the tortured and holy land of Haiti, for long the cradle and bulwark of negritude in America, so often burned, ravaged and bathed in blood, sweat and tears, but which continued to nourish that mysterious 'tree of black freedom', the trunk of which, although hacked and scattered to the winds, still each time grows again from its many deep roots.

Ladies and Gentlemen, participants and observers, we welcome you with respect, trust and friendship. You will find here surprising survivals from our Mother Africa in gestures, words, songs, dances and many other significant details. You will also find kindness which reflects a real wish to please, but which does not exclude dignity and self-control, a welcome full of the warmth of easy-going human friendliness which does not exclude respect for others; a sense of solidarity born of long suffering which does not exclude independence of character; a way of smiling tinged with melancholy and dreaminess, the gaiety of laughter clothed in light, music, colour and dancing which does not exclude clear-headedness and is often a mask behind which life's aggressions can be challenged. There is also the faithfulness to ourselves and our values born of our determination to survive, but which does not exclude openness to human contacts and discussions.

In order to become at last truly ourselves, we know that at the crossroads of the present we still have to overcome obstacles of a new creeping and insidious kind, such as land erosion, drought, floods, the slow destruction of our historical monuments, the unsuitability of our educational system in comparison with our needs and aspirations, underproduction—in a word: underdevelopment.

In this new kind of struggle, applying the development strategy which we have chosen, we Haitians need sincere, understanding and reliable friends who are able to avoid wounding our native pride, to accept us as we are, and to give their friendly co-operation as we tread the difficult path ahead.

Now is the time for thought, joint effort and mutual enrichment. In this connection, the great migrations and the wanderings of those willingly or unwillingly uprooted from their native lands are particularly revealing. Man is in himself a whole universe, and even when he was transported naked, empty-handed and far from his own kin, he still kept his memories of home, his visions, his dreams, his ideas and his emotions and, in his new surroundings, his daily acts still reflected the traditions of the past, imprinted indelibly on his innermost unconscious.

By studying these movements, we get a deeper grasp of the contributions and reactions of different civilizations, and can discern through the curtain of time our ancestors kneeling to their own gods in their hidden temples.

The studies which you will undertake on the slave trade in all its aspects, implications and consequences will be both moving and valuable.

Few terms evoke in us such strong reactions, such an emotional shock, as the words 'slave trade', few terms carry such tragic memories, so indelible that no passage of time could ever quite efface them.

We, too, following on the original inhabitants of this land, have our eyes ceaselessly fixed on the ocean over which through the centuries has come so much good and so much evil. The first predators who settled on our countryside brought with them the cross in one hand and the sword in the other; in doing so they set the course of our historical destiny. The result of their despoiling passage was the slave trade, suggested and indirectly instigated by Las Casas.

You will, during these few days, identify the cultural imprint which, through their long journey, their complex process of adaptation and their protective and survival mechanisms, the victims of the slave trade clearly and indelibly impressed on the different fields of human activity in the places and societies where they had to make their lives.

This is, without doubt, an exciting and constructive task which, while there may be gaps in our knowledge and many traps to be avoided, is pregnant with unexpected discoveries that will provide the impetus for new historical, sociological and philosophical advances for the benefit of mankind.

While these remarks are not off the subject, they must seem to you who are precise men of science rather illusory and pointless.

You will have to set down the interactions, extrapolations and end results of extraordinary adventures lived by our fathers uprooted from Africa and cast into the outer darkness of slavery.

From the confrontation of your different theories and painstaking research we shall obtain a clear, precise and informative picture of the impact of the slave trade and its indelible imprint on the old as well as the new world.

I do not wish to take up more of the precious and unfortunately limited time which you have to discuss your researches and reflections on so fascinating a subject as the slave trade, but in this arduous task, you have my warmest wishes for the successful accomplishment of your task. May you have a happy and fruitful stay in Haiti.

Raoul PIERRE-LOUIS
Secretary of State
for Education, Haiti

Appendix 3: Opening speech of the Director-General of Unesco

Mr Minister,
Excellency,
Ladies and Gentlemen,

First of all I wish to express my deep gratitude to the Government of the Haitian Republic for its kindness in hosting this meeting of experts in connection with the *General History of Africa* project. I also wish very sincerely to thank Mr Raoul Pierre-Louis, Secretary of State for Education, for his personal co-operation in the preparation of this meeting and for the important address that he has just delivered. I am grateful to him for having so affectionately welcomed the Haitian lady who has shared my life and efforts for more than twenty-five years. This is the first time that Unesco has organized a meeting on this important project concerning the history of Africa outside the African continent. It was right that it should be held in Haiti. But the occasion has above all a special significance by the very reason of the topic of your discussion, the question of the slave trade. For Haiti remains a living symbol of both the sufferings and the heroic struggles of the black slaves uprooted from their African soil but never resigned to their fate. Their victorious action made possible for the first time in the history of mankind the establishment, out of the ruins of a slave society, of a State based on the right to individual freedom.

While the slave trade determined the future of the communities resulting from the African diaspora which today form the population of many Latin American and Caribbean areas, it also left a very deep imprint on the history of Africa. This means that the results of the work of this meeting will be very important for the project on the *General History of Africa*, the drafting of which has been entrusted by Unesco to an international scientific committee composed of specialists from Africa and all the other regions of the world. I have pleasure today in welcoming a number of its members here present.

To further its work the committee recommended the holding of just such meetings of experts, colloquia and seminars on certain vital topics such as that for which we are convened today.

There are five main items on the agenda for your discussion. The first is the scale of the slave trade. In the study of this subject, comparisons of the different methods employed should enable more precise statistical data to be evolved.

Following on this quantitative approach, you are called upon to discuss in substance the demographic, political, economic, social and cultural consequences of the slave trade, both in Africa and the receiving countries, particularly in the slave trade, both in Africa and the receiving countries, particularly in the Americas.

Next it is proposed that the meeting study movements of thought and ideologies, both those used to justify the slave trade and the abolitionist movements, together with the interpretation of different contemporary schools of thought and research. More particular attention will be focused on the factors which led to the abolition of the slave trade.

Finally, turning to action and the organization of future studies, you are asked to make proposals for the practical follow-up of this meeting. On its side, Unesco pledges itself to contribute its full co-operation.

While it is true that other peoples, for example the Amerindians, have suffered at one time or another in history from violent oppression which forced them into a situation of slavery, it is essentially the Africans who, in modern times, were reduced to slavery and transported in large numbers to other continents by means of an organized movement. The slave trade, of which it has been said that it was an endless bloodletting, drained the African continent of a large part of its vital resources, for it was generally of their youngest and strongest members that their peoples were bereft.

The slave trade therefore had far-reaching consequences for the economic, social, cultural and even political life of Africa, although it is not yet possible to quantify them precisely. A great deal has been said and written about the slave trade but, in fact, there is still no satisfactory answer to a number or questions, starting with the far-off origins of the traffic in African slaves, which probably go back as far as the beginning of Mediterranean history. Similarly, still too little is known about the traffic through the Sahara or that via the east coast of Africa across the Indian Ocean in the direction of India, Indonesia and as far as China. There is indeed evidence that black slaves were presented to the Emperor of China in the seventh century, while African slave labourers are reported in Canton in the twelfth century.

It would seem that in the eleventh and twelfth centuries, after the conquest of the north of India by the Muslims, power was in the hands of an 'African slave dynasty'.

The African slave presence in Asia was reinforced in the fifteenth century, particularly in Bengal where social, economic and political life is said to have been enlivened by the activities of some 8,000 black slaves.

The traffic grew between the seventeenth and eighteenth centuries, when Portuguese and Dutch traders selected Antongil Bay in Madagascar as the bridgehead in the direction of Sumatra. Little has been written about this period and we must wait until various archives give up their secrets. These include the Portuguese and Arab records, documents which may exist in countries lying between Mozambique and the Red Sea, archives in the Seychelles which served as a staging-post between Africa and the other Mascarene Islands, plus archives in India and the Indonesian archipelago.

However, the real slave trade which was to have far-reaching repercussions may be taken as that which developed across the Atlantic. Quantitatively large, it was also important by virtue of its organized character and no doubt also because of the extent of its manifold consequences.

The most recent research, even that which has made use of the most modern technology such as computerization, is still far from providing complete information on the loss of human resources forced upon Africa. The figures put forward so far remain approximations. Methods of estimation, moreover, vary from one school to another. You are therefore asked to compare the different approaches followed by establishing statistics and to suggest a method that might provide more precise results.

But apart from methodological problems, there still remains a question of scientific interpretation. Here again, your meeting has an important task to perform. This is to find a way to deal with certain basic questions, from the standpoint of the strictest objectivity, through use of more varied and more numerous data, drawing on all the sources that have remained hitherto inacessible or have rarely been consulted, or those containing information which has been wrongly interpreted. Such sources include oral tradition, an invaluable store of ethnic memories.

In connection with the very substance of your meeting, I should myself like, in a very personal way, to lay before you a number of questions.

First, what were the circumstances in which the slave trade was carried on in Africa itself? It is important ot get a clear idea of what is known about the trading posts and holding areas in which the captives were assembled in conditions such that some died even before embarkation on the slave-ships. It would, no doubt, be advisable to have recourse to sources hitherto inadequately investigated, and to cross-check information supplied by the various documents, such as the records of ship-owners, slavers, the big monopoly companies and national naval archives. In particular an even closer analysis should be made of ships' articles which provide valuable evidence concerning the loading, travel and unloading of slaves; and court records of civil and criminal proceedings concerning slaves and slave-traders should be more thoroughly studied.

It is also desirable to sum up present knowledge concerning the way in which the man-hunts were carried out, the victims captured and reduced to slavery on the African continent, and to study completely objectively the role both of foreign powers and of the local authorities.

One of the too little known and yet real aspects of the subject on which fresh and more thorough research is required is the topic of domestic anti-slavery and anti-slave-trade movements. The resistance struggles leading to the victorious winning of independence in America have their early roots in this determination on the part of the victims of the slave trade to maintain their human dignity and safeguard their existence.

While new life can thus be instilled into the study of the circumstances of the slave trade, there is also need for a more precise appraisal of its consequences in Africa. The foremost of these are in the human context. There was a terrible loss of life, which, as I have said, literally drained the blood of Africa and also, no doubt, left huge stretches of land uncultivated, seriously interfering with social and economic life and hindering cultural development and technological progress.

Thus for more than four centuries, population growth in Africa lagged greatly behind that in any other continent over the same period.

While these losses, in terms of human life, are, if not precisely, at least with increasing accuracy, being quantified in all their tragic reality, other, and not the least important, effects have not yet been elucidated. Examples of such effects are the perversion of men's minds caused by the slave trade and interferences of all kinds which had a direct impact on the normal development of Africa. The fact that there were some Africans who turned into accessaries to the heinous crimes committed in the course of the slave trade, so becoming the suppliers of the slave-traders, deserves further elucidation. But at the same time it is important to give consideration to a basic fact, namely the strength of the spiritual and moral values, and the peoples' powers of resistance, which gave rise in Africa itself to opposition movements.

Thus these values survived, and cultural identity persisted through all the sufferings of enslavement and transportation. This is because this culture was deeply rooted in the heart of men's innermost consciousness, an integral part of the very existence of the communities concerned. It formed the very essence of their lives. It was thus able to stay alive during exile, preserve dignity in servitude, and supply the inspiration for revolt and the conquest of freedom and independence.

The qualitative factors connected with the study of social systems and of spiritual, moral and cultural values thus have a part in your work alongside the quantitative factors being determined under increasingly strict control and with ever greater precision.

This work, while essential for a proper African epistemology, is also of prime importance in throwing light on the history and the present situation of Europe and, of course, Africa.

It is becoming increasingly clear that the slave trade had a fundamental part to play as far as Europe was concerned, for the first industrial revolution can no longer be isolated from the primitive capital accumulation deriving from the 'triangular trade' and the monopoly system. In recent years many historians and economists, belonging to different schools of thought, have endeavoured to ascertain how his kind of trade, based on the exploitation of slave labour, can have stimulated the technological explosion.

These studies have clearly shown that the contribution of the slave trade to the industrial and commercial development of countries embarked on an era of capitalist expansion was decisive, as was therefore its influence on the socio-economic and political institutions of Europe and North America.

Thus, to paraphrase Aimé Césaire, 'those who invented neither gunpowder nor electricity' were, whether they liked it or not, at the origin of the extraordinary economic drive which produced modern technological civilization; it can be said of them, to quote the poet again, that 'without them the earth would not be the earth'. Maybe it will be for them to contribute now to bringing this civilization into better balance and harmonizing it so that the earth may be a better place for each individual and for all mankind.

As regards Latin America and the Caribbean, by a happy chance the Intergovernmental Conference on Cultural Policies, held by Unesco for the first time in this region, and which has just ended in Bogotá, almost coincided with your meeting. In the course of that conference a number of delegates stressed that many liberation movements had started in the Caribbean and then spread to the continent, thus sealing the historic link of unity between the Islands and Latin America. In an initial summing up of the situation on the closing day of the conference, I myself made a point of stressing the pioneer role of Haiti and the value of the example set by its struggles, which indissolubly linked together liberation from slavery and the winning of political independence.

There is one other basic feature of the Caribbean to which I should like to draw attention here. This is the welding into an original identity of the differing cultural traditions coming from Africa and elsewhere. The old-time slave-traders were accustomed to split up ethnic and linguistic units so as to dominate more easily the groups subjected to the slave trade by reducing them to the single elementary status of slave. However, by some miracle, despite this forced separation, a real cohesion survived. This miracle is essentially that of culture, a community of culture. It was linked to shared values and beliefs, and to religious, spiritual and artistic forms of expression which made it possible to create a sense of common origin and active solidarity. Thus, through this very uprooting, culturally integrated communities were created all over again; while they used borrowed languages, they none the less provided the foundation for the awareness of a collective consciousness, which itself became the basis for a will to common action.

This meeting will also have to take into account this cultural integration both to understand the past with its independence and abolitionist movements and to look into the future. Your meeting is indeed called upon at the end of its work to frame practical plans for future action. The results of your work will primarily contribute to the drafting of the chapters and sections concerning the slave trade in the *General History of Africa*. However, they should also open up new avenues of research, including the organization of collective undertakings and the publication of books intended for the general public, and works of reference. In this connection, I have asked for a study to be made of the possibility of supplementing the *Guide to the Sources of the History of Africa* series published under the auspices of Unesco, with a publication on archival sources relating to the slave trade to be found in the Americas and the Caribbean.

In addition, organized efforts to stimulate the collection of historical documents, and the reproduction of texts which are difficult to find could supplement documentation now available.

Your recommendations should also be directed towards strengthening Unesco's programmes concerning relations between Africa and the Caribbean and, I would say, America in general. These programmes should, moreover, help to increase our understanding of the way in which ethnic groups and peoples transported from different African regions were welded into a national community.

I have the intention of proposing, at the next session of the Unesco General Conference, the convocation of a meeting of experts on the black African cultural presence in the Americas and the Caribbean. It would be the purpose of such a meeting to facilitate the framing of a research and cultural dissemination programme on the African diaspora.

Arrangements are also being made to assemble and translate for publication oral traditions transmitted in the African languages. At the same time the exchange of information and cultural programmes, specialists and students, between Africa and the African diaspora will be encouraged. This will contribute by the same token to strengthening the bonds of solidarity existing between Africa and the peoples of the diaspora, who continue, with an acute consciousness of their history, to bear witness to the originality and vital strength of black African cultures and values.

Unesco is, moreover, planning in the years to come to lay particular stress on the study of Caribbean cultures. This will involve the framing and implementation of a complete research and publication programme concerning the Caribbean cultures in all their component parts—autochthonous or Amerindian, Asian, European and African.

In the context of African contributions to cultural identity and the struggle for freedom in the Caribbean, it is impossible not do commemorate those leaders of independence movements and protagonists of human dignity, Toussaint Louverture and Jean-Jacques Dessalines, the incarnation of the will and aspirations of all those peoples uprooted from Africa who were none the less able, despite their oppression, to create new nations out of the strength which they found by drawing on their ancestral values.

Excellencies, Ladies and Gentlemen, I hope that with these brief remarks I have been able to indicate the importance of the meeting that is opening today. The meeting is made up of the contributions and the whole accumulated experience of specialists from the Caribbean, Africa and other regions of the world. I also wish to welcome members of the diplomatic corps, the observer from the Holy See and the representatives of the Gulbenkian Foundation and the International Council for Philosophy and Humanistic Studies, which contributed to the organization of this meeting. I also welcome among us the representatives of the Ménil and Leopold Sedar Senghor Foundations, and of the African Culture Society, who have been good enough to join us in our work.

In conclusion, I reiterate my gratitude to the host country, to the Haitian people, to its government, and in particular to H.E. Jean-Claude Duvalier, President of the Haitian Republic, who, by granting his patronage to this meeting, has given it still deeper significance.

To you who are the experts, I wish to say that, through your study of the modalities and consequences of the slave trade, you will not only be helping to throw further light on a historical problem: you will be making a personal contribution to thought on a scandalous practice contrary to the most elementary human and national rights.

In this way, your work will be a factor in the awakening of concern about injustices and inequalities which still in our time oppress many peoples and which can only be brought to an end as the result of a real determination to establish a world of justice, solidarity and peace in which progress would, in a spirit of rediscovered fraternity, be guaranteed for all countries and all men.

It is with this hope that I give you my warmest wishes for the complete success of your work.

Amadou-Mahtar M'Bow
Director-General of the United
Nations Educational, Scientific
and Cultural Organization

Part II
Supplementary papers

In order to promote a fuller exchange of views during the meeting, each partici-
pant was requested to submit, in the space of a few pages, the following:

An account of research in his country, to include: a bibliography, including theses;
work in progress; areas of research to be explored and gaps to be filled; a
list, with addresses, of national and foreign specialists working on the problems
of the slave trade.

Statistics on the slave trade.

Principal ports or trading-posts in Africa, serving as outlets to America or to
the countries of the Indian Ocean, and in the receiving countries.

A list of archives (public archives in North America, Latin America, the Caribbean, Europe and Asia; private archives (individuals or families, commercial
firms, churches, etc.).

The role and impact of slaves: economic—contribution to the development of the
receiving country (e.g. the sugar industry, the coffee industry, etc.); cultural—
the African influence, through slavery, on many countries of the Western
hemisphere; political—the participation of Negroes in the social and political
strife and the wars of independence of the receiving countries, and in the
building of new nations.

The reports submitted are reproduced below and arranged alphabetically by
author.

An account of research on the slave trade in Nigeria

J. F. Ade Ajayi and J. E. Inikori

Whereas a number of Nigerians have made important contributions to African history, for reasons that are difficult to explain, the slave trade is a neglected theme in Nigeria. However, there are one or two specialists who have specifically treated some of its aspects and a number of others have dealt with issues and periods closely connected with it.

Taking the second group first, we have Professor K. O. Dike (now at the Department of History, Harvard University, United States) whose book, *Trade and Politics in the Niger Delta*, touches on a number of issues relating to the slave trade, especially the impact of abolition. Professor E. J. Alagoa of the University College, Port Harcourt, has done a large amount of work on the history of the Niger delta during the slave-trade era. Dr K. Princewill of the Department of History, University of Ibadan, wrote her Ph.D. thesis on the impact of external trade on the Fante during the slave-trade era. Dr I. U. A. Musa of the Department of History, Ahmadu Bello University, Zaria, has worked largely on issues closely related to the trans-Saharan slave trade. Dr Mahdi Adamu of the Department of History, Ahmadu Bello University, Zaria, has studied the contribution of the central Sudan of West Africa to the transatlantic slave trade.[1]

The present limited researches in Nigeria have raised a number of issues which should be pursued further. In particular, more work should be done on the economic and social impact of the slave trade on West African societies. Of particular interest are the following: (a) export slave trade and the incidence of wars in West Africa; (b) export slave trade and the expansion of internal slavery in West Africa; (c) export slave trade and demographic processes in West Africa; (d) export slave trade and the pattern of settlements in West Africa; and (e) the economic consequences of the export slave trade, especially the opportunity cost of the trade for West African economic development.

Research work relating to these topics should be based on a thorough examination of archival materials and oral evidence. Wherever possible quantitative analysis should be applied. The application of social and economic theory will be particularly helpful both in the selection and evaluation of facts as well as in the analysis of the ascertained evidence. For this reason, scholars in disciplines such as sociology and economics should be encouraged to take an interest in such research work. More important, undergraduate and post-graduate programmes in history departments should be structured in such a way that interested students can acquire the analytical tools needed for a proper study of the slave trade along the lines we have suggested.

Statistics on the slave trade

Professor Curtin's book, *The Atlantic Slave Trade: A Census* (1969), has stimulated a great deal of quantitative research relating to the slave trade. One recent contributor to the debate is Leslie B. Rout, Jr,[2] who shows that Curtin's estimate of slave imports into Spanish America up to 1810 is about 67 per cent too low. On present evidence it would seem that Curtin's global estimate for the Atlantic trade may be at least 10 per cent too low. We think therefore that it would be more realistic for the moment to raise Curtin's figures for the Atlantic trade by 40 per cent, making total exports from Africa by way of that trade 15.4 million.

From the comments of Professor Hubert Gerbeau who is familiar with the slave trade from the East African coast, the figure for the Indian Ocean trade is about 4 million. On present evidence, the figure for the trans-Saharan and Red Sea trades may be put at about 10 million. This brings the total to about 29.4 million. The present evidence permits us to say, therefore, that 19 million represents the lowest possible number and 30 million, the highest.

New research should provide more statistical information, especially on mortality between the time of capture and the time of departure from Africa. While in some aspects of the slave trade the total numbers may not be very important, in other aspects a proper understanding of the issues requires a quantitative analysis.

Notes

1. Of the specialists who have worked specifically on some aspects of the slave trade, we have the following:

   J. U. J. Asiegbu, University College, Port Harcourt, whose main work on the subject is *Slavery and the Politics of Liberation 1787–1861*, London and New York, Longman, 1969.

   E. A. Oroge, formerly of the University of Lagos, Lagos, whose main work is 'The Institution of Slavery in Yorubaland with Particular Reference to the Nine-teenth Century' (University of Birmingham, Ph.D. thesis, 1971).

   J. E. Inikori of the Department of History, Ahmadu Bello University, Zaria, whose main works relating to the slave trade are: 'English Trade to Guinea: A Study in the Import of Foreign Trade on the English Economy 1750–1807' (University of Ibadan, P.D. thesis, 1973); 'Measuring the Atlantic Slave Trade: An Assessment of Curtin and Anstey', *Journal of African History*, Vol. XVII,

No. 2, 1976, p. 197–223; 'Measuring the Atlantic Slave Trade: A Rejoinder',
Journal of African History, Vol. XVII, No. 4, 1976, p. 607–27; 'The Import of
Firearms into West Africa 1750–1807: A Quantitative Analysis', *Journal of African
History*, Vol. XVIII, No. 3, 1977, p. 339–68; 'The Origin of the Diaspora: The
Slave Trade from Africa', *Tarikh*, Vol. 5, No. 4 (in press); 'West African Import
and Export Trade 1750–1807: Volume and Structure *Essays in Honour of Profes-
sor K. O. Dike*, edited by professor Obaro Ikime, Ibadan University Press (in press);
'Slave Trade: A Retardative Factor in West African Economic Development'
(paper presented at the Seminar on Economic History of the Central Savannah
of West Africa, Kano, 5–10 January 1976.
2. *The African Experience in Spanish America 1502 to the Present Day*, p. 61–6, Cambridge,
Cambridge University Press, 1976.

Portuguese research on the slave trade

Antonio Carreira

Bibliography

Most of the literature on the subject is listed in the short essays recently published under the title *Notas sobre o Tráfico Português de Escravos na Costa Occidental Africana*. The only authoritative work is Edmundo Correia Lopes' *Escravatura—Subsídios para a Sua História*, Lisbon, 1944.

Current research

Various occasional research projects of a purely bibliographical nature have been undertaken recently by students of the Faculadade de Letras de Lisboa. To the best of our knowledge, there are no other Portuguese research projects in progress specifically on the slave trade. For reasons which are irrelevant here, the limited number of Portuguese studies on slavery have generally formed part of broader-based works in which they have been included with a view to corroborating and clarifying (or complementing) other material (V. Magalhães Godinho, Texeira da Mota, Oliveira Marques and a few others). In concrete terms, the only studies on the slave trade known to us are limited to the activities of the Companhias Pombalinas (first dealt with by Cunha Saraiva in 1938 and 1940), the studies by Dias Nunes (Brazilian) in 1965, and our own works in 1968, 1969 and 1972. A number of these works relied (for the most part) on the wealth of documentation available in Lisbon: accounts and records of the Companhia do Grão Pará e Maranhão and the Companhia de Pernambuco e Paraíba. However, these sources have not yet been explored in relation to the main economic aspects of the slave trade. We embarked upon such a project, but were forced to abandon it owing to a lack of funds and other forms of support.

We have, however, accumulated a considerable amount of material from the archives in Lisbon and Cape Verde, with a view to studying the subject in greater depth (and more extensively). Other activities have prevented us from pursuing our research and analysis as rapidly as we would wish.

Areas of research and gaps to be filled

In our view, a major research project should be set up to study records and accounts connected with the slave trade. Such a project would also involve an overall survey of the economics of the slave trade: vessels used, products and goods transported, origins and destinations, costs at the places of origin and selling prices on the consumer markets, the purchase and selling prices of slaves and, lastly, all the factors that would facilitate an appraisal of the significance of this movement of goods and persons and its repercussions on the economic, social and political lives of the nations which benefited from it.

This is a difficult and exacting task, but it could be accomplished by a number of research teams if the necessary funds were made available.

In our view, this is the only way to fill the large gaps in practically all the data available for each area, particularly in regard to the number of slaves shipped from each sector (and, where possible, the various ethnic divisions), and mortality at the ports of embarkation, during the voyage and at destinations. With such information (if obtained) we could attempt more accurate estimates of the numbers of slaves shipped and correct points of view expounded in the existing literature.

Portuguese research specialists working on questions connected with the slave trade

As we have already mentioned, Portugal's contribution to the study of the slave trade has been fairly negligible. The studies carried out are quite fragmentary and tend to concentrate on specific areas, without the overall approach which is to be desired in this type of research. The most significant study of the slave trade is the work by Correia Lopes, to which we have already referred. Various research specialists in history, economics, sociology and other fields can also make a valid and significant contribution to the clarification of questions associated with the slave trade.

In this connection, we would like to mention the following research specialists: Professor Dr Vitorino Magalhães Godinho, Professor Dr A. H. de Oliveira Marques, both at the Universidade Nova de Lisboa (Faculdade de Ciencias Humanas e Sociais, Avenida de Berna, Lisboa) and Comandante Avelino Teixeira da Mota, Avenida do Restelo, 46 Lisboa 3.

Statistics on the slave trade (Portuguese)

Our studies over the past ten years would suggest that the biggest gaps in our knowledge relate to the seventeenth century. Until now, the figures for this period have been no more than estimates—at times of a dubious nature. The figures which we give further on in this study show glaring disparities in the volume of the slave trade in each of the areas of the different traders and/or contractors. As a basis for our work, we divided the west coast of Africa into three sectors. This should provide a framework for examining the disparities in the various figures (whether estimated or available from the customs records).

First sector

From the Bay of Arguim and the mouth of the Senegal River to Cape Palmas (the southernmost part of Sierra Leone) or the rivers of Guinea and Cape Verde.

The slaves taken here (fifteenth century) were legally shipped to Portugal, Madeira, Cadiz, Seville, Sanlucar de Barrameda and other ports in southern Spain. Slaves were also shipped illegally to the West Indies. The slave raids and sale transactions occurred in Argium, around the mouth of the Senegal River and the ports of Sine, Salum, Cacheu, Bissau and Ribeira Grande (Santiago Island, Cape Verde). However, there are no accurate figures for this traffic; there are estimates for the years 1455–99 and for the entire sixteenth century (see Table 1). Figures are available only for the period 1757–94 when a total of 24,594 adults and seventy-two children were dispatched to Bahia, Pernambuco, Pará and Maranhão from Cacheu and Bissau. With respect to the eighteenth and nineteenth centuries we have only passing references to the fierce slave wars waged against the populations in large areas of Senegal (south), Gambia, Firdú, Casamansa (including Futa Toro and Futa Djaló), Guinea and part of the interior of the continent. One of the main aspects of these wars was the involvement of the dominant classes seeking to gain political power and further the cause of Islam. Religious interests were more powerful than political and social considerations. From 1840 onwards, the slaves were practically always sent to Cuba or another Caribbean island down the Gambia, Casamansa and other rivers. One of the main reasons for this was the war between the emancipated Fulas and the black (i.e. captive) Fulas which lasted from 1863 to 1888.

From our knowledge of the region and its history, we are convinced that, of the three sectors, this area supplied the lowest number of slaves for foreign markets. Towards the end of the eighteenth century, Oliveira Mendes wrote:

Bissau, Cacheu and some other islands are hardly worth mentioning. While there are blacks in the backlands those who could be taken into slavery are *barely sufficient for working the land on the islands*.

The social and political organization of the peoples in the area did not favour (but rather went against) any significant volume of slave trading with other countries. Considerable numbers of slaves were absorbed by the home markets.[1]

TABLE 1. Summary of the slave traffic [1]

Periods	From Bay of Arguim to Cape Palmas		From Cape Palmas to Cape Lopo Gonçalves		From Luanda and Benguela	
	Adults	Children	Adults	Children	Adults	Children
Fifteenth century (1455–99) [2]	33,750	...	...	...	...	...
Sixteenth century [3]	350,000	...	...	...	...	...
Sixteenth and seventeenth centuries (1531–1680) [4]	...	...	...	...	927,000	...
Eighteenth century (1726–32 and 1797–1806)	...	...	158,291	...	...	...
(1756–94) [5]	24,594	72	312,403	169	943,182	17,788
Nineteenth century (1800–36) [6]	...	...	...	...	494,529	263
(1837–50) [7]	...	...	62,786	...	623,214	...
TOTAL	408,344	72	533,480	169	2,987,925	18,051
Assuming that contraband traffic amounted to around 50 per cent of the total shown in customs records and that other traffic was outside the control of the Portuguese we may add a further	204,172	36	266,740	84	1,493,962	9,025
GRAND TOTAL	612,516	108	800,220	253	4,481,887	27,076

1. Most of these figures were obtained from the available Portuguese literature and through my own research in the Lisbon and Cape Verde archives. Certain details may have to be corrected or altered (figures, and origins and destinations) in the light of a study of the sources of the various authors. The figures for children include babies.
2. Figures estimated on the basis of 750 slaves shipped a year × 45 years.
3. As above on the basis of 3,500 slaves a year.
4. Statistics from Abreu e Brito and estimate by Cadornega.
5. 19,940 shipped by the Companhia de Grão Pará and the Companhia de Pernambuco e Paraíba; and 4,654 slaves shipped by individual traders in the period 1778–94.
6. The total number of slaves shipped from Angola in the nineteenth century was 1,117,743 adults and 263 children. The legal traffic (over 28 years) amounted to 494,529 adults and 263 children (= 494,792) giving an annual average of 17,691.
7. In the 12-year period of illegal traffic in Angola, an average of 51,934 slaves a year were shipped, which adds 20.7 per cent to the legal traffic.

From Cape Palmas to Cape Lopo Gonçalves, comprising the area which used to be known as Costa da Mina (Malagueta Coast—Liberia, Ivory Coast, the Gold Coast (now Ghana), and the Slave Coast including the Forcados, El-Rei and Escravos rivers).

Trafficking began here very early (1482–85), but the Portuguese were so obsessed with the idea of gold that they failed to develop the slave trade. Subsequently, the problems arising from the conflict of interests between the British, Dutch and others led to a climate of instability and the decline of the Portuguese slave trade. The figures compiled relate to the period 1726–1806 when 470,694 adults and 169 children were shipped through Cotonou, Popo, Lomé, Badagri and other ports. In the nineteenth century only 62,786 adults were shipped (giving a total of 533,480 adults and 169 children). We do not know the relevant figures of the trade carried on by the British, Dutch and others.

Most of the slaves were sent to Bahia, Pernambuco, Rio de Janeiro, Pará and Maranhão (with smaller consignments going to Pará and Maranhão than to the other States).

Third Sector

From Cape Lopo Gonçalves (more specifically from Loango) to the Coporolo River (to the south of Benguela) including Luanda and Benguela, the most prominent slave-trade area.

Most of the available figures relate to this sector, particularly the area between the Dande Straits (to the north of Luanda) and the Coporolo River, which came under the jurisdiction of the Luanda and Benguela customs inspectorates. The entire sector to the north—from Luanda to Loango—was practically always outside the control of the Portuguese authorities. It was dominated by more powerful nations with a greater interest in the slave trade. Few, if any, figures are available for this area. Even so, we may say that, overall, Angola was the sector where the 'hunt for the African' was carried on with the greatest intensity.

According to the records of the Feitorias of Luanda, 79,052 adults were shipped to Brazil or the Spanish West Indies in the years 1575–91. It is also estimated that another 847,848 adults were shipped to these destinations, making a total of 927,000 for the period in question.

In the eighteenth century (from 1726 onwards, although figures are missing for certain years), 943,182 adults and 17,788 children (including infants) were exported to the above destinations. These figures are taken from the customs records, governors' reports and official correspondence. In the nineteenth century, during the period when the slave trade was still legal (1800–36), 494,529 adults and 263 children were dispatched (giving an annual average of 17,691). Between 1837 and 1850 when slave traffic went on illegally, a further 623,214 adults (an annual average of 51,934) were shipped, that is 20.7 per cent of those transported during the period of legal slave trading.

From the three sectors, 3,929,749 adults and 18,292 children were shipped (making a total of 3,948,041). However, if we accept, as a working hypothesis for purposes of appraisal, that during the slave-trade period the clandestine shipments may have totalled roughly 50 per cent of the legal traffic entered in the customs records (plus the slaves taken by other nations engaged in the African slave trade) it is probable that a further 1,974,019 adults were shipped, giving a total of at least 5,822,060 slaves (adults and children).

Up until 1578, the slaves taken from Angola (Luanda and Benguela and to a certain extent from Loango and other river areas) were assembled on the island of São Tomé from where they were exported to Brazil and the Spanish West Indies. Subsequently, the slaves were shipped directly from Pinda, Luanda and Benguela to Central and South America (particularly Brazil). Spanish domination (after 1580)—particularly in the seventeenth century— resulted in the shipments of slaves to the River Plate (Montevideo and Buenos Aires) being stepped up in view of the better prices and the fact that the transactions were settled in silver coinage (pataca and peso), whereas at most other destinations they were bartered for goods (cloth, beads, ornaments, iron bars, guns, spirits, etc.).

In all the sectors (besides omitting the ethnic origins of the slaves) the records generally fail to indicate embarkation and destination ports. This makes it difficult to arrive at specific figures. In other instances, there is considerable confusion over the names of the ports of disembarkation. Alongside these irregularities, we must also consider the fact that vessels often made out their papers for a certain port and then diverted their consignments to other ports where the prices were higher. These diversions were justified by 'protests' stating that they were forced to put into port.

Other questions which need to be clarified, particularly in relation to Angola, are: the organization of the markets where slaves and produce were sold, which date from the early seventeenth century at least; and the activities of the *Pumbeiros*, *Aviados*, *Funantes* and others involved in slave trading in the backlands, who sometimes acted as allies and other times as enemies of the captains and majors. The same applies to the role of these agents in setting off tribal wars with the aim of buying up prisoners and shipping them into slavery. These aspects are dealt with in *Angola—da Escravatura ao Trabalho Livre* (1977).

Table 1 gives a clearer picture of the development of the slave trade in these three sectors.

Archive materials

Public archives

Generally speaking, the public archives in Lisbon are badly organized and in some cases to not have the catalogues and index-cards which would facilitate research work. In some archives, the documentation is arranged somewhat haphazardly and without any respect for chronological order. This is due to a lack of trained personnel and financial resources. Despite this, most of the documents are in a good state of preservation. Research into the slave trade basically involves going labouriously through thousands of records and account books.

The most important repositories of documentation in Lisbon are: (a) Arquivo Nacional da Torre do Tombo; (b) Arquivo Histórico Ultramarino; (c) Arquivo Histórico do Ministério das Finanças (covering a specific period); (d) Biblioteca Nacional (particularly in the reserve stock); (e) Biblioteca do Ministério da Marinha; (f) Biblioteca da Ajuda (the latter two are not all that important); (g) Biblioteca da Câmara Municipal de Lisboa; (h) Fundo do Erário Público (the latter two house only certain types of documentation).

It would be extremely useful if Spanish research specialists were interested in this subject. This would facilitate access to the Madrid, Simancas and other archives. In view of the obstacles involved, this kind of archive research can only be undertaken with positive government support.

Private archives

To the best of our knowledge, there are few private archives in Portugal (on family estates, in churches, etc.) apart from the archive at the home of the Marques do Lavradio (which has been the subject of research projects and a number of brief publications). If any other private archives do esist, they are not likely to house any significant material concerning the slave trade.

In the former Portuguese colonies (Cape Verde, Guinea, São Tomé and Angola), there is hardly any documentation available on the slave trade, if we discount Angola. A wealth of material (historical and recent) has been destroyed through lack of suitable premises, indifference on the part of the public authorities, the climate (hot and humid) and the usual pillagers. Coupled with this, there is the difficulty (or impossibility) of reconstructing many of the relevant facts. In Angola (and to some extent on São Tomé), a fair number of documents have yet to be examined. This is not the case with Cape Verde. Much of the Angolan archive material would have been lost had it not been for the far-sightedness of a dedicated group of civil servants, who published part of the catalogued documentation. We are referring to the publication *Arquivos de Angola*, founded in 1933, which appeared fairly regularly over a period of thirty years. It is the most important repository of documents relating to the slave trade, the markets and the economic life of the territory since the sixteenth century.

The parish registers in Portugal and in her former overseas territories are another valuable source. These registers should contain useful information on the slave trade.

The role and impact of the slaves

In economic terms

It would be quite impracticable to give a detailed account of the role of the African slave in the development (in its various aspects) of all the territories with slave-based economies. For this reason we endeavoured to give a very brief (and incomplete) description of this subject in *Notas sobre o Tráfico Português* . . . (p. 9–12), so far as the form of such an essay would allow. It is a subject that calls for much more research and analysis.

The forced transfer of vast numbers of Africans to sparsely populated areas brought about changes in local life and had various other repercussions. One of the most notable of these repercussions was the extensive population of unoccupied areas, and farming and mining on a scale which would have been out of the question with the local populations of each region. The other signicant repercussion was the retreat (or stamping out) of the indigenous populations who had to take refuge in an alien and in some cases hostile environment, which served only to hasten their decline or disappearance.

It is difficult (or impossible) to single out every aspect of the influence exerted by slave labour in the general economic development of these areas. For this reason we are confining our study to Brazil and, specifically, to a survey of certain products exported in the sixteenth and seventeenth centuries. This should give us a clearer idea of the way things developed.

Sugar

In 1591, Abreu e Brito drew up an inventory recording the existence in Pernambuco of sixty-three sugar plantations with an annual production of 378,000 *arrobas* of 'brown sugar' worth 75,600 *cruzados* (one *cruzado* = 400 *reis*). In 1629 (Mauro), the number of sugar plantations rose to 346; and in 1761 (Antonil), exportable production (*batido*, white, *macho* and brown) accounted for the following quantities and values:

Bahia: 14,500 35-*arroba* chests = 507,500 *arrobas*. 1,070,204,400 *reis*.
Pernambuco: 12,300 35-*arroba* chests = 430,500 *arrobas*. 834,140,000 *reis*.
Rio de Janeiro: 10,220 35-*arroba* chests = 357,700 *arrobas*. 630,796,400 *reis*.
Total: 37,020 35-*arroba* chests = 1,295,700 *arrobas*. 2,535,142,800 *reis*.
In 1638, exports were in excess of 1,800,000 *arrobas* (Mauro).

Hides (sole leather)

Bahia: 50,000. 99,000,000 *reis*.
Pernambuco: 40,000. 70,000,000 *reis*.
Rio de Janeiro and other captaincies: 20,000. 32,800,000 *reis*.
Total: 110,000. 201,800,000 *reis*.

These figures also give an idea of the volume of cattle production, particularly in the north-east of Brazil.

Tobacco
Bahia: 25,000 rolls. 303,100,000 *reis*.
Alagoas and Pernambuco: 2,500 rolls. 41,550,000 *reis*.
Total: 27,500 rolls. 344,650,000 *reis*.

Gold
100 *arrobas* 'apart from what was extracted (and is till extracted) secretly from
   other streams which the miners did not declare as they did not wish them to
   be taxed', 614,400,000 *reis*.
      Between 1721 and 1754, the gold sent from Brazil to Portugal fluctuated
between 11,000 to 20,000 *arrobas* a year (Magalhães Godinho).
      In the space of a century sugar took over as the leading export product.
It supplied vast sections of the European market, and brought about a radical
change in eating habits. Sugar exports rose from 378,000 *arrobas* a year at the
end of the sixteenth century to 1,295,700, which means that they increased
around three and a half times.
      These five key products had a total value of 3,743,992,800 *reis*. They all
relied heavily on slave labour.
      We should also mention the discovery of diamonds (1729). They proved
to be a further source of revenue. But like gold they were badly used. They
enabled the Portuguese aristocracy and upper middle classes to give full rein
to their propensity for ostentation, vanity and luxurious living. The country
began to import somewhat wildly (especially from Great Britain) a whole
range of useful, essential and superfluous consumer goods as a form of regale-
ment for the privileged classes, thus mortgaging Brazil's production. Great
Britain recognized an easy way of advancing the 'Industrial Revolution', by
having the Portuguese trading deficit settled in gold and diamonds.
      We should mention two other Brazilian products: cotton and coffee.
In 1776, the exportable cotton production was 42,664 *arrobas;* it had risen to
560,000 *arrobas* by 1796 (Borges de Macado).
      Coffee growing, which dates from the end of the eighteenth century,
relied just as heavily on slave labour. The slave was responsible for clearing
and setting out the plantations, tending the seedbeds, weeding, and cultivating
the coffee plants. In the space of a hundred years, coffee rose to head the list
of exports, taking over from sugar which had begun to feel the effects of competition from producers in the West Indies. In regard to coffee, we should also
note the influence of the European immigrant, who arrived at the dawn of
the nineteenth century to contribute to the development of the south of Brazil
at the very time when it was recognized that the slave trade and African forced

labour had to end. But we should not forget that the slave was an important factor (indirect, to be sure) in the recruitment and transportation to Brazil of European immigrants. Recruitment was financed from a percentage of the customs duties levied on the slave trade. Coffee proved to be a turning-point in the Brazilian agricultural economy and superseded sugar as the country's leading product. Conditions favourable to increased coffee consumption had developed in Europe (and elsewhere). Coffee became widely drunk for its stimulative effects at the expense of tea, which until then had been drunk throughout Europe.

The economic development of Brazil has to be ascribed in part to voluntary and involuntary immigration. Voluntary immigration, in particular, may be considered a constant feature of Portuguese life.

The African slaves working on the plantations and in the mines soon began (in the seventeenth and eighteenth centuries) to disturb agriculture and other forms of economic activity. They destroyed farms and settlements; they established *quilombos* with the aim of shaking off the yoke of slavery and trying to wipe out or reduce the effects of their submission to the white man. Slave rebellions occurred here and there and became common, or very frequent, in the nineteenth century. It is our view that they were fomented, led and directed by Muslim slaves, many of them learned man from the Costa da Mina, where there was a struggle to impose the Islamic doctrine.

Gold and diamonds also brought about an unaccustomed upsurge of wealth, which unhinged the economy of regions specializing in sugar cane, tobacco, manioc and the manufacture of sugar and spirits, because of the high cost of slaves. With his highly valuable products, the miner could buy his labour force at prices which the farmer could ill afford. The miner did not haggle over prices. A slave costing from 150,000 to 200,000 *reis* in Bahia would fetch, in the mining areas, between 250 and 500 *oitavas* of gold (an *oitava* generally equalled 1,400 *reis*) which was between 310,000 and 700,000 *reis* (1700–03). Agricultural production could not support a similar increase in labour costs. The price disparity led to the emergence of 'the poor [or impoverished] farmer or plantation owner' and the wealthy miner or prospector. Panic broke out in many agricultural regions; the cost of essential foodstuffs soared out of all proportion in the ports and in the interior. In many respects, the situation of the poor and the middle classes became critical. The less-well-to-do farmers and plantation-owners were forced to sell their slaves. It was not that they had to realize their capital; they could simply no longer afford to feed and clothe them. However, apart from these considerations, they also had to cope with the continual problem of runaway slaves and incitement by trouble-makers. When slaves escaped, a double loss was usually involved: the loss of the labour force and the capital investment which it represented; the need to replace that labour force and the corresponding new investment.

For a brief period the mining area was invaded by a legion of runaway slaves and others, brought from the north-east by the *atravessadores* (contrabandists). In 1735, a government census showed that there were 101,651 slaves in the mining areas; by 1750, this figure had risen to over 150,000. And we have no idea how many slaves who escaped from the farms and plantations of the north-east took to the backlands, the rivers and *igarapés* and hid there.

The euphoria over the gold and diamond discoveries was felt at all levels of society. Contraband trade went on unchecked and developed its own organizational structure. This phenomenon resulted in a spread of highway robberies, killings and many other forms of violence. The entire mining and prospection area became unsafe.

At the same time, Portuguese emigrants flocked to the Brazilian mining areas from Europe in the hope of striking it rich, or just to escape poverty, the hardships of rural life or even the persecutions of the Inquisition.

From Trás-os-Montes, das Beiras, do Minho, etc., virtually anyone who had the price of a ship's passage embarked in search of his 'bonanza'. People from the most varied walks of life headed for the mines: gypsies, vagrants, New Christians and Jews, rural labourers, craftsmen, small farmers and small traders, mixed with adventurers and criminals. They all sold their belongings and set their sights on Brazil. Crews went missing immediately after their ships put into port and hid with friends or acquaintances in the backlands. In this way, around 800,000 Portuguese migrated to Minas Gerais and other regions in southern Brazil between 1705 and 1750; and this was at a time when Portugal's population numbered only a little over 2 million. Faced with such a large-scale abandonment of the country, the Portuguese Government introduced various measures aimed at controlling embarkations and the issue of passports.

The wave of emigration in the eighteenth century proved to be a decisive factor in the 1822 Secession.

In the main, it was Brazil that benefited from the economic progress made in the country with the aid of slave labour. Only the occasional 'crumbs of wealth' reached Portugal, and even these were badly used, as already mentioned. A sizable portion was simply given away to Great Britain, while another part went to various other European countries. In many of these countries a class of *nouveaux riches* burgeoned, engaged in the slave trade; the shipping and trading companies connected with the slave traffic also flourished. This prosperity is quite evident in the movement of ships and goods in the ports of Great Britain (Bristol, Liverpool and others), France (Bordeaux, Marseilles, Nantes, etc.) and Holland.

All in all, the (limited) benefit which the Portuguese derived from all these ventures is reflected in the sweat and toil of the immigrant, whose main concern was to save up enough money to support his family in Portugal, to acquire a plot of land (or increase it if he already had one), to buy a few teams of oxen, and to improve his house or build a new home. Relatively few immigrants made their fortunes in a big way. Those who did, bought or built manor houses—especially in the north of the country—or invested their capital in the trading and slave-trafficking operations which were set up in the middle of the eighteenth century, Such was the background to the emergence of the rural and merchant middle classes in northern and central Portugal and the 'joke' of our second-rate capitalism. The fact that so few Portuguese became rich in Brazil gives a certain idea of the cultural standing of the vast majority of emigrants, particularly those who went to South America. Emigration proceeded without any reference to qualitative considerations; it was a purely quantitative phenomenon, and the majority of emigrants were unskilled or minimally trained workers who were as a rule illiterate. Brazil accepted anyone who was willing to work in the country, as it was interested in building up the Brazilian population. Hence most of the Portuguese found themselves on the lower rungs of the employment ladder. This is borne out by the kind of epithets with which the Portuguese immigrant was tagged, many of which were disparaging. These workers were never afraid to take up a new type of work and could turn their hand to anything that came along.

Despite all this, emigration was largely responsible for the fact that the Portuguese acquired new habits and new forms of behaviour, and evolved a different view of the world and other peoples, which was much broader and more enlightened than the narrow-minded approach characterizing life in Portugal. The Portuguese acquired a new mentality and raised his own cultural level. We should also mention eating and other habits in European countries, which were the outcome or the large-scale introduction of tropical products: sugar, coffee, cocoa (hence chocolate), peanuts, piñon seed, palm oil and coconuts, etc. Most of these foodstuffs entered Europe as raw materials and were then processed. Sugar had to be refined and purified; peanuts were imported for their edible oil (in view of the growth of the population and the inadequate olive-oil production) and for their bagasse which was used in soap-making; piñon seed was also used in soap-making; palm oil and coconut oil were used in the manufacture of margarine and in the soap industry. The processing operations required the construction of large factories (for processing oils, cocoa and chocolate). Cocoa and chocolate became very popular in Europe.

The peanut, introduced into Africa in the first half of the nineteenth century, became a leading crop within little over fifty years. The seed headed the list of exports in Senegal, Gambia, Guinea-Bissau and other areas. The expansion of peanut farming brought about a radical reorganization of local economies and significant social and political changes in practically all the areas concerned.

Cocoa, which was originally a leading crop on the islands of São Tomé and Principe, was also introduced on the island of Fernando Po, on the Ivory Coast, the Gold Coast, now Ghana, and other places; a very high volume of production was achieved, particularly in the Ivory Coast and in the Gold Coast.

This kind of agriculture and mining could only be developed because of the huge demand on the European and American consumer and producer markets.

These products were grown in the tropics for two reasons: first, to meet the demand on the domestic consumer market and/or the export markets; second, to obtain the revenue which would enable African producers to engage in the trade from which they were practically excluded during the slavery era. These products served as a basis for the fiscal systems necessary to the European administrations in the various territories (through the hut levy, taxes, licences and other forms of taxation). The administrations also resorted to indirect strategies, such as creating a demand for certain essential goods among African populations who had never or hardly ever felt the need for them. This was the practical way to control the African markets and import European and American manufactured products.

These processes occurred persistently over a long period of time. However, they only gained a certain momentum in the second half of the nineteenth century, at a time when European policies on the domination of the African continent were clarified and defined. The main historical development in this lengthy process of evolution was the political and social crisis of the eighteenth century (the French Revolution, the Napoleonic Wars, etc.) which culminated in the General Act of the Berlin Conference (1884–85) with all its political and economic implications.

There is no doubt that a number of European countries derived considerable wealth from Brazilian gold and diamonds; raw materials (especially those we have listed) brought them even greater prosperity. Portugal benefited the least from all this trade. Despite her pioneering activities, she received a very small slice of this prosperity. The blame for this phenomenon may be laid squarely upon the society of the day, which saw everything purely in terms of territorial occupation.

Cultural considerations

In a limited study such as this, it would be quite impracticable to attempt even a brief survey of the impact of the slaves on the cultural life of each area where slave-holding was a common practice.

We shall confine ourselves to a number of passing references which are necessarily incomplete and do not therefore give a full and accurate picture of the cultural interchange and miscegenation which occurred.

Would Central and South America be as they are today without the contribution made by the African, whether as a slave or as a free man? The answer is obviously no.

Brazil, for example, was profoundly influenced by the Bantu culture (which in certain aspects was far more influential than the Sudanese culture) in the areas of music, language, food, magical and cult practices, even though the latter are quite syncretistic. Most Brazilian musical instruments are nothing other than adaptations of Angolan instruments. Another sign of this influence is the way society was organized at the time when the 'Casa Grande' was one of the prominent social features. Apart from these generic aspects, the most 'vital' sign of African cultural influence is the presence in Brazilian society of the Negroes and mestizos (individuals of mixed blood: from a white man and Negro woman, or even from two mestizos). Despite the 'injection' of white blood, Negro blood is still very strong in Brazil.

Another, perhaps more interesting, example is the creole islands: Cape Verde, practically all the West Indian islands and, on another level, São Tomé. Generally speaking, these islands have a creole population with a creole language and a creole culture. The degree of miscegenation, and linguistic and cultural intermixture may vary. Nevertheless, the reality of these islands should not be underestimated or denied.

The creolization, in the broadest sense of the term, of the inhabitants of the Cape Verde islands has the Portuguese language and culture as its base, just as the creolization of Haiti, Guadeloupe and Martinique is based on the French language and culture, and the creolization of the Dominican Republic on the Spanish language and culture. The same applies to other islands and areas which we are unable to mention owing to lack of space.

In all these areas, the dominant human type is markedly African, although there is evidence of hybridism. Apart from physical appearance, we should consider the main aspect of culture: the language. To give an example, the Cape Verde creole, spoken by all the inhabitants (although the majority understand Portuguese), has a vocabulary which is 90 per cent Portuguese (including various archaic forms), 5 per cent Mandingo or Fula, with the remaining 5 per cent being derived from various other European languages. However, the basic grammar of the language is of African origin.

The same sort of situation may be encountered in Haiti where 90 per cent of the population speak a creole French, and in the Dominican Republic where the language is a creole Spanish.

Various European languages, and Portuguese in particular, were in some degree influenced by the African languages. However, this influence was confined to the acceptance of a limited number of words which today form part of the national vocabulary. Such a phenomenon is the normal outcome of this type of relationship between peoples who speak different languages.

We have focused on the language question as language is one of the fundamental aspects of the culture of a people.

Note

1. See *Notas sobre o Trafico Português de Escravos na Costa Occidental Africana*, p. 33–4.

The Catholic Church and the slave trade

Luigi Conti

The official position of the Church towards the slave trade is the same as its position with regard to slavery in general.

The Catholic Church's action concerning the slave trade has been both direct and indirect.

Direct action

Scientific research, when conducted in depth and without ideological prejudice, shows that the action of the Popes and the missionaries played a decisive part in the abolition of slavery and of the slave trade.

It is worth while remembering that Pope Calixtus I (218–22) himself bore the stigmata of slavery.

On 7 October 1462, at the very beginning of the slave trade to Europe Pius II rose in defence of Negroes reduced to slavery and denounced the trade as 'magnum scelus' (a great crime), ordering the bishops to inflict ecclesiastical sanctions on those who practised it.[1]

Paul III (1534–49), in a Brief on 29 May 1537 to Cardinal Juan de Tavera, Archbishop of Toledo, forbade on pain of excommunication that American Indians should be reduced to slavery or despoiled on any pretext whatsoever of their possessions ('ne praefatos Indios quomodolibet in servitutem reidgere, aut eos bonis suis spoliare quoquemodo praesumat').[2] A few days later, at the beginning of June 1537, the Pope in the Bull 'Veritas Ipsa', addressed to all Christendom, proclaimed the absolute condemnation of slavery and annulled retrospectively all contracts providing for it, so that slaves had the right to free themselves from their state of servitude.

Urban VIII (1623–44), in his Letter of 22 April 1639 to the Representative of the Holy See in Portugal during its union with Spain, condemned slavery in his turn, threatening all those who practised it with excommunication.[3]

But people did not take sufficient notice of these papal documents. The missionaries, in their letters to the Sacred Congregation 'de Propagande Fide' (founded 6 January 1622), were always describing the dire effects of slavery on their evangelical mission and pressing for a fresh condemnation. This was issued by the Holy Office on 20 March 1686.

At the beginning of the eighteenth century, during the pontificate of Clement XI (1700–21), Rome was forced to take more severe measures: despite all the previous documents on the subject it was clear that slavery continued to exist and was even spreading. But Rome was convinced that no improvement was possible without the real co-operation of the King of Portugal, whose colonial Empire included a large part of the New World. So in 1707 the Sacred Congregation 'de Propaganda Fide' adjured the Papal Nuncios in Lisbon and Madrid, and all those in a position to do so, to act so as to bring about the abolition of slavery—'di procurare in ogni canto l'estirpazione degl'istessi gravissimi sconcerti'. But this appeal met with practically no response.

In the Instruction sent by the Sacred Congregation 'de Propaganda Fide' to the new Papal Nuncio in Lisbon, Vincenzo Bichi, the question of slavery was dealt with at length. The Congregation required slaves to be given a holiday not only on Sundays and feast days but also on Saturdays. This is probably the first demand in history for a five-day week.

In their meetings on 15 December 1738 and 28 November 1741, the Cardinals of the Sacred Congregation 'de Propaganda Fide' again dealt at length with the question of slavery. Thus on 22 December 1741, Pope Benedict XIV (1740–58), in the Papal Constitution *Immensa*, once more condemned slavery in the same terms as Paul III and Urban VIII. Although the Constitution referred specifically to the enslavement of the American Indians (and, as a result, the king of Portugal, by the law of 6 June 1755, forbade the enslavement of the Indians and ordered them to be set free), it was also applied to the enslavement of Negroes. In several other documents the Sacred Congregation extended the ban on slavery among the Indians to slavery among the blacks. In 1758 a copy of the Constitution *Immensa* was sent to the Prefect of the Capuchins in the Congo.

When the anti-slavery movement was gaining ground in Europe and Africa at the end of the eighteenth and the beginning of the nineteenth century, the Popes and the Sacred Congregation 'de Propaganda Fide' contributed amply to the eradication of slavery and the awakening of consciences.[4]

Pius VII wrote to the governments of Spain, Portugal and Brazil. In 1823, in a letter to the king of Portugal, Pope Pius VII again insisted on the abolition of slavery in the king's colonial empire.[5]

Any scientific inquiry on the subject should appraise the decisive part that Pope Pius VII played through his Representative at the Congress of Vienna (1814–15) to bring slavery to an end. It was through this Congress that Pius VII brought the full weight of his authority to bear on the subject. And in fact he did bring about abolition.

On 3 December 1837, Gregory XVI, in the Brief 'In Supremo Apostolatus Fastigio', after listing his predecessors' provisions with regard to slavery, went on to condemn it severely in all its forms. The reference to the trade in black slaves is clear, for it was still widely practised despite the fact that it had been legally abolished by the Congress of Vienna.[6]

Pius IX raised his voice against slavery in 1851 at the beatification of Pierre Claver (1580–1654), a Jesuit missionary known as 'the Negroes' apostle'.

On 5 May 1888, Leo XIII, in a letter to the bishops of Brazil, congratulated them warmly on what they had done to abolish slavery, and recalled the teaching of the Church in this matter.[7]

Throughout the period in which the slave trade was being carried on the missionaries, also encouraged by the declarations of the Popes and of the Sacred Congregation 'de Propaganda Fide', tried with all the means at their disposal to teach slaves, both Indians and blacks, to baptize them and set them free. The Sacred Congregation 'de Propaganda Fide' and the Charity of the Holy Child frequently provided money for this purpose. A well-known example of this kind of activity is the mission at Bagamoyo in East Africa.

Naturally, after the abolition of slavery among the American Indians, the Church's activities in this field turned more towards slavery among the blacks.

The work of the missionary bishop Cardinal Lavigerie (1825–92) for the abolition of slavery is well known.

It should be noted that the missionaries—Dominicans, Franciscans, Jesuits and others—who went to the New World soon found themselves fighting against those who exploited first the Indians then the blacks. Many of them were tortured or even killed by the settlers.

The bad example set by those owners receives a good deal of attention, but this cannot detract from the vast and beneficent work carried out by the Church among the Indians and the Negroes.

Indirect action

As some people nowadays deplore, the Church did not organize crusades or stir up revolutions against the various forms and manifestations of slavery. But the Church did act, in obedience to Christ and to the Gospel, in an indirect, patient, constant, planned and effective manner—one which was the more likely to succeed because it could create an environment and conditions favourable to the abolition of the slave trade in general and of the trade in African Negroes in particular.

The Church has always preached monogenism, and so has taught and practised the principles of equality and fraternity between men in the universal fatherhood of God. The Church has done this despite and in the face of times conditioned by the human and social sciences.

If the Church urged slaves to be patient, it also demanded that masters should consider them and treat them like men, like brothers, for before God 'there is neither bond nor free ... for ye are all one in Christ Jesus'.

Furthermore, if the Church was careful to baptize slaves it was because it considered them to be men, or rather sons of God. But the spreading of the Gospel also meant developing them as human beings, giving them a greater awareness of their dignity, which would lead them to accept the responsibility for their own liberation. This is the reason for the hostility that existed between settlers and missionaries, and for the resistance of the latter, which finally aroused or fostered liberation movements among the slaves themselves.

The Church's missionary activities in this field can be seen in detail in the archives of the religious orders and institutes which throughout the centuries of slavery devoted themselves, sometimes in tragic circumstances, to preaching the Gospel to the Indians and the Negroes, and to promoting their human dignity.

Notes

1. O. Rainaldi, *Annales*, X (a. 1482), Lucca 1752, p. 341–2.
2. *Bullarium Taurinense*, XIV, Turin 1868, p. 712–13.
3. ibid., p. 712–14.
4. In a letter of 20 September 1841 addressed to the king of France, Pius VII wrote: 'Ad interponenda vero huiusmodi officia religio ipsa nos movet, quae improbat execraturque turpissimum illud commercium, quo Nigritae, tamquam si non homines sed pur putaque animantia forent, emuntur, venduntur, ac miserrimae vitae durissimisque laboribus usque ad mortem exantlandis dovoventur. Itaque inter maxima, quae sanctissima eadem religio orbi contulit, hona, servitutis magnam partem abrogatae aut mitius exercitae beneficium merito ab omnibus recensetur.' In the same Letter Pope Pius VII addresses both churchmen and laymen in these terms: 'And we forbid any ecclesiastic or layman to dare on any pretext whatever to maintain that this trade in Blacks is allowed, or to preach or teach in public or private, in any manner whatsoever, anything in contradiction to this Papal Letter.'
5. Itaque ad maiestatem tuam, cuius egregiam erga nos voluntatem cognitam penitus planeque perspectam habemus, paterna haec officia dirigimus, maeque intomo cordis affectu hortamur in Domino atque obsecramus, ut, singulari sua prudentia in consilium advocata, omnem det operam, uti opportunae illae hac de re legum poenarumque sanctiones in omnibus suarum, qua late patent, ditionum partibus accurate serventur, ac probrosum demum Nigritarum commercium summo cum religionis atque humani generis commodo radicitus extirpatur.'
6. *Acta Gregorii XVI*, II, Rome 1901, p. 387 et seq.
7. *Acta Leonis XIII*, VIII, Rome, 1889, p. 169–92.

Supplementary report on slave-trade studies in the United States

P. D. Curtin

Research on the slave trade in the United States is now very extensive and I cannot know all of it. But the most recent bibliography is:

Hogg, Peter C. *The African Slave Trade and its Suppression. A Classified and Annotated Bibliography of Books, Pamphlets, and Periodical Articles*. London, 1973.

Other more recent important contributions have been:

Rubin, Vera; Duden, Arthur (eds.). *Comparative Perspectives on Slavery in New World Plantation Societies*. New York, New York Academy of Sciences, 1977. (Annals of the New York Academy of Sciences, Vol. 292.)
Drescher, Seymour. *Econocide. British Slavery in the Era of Abolition*. Pittsburgh, University of Pittsburgh Press, 1977.
Gemery, Henry; Hogendorn, Jan. A volume containing papers originally presented at a slave-trade conference in Waterville, Maine, in August 1977, published in 1978.
Klein, Herbert. S. *The Middle Passage; Comparative Studies in the Atlantic Slave Trade*, Princeton, N. J., Princeton University Press, 1978.
Villa Vilar, Enriqueta. *Hispano-America y el Comercio de Esclaves*. Seville, 1977.

Other important ongoing research is being carried out by David Eltis, Department of Economics, Rochester University, Rochester, N.Y.; Stanley Engerman, Department of Economics, Rochester University, Rochester, N.Y.; and Joseph Miller, Department of History, University of Virginia, Charlottesville, Virginia.

The slave trade and the peopling of Santo Domingo

Jean Fouchard

Contemporary accounts and recent studies alike have provided us with generally accurate information about the living conditions of the Negroes who were imported into Santo Domingo, their physical and moral characteristics, their temperament, age, stature, reactions to slavery, religious beliefs, food, housing, furniture, names, physiological condition, artistic sense, tastes, customs and so on.

But there are two main questions which still preoccupy historians and ethnologists: how many slaves were imported into Santo Domingo, and what were the relative proportions of the different ethnic groups among the Africans who formed the island's population?

We still have no answer to the first question. Statistics relating to the slave trade in Santo Domingo are too partial and fragmentary. We do know that at certain periods in the history of the colonization of the country, the southern strip was supplied principally through the illicit slave trade, which increased considerably during the American War of Independence and towards the end of the official slave trade; but we do not possess the figures that would enable us to estimate the size of this parallel traffic.

From the beginnings of colonization up to 1764, all we have to go by is scattered information, incomplete and occasional statistics, and necessarily partial estimates. Between 1764 and the end of the official trade in the island in 1793, the Santo Domingo newspapers supply us with invaluable information about the arrival of the slave-ships.

We are thus reduced to a rough estimate, but one which confirms the 'dreadful number' of deaths and the fact that Santo Domingo 'devoured' its slaves at a terrifying rate. Neither the ridiculously low birth rate nor the increasingly large consignments of imported slaves could compensate for the high rate of consumption, which was due to harsh conditions, forced labour driven to inhuman limits, tyranny and cruelty, not to mention almost universal and permanent malnutrition.

Hilliard d'Auberteuil, a notary at Cap Haïtien for twelve years, gives a horrifying account:

A third of the negroes from Guinea die normally during the first three years after their transplantation, and the working life of a negro acclimatized to the country cannot be put at more than 15 years. . . . More than 800,000 negroes have been brought into the colony since 1680: so large a nursery should have produced millions of slaves, yet there are only 290,000 now [1776] in the colony.[1]

If we accept the apparently very reasonable figure of 800,000 as the total number of Negroes brought to Santo Domingo between 1680 and 1776, this means an annual intake of fewer than 8,000. If we add to this the slaves imported by most Christian Spain from 1503 on—in the year, by the way, when Leonardo da Vinci painted the Mona Lisa—and the large consignments received during the French period (sometimes amounting to more than 45,000 Negroes a year, not counting the illicit trade), we should probably be not far from the truth in estimating the total number of Negroes imported into Santo Domingo at about 2 million.

Some such number would have been needed for Santo Domingo, during three centuries of colonization, to have become the gold mine which in turn enriched the crown of Castille and accounted for almost two-thirds of the general trade of the kingdom of France. At that time, the island was the most important colony in the New World, with an economy far outstripping those of Canada and of the embryonic Confederation of the United States of America.

Two million is a reasonable estimate, taking into account the fragmentary information which has come down to us either through the works of such classic authors as Charlevoix, Moreau de Saint-Méry and d'Auberteuil, or through the data provided by Bryan Edwards and, more recently, Pierre de Vaissière and Gaston Martin, or through the more detailed statistics derived from Santo Domingo's own newspapers.

The second question concerning the ethnic distribution of the African slaves who formed the population of Santo Domingo is of the greatest interest to us. It is indeed essential to know the exact origin of our forefathers, and fortunately the Haiti School has recently been able to determine this thanks to a hitherto unexploited sources: statistics on runaway slaves and their ethnic distribution based on descriptions of 48,000 runaways, announcements of slave-ship consignments as they arrived in the chief ports of Santo Domingo, and the almost daily book-keeping of the slave trade as reflected in the island's newspapers between 1764 and 1793.

The slaves imported into Santo Domingo came from a vast geographical area and an infinite number of different 'nations' or tribes with varied and imprecise designations difficult to connect with definite locations. The list put forward by Moreau de Saint-Méry, the list Robert Richard drew up from the minutes of the Santo Domingo notaries [2] and the data supplied by Descourtilz and de Malenfant reveal this diversity. I myself have added to these lists some

designations supplied by the Santo Domingo papers and apparently relating
to cantons and villages rather than to ethnic groups in the proper sense of the
term. Fortunately, from 1780 on, the newspapers of Cap Haïtien and of
Port-au-Prince began to describe slaves, maroons and Negroes for sale in
terms of the major ethnic groups to which they belonged.

Details given in notices of sale from 1764 on and descriptions of maroons
from 1780 on are more revealing. On the basis of this information, I shall try
to arrange in three categories the 'nations' which went to make up the population of the colony, using the geographical divisions put forward by Moreau de
Saint-Méry.

This classification is less hazardous than a classification based only
on religion, or on a common language, or again, on common political or
social interests.

No doubt a very exacting critic could find in the suggested classification
several details which are not entirely consistent with the norms adopted.
Nevertheless this system is the one that comes closest to the facts, and that
gives the best general outline of the origins of our ancestors.

Sudanese

This group includes the various peoples of the West African coast and the
nearby communities on the banks of the Senegal, Gambia and Niger rivers:
Senegalese, Wolofs, Calvaires; Fulani, Tukulors; Bambaras, Mandingos,
Bissago(t)s; Susus.

Guineans

These are the peoples who lived further south but still north of the Equator,
in the whole of the area round the Gulf of Guinea, including the Ivory Coast,
the Slave Coast and the Gold Coast (now Ghana): Kangas, Bourriquis, Misérables, Mesurades, Caplacus, Nagos, Mines, Minas, Yorubas, Thiambas;
Fons, Agousas, Socos, Fantins, Mahis, Dahomans, Aradas, Cotocolis, Popos,
Fidas, Hausas, Ibos, Mokos of Benin.

Bantus

These peoples lived south of the Equator, chiefly in the kingdoms of Congo
and Angola, which marked the limits of the French slave trade. They included:
Kongos, 'Francs Kongos', Musombis, Mondongos, Malimbas, Angolas.

To these were added, towards the end of the colonial period, large numbers of Mozambicans (especially from 1773 on), together with a very few
Negroes from such places as Madagascar and Mauritius—the sole contibu-
tion, though a large one, from East Africa.

It is generally agreed that the settlement of Santo Domingo was carried out in the first place by the Sudanese group, then the Guinean group and finally the Bantu group.

What is certain is that early slave consignments to Santo Domingo came from St Louis in Senegal and the island of Gorée.

Imprecision begins with the second phase of imports. We do know that the Guinea group was the first to take over from the Sudanese group as the colony's main provider of Negro slaves, but we do not know whether in the latter part of the colonial period, the Guinea group or the Bantu group predominated. The chief point of any inquiry into this subject is to find out which ethnic groups were in the numerical majority in the last half-century before independence. These groups were our most immediate ancestors, not only bequeathing us their physical and moral characteristics but also, at a deeper level, forming and influencing our cultural heritage.

Were they Guineans or Bantus?

No definite answer to this question has yet been found. Attempts had been made to solve the riddle by examining voodoo and oral tradition, settlers' correspondence, the minutes of the Santo Domingo notaries, the bills of lading of the slave-ship owners, and workshop inventories, but without being able to satisfy our legitimate curiosity.

Let us briefly examine these various approaches. Some specialists have tried to maintain that the practice of voodoo as the predominant popular religion in the colony is conclusive proof that Guinean slaves were in the majority in Santo Domingo. It is an attractive theory, but it does not stand up to analysis. Furthermore, it is contradicted by the advertised descriptions of slaves and by the workshop inventories, which on the one hand show that Kongos were in the majority among the maroons and on the other hand reveal no very considerable proportion of Dahomans (Aradas excepted). While it is true that voodoo, originating in Dahomey (now Benin), did take root and spread in the colony, this was not because of any massive presence of Dahoman slaves, for there was never any such thing. The reasons for the introduction and widespread practice of voodoo must be sought elsewhere.

In a recent paper, Lilas Desquiron[3] pointed out the considerable contribution made by Kongos of the Bantu group to the establishment of voodoo in Haiti. Moreover ethnologists have shown that voodoo had borrowed some elements from Catholicism. It thus appears that voodoo, by reason of the disparate nature of its elements, cannot indicate the predominance either of the Guinean or of the Bantu group among the early population of Santo Domingo. True, the word 'Guinea' for a long while symbolized Africa, but so, towards the end of the colonial period, did the word 'Congo'. The runaway chief Macaya recognized the king of Congo as 'born master of all blacks', and even before the ceremony at Bois-Caiman a Congolese song was adopted as an anthem for the rebels and for voodoo assemblies.

Be that as it may, while the voodoo songs with their many verses refer to the gods or *loas* of Africa, in terms either of the *rada* or of the *petro* ritual, they always refer to them together, for instance:

Mrin sôti lan Guinin, mrin sôti Guéléfé [Ifé] . . . palez hounsis congos lan Guinin . . . of té-léguey . . . Legba Petro, Legba Ibo, Legba Dahoumin, Legba Allada, Legba Badagri . . .

The litany known as the 'Prayer of Djor' shows even more clearly the number of 'peoples' which combined to form the Haitian community:

Rélé toutes toutou l'Afrique Guinin, toutes nanchons [nations] rada [Aradas], ibo, caplaou, en-mine [Amine, Mine], mondongue, mandingue, sinigal [Senegal], canga, congo, nago, danhomé, wangol, mahi, foulah, mayoumbé, fon, bambara, haoussa, congo-franc . . .

The voodoo songs thus reflect a recognition of the original *loas* of all the 'nations' contributing to the peopling of Santo Domingo and of the many different contributions to the growth of voodoo itself, rather than any ethnic distribution.

Does an examination of the settlers' correspondence, of the accounts of contemporary historians, of workshop inventories or of bills of lading give any better results? No—colonial documentation provides no exact answer to our questions as to whether the Guineans or the Bantus were in the majority at the end of the colonial period.

But it is certain that if workshop inventories, for example, are analysed systematically as more and more archives are discovered, we shall obtain an increasingly accurate picture. In the end we shall know what was the most usual 'distribution' for the period we are concerned with, in the workshops and in the sugar, indigo and coffee mills and plantations. Were the Aradas in the majority in the sugar industry, and the Kongos in the coffee industry? What was the real proportion of *bossales* (newly imported slaves) and 'creoles' (born in the colony) used in agricultural labour, domestic service and factory work at the end of the colonial period, even before the slackening off and eventual abolition of the official slave trade?

The inquiry is only just beginning. It will be a long and difficult one: workshop inventories do not abound. Every so often a fresh bundle of them is found in some dusty old cupboard.

M. Debien has analysed several hundreds of workshop inventories and brought together an invaluable source of documentation. At the same time, in order to find out the origins of the West Indian slaves, he also consulted the even rarer bills of lading of slave-ship owners, but came to the conclusion that these documents threw no light on the subject. None of the bills of lading consulted so far has shown the cargoes broken down in terms of ethnic groups, though they do tell us the names of the slave-ships' home ports (Nantes, La Rochelle, Le Havre, Bordeaux, Lorient, Marseilles, St Malo, Honfleur) and sometimes the ship's tonnage and the length of the crossing.

There still remain the announcements and advertisements in the Santo Domingo press. These notices are of two kinds. One group refers to slaves who are up for sale as the result of the temporary or permanent return of some settler to France. Unfortunately, these advertisements do not give exact descriptions of the slaves. Moreover they relate to only a tiny fraction of the total number of slaves, and generally to domestics. More interesting for us are the notices about slaves who had run away, who were in prison or were up for sale for having attempted to run away. These advertisements are numerous enough to provide a very serious basis for investigation. We possess no fewer than 48,000 of them spread out over some thirty years. With a few exceptions they all indicate the 'nation' the fugitive belonged to. It might be objected that, since such advertisements refer to maroons, they necessarily make no reference to the 'peoples' who were not given to running away. But there were no such peoples. A more serious drawback is that the lists of runaways do not show the actual proportion of each 'nation' in relation to the total slave population of Santo Domingo, but merely the proportion of each 'nation' in relation to the total number of runaways. But this information is in itself very important, because it reveals that Kongo slaves were in a clear majority among the runaways. This remained true almost without exception from 1764 to 1793, i.e. throughout the last phase of the colonial period.

So were Kongo slaves in general in the majority, or were they merely the 'people' most given to escaping, despite their reputation in the colony for being 'the most lively and the readiest to submit to servitude'?

The table appended to this paper shows how Kongos were in the majority among the runaways for the years 1764, 1765 and 1766 for example, while in the same years the slaves imported came largely from the Guinea and Gold Coasts.

The notices of slave-ship arrivals in the colony provide another source of information. These represent the actual voices of the colonists, the evidence of the slave-traders themselves, the day-books of Santo Domingo's trade in slave labour.

Here too there will be certain instances of lack of precision, but fortunately these do not invalidate the overall information supplied; and the great majority of these notices are absolutely exact. Only the professional scruples of the historian compel me to quote the few exceptions.

At all events, the arrival notices of the slave-ships enable us to conclude with certainty that Bantus were in the majority in the final peopling of Santo Domingo. They almost always say where the cargo is from, or give the name of the African port from which the ship sailed.

Unfortunately, the Santo Domingo newspapers often give somewhat contradictory information. Towards the end of the colonial period, and more especially between 1783 and 1785, the papers habitually ascribed to the 'Gold Coast' not only cargoes of Guinean Ardas but also Kongos from the Bantu group and Senegalese from the Sudanese group. The term 'Gold Coast' was sometimes used to mean the Congo, Angola, Senegal, Dahomey of even Mozambique, and to cover slaving centres such as Malimbe, Porto Novo, Ardre or Adra, Aunis, Juda, Anamabou, Gorée and Badagris, which by no means all belong to the geographical or ethnic region of the Gold Coast. We also see, though this is not so serious, the term 'Kongos' applied to cargos from Angola and Mozambique—people belonging, it is true, to the same Bantu group.

The Santo Domingo newspapers and slave-traders were aware of these occasional distortions. That was why they sometimes took the precaution of specifying that some cargoes came from 'the real Gold Coast'.

We can therefore reach the following conclusions: from St Louis and later from Gorée came the Senegalese, the Bambaras, Quiambas, Sudanese and Fulani from Futa; the Mandingos were supplied by Gambia; the Aradas represented the real Gold Coast or Slave Coast from Dahomey to eastern Nigeria, and were grouped in the slaving centres of Juda, Porto Novo, Ouidah, Abomey and Allada.

The Mines and the Thimbas came from present-day Ghana, the Mocos from Gabon, the Cotocolis from Togo, and the Nagos from south-west Nigeria.

The Misérables and the Bouriquis came from the Malaguette Coast (present-day Liberia), and the Mondongos from the kingdom of Benguele; Angola's slaving ports were Cabinda and Loango. The Mandongos were wrongly put in the same category as the neighbouring Kongos from the kingdom of Congo, which lay between Capes Lopes and Negre, and thus between Gabon and Angola.[4]

On this basis we can rectify the few minor errors and inaccuracies previously referred to. This is what I have tried to do in my appended summary account of the slave trade based on notices of slave-ship arrivals in the various ports in Santo Domingo and of advertisements of public sales of their cargoes.

According to the results of this inquiry, therefore, the Haitian community's most immediate ancestors were mostly slaves belonging to the Bantu group, which reinforced and then predominated over slaves imported from the Guinean group and over declining supplies from the Sudanese group.

These three groups have fashioned our people and, via the strangest of melting-pots, have stamped it for ever. They came to sow and quicken our land, and they worked in blood, sweat and tears to produce stitch by stitch, with French thread and Bantu spindle, a new ethnic fabric, without ever cutting the umbilical cord that links us forever to Africa.

Notes

1. *Considérations sur l'État Présent de la Colonie Française de Saint-Domingue*, II, p. 62–3.
2. *Revue d'Histoire des Colonies*, No. 135, 3rd quarter, 1951, p. 310.
3. *Evolution Historique d'une Religion Africaine : Le Voodoo* (paper presented by Mrs Lilas Desquiron de Heusch at the Free University of Brussels for the academic year 1967–68).
4. See Moreau de Saint-Méry, I, 52 et seq., and Rosseline Siguret, 'Esclaves . . . au Quartier de Jacmel', *Revue Française d'Histoire d'Outre-Mer*, No. 2, 1968, p. 224.

Appendix: Summary account of the slave trade to Santo Domingo, 1764-93

1764

Papers consulted: Gazette de Saint-Domingue, various announcements and *Affiches Américaines*.
Number of slave-ships : 31.
Declared provenance: (a) Guinean group (Gold Coast, 10; Guinea Coast, 9); (b) Bantu group (Angola Coast, 10); (c) Sudanese group (Gorée, Senegal, 1) and (d) other places (bought in Martinique, 1).
Group providing most imports: Guinean group (Guinea and Gold Coasts), 19, as against 10 ships from the Angola Coast (Kongos, 'Francs-Kongos') dealing in slaves from the Bantu group.
Number of Negroes declared:[1] 6,681.
Group providing most runaways in same year: Bantu group; out of 405 announcements, the majority already related to Kongos.[2]

1. While the gazettes usually give the slave-ships' provenance, they often omit to show how slaves there were in each cargo. So the number of Negroes declared every year does not always correspond to the volume of imports. But it does give some idea of which group predominated at the time in the peopling of the colony.
2. The figures given here for runaways are not always strictly accurate. For most years I have preferred to give only an estimate, since there was not time to examine one by one the 48,000 announcements spread over some thirty years.

1765

Papers consulted: Various notices and *Affiches Américaines*.
Number of slave-ships: 15.
Declared Provenance: (a) Guinean group (Gold Coast, 6; Guinea Coast, 6); (b) Bantu group (Angola Coast, 3); and (c) Sudanese group, 0.
Group providing most imports: Guinean.
Number of Negroes declared: Only 2,180, whereas for the ports of the Cape and Port-au-Prince alone the real total was 11,900 (*Affiches Américaines*, 12 March 1766).
Group providing most runaways: Bantus, (Kongos), out of about 600 announcements.

1766

Papers consulted: Affiches Américaines
Number of slave-ships: 35.
Declared provenance: (a) Guinean group (Gold Coast, 11; Guinea Coast, 7); (b) Bantu group (Angola group, 15); and (c) Sudanese group (Gorée, Senegal, 2).
Group providing most imports: Guinean: 18.
Number of Negroes declared: 9,602.
Group providing most runaways: Bantus (Kongos), out of about 800 announcements.

1767

Papers consulted: Affiches Américaines.
Number of slave-ships: 52.
Declared provenance: (a) Guinean
group (Gold Coast, 21; Guinea
Coast, 4); (b) Bantu group (Angola
Coast, 27); and (c) Sudanese group,
0.
Group providing most imports: Bantu
group.
Number of Negroes declared: 15,293.
Group providing most runaways: Bantus
(Kongos), out of 1,095 announce-
ments.

1768

Papers consulted: Affiches Américaines
and *Avis du Cap.*
Number of slave-ships: 39.
Declared provenance: (a) Guinean
group (Gold Coast, 11; Guinea
Coast, 6); (b) Bantu group (Angola
(Coast, 20); and (c) Sudanese group
(Gorée, Senegal, 2).
Group providing most imports: Bantu.
Number of Negroes declared: 8,841.
Group providing most runaways: Bantus
(Kongos), out of 1,100 announce-
ments.

1769

*Papers consulted: Affiches Américaines,
Avis du Cap,* and *Supplément aux
Affiches Américaines.*
Number of slave-ships: 37.
Declared provenance: (a) Guinean
group (Gold Coast, 13; Guinea
Coast, 2); (b) Bantu group (Angola
Coast, 21); and (c) Sudanese group
(Gorée, Senegal, 1).

Group providing most imports: Bantu.
Number of Negroes declared: 7,950.
Group providing most runaways: Bantus
(Kongos), out of about 1,250 an-
nouncements.

1770

*Papers consulted: Affiches Américaines,
Supplément aux Affiches Amécicaines.*
Number of slave-ships: 36.
Declared provenance: (a) Guinean
group (Gold Coast, 18; Guinea
Coast, 1); (b) Bantu group (Angola
Coast, 15); (c) Sudanese group
(Senegal, 2).
Group providing most imports: Guinean.
Number of Negroes declared: 8,768.
Group providing most runaways: Bantus
(Kongos), out of about 1,300 an-
nouncements.

1771

Papers consulted: Affiches Américaines
and *Supplément aux Affiches Américaines.*
Number of slave-ships: 30.
Declared provenance: (a) Guinean
group (Gold Coast, 9; Guinea Coast,
1); (b) Bantu group (Angola Coast,
17); and (c) Sudanese group (Gambia
and Senegal, 3).
Group providing most imports: Bantu.
Number of Negroes declared: 6,990.
Group providing most runaways: Bantus
(Kongos) out of about 950 announcements.

1772

Papers consulted: Affiches Américaines
and *Supplément aux Affiches Américaines.*

Number of slave-ships: 39.

Declared provenance: (a) Guinean group (Gold Coast, 11; Guinea Coast, 5); (b) Bantu group (Angola Coast, 21); and (c) Sudanese group (Gambia and Senegal, 2).

Group providing most imports: Bantu.

Number of Negroes declared: 8,821.

Group providing most runaways: Bantus (Kongos), out of about 1,000 announcements.

1773

Papers consulted: Affiches Américaines, Supplément aux Affiches Américaines, and various announcements.

Number of slave-ships: 35.

Declared provenance: (a) Guinean group (Cold Coast, 15; Guinea Coast, 0); (b) Bantu group (Angola Coast, 19); and (c) other places (Mozambicans, 1).[1]

Group providing most imports: Bantu.

Number of' Negroes declared: 6,270.

Group providing most runaways: Bantus (Kongos), out of about 1,000 announcements.

1774

Papers consulted: Affiches Américaines and *Supplément aux Affiches Américaines.*

1. This is the first declared import of Negroes from East Africa. From now on, slaves from Madagascar and above all from Mozambique became more numerous. (The *Supplément aux Affiches Américaines,* 24 July 1773, cargo unloaded on the 18th of the same month.) Despite the difficulties of carrying on the trade in this area, Quiola and other East African slaving centres were often preferred to the Gold and Angola Coasts.

Number of slave-ships: 35.

Declared provenance: (a) Guinean group (Gold Coast, 7; Guinea Coast, 2); (b) Bantu group (Angola Coast, 24); and (c) Sudanese group (Gorée, Senegal, 2).

Group providing most imports: Bantu.

Number of Negroes declared: 7,629.

Group providing most runaways: Bantus (Kongos), out of about 1,600 announcements.

1775

Papers consulted: Affiches Américaines and *Supplément aux Affiches Américaines.*

Number of slave-ships: 44.

Declared provenance: (a) Guinean group (Gold Coast, 19; Guinea Coast, 1); (b) Bantu group (Angola Coast, 20); and (c) Sudanese group (Gorée, Senegal, 4).

Group providing most imports: Bantu.[2]

Number of Negroes declared: 7,965.

Group providing most runaways: Bantus (Kongos), out of about 1,300 announcements.

1776

Papers consulted: Affiches Américaines and *Supplément aux Affiches Américaines.*

Number of slave-ships: 58.

Declared provenance: (a) Guinean group (Gold Coast, 26; Guinea

2. As the Guinean and Bantu groups were equal this year as regards provenance, I was obliged in this case to use the list of Negroes declared to arrive at the relative numbers of Guineans and Bantus. Out of 7,965 Negroes declared, more than half are said to come from the Angola Coast.

Coast, 1); (b) Bantu group (Angola Coast, 30); and (c) Sudanese group (Gorée, Senegal, 1).
Group providing most imports: Bantu.
Number of Negroes declared: 10,921.
Group providing most runaways: Bantus (Kongos), out of about 2,100 announcements.

1777

Papers consulted: Affiches Américaines and *Supplément aux Affiches américaines.*
Number of slave-ships: 50.
Declared provenance: (a) Guinean group (Gold Coast, 20; Guinea Coast, 1); (b) Bantu group (Angola Coast, 22); (c) Sudanese group (Gorée, Senegal, 5) and (d) other places[1] (Mozambicans, 2).
Group providing most imports: Bantu.
Number of Negroes declared: 11,387.
Group providing most runaways: Bantus (Kongos), out of about 2,000 announcements.

1778

Papers consulted: Affiches Américaines and *Supplément aux Affiches Américaines* (double supplement)
Number of slave-ships: 49.
Declared provenance: (a) Guinean group (Gold Coast, 28); (b) Bantu group (Angola Coast, 17; Mozam-

1. The Mozambicans belong to the Bantu group.

bicans, 2); and (c) Sudanese group (Senegal, 2).
Group providing most imports: Guinean (Gold Coast).
Number of Negroes declared: 10,336.
Group providing must runaways: Bantus (Kongos), out of about 1,700 announcements.

1779

Papers consulted: Affiches Américaines and *Supplément aux Affiches Américaines* (double supplement).
Number of slave-ships: The long American War of Independance disrupted the slave trade. Because of insecurity at sea there are practically no announcements of slave-ship arrivals, apart from the following three, from which it is not possible to determine the respective size of the groups: (a) 2 March 1779—The *Négresse* of Le Havre, coming from the Gold Coast and arriving at the Cape on 25 February. Out of this cargo, 89 Negroes are announced for sale; (b) *Affiches Américaines*, 15 June 1779—'Two English ships with cargoes of Negroes from captures made in the rivers of Gambia and Sierra Leone in Africa by the division commanded by M. de Pondevis-Gren. The names of these ships are the *Providence* and the *Herifort.*' *Affiches Américaines*, 17 August—The *Nymphe* coming from the African coast.
Group providing most runaways: Bantus (Kongos), followed first by a higher than usual percentage of creole or West Indian Negroes, and then by Nagos and Mondongos; out of about 1,300 announcements.

1780

Papers consulted: Affiches Américaines
and *Supplément aux Affiches Américaines* Santo Domingo was still
feeling the effects of the war and of a
blockade which paralysed the arrivals
of slave ships. The gazette still kept
the heading 'Arrivals of shipping'.
Some escorted convoys were described as 'coming from France or
'having called at Martinique', or
'coming from the Windward Islands',
but not a single ship is noted as
coming directly from the coasts of
Africa.
Group providing most runaways: Bantu
group (still the Kongos), And among
the runaways there are still more
Bossales than creoles. The number
of runaways noted for the year is
about 1,250.

1781

Papers consulted: Affiches Américaines
and *Supplément aux Affiches Américaines* (reduced format).
Number of slave-ships: Hostilities continued and maritime transport still
encountered the same difficulties,
although many merchant ships coming from France arrived under escort
at the Cape and At Port-au-Prince
—veritable caravans, with sometimes
as many as sixty-nine ships anchored
off the Cape at the same time.

The slave trade consisted of a few
ships that managed to get through the
blockade, and of a few neutral ships,
Danish or Spanish for example,
which called at Havana and brought
small consignments of Negroes to
Santo Domingo.

More new names occur among the
runaways: Mandingos, Minas, Mozambicans, Nagos, Thiambas. This
suggests that it had become difficult
to supply slaves, and to provide them
in quantities adequate to the colony's
requirements. Such supply as there
was Santo Domingo owed to the
illicit trade rather than the official
traffic, which had become dangerous
if not impossible.

Kongos are still in the majority
among the runaways, followed by
creolized Bossales no longer labelled
as new Negroes; large numbers of
creoles belonging to Santo Domingo
itself or to the neighbouring West
Indies (Dutch and Spanish Negroes,
creoles from Curaçao and Martinique); and Mississippi Negroes,
together with Nagos, Mandingos,
Ibos and other Bossales given to
escaping.

Another source of supply was the
occasional capture on the high seas.

It is also interesting to reproduce
the announcements in the *Affiches
Américaines*, which show better than
any commentary the small number
of Negroes arriving in 1781:

*Supplément aux Affiches Améri-
caines*, 27 February 1781: 'On
28 February 1781, at the Cape, at the
request of Bernard Lavaud [agent
representing the captains responsible
for the capture], sale and auction of
202 new head from the Gold Coast,
taken from the *Diamant* of London,
captured from the enemies of the
State by the frigate *Saratoga* of the
United States of America together
with two frigates, a privateer brigantine of Philadelphia and the King's
brigantine the *Chat*.' Also sale and
auction of the ship *Diamant*, known
as the *Duc de Laval*, a slave-ship of
La Rochelle.[1]

Affiches Américaines, 29 May: The *Lion*, privateer of the Cape, has taken and brought to Les Cayes a *fénau* [?] with a cargo of Negroes being sent from St Lucia to Jamaica under the Portuguese flag.

Supplément aux Affiches Américaines, 24 July: 'The *Senac* arrived at the Cape coming from Senegal with a cargo of 56 blacks.

'217 blacks traded on the coast of Mozambique introduced into this port by the *Gànge*, from Lorient.'

Affiches Américaines, 16 October Stanislaus Foache, Hellot and Co., 'hold a sale from the slave-ship *Acrā* coming from the Gold Coast'.

Affiches Américaines, 20 November: The Danish ship *Kristiansborg* 'with a very fine cargo of 200 Negroes from the Gold Coast' to be disposed of by Foache, Hellot.

Group providing most imports: Guinean (Gold Coast), but this cannot be vouched for because of the irregularity of the announcements.

Group providing most runaways: Bantu (Kongos), out of about 1,900 announcements.

1782

Papers consulted: Affiches Américaines and *Supplément aux Affiches Américaines*

Number of slave-ships: The list below includes all the announcements relating to the slave trade for 1782:

1. Out of the 202 Negroes in this cargo, seven ran away soon after arrival: [Seven runaways new Negroes of the Mandingo nation, unbranded, from the sale of the slave ship captured from the enemies of the State early last month; they ran away from the domicile of M. Sainte-Marie in the district of Le Borgne in the night of the 16th to the 17th.'

'The *Fleurie* of Nantes, coming from Senegal with 130 Negroes.

'The *Chambellan Schask*, a Danish ship with a cargo of 400 blacks from the Gold Coast for Foache, Hellot and Co.

'The *Patience* of St Thomas, with a fine cargo of 200 Negroes from the Gold Coast for Lory, Plombard and Co.

'Foache, Morange and Co., announce that they have just received a very fine cargo of 271 Negroes from the Gold Coast.

'Lory and Plombard announce that they have for sale 31 head of new Negroes of the Arada nation, and in the following week 59 other new Negroes, also Aradas.

'Foache, Morange announce the arrival of a very fine cargo of 207 Negroes from the Gold Coast.

'Abeille and Guys have for sale 12 fine Negroes from the Angola Coast, and Foache has 50 head of Negroes from the Gold Coast.

'The *Duchesse de Polignac* of St Malo, coming from Gabinde, with arrival of 800 blacks from the Angola Coast.

'Martineau and Blanchard have 50 fine new Negroes for sale.

'Roux and Rivière have received a cargo from the brigantine *Elsinore*.'

Group providing most imports: Guinean.

Group providing most runaways: Bantu (Kongos), out of about 1,000 announcements.

1783

Papers consulted: Affiches Américaines, and *Supplément aux Affiches Américaines*

Number of slave-ships: 29.

Declared provenance: (a) Guinean group (Gold Coast, 13; Guinea Coast, 1);[1] (b) Bantu group (Angola Coast, 9); (c) Sudanese group (Senegal, 3); and (d) other places (Porto-Cabello, Cape of Good Hope, 3).

Group providing most imports: Guinean.

Number of Negroes declared: 5,531.

Group providing most runaways: Bantu (Kongos), out of 1,386 announcements.

1784

Papers consulted: Affiches Américaines and *Supplément aux Affiches Américaines.*

Number of slave-ships: 71.

Declared provenance: (a) Guinean group (Gold Coast, 27; Guinea Coast, 0); (b) Bantu group (Angola Coast, 37); and (c) Sudanese group (Senegal, 7).

Group providing most imports: Bantu (Angola Coast).

Number of Negroes declared: 14,767.[2]

1. This cargo is said to the 'from the Coast of Guinea', but at the sale the same cargo is referred to as 'Negroes from the Gold Coast'. Similar errors in the location of certain ports or even of certain ethnic groups are corrected in the statistics which follow.
2. A table showing arrivals of slave-ships for 1784 was published in the *Affiches* in 1785. This table shows 82 ships, a figure fairly near the one given above, but as against the 14,767 Negroes indicated above as put up for sale, it says that 22,830 were obtained for the trade, of whom 3,578 died during the crossing. This brings the real number of imports to 19,252. The table deals only with sales of Negroes in the ports at the Cape and at Port-au-Prince, omitting other slaving ports in Santo Domingo such as Saint-Marc, Léogâne, St Louis, etc.

Group providing most runaways: Bantu (Kongos), out of 1,489 announcements.

1785

Papers consulted: Affiches Américaines and *Supplément aux Affiches Américaines* (enlarged format from 1785 on).

Number of slave-ships: 50.

Declared provenance: (a) Guinean group (Gold Coast, 20; Guinea Coast, 1); (b) Bantu group (Angola Coast, 23); (c) Sudanese group (Senegal, 5); and (d) other places (Mozambique, 1).

Group providing most imports: Bantu (Angola Coast).

Number of negroes declared: 12,148.[3]

Group providing most runaways: Bantu (Kongos), out of about 2,400 announcements.

1786

Papers consulted: Affiches Américaines, Supplément aux Affiches Américaines, Feuille du Cap-François and *Feuille du Port-au-Prince* (with supplement).

Number of slave-ships: 62.

Declared provenance: (a) Guinean group (Gold Coast, 22; Guinea Coast, 0); (b) Bantu group (Angola Coast, 27); (c) Sudanese group (Senegal, 11); and (d) other places (Mozambicans, 2).

3. The *Affiches* published in 1786 a summary table for 1785 with the following figures: number of slave-ships, 65; number of slaves sold, 21,652. This time it is specified that this figure concerns the ports of Port-au-Prince, the Cape, Léogâne, Les Cayes, Saint-Marc and Jacmel.

Group providing most imports: Bantu (Angola Coast).
Number of Negroes declared: 17,432.[1]
Group providing most runaways: Bantu (Kongos), out of about 2,600 announcements.

1787

Papers consulted: Affiches Américaines, Supplément aux Affiches Américaines, Feuille du Cap-François and twice-weekly supplement.
Number of slave-ships: 87.
Declared provenance: (a) Guinean group (Gold Coast, 44; Guinea Coast, 0); (b) Bantu group (Angola Coast, 20); (c) Sudanese group (Senegal, 14); and (d) other places (Mozambique, African Coast, Sierra Leone, Gabon, Quiola.
Group providing most imports: Guinean (Gold Coast).
Number of Negroes declared: 22,726.[2]
Group providing most runaways: Bantu (Kongos), out of about 2,500 announcements.

1788

Papers consulted: Feuille du Cap-François and *Affiches Américaines,* published Thursdays and Saturdays.
Number of slave-ships: 36.

1. The total number of negroes imported in 1786 is 27,648, i.e. 2,592 at Léogâne, 873 at Jacmel, 385 at Les Cayes, 2,014 at Saint-Marc, 12,319 at the Cape, and 9,465 at Port-au-Prince *(Affiches Américaines,* 10 March 1787).
2. Bryan Edwards gives a figure of 30,839 for Negroes imported in 1787. The nine cargoes shown under 'other places' include 4 from Mozambique, 4 from the Gold Goast, and 1 from the coast of Africa.

Declared provenance: (a) Guinean group (Gold Coast, 16; Guinéa Coast, 0); (b) Bantu group (Angola Coast, 19); and (c) Sudanese group (Senegal, 1).
Group providing most imports: Bantu.
Number of Negroes declared: 12,048.[3]
Group providing most runaways: Bantu (Kongos), out of about 2,800 announcements.

1789

Papers consulted: Affiches Américaines, Supplément aux Affiches Américaines, Feuille du Cap-François and supplement; various other news items.
Number of slave-ships: 120.
Declared provenance: (a) Guinean group (Gold Coast, 48; Guinea Coast, 2); (b) Bantu group (Angola Coast, 44; Mozambique, 10); (c) Sudanese group (Senegal, 6; Gambia, 1); and (d) other places (not specified, 4).
Unusual provenances: Isles of Los (at the entrance to the port of Conakry, Guinea), 1; Cape of Good Hope (Bantu), 1; Ile de France (east of Madagascar; now Mauritius), 2; Prince's Isle (gulf of Guinea); 1; a total of 5, of which 3 are Bantu.
Group providing most imports: Bantu.
Number of Negroes declared: 33,937.[4]
Group providing most runaways: Bantu (Kongos), out of about 3,150 announcements.

3. Bryan Edwards gives 29,506 Negroes imported in 1788. At least two cargoes declared as being from the 'Angola Coast' were from Mozambique.
4. The announcements of slave-ships arriving in 1789 mention the Cape, Port-au-Prince, Les Cayes, Jérémie, Jacmel, Léogâne and Saint-Marc.

1790

Papers consulted: Affiches Américaines, Feuille du Cap-François, various news items, *Supplément aux Affiches Américaines* and *Journal Général de Saint-Domingue* (October to December).
Number of slave-ships: 170.
Declared provenance: (a) Guinean group (Gold Coast, 68); (b) Sudanese group (Senegal, 3); (c) Bantu group, (Angola Coast, 68; Mozambicans, 26; and (d) other places (unspecified, 3; Ile-de-France (Mauritius), 2).
Group providing most imports: Bantu (Kongos and Mozambicans).
Number of Negroes declared: 46,471.[1]
Group providing most runaways: Bantu closely followed by Mozambicans), out of about 3,500 announcements.

1791

Papers consulted: Gazette de Saint-Domingue, Politique, Civile, Économique et Littéraire, Affiches Américaines (Wednesdays and Saturdays, plus a supplement), *Journal Général de Saint-Domingue* (January to March), *Courrier de Saint-Domingue, Courrier National de Saint-Domingue, Journal de Port-au-Prince* and *Assemblée Coloniale de la Partie Française.*
Number of slave-ships: 58.
Declared provenance: (a) Guinean group (Gold Coast, 22; Guinea, Isles of Los, 1); (b) Bantu group (Angola Coast, 24; Mozambicans, 3); and (c) other places (African

coast, 2, Ile-de-France (Mauritius), 1; unspecified: 3).
Group providing most imports: Bantu.
Group providing most runaways: Bantu (Kongos, followed by many Mozambicans), out of about 4,600 announcements.

1792 and 1793

Papers consulted: Journal Politique de Saint-Domingue (edited by a member of the Colonial Assembly), *Affiches Américaines, Journal des Révolutions de la Partie Française de Saint-Domingue, Moniteur de la Partie Française de Saint-Domingue* (daily and supplement), *Observateur Colonial* and *Gazette des Cayes.*[2]
Number of slave-ships: The official slave trade was coming to an end, amidst serious upheavals in Santo Domingo and increasingly vigorous activity on the part of the abolitionists. Announcements of slave-ships' arrivals become more and more rare, as if the new spirit forbade too much attention being paid to this controversial traffic. But slave ships with well-known names continued to come and go to and from the Cape and Port-au-Prince. The papers show that it is a slave ship by the length of the crossing, but the ships' provenance and the size of their cargoes are not mentioned. The runaway lists include creoles from Martinique, Charleston and Marie-Galante (showing that some slaves were supplied by these neighbouring countries) as well as new Negroes, some-

---

1. Both this figure and that for the number of slave-ships are very large. Between 14 October, 17 slave-ships are announced as arriving at the port of the Cape alone.

2. These papers form part of the Moreau de Saint-Méry Library, Archives de la France d'Outre-Mer.

times not yet branded and unable to speak French: the newly imported Negroes included Kongos, Mozambicans, Nagos, Senegalese, Mandingos and Ibos. All this confirms that the slave trade was still going on in 1792 and even up to the end of March 1793.

It would be especially interesting to know more about the slave trade in its final manifestations. But, unfortunately, for these last two years the evidence of the newspapers is limited to just a few announcements: the *Sérapis* coming from Mozambique; a cargo of 282 Negroes from the Gold Coast; three others from the same place (Gold Coast); Nine cargoes coming from the Angola Coast.

In 1792 the press was generally silent about the composition of cargoes, and the number of Negroes announced did not exceed 2,000.

In 1793 the *Moniteur Général*, though a daily paper carrying a supplement, made only the following announcements: (a) 14 January 1793 —3 Kongos, new Negroes from on board the *General Washington*; (b) 20 February 1793—Sale of Bossales from Senegal from a boat coming from Havana; (c) 22 March 1793— 'The *Nouvelle Société* of Nantes arrived from the Zaire River, Angola Coast, with a very fine cargo of 331 head of Negroes for Demonhaison Lelong and Co., who will start putting them up for sale the 25th inst.'; (d) 25 March 1793—'The *Bonne Henriette* of Bordeaux with a superb cargo of 378 blacks coming from the Angola Coast'; (e) 27 March 1793—'The *Postillon* of St Malo coming from Senegal for Foache, Morange, Hardivillier.

This annoncement is the last to appear about the official slave trade.[1]

Curiously enough it ended with an uprooting of the same Senegalese Negroes as those with which it had begun a century and a half earlier. It was the firm of Stanislas Foache —the biggest slaving company in Santo Domingo—which had the melancholy distinction of being responsible for the final crime, so nonchalantly recorded in the colonial gazettes.

Group providing most imports: Bantu (Kongos and Mozambicans), followed by cargoes from the Gold Coast and Senegal.

1. The illicit trade was to continue a little longer. In this last brief period supplies came largely from neighbouring countries. The trade ended as it had begun, with slaves sent from the nearby islands, as in the early operations before the foundation in 1664 of the West India Company.

Bibliography

My main documentation came from the Santo Domingo newspapers (Moreau de Saint-Méry Collection in the Bibliothèque National in Paris and the Archives de la France d'Outre-Mer).

Following the early studies of Père Gabon, Gabriel Debien and Marie-Antoinette Ménier drew up a complete list of these journals in the *Revue Historique des Colonies*, Vol. XXXVI, 3rd and 4th quarters 1949, p. 424–75.

All these newspapers were consulted for this article, which supplements and summarizes some of my own earlier work on Santo Domingo, especially that on slavery and runaway slaves, to be found chiefly in two books: *Les Marrons du Syllabaire*, Port-au-Prince, Imprimerie Deschamps, 1958; and *Les Marrons de la Liberté*, Paris, Éditions de l'École, 1972.

Note: The Congrégation des Frères de l'Instruction Chrétienne, established in Haiti in 1864, has a Bibliothèque Haïtienne (Haitian Library) in Port-au-Prince which contains only books by Haitian authors or written about Haiti by foreign authors. It is the biggest library in the country and includes some 20,000 volumes and documents.

A commentary on the slave trade[1]

Joseph E. Harris

A major problem the historian confronts in assessing the scope and impact of the slave trade is the quantitative factor which of course relates to the scope and qualitative impact. Joseph E. Inikori,[2] among others, has commented in several places on this critical issue, focusing particularly on efforts to quantify the Atlantic slave trade. His criticisms of the pioneer book, *The Atlantic Slave Trade: A Census*, by Philip Curtin, seem to be basically sound and underscore the dilemma historians of the slave trade face, namely, the need to develop numerical guidelines or parameters while at the same time guarding against presenting unjustified figures.

Whatever one may think or say against existing estimates for the Atlantic slave trade, and there are grounds for scepticism, such figures do serve the vital function of providing a basis for critique which should clarify problems so that additional research might bring us closer to truth.

It seems to me that such a point might now have been reached for the Atlantic slave trade so that within a few years there should be a greater consensus. However, estimates for the trans-Sahara, Red Sea and Indian Ocean trades still lack the documentation even to propose a base figure which would very likely assume undue acceptance as authoritative. The data for those areas are just too scattered and insufficient to warrant an overall estimate at this time. Simply to conclude that the likely underestimation or overestimation may be compensated for by some other more plausible, but still unsure, factor should be undertaken with great caution, especially in publications.

The preferred data for estimates are records of companies, government customs and census bureaux. Up to the nineteenth century, these kinds of evidence hardly exist for the Indian Ocean, Red Sea and Mediterranean trades. After 1800, there are still virtually no company records; and census data for recipient countries do not seem to be much better. However, European observers recorded some customs returns of a few African and Arabian ports, and some counts have been made of slaves on captured vessels. But this still leaves us with very little direct evidence for the Indian Ocean and Red Sea trade. This has not, however, prevented a controversy over the scale of the trade.

For the Red Sea area, estimates have been made by Richard Pankhurst

(1964) who averaged reports for ports and noted a likely high count of 1 million for the nineteenth century. For the southern (Swahili) coast, nineteenth-century data came from British consular reports in Zanzibar and the navy patrols. Most estimates have been based on those reports, which are criticized as reflecting abolitionist proclivity for high figures to justify greater vigilance for suppression. Some observers have argued further that abolitionists also did not take into account the demand for slaves for plantation labour in East Africa and thus assumed that all slaves were for export when in fact some were kept in Zanzibar and Pemba. A distinction should therefire be made between local and export trade for Zanzibar which seems hard to establish at this point, especially since the Zanzibar archives have been closed to researchers since 1964.

The problem of quantifying becomes greater at the Asian points of entry. In the Persian Gulf for example, one of the most active ports, Sur, had no customs office, and Muscat's records are scattered and difficult to obtain. In addition, quantification is hampered by the inability to distinguish between sales and resales. Slaves were frequently moved from Mecca, Jidda, Sur, Muscat and other points to Basra, Bushire, and on to India which itself received some direct shipments.

Indian shipments came through several small areas in the north-west, Gujarat in particular, but estimates are virtually non-existent. For at least two depots, Surat and Bombay, there are scattered documents in the East India Company records which are available in India; police records are also useful since the Commissioner of Police was charged with the responsibility of monitoring the import of slaves and later with the distribution of freed slaves among families in India or placing them in mission stations or on government farms.

The argument here is for the organization of a concerted approach to these problems in a number of key locations known to have been important slave depots, markets, etc. Critical aspects of this would be the identification of all available official and unofficial records in East Africa and across the length of Asia. This obviously would require the involvement of researchers in the affected areas; and the search should not be limited to coastal regions. Indeed, my research in India, Hyderabad in particular, revealed the importance of the slave trade and documentary evidence in an interior centre. Repositories in Hyderabad contain numerous uncounted stacks of uncatalogued documents on political, economic, and military matters written in Arabic and Urdu. A cursory examination of a sample of those documents by an informant confirmed their relevance to the slave trade and the African presence in the area. A somewhat similar situation exists in Iran, Kerman province and the area around Bandar Abbas in particular, where evidence in Arabic and Farsi needs to be identified and made available to interested researchers.[3]

Related to the problem of sources are the communities of African descent in various parts of Asia. Here again, those communities may have documents or know where pertinent material exists; and the inhabitants of those communities can provide oral accounts useful for the nineteenth century and perhaps earlier. My experience in some of those areas confirmed the presence of people who acknowledged their slave heritage and African links. Without a doubt, this approach would provide valuable data on the slave trade.

The cities of Bombay and Surat in India include uncounted persons of African descent, and while it would be time-consuming and difficult to locate them to establish their African identity, a rewarding effort is still possible. One starting-point should be the early census records which are available from the seventeenth century. Africans may be listed as African, Siddi, Habshi, or Hubshi. One set of records I studied, for example, referred to a seventeenth-century settlement of africans in Bombay being forced to move so that Europeans could settle in the area.[4]

On several occasions Indians returning from East Africa and Madagascar brought African servants who often remained in Bombay or Surat as runaways or attached to a family in India. In either case they cultivated links with other Africans in the city.

Still another approach would be a meticulous investigation of East India Company records which contain data collected by company agents involved in attempts to control and later suppress the slave trade in the Indian Ocean. Those agents sometimes co-ordinated activities in India and the Persian Gulf and Red Sea areas. These records help to quantify the trade, identify dealers, origin and the ethnicity of the slaves, and overland slave routes. In addition, one could expect to find data on the extent to which Africans were sold in India where Hindu women were purchased or kidnapped and taken to the Persian Gulf and Arabian regions for sale.

Impact on non-African countries

Economic Consequences

Agriculture
Although little has been done, we do know that African slaves worked on date and coconut plantations around Basra (Iraq), Bandar Abbas and Minab in Persia, and the Batinah or Trucial coast on the Persian Gulf. The relationship between date plantations and the slave trade needs serious investigation; indeed, dates were exchanged for slaves. What other sources of demand existed? How and when did that demand impact on the slave trade and slavery —and what were the economic benefits for the producing economies?

There is a very valauble source I should mention here: J. G. Lorimer,

A Gazetteer of the Persian Gulf, Oman and Central Arabia, Vol. II, Calcutta, 1908. In that *Gazetteer,* Lorimer provides estimates of Africans in certain areas. For Bahrein he estimates some 11,000 Africans; Kuwait, 4,000; Lingeh, 1,500; Qatar, 6,000; for Oman he simply notes, 'exceptionally numerous'. His counts were based on various British reports for 1905–07. We should note that some of these figures are for areas in which intensive date-palm cultivation occurred—Bassa, Qatar, Oman, for example.

Pearl Diving

The other area with a high African population in Lorimer's survey is Bahrein. Here several nineteenth-century observers noted the major economic activity for African slaves in Bahrein was as pearl divers. The demand for them was reportedly very high, as was the mortality rate. Captain Prideaux reported that pearl diving was so deleterious to the health in the 1840s that middle-aged Africans were hard to find, and a Bahrein Sheik told the British political-officer in the 1890s that the demand remained great. Lorimer simply observed that 'free negroes or negro slaves' were a large proportion of the divers.

What needs to be determined is the specific relationship between the Persian Gulf pearl industry and companies in Europe and elsewhere. And what about the profitability of the industry, whether it was of long standing—that is, prior to the 1840s when observers seem to have been noticing it? For the present, no conclusion is made here other than that African labour made this economic contribution. The extent must await further research.

African crews

In addition to agriculture and the pearl industry, I will comment briefly on African crews serving on Arab and European vessels. There may be studies on this subject, I just do not know since I have not devoted much attention to it. But there are frequent references to the African crews on dhows going to and from East Africa, and one British official in India observed the large number of Africans in the British navy during the 1850s. Africans also worked on the docks at several ports on the Persian Gulf and Indian Ocean. These occupations certainly contributed to economic development in affected regions.

Military

One final area is the military. Of course the use of African soldiers contributed to political and economic development in several Asian areas, India in particular. There is some documentation for this in general histories of India and travel accounts of Ibn Batoutah and others. But I prefer to call attention to two examples. The first is to Malik Ambar, the Ethiopian who usurped power in central India in 1602 and governed until 1626. A bit has been written on him and his achievements, including the expansion of trade, construction of roads, canals, mosques and public buildings, etc. He also imported Africans to serve in his army, a point of interest in terms of African settlers in India.

But the key point I wish to make here is that in addition to promoting trade with Persians and Arabs, he negotiated also with the Portuguese and British and this aspect of Ambar's contribution has not received much attention to my knowledge.

A different aspect of this relates to relations between Ambar and another area ruled by Africans, Janjira Island which emerged under Africans (Siddis) in the late fifteenth century and became a critical naval force on the north-west coast of India. Ambar sought an alliance with them in 1616 and failed; the Moguls negotiated an alliance about which an Indian military historian has written:

It is only when the Siddis of Janjira offered their services to the Moguls against the Maratha power on the sea that Arangazib (the Mogul emperor) gave half-hearted recognition to a fleet being organized on a reasonable scale. During 200 years of Mogul greatness, the Indian Sea was under alien control.[5]

The Moguls thus began to subsidize the navy of the Janjira Siddis in exchange for an alliance.

Another Indian scholar, Jadanath Sarkar, has written that Shivaji, the Maratha hero:

achieved this [building a Maratha nation] in the teeth of the opposition of four mighty Powers like the Mogul empire, Bijapur [another Indian kingdom], Portuguese India, and the Abyssinians of Janjira.[6]

The Janjira Siddis were subsequently wooed by several European powers —Portugal, Holland, Great Britain. Alliances were made during the seventeenth, eighteenth and nineteenth centuries for the protection of European trade in north-western India before Janjira succumbed to British colonial rule in 1834. There is clearly a need to investigate these economic, political and diplomatic dimensions of Africans in India.

The better known revolts of Africans in Bengal Province during the fifteenth century, as well as Ambar's usurpation of power deserve intensive research.

In addition to economic effects, certain social and political consequences should be explored more intensively. How and why did African slaves rise to economic and political power in various parts of Asia? They acquired power, frequently if not always with Arab support, among the northern Aryans and among the darker southerners, of present-day India in particular. Yet, full assimilation has not occurred, nor has it been an expressed policy goal of present leaders. Why? And how significant is the fact? What have been the

effects of miscegenation and the appearance of mulattos on relations between
Afro-Asians and Asians and how do these groups perceive Africa and Africans?
What is the ethos of Afro-Asian communities?[7]

We know that some Africans liberated in Asia returned to Africa. But
to what extent? For what reasons? And with what effects? This subject is in
great need of research. My own work has revealed links between present-day
families in Kenya and Africans liberated from slavery in India. Descendants of
liberated Africans have been pioneers in Kenya as teachers, preachers, jour-
nalists, trade unionists, and politicians since the last quarter of the nineteenth
century;[8] and there is some indication that a somewhat similar situation
developed in Tanganyika and Zanzibar (now the United Republic of Tanzania),
and possibly Ethiopia. While those examples may not compare in scale with
Sierra Leone and Liberia, they share with their West African counterparts a
link with the slave trade and slavery and had a similar local impact. Furthermore, such a study may produce results of surprising importance.

Let me now conclude with a personal experience. While conducting
research among repatriated Africans in Kenya I discovered two rather obscure
small books of highly significant relevance for the study of the slave trade in
East Africa.[9]

Both works are about Yaos; Chengwimbe in Rempley's book and
Mbotela by Mbotela; both were in the Lake Malawi area and provide physical
and historical continuity for the slave trade because they experienced the first
stage of the capture and sale in East Africa, the subsequent sea voyage, eventual
abolition, and repatriation. One of them, Chengwimbe, also experienced freedom and education in India prior to repatriation. These two cases, therefore,
are especially valuable in that they reveal the personal insights of victims of
the slave traffic and also because they help to illustrate some of the broad
generalities so common in studies of the slave trade, especially for East Africa.
Indeed, the whole story of the slave trade and repatriation in Kenya become
more vivid and real as one follows Chengwimbe and Mbotela, and their
descendants, through their experiences of the slave trade, freedom, repatriation
and nation-building in Kenya.

In sum, we know much about the slave trade and its consequences, but
the need for continued investigation, critique, and publication remains substantial.

Notes

1. 'Black American Diasporic Relations'. I would like to make this observation on the
   American diaspora. When Africans liberated Haiti in 1804, that country emerged
   as a symbol and rallying point for the evolving black identity in the American
   hemisphere. Whites in the United States were fearful that the Haitain example
   would spill over into the United States and blacks began to establish Haiti and its

revolutionaries as legends in song and literature; and the 1820s witnessed United States blacks migrating to Haiti, a continuing tradition in the American black diaspora.

2. Joseph E. Inikori, 'Slave Trade and the Atlantic Economies, 1451–1870'; and 'Measuring the A tlantic Slave Trade', *Journal of African History*, Vol. XVII, No. 4, p. 495–627.

3. Joseph E. Harris, *The African Presence in Asia: Consequences of the East African Slave Trade*, Evanston, Ill., Northwestern University Press, 1971.

4. ibid., p. 69.

5. K. M. Panikkar, *India and the Indian Ocean*, London, 1945, p. 8.

6. Jadunath Sarkar, *History of Aurangzib*, Calcutta, 1919, Vol. IV, p. 237–8. Note that Janjira is regarded as a 'Mighty Power'.

7. In recent years Afro-American historians have contributed much to the understanding of the ethos of black Americans by studying their songs and literature. See: Sterling Stuckey, 'Through the Prism of Folklore: The Black Ethos in Slavery,' *The Massachusetts Review*, IX, 3, 1968; and John Blassingame, *The Slave Community* (Oxford University Press, 1972). Perhaps these works could serve as models for similar studies of Afro-Asian communities.

8. Harris, *The East African Slave Trade and Abolition in Kenya*, Department of History Howard University, 1974; 'Blacks in Asia,' *World Encyclopedia of Black Peoples*, Algonac, Michigan, 1975; *Abolition and Repatriation in Kenya*, Nairobi, East African Literature Bureau, 1977.

9. One is the biographical study: W. J. Rampley, *Matthew Wellington: Sole Surviving Link with David Livingstone* (London, n.d.); and the other is autobiographical, James Juma Mbotela, *Uhuru wa Watumwa* (London, 1934) and translated as *The Freeing of the Slaves in East Africa* (London, 1956). Both of these studies had a limited circulation, mainly in London and East Africa, and are now out of print, except for the Swahili account. Both studies contain valuable data pertinent to the East African slave trade and to the repatriation of ex-slaves on the Kenyan coast during the nineteenth century.

The present state of research in Brazil

Waldeloir Rego

It was on the Bahia coast that the Portuguese discoverers and colonizers landed, and it was there, in 1549, that Brazil's first town was founded, later to become the first capital and the centre of important events. So it was from Bahia that the African slaves spread outward over the rest of Brazil. It should be noted, however, that most of them stayed in Bahia, where one still meets with survivals of Dahoman religious rites. Bahia is also the only place where religious ritual is practised in the Fon language. One can still distinguish rituals which originated in Mahis, Savalu, Abomey and many other places in Dahomey. Traces of Nigerian ritual, in the Yoruba language, are even more marked. Until recently a Nigerian teacher was giving lessons in the Yoruba language, and innumerable foreign researchers (mostly African) come to Brazil, and to Bahia more especially, to study the African diaspora.

Studies concerning black people are very inadequate in Brazil. Genuine specialists are rare, though many people toy with the subject who are not really interested, who have not the necessary training for scientific work, and who really pursue other, sometimes commercial, ends. Some use the subject just to lengthen their *curriculum vitae* or to obtain grants for travel abroad, using studies about the black people as a pretext. Others again have purely political aims.

The Brazilian Government gives some support, though it is still modest, to studies on this subject, especially through the Cultural Department of the Ministry for Foreign Relations. The Joaquim Nabuco Research Institute in Pernambuco has long been interested in the question of the black people in Brazil. In Bahia, where most of them are concentrated, a section of the Federal University of Bahia, the Centro de Estudos Afro-Orientais (Centre of Afro-Oriental Studies) enjoys limited support from the Ministry of Education and Culture. But lack of resources has so far prevented it from achieving anything of importance, apart from a course in the Kikongo language given by a teacher from Zaire, N'Landu Ntotila. This is a high-level course, but it is in danger of being dropped this year through lack of funds. As for the course in the Yoruba language mentioned above, that has already been suspended despite the interest it aroused among students and followers of the Yoruba religion.

São Paulo has a Centre of African Studies (Centro de Estudos Africanos) which has a different policy from that of the centre in Bahia; under the administration of Professor Fernando Augusto Albuquerque Mourão it is carrying out word of the highest quality. The centre is a section of the University of São Paulo. It has just brought out the first volume of its periodical, *Africa*, which makes a valuable contribution to studies on Brazil's black culture.

In Bahia a Black Museum, built at the suggestion of the Brazilian Ministry of Foreign Relations, is soon to be opened. It will be attached to the Ministry of Education and Culture, through the Federal University of Bahia.

Steps that need to be taken

Create a scientific body able to collect as quickly as possible all the available material on existing black culture, some of which is in the process of disappearing.

Make all Brazilian archives concerning black people available without restriction, whether the material is held publicly or privately.

Finance, through public or private, State or para-State institutions, visits by experts to countries where studies on the blacks are necessary.

Help researchers in their studies by providing them with the facilities needed for their work, copies of documents, etc.

Recruit as quickly as possible Yoruba-, Fon- and Kikongo-speaking African teachers to give courses in Bahia.

Keep African specialists in touch with Unesco activities in this field.

The state of research in Guyana

Walter Rodney

Guyana has no past or ongoing research into the history of the slave trade to Guyana. Historical work on the regime of slavery itself is dated and superficial.[1]

Rodway's *History* was based on secondary sources and translations from the Dutch. General texts compiled in the present century have not gone beyond this point.

A number of theses have been concerned with economic and social life in Guyana in the nineteenth century, with emphasis on post-Emancipation developments. They provide only brief introductions to the last years of slavery. References to slavery in British Guiana are also to be found in reconstructions of Caribbean history and of the history of the British West Indies in particular.

In effect, therefore, the field is still completely open and the areas of research correspondingly wide. As an exception to the prevailing neglect, there is a researcy project into the phenomenon of escaped slaves in British Guiana conducted by Alvin Thompson of the University of the West Indies, Barbados.

The development of slave society in Guyana is assumed to have followed the same patterns as that of slave societies emerging under similar conditions in the Caribbean. The crops were cotton, coffee, cocoa and above all sugar. Slaves grew their own provisions and were also briefly engaged in gold-mining in the eighteenth century. The only unusual activity in British Guiana (relative to the Caribbean islands) was the creation of polders on the swampy coastal environment.

The Guyana National Archives house documents which relate mainly to the British period of slavery. Efforts are being made to recover copies of relevant documents in the Netherlands and the United Kingdom.

1. See, for example, James Rodway, *A History of British Guiana*, Georgetown, 1890, 3 vols.

The slave trade from the fifteenth to the nineteenth century

Y. Talib

Documentary sources

Accounts and Papers (1837–38). Vol. II, Paper 697, House of Commons, Slave Trade. Correspondence, orders and regulations.

Accounts and Papers (1841). Vol. XXVIII, Paper 238.

Slave-trade correspondence presented to Parliament in 1842. (F.O. 54/5.)

Public Record Office, London. (F.O. 84) Slave Trade. 'Up to 1840 this series contains little material on the Arab slave trade from East Africa and Abyssinia; after that date the volume of relevant correspondence increases greatly. Slave-trade correspondence between the Foreign Office and the other departments of State before 1839 is collected in the "Domestic Various" volumes of the series; but after that year the concentration of the direction of slave-trade policy in the Slave Trade Department of the Foreign Office brought such an increase in the volume of correspondence that the "Domestic Various" category had to be replaced by a number of new categories, "India Board", "Admiralty", "Colonial Office", etc. From 1840 onwards all correspondence on the slave trade received at the India Board from the Indian Presidencies was passed to the Foreign Office, to be dealt with in the Slave Trade Department.—J. B. Kelly, *Britain and the Persian Gulf, 1795–1880*, p. 868, Oxford, 1968.

Report from the Select Committee on the Slave Trade (E. Coast of Africa). Parliamentary Paper, XII (1871), United Kingdom.

Report addressed to the Earl of Clarendon by the Committee on the East African Slave Trade, 24 January 1870, LXII, 1871.

Correspondence respecting Sir Bartle Frere's mission to the East Coast of Africa—1872–73, Parliamentary Paper, LXI, 1873.

Correspondence respecting the abolition of the legal status of slavery in Zanzibar and Pemba (C.8858) (1898), London.

Enclos to Bombay See. Letters, Vol. 51, enclos to See. Letter 115 of 15 Oct., 1842. Report on the Slave Trade of Abyssinia by Capt. W. C. Harris, enclosed in Harris to Willouby, 20 July 1842 (No. 37, Sec. Dept.). Enclosed with the report is a map of the slave routes through Sheoa. See also Vol. 34, enclos to See. Letter 59 of 17 July 1841, Haines to Willouby, Aden, July 1841 (No. 54 Sec. Dept.).

SALDANHA, J. A. (ed.). *Precis on the Slave Trade in the Gulf of Oman and the Persian Gulf—1873–1905, with a retrospect into previous history from 1882, Calcutta, 1906.* (A principle source for the history of the slave trade of East Africa with the Arabian peninsula.)

Archive du Ministère des Affaires Étrangères (Aff. Étr.) Paris. (Mémoires et documents, Série Afrique (Mémo et doc. Afrique). Boutres Françaises, Recrutement de Travailleurs pour les Colonies Françaises de l'Océan Indien.)

Bibliography on slavery in the Indian Ocean and the Red Sea (general works)

Africans in India (with some items on West Africa, South America and West Indies)

BANOJI, D. R. *Slavery in British India*. Bombay, 1933.
BURTON PAGE, J. Habshi. *Encyclopaedia of Islam*. New ed., p. 14–16. Leiden and London.
FREEMAN-GRANVILLE, G. S. P. The Sidi and Swahili. *Bulletin of the British Association of Orientalists*. Vol. 6, 1971, p. 3–18. (New series.)
HARRIS, Joseph E. African History from Indian Sources. *Africa Quarterly*, 1961, p. 4–9.
PANKHURST, R. The Habshi of India. *Introduction to the Economic History of Ethiopia*. p. 409–22. 1961.
PESCATELLO, Ann M. The African Presence in Portuguese India. â*ournal of Asian History* (Weisbaden), Vol. II, No. 1, 1977, p. 26–48.
POSTANS, T. *Personal Observations on Sind*. London, 1843. (See esp. p. 358–9.)
RAO, Vasant D. The Habshis, India's Unknown Africans. *Africa Report*, September/October 1973, p. 35–8.

Malay Archipelago

MAXWELL, R. J. The Law Relating to Slavery among the Malays. *Journal of the Malayan Branch of the Royal Asiatic Society*, Vol. X, Part I, 1932. (p. 254 refers to 'Habshis' as a separate category of slaves.)

The Red Sea

Sudan

STACK, (Sir) Lee. The Slave Trade between the Sudan and Arabia. *Journal of the Central Asia Society*, Vol. 8, 1921, Part 3, p. 163–4.
YUSUF FADL HASSAN. The Slave Trade. *The Arabs and the Sudan*. p. 42–9. Edinburgh University Press, 1967.

Ethiopia

PANKHURST, R. The Ethiopian Slave Trade 1800–1935. A New Assessment. *Journal of Ethiopian Studies*, 1964.
SERJEANT, R. B. South Arabia and Ethiopia—African Elements in the South Arabian Population. *Proceedings—3rd International Conference of Ethiopian Studies*. Vol. I, p. 25–33. 1966.

Arabia

ARNAUD, T. H. J.; VAYSSIERE, A. Les Akhdam de l'Yemen, leur Origine Probable, leur Mœurs. *Journal Asiatique*, Vol. XV, 4th series, p. 375–87. Paris, 1850.
BURTON, Richard. *Pilgrimage to al-Madinah and Meccah*. Vols. I and II. Dover Edition, London, 1964. (Slaves, trade in, at Jeddah and in Egypt, i, 47. Refrom in slave laws throughout the East much needed, 49. The black slave girls of Al-Madinah, ii, 12. Value of slave boys and eunuchs, 12. Value of galla girls, 13. Female slaves sat Meccah, 233. The Slave Market of Meccah, 252.)
DOUGHTY, Charles. *Travels in Arabia Deserta*. Vol. I, p. 553. London, 1926.
FRERE, Sir B. Memorandum regarding Banians or Natives of Indian in E. Africa, Oct. 1873. In: J. A. Saldanha (ed.). *Precis on the Slave Trade in the Gulf of Oman and the Persian Gulf 1873–1505*. p. 7–13, Simla, 1906.

HAFIZ WAHBA. (Slavery in Mecca). *(The Arabian Peninsula in the 20th Century)*. p. 36–8. 1935.

HURGRONJE, S. *Mecca in the Latter Part of the 11th Century*. Leiden and London, 1931. (On slavery and the place of slaves in Meccan society, see p. 11–15, 17–19; on Abbyssins (Habsh), p. 13, 107, 109, 182.)

——. Abd. *Encyclopaedia of Islam*, New Edition, Leiden and London, 1960.

LANDON. The Domination of Commerce by Indian Merchants. *Oman Since 1856*. p. 131–56. Princeton, 1967.

LA ROQUE. *Voyage to Arabia the Happy by the Way of the Eastern Ocean and the Struggle of the Red Sea, performed by the French for the First Time. A.D. 1708, 1700, 1710 etc.* London, 1726. (English translation.) On the Baniyans see p. 123–7.

NEIBAHR, M. Le Rôle des Baniyans comme Intermediaires dans le Commerce. *Description de l'Arabie*, Vol. II, 1779, p. 134.

REUBEN, Levy. Slavery. *The Social Structure of Islam*. Vol. I, p. 117–27. Cambridge, 1957.

RIGBY. Report on Zanzibar. *Records of the Bombay Govt.*, No. LIX, 1861, p. 9–12.

Role of Indians in the Slave Trade. (A necessary cog in the slave trade was the Indian Merchant since the Indians financed the Arab slave-brokers. This was especially so as far as the trade is concerned in southern Arabia, Ethiopia, East Africa.)

SERJEANT, R. B. Forms of Plea, A Shafi'i Manual from al-Shrih. *Revista degli Studi Orientalia*. (Rome), Vol. XXX, p. i–ii, 1955.

——. *The Portuguese off the South Arabian Coast: Hadrani Chronicles, with Yemeni and European Accounts of Dutch Pirates off Mocha in the Seventeenth Century*. Oxford, 1963. (On Banians, see p. 32–4.)

VAN DEN BERG. *Le Hadramout et les Colonies Arabes dans l'Archipel Indien*. Batavia, 1866. (See *Domestiques et Esclaves*, p. 46, 69–70.)

Arab Slave Trade in the Indian Ocean and the Persian Gulf

AL-MUKHTAR B. AL-HASSAN B. BUTLAN (d. 455/1063), *Risala fi Sharyy al-Raqig wa taglib al-'abid.* [On the qualities, uses and methods of sale of various slaves.] (In Arabic.)

BARASSIN, J. Une République Noire à Bourbon au XVIIIᵉ Siècle. Les Marrons. *4ᵉ Congrès de l'Association Historique Internationale de l'Océan Indien*. Saint-Denis de la Réunion, 3–9 August 1972.

CHATELAIN, Nicolas. *De l'Immigration Africaine dans les Colonies Françaises*. Saint-Denis de la Réunion, 1882.

COLOMB, P. *Slave Catching in the Indian Ocean*. London, 1873. 503 p. (Still the best general account on the subject.)

DU CASSE, André. *Les Négriers ou le Trafic des Esclaves*. Paris, 1938.

GAVIN, R. J. The Bartle Frere Mission to Zanzibar. *The Historical Journal*, Vol. 2, 1962.

HOLMWOOD, F. Africa and the Slave Trade. In: J. F. Elton (ed.), *Travels and Researches among the Lakes and Mountains of Eastern and Central Africa*. London, 1879.

HUTCHINSON, Edevard. *The Slave Trade of East Africa*. London, 1874.

KELLY, J. B. The Arab Slave Trade 1800–1842. *Britain and the Persian Gulf 1795–1880*. p. 411–51. Oxford and London, Oxford University Press, 1968. (An important study based on archival sources.)

——. The Attack on the Slave Trade—1842–1873. *Britain and the Persian Gulf*, p. 576–637. 1968.

LUGARD, F. D. *The Rise of our East African Empire*. London, 1893. (Reprinted, Frank Cass, London 1968.) (Chapter VII, African Slavery; Chapter VIII, Methods of Suppressing the African Slave Trade; Chapter XVIII, The Labour Supply in East Africa.)

LLOYD, Christopher. *The Navy and the Slave Trade*. London, 1968. (East African Slave

Trade, p. 187–202, The Portuguese East African Slave Trade, p. 217–28. The Attack on the Arab Trade. First stage. The End of the Arab Trade, p. 259–74, Appendix B. Captives from the Arab Slave Trade.)

MALECOT, Georges. Bourbon et l'Abyssinie: Les Tentatives de Recrutement de Travailleurs Le Problème de Main-d'Oeuvre à la Réunion. *Les Voyageurs Français et les Relations. entre la France et l'Abyssinie de 1835 à 1870.* p. 72–93. Paris, Société Française d'Outre-Mer, 1972.

MARITEAU J. *Life of Sir B. Frere.* London, 1895. 2 Vols.

MARTIN, Gaston. *Histoire de l'Esclavage dans les Colonies Françaises.* Paris, Presses Universitaires de France, 1948.

MARTIN, Jean. La Révolte Servile de 1891 à Anjouan. *Revue Française d'Histoire d'Outre-mer,* No. 218, 1st quarter, 1973, p. 45–85.

NIWULIA, Moses D. E. *Britain and Slavery in East Africa.* Washington, D.C. 1975. 274 p.

——. The Role of Missionaries in the Emancipation of Slaves in Zanzibar. *Journal of Negro History* (Georgia), Vol. LX, No. 2, April 1975, p. 268–87.

O'NEILL, H. E. *The Mozambique and Nyasa Slave Trade.* London, 1888.

PEYTRAUD, Lucien. *L'Esclavage aux Antilles Françaises avant 1789,* Paris, 1897.

POPOVIO, A. *La Révolte des Esclaves en Irak aux IIIe/IXe Siècles.* Paris, Paul Geuthner, 1977.

RUSSEL, Lilian. *General Rigby, Zanzibar and the Slave Trade.* London, 1938. (Christopher Rigby was the British Consul and Political Agent in Zanzibar from 1858 to 1861.)

SULLIVAN. *Dhow Chasing in Zanzibar Waters.* London, 1873.

WICKERS, Lucien. L'Immigration Réglementée à l'Ile de la Réunion. Faculté de Droit de l'Université de Paris. (Doctoral thesis.)

West Indies, South America

BOUVT WILLAUMEZ, E. *Commerce et Traite des Noirs aux Côtes Occidentales d'Afrique.* Paris, 1848.

KILLON, Martin L.; ROTHBERG, Robert I. *The African Diaspora: Interpretive Essays.* Harward, 1976. 570 p.

GASTON, Martin. *Nantes aux XVIIIe Siècle, l'Ère des Négriers.* Paris, Alcan, 1931.

MELLAFE, Rolando. *La Introducción de la Esclavitud Negra en Chile—Trafic y Putas.* Santiago de Chile, 1959.

PATTERSON, Orlando. *The Sociology of Slavery. An Analysis of the Origins, Development and Structure of Negro Slave Society in Jamaica.* London, 1967. 310 p.

Madagascar and the Indian Ocean Islands

ANON. *L'Esclavage et son Abolition à Madagascar. Paris Rev. Polit. et Littér.,* 2 April 1898, p. 436–42.

CURT, Rev. Needham, Madagascar: Slavery and Christianity. London, *Mission Life.* Vol. IV, p. 193–200. 1883.

DEHERAIN, Henri. La Traite des Esclaves à Madagascar aux XVIIe Siècle et XVIIIe Siècle. *La Nature,* Paris, 28 May 1904, p. 401–3.

——. L'Esclavage au Cap de Bonne-Espérance aux XVIIe Siècle et XVIIIe Siècle. Paris, *Journal des Savants,* September 1907, p. 488–502.

——. *Le Cap de Bonne-Espérance au XVIIe Siècle.* Paris, 1909. 256 p. (L'Esclaves Importés de Madagascar, p. 202–9.)

GRANT, Charles, Vicount de Vaux. The Malagasy Slaves in the Isle de France. London, *History of Mauritius,* p. 75–8, 297–8. 1801.

LANUX, Jean Baptiste de. Mémoire sur la Traite des Esclaves à une Partys de la Coste de l'Est de l'Isle de Madagascar (1729)—L'impression d'un Mss—Conservé au Musée Leon Dieux, St. Denis, La Réunion, *Recueil de Doc. et Trav. Inédits pour Servir à l'Histoire des Mascareignes Françaises*. October–November. 1932, p. 79–85.
LAVIGNE, R. P. Louis. La Traite dans les Parages de Madagascar [aux Comores etc.]. *Ann. de la Sainte Enfance*. Paris, 1868, p. 191–6.
REYNAUD, Et. Journal de Bord du Négrier 'Marengo' Cape Reynaud, allant de l'Isle de France à Sansibar et de Retour, 1804, 101 p. (Original Ms.).
VIDAL (ed.). *Bourbon et l'Esclavage* Paris, 1847. 64 p.

Additional bibliography

Slavery
CRATON, Michael; WALVIN, James; WRIGHT, David. Slavery, Abolition and Emancipation. *Black Slaves and the British Empire*. London, 1976.
EDMONDSON, L. Transatlantic Slavery and the Internationalization of Race. *Caribbean Quarterly*, Vol. XX, Nos. 2 and 3, June–September 1976.
ELTIS, D. The Traffic in Slaves between the British West Indian Colonies, 1807–1833. *Econ. Hist. Rev.*, Vol. XXX, 1972, p. 55–64.
GOITIEN, S. D. Slaves and Slavegirls in the Cairo Geniza Records. *Arabica*, Vol. 9, 1962, p. 1–20.
GREEN, William A. *British Slave Emancipation : the Sugar Colonies and the Great Experiment, 1830–1865*. Oxford, Clarendon Press, 1976.
TEMPERLY, Howard. Capitalism, Slavery and Ideology. *Past and Present*, No. 75, May 1977, p. 94–118.
WHEATLEY, Paul. [Nu Pi] Slaves. Geographical Notes on Some Commodities Involved in Sung Maritime Trade. *Journal of the Malayan Branch of the Royal Asiatic Society*. Vol. 32, Part 2, No. 186, 1961, p. 54–5.

Statistics

East Africa to the Persian Gulf

Few figures are available on this aspect of the slave trade and they vary greatly.
Kelly quoting nineteenth-century sources, gives the figure of 8,000 to 15,000 slaves exported annually from the East African littoral to the southern Arabian coast and the Persian Gulf. R. M. Colomb gives the figure of 10,000 to 20,000 slaves exported from Zanzibar to the Persian Gulf annually.

Mozambique

William Wilburn (*Oriental Commerce*, London, 1813, Vol. I, p. 60) mentions that the principal trade of Mozambique is slaves, of which about 10,000 are annually exported at an average of from $40 to $50 each.

Cape Town

In 1801, 'the population of Cape Town is estimated at 6,000 whites, inclusive of the military, and 12,000 slaves' (William Wilburn, op. cit., p. 35).

304   *Y. Talib*

Mauritius

'En 1820 il n'y avait pas moins de 16,000 esclaves malgaches à l'île Maurice.' Hilsenberg, *Noue. Ann. Vay.* Vol. XI, 1829, p. 160.

List of specialists on the slave trade

Ann Pescatello, 8 William Street, Paw Catuck Conn, Los Angeles. (Has made partial study of the Historical Archives of Goa—relating to the place of the African in the Portuguese colonial structure.)
Moses D. E. Nwulia, Howard University, United States. (Especially interested in the Church's role in the abolition of the slave trade—worked on archival sources of *CMS*.)

Work in progress

I am at present conducting research on the theme 'Africans in South-West Arabia, the Yemen and the Hadramaut. A Critical Survey'.

New lines of research

List of archival sources relating to African slavery, awaiting publication
Arabic manuscripts having references to Africans and slavery.
    Archives of the *Estado da India* (Goa) touched upon by Dr Ann Pescatello needs a fuller study. Several important guides on this collection have already been published, namely: BOXER, C. R. A Glimpse of the Goa Archives. *Bulletin of the School of Oriental and African Studies*, Vol. XIV, June 1952; PISSURLENCAR, P. S. S. *Roteiro dos Arquivos da India Portuguesa* (Bastora Goa) 1958.
    The India Office Records, studied partially by J. B. Kelly in preparing his monumental work, *Britain in the Persian Gulf*, should be thoroughly searched for items relating to Africa and slavery.
    Information on the 'African diaspora' obtained through oral tradition is extremely valuable as in the case of Arabia, where slavery was a continuing institution until very recent times. Information thus collected would supplement valuable data collected on the attitude of the local inhabitants vis-à-vis Africans not to be found in published texts or in archives.
    I would like here to make a special plea for the study of the slave trade and slavery as an institution in the Island of Madagascar. These aspects were overlooked during the meeting of experts in Haiti: French, British, Danish, Dutch and Arab slavers with the collaboration of local rulers exported slaves from Madagascar to Cape Town, islands in the Indian Ocean (Réunion, Mauritius, Seychelles, etc.) and even as far away as Batavia— the former Dutch colonial capital in the island of Java.
    H. and G. Grandidier in their monumental *Histoire Physique, Naturelle et Politique de Madagascar*, Vol. 4, *Ethnographie de Madagascar*, Vol. 1, Parts 1 and 2, Vol. 4, Paris, 1908, 1914, made valuable allusions to these aspects of slavery, using both archival and published sources.

Principal ports of trading-posts in Africa, serving as outlets to America or to the countries of the Indian Ocean, and in the receiving countries

Ports—Africa facing the Red Sea
Zeila, Massawa, Tajura, Berbera, Suakin, Roheita.

East African littoral

Quilimane-Mozambique, Kilwa, Zamzibar, Pemba, Lamu, Mombasa, Juba, Brava.

Islands of the East African littoral (Madagascar)

Mahajamba, Boina, Bombetoke, Antongil, Fort-Dauphin, Tamatave, Saint-Augustin, Narendry.

Ports in receiving countries

Middle East
Jeddah, Mukalla, Shihr, Muscat, Bushire, Basra, Mocha, Hodeida, Qatif, Sur

India

Sind, Kutch, Kathiawar, Bombay Presidency, Portuguese India (Diu, Goa, Denam),

Mauritius

Port-Louis

Réunion

St. Denis

South Africa

Cape Town

Research on African influence in the Dominican Republic

Hugo Tolentino Dipp and Rubén Silié

Introduction

The Dominican Republic is perhaps one of the countries in which detailed studies on the contribution made by African culture to its national formation are most necessary, as a series of historical factors caused it very early on to forget its direct link with the African continent.

This was because the Spanish colony of Santo Domingo very quickly became a forgotten region of the Iberian metropolis, breaking off its connection with the slave trade owing to the fact that the sixteenth-century type of sugar-plantation economy requiring considerable slave manpower was not established there. The subsequent development of a cattle-raising economy in a situation of unlimited supply of land and with a very scattered white and black population provided the basic conditions for a vigorous racial miscegenation.

When in a second phase, towards the end of the eighteenth century, the French colony of Santo Domingo became one of the wealthiest on the continent and its type of economy called for a massive influx of African slaves, the eastern part of the island, which was still in Spanish hands and where the above-mentioned type of economy prevailed, became a place of refuge for slaves brought over from Africa and desperately seeking their freedom. Thus was developed what we have described as a 'strong migratory current towards the eastern part', composed of fugitive slaves.

These fugitive slaves were to increase the black population in that part of the island. What interests us here is precisely the study of how those same fugitive slaves, while forming the black population of the east, systematically allowed the basic and original values of their mother country to fall into oblivion; ideological propaganda on the part of the Spanish colonizers was, of course, a contributory factor; for, unable to obtain the services of black people in any other way, they openly abetted the movement in escaped slaves.

From then onwards, the escaped slave who managed to reach freedom in the Spanish part of the island had a certain interest in forgetting his past and, so as not to be confused with the French slaves, began to adopt the idea that he hailed from the Spanish part, which meant identifying himself directly with the aboriginal inhabitants of the island. At the same time, by so doing, he denied his origins as he placed his ancestral memory in the hands of a new type of colonizer who subjected him to a rather less rigid form of slavery.

In addition, owing to the fact that the Dominican Republic achieved its independence in a struggle against the Haitian occupation, the problem of racial prejudice and, consequently, a more pronounced repudiation of African origins was considerably accentuated.

Hence our ruling classes largely identified themselves as a national entity negatively with respect to Haiti, creating from then onwards a strong anti-Haitian feeling and, through this feeling, bringing about an anti-African psychological projection. Thus of all the cultural contributions which go to make up Dominican national identity today least is known about the African, and it is the one about which Dominicans in general feel a certain shame.

Such an attitude, as we know, merely helps to strengthen the bonds of social domination over a people which, being for the most part mulatto, is discriminated against on account of the colour of its skin and, in its rush to acquire Spanish characteristics, has succeded in creating a new colour—that of the 'Indian', which is what all Dominican mulattos call themselves. This is a way of solving the problem of origins by eliminating the black and recuperating the autochthonous population element only.

That is why when we visit Dominican museums African history is shown as something incidental and in history textbooks the part played by Africans is not mentioned except with reference to their backwardness.

Concrete suggestions for a study in depth of African influence in the Dominican Republic

An exhaustive study of the national archives is necessary to select the documents to be found in them—work of great importance but difficult to carry out owing to the present state of our archives. However, it is possible to do so if the necessary institutional support and material resources are forthcoming. Little study has been made of the archives of the Cathedral of Santo Domingo, which are likely to provide much information on the religion of the slaves, parish registers, freeing of slaves, purchase and sale of slaves, wills, etc.

Among municipal archives, we have those of Bayaguana which have been consulted sporadically; up to now information has been found on purchase and sale of slaves, day labourers' wages, etc.

The Archivo General de Indias in Seville (Spain) also requires to be visited. Here most of the documentation on the problem of the black people of Santo Domingo in colonial times is to be found, also documents dealing with the economic, political and social activities of the colony in which the relations with the slaves and freedmen of African origin are necessarily relevant.

Also to be consulted are: *Expedientes de Negros y Desertores Franceses Refugiados* (Records Concerning Black People and Refugee French Escapees), 1776; *Expediente Integro sobre la Reducción de los Negros de Maniel* (Complete Records Concerning the Black Settlement of Maniel), 1795. The latter refers to a group of runaway slaves who spent the whole of the eighteenth century in the Bahoruco Mountains.

We have little information on what the Archivo Histórico Nacional, Madrid (Spain) contains with regard to the black people of Santo Domingo, but we do know that quite a lot of information on other West Indian countries is to be found there.

Function and influence of the slaves

From the economic aspect—contribution towards the development of the host country (sugar industry, coffee industry, etc.).

From the cultural aspect—African contribution through the institution of slavery to several countries in the western hemisphere.

From the political aspect—black participation in social and political movements, in the wars of independence of the host countries and the building of new nations.

The special interest shown by Unesco and by all those of us who are dedicated to the study of African culture in Latin America can only produce positive results on the basis of such documentary research.

It should be pointed out that in other Latin American countries where a more lively awareness has been shown by the authorities than in our own, documentary material has been compiled in various national and foreign archives as is the case with Porto Rico and Venezuela: in Porto Rico—*El Proceso Abolicionista en Puerto Rico: Documentos para su Estudio* (Abolition Process in Porto Rico: Relevant Documents); Vol. 1, *La Institución de la Esclavitud y su Crisis: 1823–1873* (Crisis of Institution of Slavery). So far only the first volume has been published and the remaining two volumes to complete the collection are awaited. The work has been carried out by the Historical Research Centre of the Faculty of Arts of the University of Porto Rico and the Porto Rican Cultural Institute, San Juan, Porto Rico, 1974.

In Venezuela—*Documentos para el Estudio de los Esclavos Negros en Venezuela* (Documents for the Study of Black Slaves in Venezuela), selection and introductory study by Emilia Troconis de Veracoechea. Caracas, Bibliotheca de la Academia Nacional de la Historia, 1969. (Colección de Fuentes para la Historia Colonial de Venezuela).

In the case of Santo Domingo, as we have already proposed, Unesco might possibly take the initiative in carrying out this work, trying to supply at the same time the material together with an introductory study concerning it.

A similar proposal was made at the Symposium on African Cultural Contributions in Latin America and the Caribbean, held in Havana (Cuba) from 17 to 21 December 1968, at which one of the recommendations submitted and approved by the experts present was the following: 'to promote the carrying out of systematic studies in those parts of America in which the Africans and their descendants have been little studied or analysed by specialists, with a view to augmenting the material likely to be of help in drawing up an inventory of Afro-American cultures'.[1]

In the event of Unesco deciding to sponsor the research on the black problem in Santo Domingo we could secure the backing of such Dominican institutions as the Autonomous University of Santo Domingo and the Dominican Museum of Mankind, both of which are deeply interested in the discovery of data concerning a subject of such importance as the revelation of our true national identity.

Bibliography on the problem of the black population in Santo Domingo in colonial times

ALFAU DURÁN, Vatilio. Documentos Históricos. Ordenanzas para el Gobierno de los Negros de la Isla Española. *Anales de la Universidad de Santo Domingo*, Nos. 57–60, January–December 1951, Santo Domingo, 1961.

ALVAREZ, José de Jesús. *La Mezcla de Razas en Santo Domingo y los Factores Sanguíneos*. Santiago, 1973.

BERNALDO DE QUIROS, Constancio. Penalidad en el Código Negro de la Isla Española. *Boletín del Archivo General de la Nación*, 5th year, No. 23, 1942.

CORDERO, Walter. El Tema Negro y la Discriminación Racial en la República Dominicana. *Revista Ciencia*, No. 2. Dirección de Investigaciones Científicas. Universidad Autónoma de Santo Domingo, March 1975.

ESTEBAN DEIVE, Carlos. *Vodú y Magia en Santo Domingo*. Edit. Museo del Hombre Dominicano, 1975.

FRANCO, Franklin. *Los Negros, los Mulatos y la Nación Dominicana*. Santo Domingo, Edit. Nacional, 1969.

LARRAZABAL BLANCO, Carlos. *Los Negros y la Esclavitud en Santo Domingo*. Colección Pensamiento Dominicano. Santo Domingo. Julio de Postigo, 1967.

LIZARDO, Fradique. Cultura Africana en Santo Domingo. *Eistin Diario*, 1978.

MALEGÓN Barceló, *Código Negro Carolino*. Santo Domingo, Edit. Museo del Hombre Dominicano, 1974.

MOYA PONS, Frank. La Primera Abolición de Esclavitud en Santo Domingo. *Eme y Eme*, No. 13, July–August. 1974.

ROSARIO CANDELIER, Bruno. Los Valores Negros en la Poesía Dominicana. *Eme y Eme*, No. 15, 1974.

SILIÉ, Rubén. *Economía, Esclavitud y Población. Ensayos de Interpretación Histórica del Santo Domingo Español en el Siglo XVIII*. Edit. Universidad Autónoma de Santo Domingo, 1976.

TOLENTINO DIPP, Hugo. *Raza e Historia en Santo Domingo. Los Orígenes del Prejuicio Racial en América*. Vol. I. Edit. Universidad Autónoma de Santo Domingo, 1974.

TOLENTINO⸺ DIPP, Hugo. La Trata de Negros en Santo Domingo. *Revista Ciencia.* Vol. I,
No. 3, Santo Domingo, 1975.
⸺. Indio. Color ó Una Categoría Social (sobre el Prejuicio de Color en Santo Domingo).
Impacto Socialista, 1975.
UTERA, Fray Cipriano. La Condición Social del Negro en la Época Colonial. *Eme y Eme,*
No. 17, March–April 1975.

Persons who are currently studying the subject of African influence in the Dominican Republic

Hugo Tolentino Dipp. Is finishing the second volume of his work *Raza e Historia en Santo Domingo.* Occupies the post of research professor in the University of Santo Domingo.

Rubén Silié. Is finishing a study on fugitive slaves in the frontier region; he also directs a study on 'anti-Haitianism' in the Dominican Republic. Occupies the post of research professor in the University of Santo Domingo.

Fadrique Lizardo. Is finishing a study on the influence of African culture in Santo Domingo; also engaged in systematic research on general themes concerning the country's folklore directly connected with African influence.

Carlos Esteban Deive. Has just started a research on slavery in the Dominican Republic. Has also carried out studies concerning the question of popular religiousness from the point of view of African influence on it. Occupies the post of researcher on contract at the Dominican Museum of Mankind.

Brazilian and African sources for the study of cultural transferences from Brazil to Africa during the nineteenth and twentieth centuries

J. Michael Turner

This article seeks to be a panorama or general overview of the various sources of information and research possibilities for study in the field of African-Brazilian studies, treating archives and other sources of documentation in Brazil, countries in West Africa and a small selected group of European sources. For the purposes of this brief survey, centres of documentation consist of national, State and local archives, national and local libraries—research institutes and collections which pertain to government offices. Certain private collections of manuscripts and documents will also be presented for discussion as they include useful, often rare information which cannot be duplicated in the public collections and archives. While the primary research for this general study was based on essentially historical methodology and sources, it is evident that the research facilities employed hold useful information for research in other academic disciplines, particularly those involving the social sciences. The uses of oral history, its possibilities in complementing more traditional historical sources constitute a subsidiary theme of the present essay.

The great scope and depth of the current research in African-Brazilian studies will be illustrated by a brief description of some of the more recent projects conducted by interested 'Africanists' in Brazil and West Africa; these various studies are related in that they are based in the complicated and varied set of historic-cultural relations which link Brazil and the African continent. The projects range from cultural anthropology and linguistics to race relations, comparative government to intellectual and social history. Those involved in the research are Brazilian, African, European and North American. As the group of researchers in African-Brazilian studies as yet remains relatively small, the opportunities for joint studies and comparative research remain good. Combined efforts in the selecting of data and sharing of informational holdings by the various documentation centres is a real possibility, particularly as their efforts to receive funding may be successful only as a function of institutional co-operation. Future research projects and possibilities, which form the final part of the essay, despite the enormous costs in field research, dealing often with three continents—should be considered with cautious optimism based on the totality of subjects and themes yet to be sufficiently researched and analysed. Of importance also is the fact that these themes often have a direct as well as indirect bearing on certain foreign policy strategy that is currently under consideration by governments, thereby not being relegated to forgotten library shelves or local archives. The contemporaneousness of African-Brazilian studies should also be considered a point of interest and emphasis.

Salvador, Bahia serves as a point of departure for any study concerned with African-Brazilian cultural and historical connections. Bahia because of its economic importance during the era of the Atlantic slave trade received large numbers of African slaves, who in coming to Brazil brought not only their ability to work in the sugar-cane fields, but also their varied African cultures and personalities. These cultural traits were representative of different ethnic groups from Senegal to the Cameroons, and also from Angola and Mozambique, all mixing racially and socially with Portuguese and Amerindian cultures with the result being the cultural heterogeneity which is today's almost mythic Bahia, a region considered both by its native Bahians and the rest of Brazil as an area apart and culturally special from the rest of the country.[1] Research on Afro-Brazilian culture, as manifested in the various cults and sects of Afro-Brazilian religion has tended to focus upon the city of Salvador and to a lesser extent upon the interior of the stade of Bahia. The literal 'centre' for research in Bahia concerning African influence in Brazil is the Centro de Estudos Afro-Orientais, CEAO, semi-independent from the Federal University of Bahia. Founded in 1959,[2] the centre was the first institute in Brazil to be concerned with Africa and African studies. Being situated in Salvador, quite logically it concentrated its research interests on the city and the constellation of African retentions in that particular urban environment. Its library facilities during the 1960s represented the most comprehensive collection of books and periodicals concerning Africa to be found within Brazil. As many of the first research fellows of the centre were trained ethnologists and anthropologists the library tended to mirror these interests, ethno-cultural studies being more numerous than political and economic monographs. Important as the centre's organ of diffusion and medium of information expression within Brazil of the international research concerning Africa is its journal, *Afro-Asia*. This remains the sole Brazilian-African studies journal.[3] Despite a series of economic vicissitudes the CEAO and its journal have continued with pioneering work, while having to deal with the problems of having been the first in the field.

For researchers in Bahia who wanted to concern themselves with African influence within Brazilian, perhaps more specifically Bahian, culture the centre proved an invaluable agent. But if the research was of a more general nature concerning Afro-Brazilian history or a more global project concerning the African continent the research facilities of CEAO by 1970 were seen to be increasingly inadequate, as for reasons of financial exigency the latest publications were not being purchased. There was a certain introspection within the centre and its research which tended to define Africa as being a coastal strip between Ghana and the Cameroons, with heavy emphasis being given to the cultural transferences between Benin, Nigeria and Bahia.[4] Researchers, particularly foreign researchers were guided into certain cultural areas and during the early 1970s the orientation of CEAO seemed to be linked to a series of repetitive studies of *candomblé* cults and rites located in Salvador and its environs.[5] Certain transformations occurred in the mid-1970s and the centre's definition of Africa also changed as a new cultural axis was established between CEAO and the Université Nationale du Zaïre, with an exchange of language professors, Portuguese being taught in the African country, a Bantu language in Bahia. The major influence within the Bahian African Studies Centre remains ethno-cultural, with linguistics occupying a major portion of the research time of the centre's members.[6]

Researchers whose concerns are more directly related to themes within Afro-Bahian, Afro-Brazilian history are to be directed to the Archive of the State of Bahia and to the Municipal Archive in Salvador. Despite the tragic loss for researchers in the burning of documents relative to Brazilian slavery in 1890,[7] ample material relative to property exchanges, sale of slaves, Church ownership and African commerce to Bahian ports can be obtained in the two major public archives. Classification of documents, seemingly the bane of researchers in any country, remains a problem in the Bahian archives, although incomplete guides are available. Because of interest in the subject of Bahian slave rebellions and revolts, particularly in the nineteenth century, a brief collection of holdings of the State Archives is available to researchers, although personal experience of the writer has attested to the limitations of that particular guide and the necessity of direct 'attack' upon the shelves of the archives for unearthing potentially useful cartons of information. Another problem of a logistical nature for the researcher in Salvador archives is the daily operating schedule, 2 p.m. to 6 p.m. on weekdays. Fortunately one other important source of research material for Afro-Brazilian history has morning work hours—the State Library—thus allowing for organization of a full workday.

The new State Library was completed in 1971, and at the time of utilization by the writer, was still in a test phase, surely concluded with refinements in the institution's workings and organization, five years later. The newspaper holdings of the library are of interest as they date from the nineteenth century, with also a rather complete collection of twentieth-century newspapers from throughout the state of Bahia, particularly Itabuna and Ilhéus. An unexpected discovery while reading newpapers from Ilhéus for the 1930s was the presence of an Afro-Brazilian organization in that city, ideologically linked to the United Negro Improvement Association of Marcus Garvey and his 'Back-to-Africa Movement' that had attracted Afro-Americans in the United States during the 1920s.[8] During my research visit to Salvador in 1971, plans were being made for the transference of quantities of State newspapers, miscellaneous periodicals and journals, and magazines pertaining to Bahia and its history. Mechanisms were being installed for microfilming and reading of microfilms, the catalogue system of the library was both logical and useful to the novice researcher. Important also is the fact the complex was seen to be a model of new bibliographic techniques, a break in the traditional information sources represented both by the archives and the Geographical and Historical Institute of Bahia, a monument to Bahia's past historic culture and at present, dimished grandeur.

The Bahia Institute, in common with many historical monuments is exhibiting tangible signs of old age and disrepair. However, for its collection of nineteenth-century Salvador newspapers, rare books and manuscripts the institute demands consultation from the serious historical researcher.[9] Salvador is a citadel of tradition as apparent and representative within its intellectual and academic life as within its social institutions. One method of meeting and conversing with this academic establishment is through the institute, whose members tend to congregate for genteel intellectual exchange and *cafezinho* two or three evenings a week. The academic disciplines are not limited to only history or geography, but can include a fair range of the old guard from all areas of the humanities and the social sciences. These contacts are also useful in that they provide the possibility of gaining entrance to private library collections, which can only be consulted through personal recommendation.

Presenting a greater problem to the researcher is the actual condition of the institute and the lack of facilities for working within the ancient building. A very cramped reading room which during its single daily afternoon session occupied by the city's university and high-school students working on historical assignments, ofen requires a researcher to work with crumbling nineteenth-century newspapers or documents in a hallway or under a staircase, for simple lack of desk space. Preservation of documents is at best rudimentary, with time and small animals making irreparable inroads on the newspapers. Plans have been discussed but never initiated for a systematic microfilming of the institute's newspaper holdings, but have been indefinitely delayed for lack of financial resources. The necessity to reclassify and re-order the system of documentation has also been discussed but not enacted by those responsible for the institute. A part of the problem clearly is in the nature of the institution itself, an historical tradition attempting to function as such within contemporary society and academia; the primary characteristics of the institute are its insularity to excessively 'innovative' techniques and methodology in the humanities,[10] and in an effort of self-preservation an almost blind commitment to maintaining the Salvador academic status quo. Gaining their confidence is a researcher's decision which obviously is based on the requirements of the

particular project and the utility of the institution and members to the successful completion of the research. For studies concerning eighteenth- and nineteenth-century slavery in Salvador and surrounding area, the newspaper collections are useful. Social and family historians would also benefit from the
holdings of the institute, its collection also interesting economic historians.[11]

Private collections either owned by individuals or institutions are numerous in Salvador and also relevant to the study of Bahian slavery or Afro-
Brazilian history in various eras before and after abolition. The two major
Salvador convents, Carmo and Desterro, have official histories and substantial documentation of eighteenth- and nineteenth-century commercial transactions that shed good insights on the relationship between the Salvador Church
and the institution of slavery.[12] Also of interest is the collection of the recently
deceased professor and cocoa *fazendeiro* Frederico Edelweiss, an extensive
collection of books and documents covering a range of academic disciplines all
dealing with Bahia. He called his collection a 'Bahia Studies Programme' captured in a multi-room library;[13] in the case of Afro-Bahian Studies while dupli-
cation does exist between some of the Edelweiss holdings and that of CEAO,
there are sometimes singular holdings owned by Edelweiss not found in the
centre. His collection of Amerindian linguistic texts and tracts is unmatched,
truly invaluable. It is my sincere hope that the collection in its entirety will be
quickly moved to a special section of the library of the Federal University of
Bahia, access to be made available to all interested researchers. During the
past Edelweiss was at the disposition of all researchers who came to Salvador,
allowing one to work unrestricted in his library; as his Bahian collection was
symbolized by an inclusiveness and globality of approach, its utility to the
researcher in varied disciplines should be stressed.

Culture and cultural history clearly dominate research patterns of the
recent past in Salvador and in Bahia state. With its African studies centre
performing the function of intellectual patron, little emphasis has been placed
upon more contemporary Brazilian-African relations, something of an irony
as the centre itself was a result of the first Brazilian diplomatic initiative
towards Africa in 1960 during the government of Jânio Quadros.[14] This more
contemporary approach to Africa and Brazilian-African relations is to be
found in the African studies centres in Rio de Janeiro, (linked to the Candido
Mendes University Foundation) and São Paulo, a more integral part of USP.

The Centro de Estudos Afro-Asiáticos in Rio is administratively an
integral part of the Candido Mendes University Foundation and offers multi-
disciplinary courses concerning Africa (Asia receives significantly less attention), to any interested university student in the Rio area, regardless of the
student's institutional affiliation.[15] The heart of the Rio centre is the library,
a collection very strong in contemporary African affairs and recent African
independence movements. This contemporary interest of the Rio centre is

reflected in its director and staff, the majority with personal experience in Portuguese-speaking African countries, and countries in southern Africa. The centre has attempted to chronicle Brazil's developing relationship with Angola, Mozambique, Guinea-Bissau and Cape Verde, and is receiving ample documentation and primary sources from these countries, including newspapers. The centre has also been able to establish personal contacts with many of the leaders of these new Portuguese-speaking countries and it has served in an advisory capacity to Itamarati, the Brazilian diplomatic service, in helping to define Brazil's evolving contacts and possibilities of exchange with these countries.[16]

Some attention has been given by the Rio centre to that city's Afro-Brazilian population and it has sponsored some seminars which have allowed Afro-Brazilians an opportunity for some self-analysis and group expression. The major emphasis of the Rio centre is international relations within Africa and between Brazil and the African continent. The centre is less culturally oriented, less involved with anthropological and ethnic studies than CEAO in Salvador. The course offerings in Rio are concerned with an analysis of contemporary African political ideology and strategies for economic development, other courses tending to focus upon the problems of decolonization and neo-colonialism and the role of international cartels and multinationals on the African continent.[17] As described by its director, the major function of the Rio centre is to disseminate information about Africa, serve as an essentially neutral African information 'bank' to the Rio community; unfortunately these functions at times have tended to compromise academic excellence as a large part of the centre's time is devoted to a quasi-public-relations effort for the continent. In an effort to redress this intellectual imbalance the centre is inaugurating in November 1977 its own journal. The centre's plan for the journal is to include scholarly research papers, primary African documents and opinioned interpretations of contemporary African events all under one cover.

While admittedly courting the Rio public, the centre's staff exhibits a sound knowledge of Africa and a working experience of the continent; it has set a difficult task for itself as it has taken a middle position between a base popularization of a subject catering to a capricious public interest stoked only by media coverage of Africa and those serious students of Africa who are interested in analysing a continent of multi-cultures or attempting to understand how their own country of Brazil fits into (or is attempting to fit itself into) the overall African picture. The Rio centre because of these various contradictions is recommended to the researcher with an interest in Brazil-African relations, particularly in terms of international relations and political science. It provides alternative sources of information and a balance to the data provided by the Itamarati archives and the National Archive and Library, holdings obviously of a different value. The Rio centre is in contact with Itamarati but remains very far from being an official spokesman for Itamarati African policy, it is independent in thought and pronouncement.

Apart from the Rio centre, the city seems to be experiencing a mushrooming number of institutes, centres organizations devoted to the study of Afro-Brazilian culture. Some are con,nected with universities and institutions of higher learning (Candido Mendes Federal University of Fluminense), others more administratively independent located both in the more fashionable Zona Sul (Copacabana, Ipanema) and in the at times mythologized Zona Norte (Bangu). Newspapers, news-sheets and pamphlets are beginning to trickle forth from all of these fledgling institutes; unfortunately many of the organizations seem to be engaged in fractious internecine skirmishes one aga nst another. They are and at the same time are not members and a result of the cultural 'Black Rio' movement, however their at present fragile nature should not serve as a denial of their potential future importance and usefulness for the researcher attempting to understand the reality of the Afro-Brazilian experience. It is important to remember also that the 'Black Rio' movement is not confined solely to the carioca city, but can be encountered in Salvador, São Paulo and Brasilia; in fact in any urban area where there is a significant concentration of Afro-Brazilians. It is evident that this contemporary phenomenon or cultural movement among Afro-Brazilians will become the subject of many interpretations and intellectual analyses, as its meaning and significance become more defined in social, economic and quasi-political terms.[19] The Rio African studies centre is aware of the movement and plans in the future to involve itself more directly with the community's programme interests as expressed through 'Black Rio'.

In terms of institutional support and interest, the number and varied types of publications, diversity of groups and interests and research possibilities, it is the author's conviction that Rio de Janeiro provides the most fertile area for research on contemporary Afro-Brazilian culture and mores, serving as a kind of national centre and testing ground,[20] and also as a mirror for the rest of the national society. São Paulo while also providing a strong community has or exhibits another kind of insularity which does not permit its community to serve as a kind of mirror as that of Rio.

The third major African studies centre is located at the University of São Paulo (USP), more directly integrated into its university than either CEAO in Salvador or CEAA in Rio. The USP centre is the only African studies programme in Brazil which offers advanced degrees (masters and doctorate) to its students through direct entrance to the post-graduate departments of USP. While the centre itself is less well defined than the other two, exhibits less of a specific personality, its contacts with Itamarati, with the African diplomatic corps in Brasilia and with various African universities through the medium of professor/student exchange programmes is very far reaching and extensive. The USP centre has been active in recruiting African students to attend the University of São Paulo, has encouraged the students to make special presentations concerning Africa at the school and often served as a kind of unofficial liaison and at times ombudsman between the African students (including African diplomat-students before their entry into the Instituto Rio Branco) and Itamarati. In a manner different from the Salvador and Rio centres, the group at USP has acted in the role of government adviser for African affairs, enjoying a free and open relationship with Itamarati.[21]

The São Paulo centre has presented some public programmes concerning Africa to the city, however its major focus is academic, providing post-graduate courses and orientation within the institutional structure provided by USP. At times the centre has also provided orientation and information for São Paulo industrialists interested in the possibilities and potential growth of the so-called African markets.[22] Certain Afro-Brazilian groups in São Paulo fault the centre for its lack of interest in Afro-Brazilian affairs and needs and its overemphasis on seemingly abstract or 'theoretical' problems of African development and culture. The overall direction of the USP centre seems to be in establishing direct university-to-university links with an increasing number of African institutions in a growing exchange programme.[23] For the foreign researcher the São Paulo centre's influence and advising role with the Brazilian Government, its good reputation among Brasilia's African embassies and its reputation within African academic circles should be seen to offer a variety of useful contacts and orientation, different in nature from those available in Salvador or Rio. Obviously if time would permit the researcher to visit all three centres this diversification in orientation could prove valuable for the study as each centre exhibits a distinctly different approach to the study of Africa.

What possibilities exist for the consolidation of certain kinds of documentation and information provided by the Brazilian African studies centres? The need for a central documentation centre and a kind of research clearing house for information concerning actual research projects involving Africa and Brazil (concomittantly Afro-Brazilian studies) has been discussed by a number of researchers and continues to demand further investigation and debate.[24] While institutional co-operation is often difficult to initiate in academia, if a sufficiently strong case can be made that such sharing of resources could result in increased financial support for the various institutions involved, particularly during this period of scant finances for research—it is hoped this admittedly monetary spur would result in fresh initiatives between the major centres and some of the other more established institutes of Afro-Brazilian cultural studies.[25] Clearly the field of study is changing every day and expanding in new directions, presenting to the novitiate researcher both bewildering complexities and myriad possibilities.

On the African continent sources of documentation for the study of African-Brazilian relations are found more in traditional archives than in the research institutes connected to universities. International relations programmes exist in African universities but tend to treat and analyse problems on the continent itself, or Africa's relationship with Western Europe and/or the United States. Latin America as a research topic for international relations has been only recently discussed and analysed.[26] However with the emergence of independent Portuguese-speaking Africa, it is expected that Africa will also be re-thinking its policies towards Latin America, particularly Brazil. Conferences such as the recent Nigerian FESTAC of January 1977, the more narrowly focused Yoruba Cultural Diffusion and Diaspora Conference of July 1976 at the Nigerian University of Ife, and the African Influences in the Americas Conference, held in Colombia during August 1977 have all presented scholarly discussions of the varied cultural historical links between Africa and the Americas. Interesting to note that the basic context of these discussions has been from the African not the American side or axis.[27] Hopefully with more conferences such as the present meeting in Houston, this international forum for African-American contact and exchange can be increased.

In Dakar, Senegal, the well-organized and also well-supervised and controlled national archives provide complete documentation for what was under colonialism the French West African Empire.[28] As direct Brazilian-African historical influence was strongest in Benin and Togo (passing over into French administrative control from a defeated Germany after the First World War), the Dakar archives are a useful alternative to the Paris colonial archives located on Rue Oudinot.[29] Information which should be located in the Benin National Archives is better sought in Dakar or in Paris. Togo has yet to open a national archive, thereby also relegating strict historical research to the Senegalese repository.

French-speaking Africa is also the subject of serious study at the Institut Fondamentale de l'Afrique Noire (IFAN), located on the campus of the Université du Dakar. IFAN in 1957 in its series, *Mémoires*, published the multidisciplinary 'Les Afro-Américains', an early study of African and Latin-American cultural connections. It was IFAN which sponsored some of the early research of the photographer/anthropologist Pierre Verger, the indefatigable researcher and pioneer in the field of African-Brazilian relations, the organization also supporting at certain stages the work of the late French 'Brésilienist' Roger Bastide. The library of IFAN is excellent and quite diverse; the monograph series, while at times highly specialized and localized in terms of subject-matter also has many monographs of a more general interest. IFAN also serves as a kind of unofficial mecca for researchers involved in francophone African research and acts as a clearing-house for discovering what researchers are in what countries, working on what kind of topic and project. One can receive the names of valuable contacts in the field at IFAN, helping to orient the researcher.

Benin remains the cultural and historical centre of Brazilian influence in Africa. Despite a change in official nomenclature, (ex-Dahomey) and a radical change in national government (Marxist-socialist), this economically poor country, in particular its coastal cities, are a reflection of nineteenth-century Bahia, Brazil. Bahian culture and social divisions were all transported by the former Bahian slaves during their peregrinations to the West African coast.[30] Research was never easy to accomplish in Benin even during the period when it was called Dahomey and boasted a triumvirate presidency.[31] The National Archive has neither catalogue nor any form of organization, seemingly defying any system of organization and defying all archivists, foreign or national, to devise a suitable one. During the period before the revolution (most recent?) the researcher could travel freely throughout the country and conduct interviews, collecting oral history at will. Unfortunately this is no longer true. The National Research Institute in Porto-Novo, the Institut de Recherche Appliquée au Dahomey IRAD or IRAB, when visited by the writer in 1975 had received no new funding from the revolutionary government, and was completely paralysed, being unable to publish a new edition or number of its monograph series *Études Dahoméennes*, or its infrequent but often excellent journal of the same name. The museum in the Portuguese fort in the coastal town of Ouidah had also come under more strict government control. While many of the most valuable documents had been burned by Portuguese officials in 1963 when they abandoned the fort on demand of the Dahoman Government, in 1975 there remained some useful resources for the study of Brazilian influence in Africa. The records of the Ouidah Roman Catholic Mission (African Fathers based in Lyons, France and in Rome) while incomplete in Dahomey, remain open to public use (at least as of 1976) providing baptism, marriage, birth and death certificates for the returned Afro-Brazilians.[32]

Curbing the researcher's ability to collect oral data is obviously a handicap, particularly as the Brazilian-Dahoman families spread themselves along the coast between Benin and Togo and Benin and Nigeria. In the writer's research interviews proved critical in supplementing lacunae encountered in the documentation, not only in the African archives but also in European sources. Any study of Brazilian historical influence in Africa, also any assessment of the African reaction to current Brazilian diplomatic offensives on the continent must take into account the oral data which was collected over time and with repeated sessions between interviewer and interviewee. In Benin this is no longer possible and constitutes a serious loss to any researcher, as all research must now receive clearance from the Ministry of the Interior after the lengthy process of being approved for a research visa to work in Benin.

The situation in Togo is better than in Benin. While the absence of a central archive is a serious problem, possibilities do exist for substantial oral data-collection with Afro-Brazilian families located in the capital, Lomé, and in the small coastal towns of Porto Seguro and Anécho. As familial connections between Dahoman and Togolese 'Brazilians' are extensive, information not secured in Benin might be possible in the neighboring Togo.[33]

Ghana and Nigeria present different problems and possibilities. The Nigerian national archives located on the campus of the Federal University of Ibadan present a well-organized system and for the researcher with a fair amount of research time, the archive is a useful source to delineate the social mobility of the Afro-Brazilians during the final decades of the nineteenth century and the early part of the twentieth century in British-ruled Nigeria. For the cultural and social historian, the various Nigerian-Brazilian descendant friendly societies present varied and useful data: these organizations, while the majority are to be found in Lagos, can also be located in western Nigerian Yoruba cities such as Abeokuta, Ijebu Ode and Ibadan—their collections of old newspapers, manuscripts, programmes from anniversary meetings of the 1920s and 1930s, lists of memberships all aid the process of re-constructing the cultural history of the Afro-Brazilians.[34]

The Ghanaian archives, while well run and well staffed, yielded less concrete information about the Ghanaian Brazilians, or so-called Tabon people. Researchers with adequate research time might do well to check through all the series dealing with the Keta region (on the border with Togo and home of the Ewe ethnic group, which becomes Mina in Togo and Benin, and a major component of Afro-Brazilian culture in West Africa), might prove a valuable source. The Tabon or Brazilian society in Accra, Ghana, is fragmented and subject to serious social class divisions. When compared with Benin, Togo or Nigeria there is a lack of historical sentiment among the Ghanaian Brazilians which forces the researcher in turn to have a more one-to-one relationship with each Ghanaian Brazilian family. The research would probably be more effective in the Keta region and in the Ga ethnic regions to the west of the capital, as there was an interesting and as yet unexplained massive integration of returning Afro-Brazilians into the Ga group on the Gold Coast during the middle of the nineteenth century.[35]

Also of interest is the ethnographic work being conducted by the Ghana National Museum, whose assistant director is very interested in Brazil (having visited the country in 1974), and who is tracing historical and cultural connections between his country and Brazil. The museum has some interesting occasional papers which can be put at the disposition of the researcher. The experience of the writer was that the museum, the families themselves all proved more helpful than the moribund Institute of African Studies at Legon, the University of Ghana. Cape Coast University would be recommended over

Legon, as there is a definite interest on the part of some of its staff in Latin America, specifically Brazil.[36] Ghana is not usually considered a traditional area of Brazilian historical influence but the country proved to be an interesting source, one requiring more than the limited research time available to the writer. As a recipient of current Brazilian economic and diplomatic influence and interest, Ghana along with Ivory Coast, Nigeria, Gabon and to a lesser extent Senegal and Zaire constitute the Black African focus of Brazilian approximation towards Africa, as distinct from Brazil's special (if indeed it could be called special) relationship with Portuguese-speaking Africa.[37] What is needed is research on the African reactions to this diplomatic initiative, as seen distinctly from the African side.

Newspapers published by the Brazilian-Africans themselves also provide an excellent source for studying social and cultural history. This is particularly true in francophone Africa during the period 1920–40 with the Dahoman newspapers.[38] While some of the collection can be found among the families themselves and in the Benin archives, the most significant holdings are in the Versailles deposit of the Bibliothèque Nationale in Paris. The Afro-Brazilians are the editors-in-chief, the reporters, and are engaged in discussing events of interest to their specific community, at that time attempting to achieve vertical social mobility and class ascendency, envisioning for itself a kind of lateral group identity, an intermediary position between the African 'masses' and the European colonialist élite. The contradiction and at times evident anxiety of this position is most accurately reflected in the newspapers.[39] Family history is well served by the newspapers, as well as additional perspectives on the colonial era as witnessed by that small literate African public of the early twentieth century. They also provide data for comparative history studies (if more are needed) of models of British and French colonial patterns, cause and effect and of the influence of the different metropoles, Paris and London. As a footnote to the interest in pan-African studies, the continuing research into the historical attempt to self-define 'Africaninity', the Dahoman press again proves its utility.

If one surveys the field of African-Brazilian studies it becomes evident that the initial studies were concerned with cultural transferences from one side of the Atlantic to the other, Bastide, Pierson, even Gilberto Freyre noting the African presence generally in the Americas and specifically in Brazil. With Pierre Verger's publication of the massive *Flux et Reflux* in 1968,[40] a data bank was established for future research in the field. Verger's almost forty years of field work not only definitively established the African historical presence in Brazil, but also returned the cultural odyssey to Africa. Transatlantic cultural studies had been given a firm base. Verger, by his presence in Bahia, influenced young researchers in the late 1960s most particularly a fellow of CEAO, anthropologist Julio Braga, who did research in Benin on the Afro-

Brazilians,[41] and who is currently working in Zaire. From within an essentially anthropological matrix Braga and the current director of CEAO, Guilherme de Sousa Castro, and his wife Iêda Pessoa de Sousa Castro did research in western Nigeria on Brazilian influences in the Yoruba language and on Yoruba influences in Brazilian Portuguese. Additional linguistic work was done in Bahia in 1970 by Ebun Ogunsanya, a Yoruba student at Radcliffe College, Harvard, whose senior thesis concerned Yoruba retentions in Brazilian Portuguese. Recently the former Cultural Attaché of the Nigerian Embassy in Brasilia, Abiola Joseph has also conducted linguistic research into the Yoruba spoken in *candomblé* ceremonies throughout Brazil.

Jose Honório Rodrigues using essentially secondary sources from Brazil, in his two-volume work *Africa and Brazil* provides a general outline of Brazil's historical relationship towards the African continent. The present author taking his departure from Verger tended to focus his doctoral research on Benin, Togo and Lagos, Nigeria and the returned Afro-Brazilian slaves, while the Brazilian couple Carneiro da Cunha, who are presenting a paper at this conference, have focused their interest on the Brazilian returnees to Nigeria. Brazilian historical influence in Ghana has been the subject of a brief research trip of the author to that country in 1975.

Wayne Selcher's publications in the field of international relations have attempted to analyse Brazilian political and diplomatic interest in Africa, its relationship to Portuguese-speaking Africa beginning in the 1950s and with his latest articles and manuscripts bringing attention to the latest approximation attempts on the part of Itamarati to win support in Black Africa.[42] Also developing from his earlier interests in Brazilian race relations, specifically in Bahia, the Ghanaian social scientist Anani Dzidzienyo widened his scope of interest with a series of articles on Brazilian diplomatic approximation attempts in Africa during 1972. Dzidzienyo has gone on to analyse the at times confused role and response of the Afro-Latin to his own Latin-American culture and towards Africa. Professor Dzidzienyo is presenting a paper at this conference on that topic. Pierre-Michel Fontaine, a political scientist from Haiti, in his work for Unesco has analysed the relationship between Brazil, Africa and multinational corporations, continuing with this research now at Cornell University. Professor Roy Glasgow, currently Federal University of Fluminense, Rio, and also Boston University, has also writen on Brazil's approximation towards Africa during the period 1971–72.[43]

In discussing possibilities for further and future research I would like to mention a doctoral dissertation study of Professor Monica Schuler, completed for the University of Wisconsin. The study concerns the migration of West Africans to Jamaica as labourers during the early part of the twentieth century. There were significant parallels between the West Indian/African economic-cultural interchange, and that of Brazil and West Africa during the

late nineteenth century. Cuba also saw large numbers of its free black population leave the island and return to Nigeria during the nineteenth century. There
was significant competition between the returned Cubans and the returned
Brazilians in nineteenth-century Lagos, although both groups were less
favoured than the English-speaking returned former slaves from Sierra Leone,
the Saros.[45] The subject of African emigration, the quasi-stranger groups such
as the West Indians and Afro-Latins arriving in West Africa are deserving
of a systematic study and analysis together with the collective problems of
'the return' and re-integration which need further research and discussion. What
were the contributions of other areas in Brazil, the central–south, Pernambuco,
Maranhão to the immigrant groups that left Brazil for Africa? What apart
from the obvious slave-trade links were the relations between Angola, Mozambique and Brazil during the nineteenth century. What is the evidence of Afro-
Brazilians returning to these countries? Central Africa needs considerably
more study to determine the range and extent of its historical ties to Brazil.
Archives and sources newly available in Lisbon hopefully should provide
some of the answers, while awaiting a sincerely desired era of stability in Angola
and Mozambique which might permit access to archival sources now closed
and a population now distracted by seemingly incessant civil strife.

The much discussed Brazilian approximation towards Africa of the
1970s is still wanting much interpretation and analysis. Still to be heard from
in a significant way are the African countries themselves, to give voice to their
interest in this approximation effort, to articulate their conditions and requirements of Brazil, in particular as they relate to Brazil's relationship towards
southern Africa and to the so-called south Atlantic strategy. It would also be
instructive to study the differences and similarities between Brazilian and
United States foreign-policy initiatives towards Africa, as seen from an African
perspective or viewpoint, to determine each policy's strengths and weaknesses.
Is Brazil in a distinctly better position than the United States because of history,
culture and climate to offer to the African continent the needed technology
and resources for that continent's future development? What are the possibilities of Brazil's acting as mediator between 'north' and 'south', to the Third
and the First world? What is the image and meaing of Africa for the Afro-
Brazilian, and does this image have any bearing on Brazil's international
image within Africa?[46]

These are some of the many research-oriented questions and problems
awaiting further elaboration and work. The subject, Africa-Brazil relations
covers at multitude of countries, more than one continent and a variety of
of languages and cultures. Research costs are prohibitive, there is always the
danger of becoming a generalist as the researcher is partly involved with Africa
and partly involved with Latin America. However, the compensations in human
terms are also intercontinental and for growth and development as a field

researcher and as an individual, the transatlantic flow has much to recommend in its favour.

Notes

1. Salvador, Bahia, is called popularly *boa terra*, in part because of its being Brazil's first capital, the alleged moral laxity of many of its inhabitants, a casual attitude towards life's problems, essentially a kind of living museum, where architecture, art and the populace represent a more ancient Brazil, one lost with the coming of the twentieth century.
2. Waldir Freitas Oliveira, 'Desenvolvimento dos Estudos Africanistas no Brazil', *Cultura*, No. 23, October–December 1976, p. 114.
3. The Rio Centro de Estudos Afro-Asiáticos is planning through the series, Cadernos Candido Mendes, to begin publication of its own *Journal of African Studies*.
4. Primary study of Bahian-African cultural relations was made by Pierre Verger, *Flux et Reflux de la Traite des Nègres entre le Golfe de Bénin et Bahia de Todos os Santos du XVIIe siècle*, Paris, 1968. Iexla Pessoa de Castro and husband Guilherme tended to focus their studies studies of Portuguese-Yoruba linguistics in Ife, Nigeria, results were published in several numbers of the CEAO African Studies Journal, *Afro-Asia* (1968–69). Julio Braga, CEAO anthropologist, Didi dos Santos, *a pai de santo* and ethnologue and his wife Juanita Elbein dos Santos, anthropologist, all focused their studies of the origins of Afro-Bahian religious cults in western Nigeria and eastern Benin, period 1968–71.
5. One African researcher, Elbun Ogunsanya, a linguistics and romance languages student from Radcliffe College, Harvard, in 1970 encountered certain difficulties as she attempted to research in cults and with people not officially under the patronage of CEAO. By 1974 three or four foreign researchers began appearing at the more celebrated *candomblé terreiros* on the same evening (period June–August 1974), causing the present writer to think that the researchers would to better to research the influence of the researcher on the ritual process of *candomblé*.
6. Of importance is the work of the Swiss linguist Rolf Reichert, *Os Documentos Arabes do Arquivo do Estado da Bahia*, Salvador, 1970, who as the resident Islamicist of CEAO worked with all of the existant Arab documents from the 1836 *jihad* in Salvador, providing Portuguese translations. See Turner, review article 'Os Documentos Arabes', *International Journal of African Studies*, Boston, 1975.
7. After the end of Brazilian slavery, it was decided by the new republic that the historical blot of having had slavery as a national institution could perhaps be erased by destroying all relevant documentation, which occurred in 1893 as mandated by the State.
8. *O Commercio de Ilheus*, June–October, 1931.
9. Nineteenth-century newspapers included in the collection of the IGHB are: *Diario da Bahia* (1830s), *O Commercio* (1840s), *O Diario da Bahia* (1850s), *Journal da Bahia* (1850s–1870s).
10. In 1973 a Ph.D. candidate from Harvard University, Jane McDivitt, was doing a study of Afro-Brazilian poetry and other literature which evoked at times hostile responses from the members of IGHB who refused to admit the existence of such a field of study. The Ghanaian researcher Anani Dzidzienyo also encountered incredulity at his insistence that political behaviour of Afro-Brazilians could serve as a subject for study and analysis in 1970–71.

11. Newspapers in collection with listing of port activities in Salvador, other relevant commercial news a represent valuable secondary source or, depending upon availability of archival material, at times a primary source.

12. Study of Susan Soeiro, thesis for Ph.D. New York University, 1975, economic history of eighteenth-century Salvador as indicated by documents located in the Convent of the Desterro, research in Salvador 1970–71.

13. The Edelweiss collection for Afro-Brazilian culture was also extensive and worth a visit for encountering old and very rare books. He also had old but general works concerning Africa, most anthropological studies.

14. Freitas, 'Desenvolvimento', p. 114–15.

15. The CEAA of Candido Mendes offers a series of extension courses, open to the Rio community attracting as wide an audience as possible, charging tuition fees for each course offered.

16. In 1976 its director, José Maria Pereira journeyed on a semi-official mission to Angola, Mozambique and Guinea-Bissau to investigate the possibilities of greater cultural and educational exchange between Brazil and those countries, principally to bring African students to study in Brazilian universities, and aid in Brazilian technological assistance in African educational projects and planning.

17. Course offerings for academic year 1977, include several courses on African ideology, decolonization (the Portuguese example) and problems of African development using models from North Africa, West, Central and Southern Africa.

18. The much contested and discussed 'Black Rio' cultural social movement despite alledged foreign influence and intervention in Brazilian culture is serving to provide a sense of cultural identity to many of Rio's Afro-Brazilian residents. Much of the intellectual life of the city's Afro-Brazilians, conferences and symposiums are beginning to take into account the cultural phenomenon that began with the popularity of American 'soul' music and black American life styles but is slowly finding its own Brazilian voice and *raison d'être*.

19. The Second Annual Conference on Black (Afro-Brazilian) contributions to Brazilian culture were held at the Federal University of Fluminense, Niteroi, in November 1977.

20. In Salvador, while there is also evidence of the 'Black Rio' movement, for Afro-Brazilians of that city it is necessary to move past the omnipresent Afro-Bahian religious cult life which has so marked Afro-Bahian culture. In Rio there is not the same strong cultural tradition for that city's Afro-Brazilian population, allowing greater possibility for self-expression, for this 'Black Rio' began in Rio and not in Salvador.

21. One of the advisers to Itamarati's participation in the recent World Festival of African Art and Culture in Lagos, Nigeria, was the USP centre, whose director, Professor F. Mourão gave one of the seminar papers at the Colloquium on African Culture which opened FESTAC.

22. In October 1976, African students at USP presented an exposition on Africa, aimed at the São Paulo business community to demonstrate investment possibilities and potentialities on the continent, the exposition was held at USP, with administrative assistance by the centre.

23. In July 1977, Professor Mourão went in the company of the Rector of USP on a tour of West African universities to begin a series of exchanges between USP and these African universities.

24. One of the topics for the Fluminense Conference in November, 1977 was the need for a kind of clearing-house of information on Afro-Brazilian studies, what resources

are available in terms of documentation and what kinds of research are currently being undertaken within Brazil.

25. In São Paulo, the sociologist Eduardo de Oliveira e Oliveira is engaged in a study of Brazilian Negritude, with interested Afro-Brazilian students at Campinas, there are functioning Afro-Brazilian institutes in Joinville Santa Catarina (a week of Afro-Brazilian culture sponsored by the institute and the state of Santa Catarina was planned for July 1977), Porto Alegre, and a number of similar centres in Rio and Salvador, that of Did dos Santos, Institute of Afro-Bahian Studies.

26. Personal communication from Professor Fola Soremekua, History Department, Universite of Ife, Nigeria, 21 October 1976.

27. Paper presented by Professor Anani Dzidzienyo at Ife Conference, in July, 1976 on 'Images of African and the Afro-Latin American', paper of Dzidzienyo at South Eastern Conference on Latin American Studies, Tuskeegee, Alabama, April 1977, 'Activity and Inactivity in the Politics of Afro-Latin America'.

28. Dakar served as the administrative centre for l'Afrique Occidentale Française thereby receiving the archival collection after the dissolution of the massive African colonial empire.

29. Archives d'Outre-Mer, also called because of its Paris address, Rue Oudinot, the most complete repository of French colonial documentation.

30. See Turner, 'Les Brésiliens—The Impact of Former Brazilian Slaves Upon Dahomey', Boston University, 1975 (unpublished Ph.D. thesis): 'Os Escravos Brasileiros no Daomé', *Afro-Asia*, Nos. 8–9, 1970; Lathardus Goggins (ed.), 'Reversing the Trend: Afro-Brazilian Influences in West Africa' *The Thematic Conceptual Approach to African History*, Dubuque, Iowa, in press; 'A Manipulação da Religião: o Caso dos Afro-baianos', *Cultura*, No. 23, October–December, 1976; 'Brazilian-African Points of Contact', *Cadernos de Candido Mendes, Révista do Centro Afro-Asiático*, No. 1, November, 1977.

31. Dahomey-Benin, a country the size of Kentucky has had an unfortunate political history since its independence from France in 1960. During the period 1970–73, a rotating three-president council was enacted in an attempt to stop almost chronic coups d'état. The system ended in a coup with brought to power present military Marxist dictatorship.

32. Documents from the Cuidah Catholic mission proved invaluable in reconstructing the social life of returned Afro-Brazilians during the nineteenth century, aided by African Mission Society records in France and Italy which cover the society's nineteenth-century workings in Togo and Nigeria as well as Dahomey.

33. Example of African neighbours, the first President of Togo, Sylvanus Olympio (assassinated while in office), was born in Dahomey and is buried in Dahomey, on ancestral land of his Afro-Brazilian descendants. The De Sousa family, a key Afro-Brazilian clan, has branches in Togo as well as in Benin.

34. Of great value is the collection under the jurisdiction of Mrs Da Rocha Thomas, of Casa de Agua, Lagos, Nigeria. She is President of the Lagos Brazilian Friendly Society and provided the writer with invaluable leads during his time in Lagos in 1972.

35. Turner, 'Manipulaçâo', *Cultura*, p. 61; 'Points of Contact', *Cadernos*.

36. In personal communication from Professor Dzidizienyo, Ghanaian professor at Cape Coast University, Ghana, did a thesis on Portuguese Africa and Brazil, 15 March 1977.

37. Wayne Selcher, *The Afro-Asian Dimension of Brazilian Foreign Policy*, Gainesville, 1974.

38. Dov Ronen, 'The African Élite as Represented by the Dahomean Press', *African Studies Association Review*, Vol. XVI, No. 1, September 1973.
39. Principal Dahoman Newspapers, *La Voix du Dahomey, La Suprême Sagesse, Le Guide du Dahomey, L'Echo du Bénin*.
40. Verger's work is more a compendium of information than a synthesis and analysis of the cultural Bahian-African connections, serving as a reference work.
41. Julio Braga, 'Nota sobre o "Quartier Bresilien" em Uida, Daomé', *Afro-Asia*, 1969.
42. Selcher, op. cit.
43. Roy Arthur Glasgow, 'Brazil's Attempted African Approximation', *Issues African Studies Association Notes*, 1973.
44. Jean Herskovits Kopytoff, *A Preface to Modern Nigeria*, Chapter III, Oxford, 1968.
45. ibid.
46. During the 1950s and 1960s the image of the United States in Africa was directly linked to its internal racial problems and their attempted resolution. Africans may in the future ask Brazilians about social and economic conditions in Brazil for Brazilians of African descent, placing Brazil in a similar position to that of the United States, with its domestic affairs influencing its international image.

Appendix: Partial list of researchers working on slavery in Brazil

Leslie Bethell (author of *The Abolition of the Brazilian Slave Trade*, Cambridge, United Kingdom, 1970).

Professor Julio Braga, Centro de Estudos Afro-Orientais, Universidade Federal da Bahia, Salvador.

CEBRAP Research Centre São Paulo.

Professor Colson, Universidade de Santa Catarina.

Robert Conrad (author of *The Destruction*, Universityof California, Berkeley Press.)

Professor Carl Degler, History Department, Stanford University, Palo Alto, California.

Professor Anani Dzidzienyo, Department of Afro-American Studies, Brown University Providence, Rhode Island.

Professor Florestan Fernandes, Depto Sociologia, Universidade de São Paulo.

Professor Katharine Fringer, Depto Geog./História, Fundação Universiadade de Brasília.

Jean-Claude García-Zamor, University of Florida, Gainesville, Florida.

Professor Brasil Gerson (author), Pallas Editora, Rio de Janeiro.

Professor Roy Glasgow, Depto de História, Universidade Federal de Fluminense, Niteroí, Rio de Janeiro.

Professor Carlos Hasenbalg, IUPERJ, Rio de Janeiro.

Marvin Harris, Department of Anthropology, Columbia University, New York.

H. Hoetink, University of Puerto Rico, Puerto Rico.

Octavio Ianni, Depto de Sociologia, Universidade de São Paulo.

Dr Mary Karasch, Fulbright Professor, Universidade de Brasília.

Herbert S. Klein, Department of History, Princeton University.

Professor Jane McDivitt, Department of Portuguese, University of Iowa, Iowa City.

Professor Katia M. Mattoso, Universidade Católica da Bahia, Salvador.

Professor Corcino Medeiros dos Santos; 'GEH', Fundação Universidade de Brasíl.

Professor Michael Mitchell, Afro-American Studies Department. Department of Politics Princeton University, Princeton, N.J.

Clovis Moura c/o CEAA, Candido Mendes, Rio de Janeiro.

Professor Maria Beatriz do Nascimento, CEAA, Conjunto Universitário de Candide Mendes, Ipanema, Rio de Janeiro.

Professor L. Nieilson, Depto de História Universidade Federal de Santa Catarina, Florianopolis, Santá Catarina, Brasil.

Professor Edson Nunes e Silva, Instituto Geografico e Histórico da Bahia Piedade, Salvador (Bahia).

Professor José Honorio Rodrigues, c/o Deptº de História Universidade Federal de Fluminense, Niteroí, Rio de Janeiro.

Professor Vicente Salles, Radio-MEC, Brasília.

Professor Stuart Schwartz, History Department, University of Minnesota, Minneapolis-St Paul, Minnesota.

Professor Thomas Skidmore, History Department, University of Wisconsin, Madison Wisconsin.

Professor Leo Spitzer, Dartmouth College, Hanover, New Hampshire.

Robert Brent Toplin (author of *The Abolition of Slavery in Brazil*, New York, 1972).